ALSO BY AMANDA VAILL

Everybody Was So Young: Gerald and Sara Murphy:
A Lost Generation Love Story

Somewhere: The Life of Jerome Robbins

Hotel Florida: Truth, Love, and Death in the Spanish Civil War

Jerome Robbins, by Himself

JEROME ROBBINS,
BY HIMSELF

SELECTIONS FROM HIS LETTERS, JOURNALS,
DRAWINGS, PHOTOGRAPHS, AND
AN UNFINISHED MEMOIR

Edited and with commentary by Amanda Vaill

ALFRED A. KNOPF   NEW YORK   2019

THIS IS A BORZOI BOOK
PUBLISHED BY ALFRED A. KNOPF

www.aaknopf.com

Library of Congress Cataloging-in-Publication Data
Names: Robbins, Jerome, author. | Vaill, Amanda, editor.
Title: Jerome Robbins, by himself : selections from his letters, journals,
drawings, photographs, and an unfinished memoir /
edited and with commentary by Amanda Vaill.
Description: First edition. | New York : Alfred A. Knopf, 2019. |
"This is a Borzoi book"—Title page verso. | Includes index.
Identifiers: LCCN 2018054551 (print) | LCCN 2019014584 (ebook) |
ISBN 9780451494672 (ebook) | ISBN 9780451494665 (hardcover)
Subjects: LCSH: Robbins, Jerome—Correspondence. | Robbins, Jerome—Diaries. | Robbins,
Jerome—Notebooks, sketchbooks, etc. | Choreographers—
United States—Biography. | Dancers—United States—Biography.
Classification: LCC GV1785.R52 (ebook) | LCC GV1785.R52 A25 2019 (print) |
DDC 792.8092 [B]—dc23
LC record available at https://lccn.loc.gov/2018054551

Front-of-jacket photograph: Jerome Robbins in his 67th Street studio, New York City, 1958 by
Arnold Newman / Getty Images
Collage and back-of-jacket photographs courtesy of The Robbins Rights Trust; Photograph of
Robbins and his dog Nick: © Jesse Gerstein
Jacket design by Jenny Carrow

Manufactured in the United States of America
First Edition

To William Earle and Aidan Mooney
with love and gratitude

When I was a child, art seemed like a tunnel to me.
At the end of that tunnel I could see light where the world opened up, waiting.

—JEROME ROBBINS

CONTENTS

PREFACE xi

A NOTE ON THE TEXT xv

1 PRELUDE: 1918–1935   3

2 APPRENTICESHIP: 1935–1944   21

3 BREAKING THROUGH: 1944–1950   83

4 RISING AND FALLING: 1950–1964   111

5 CHANGING COURSE: 1964–1983   244

6 RECONCILIATION: 1983–1998   334

ACKNOWLEDGMENTS 389

CHRONOLOGY 391

INDEX 409

PREFACE

The choreographer and director Jerome Robbins was famous for many things—reinventing the Broadway musical, creating a vernacular American ballet, winning four Tony Awards, five Donaldson Awards (precursor to the Tonys), two Oscars, and an Emmy, naming names to the House Un-American Activities Committee—but a way with words was not one of them. "He was not articulate," said his frequent collaborator and occasional nemesis Arthur Laurents, a statement that was echoed by Stephen Sondheim, Harold Prince, his sometime assistant director Gerald Freedman, the critic Frank Rich, and numerous others. And indeed, for someone who dealt in the kinetic and the visual, who staged dance and action by working physically with the performers who would embody the images he had in his mind, it seems logical that being a wordsmith might not be in his job description or his skill set.

But as I discovered almost as soon as I began working on my 2006 biography of Robbins, *Somewhere,* this assumption couldn't have been more wrong. Jerome Robbins was a prolific correspondent, inveterate journal keeper, perceptive critic, dramatic scenarist, whimsical (sometimes ribald) versifier, even confessional fiction writer. He wrote about his identity (artistic and sexual), his background, his aspirations, his conflicts. He wrote to, and about, his family, his lovers, and his friends and associates—including the playwright Arthur Laurents, the choreographer George Balanchine, the ballerina Tanaquil Le Clercq, the composer Leonard Bernstein, the novelist and poet Robert Graves, the writer and impresario Lincoln Kirstein, the actor Laurence Olivier, the novelist Edna O'Brien, the director Ingmar Bergman, and scores of others, some professionally connected to him, some not. He wrote in airplanes and on trains, at home and while traveling. He wrote for his correspondents, for the public, and for himself. His personal papers consume 100 linear feet of shelf space, and the professional papers take up a further 141; this archive, which is part of the Jerome Robbins Dance Division at the New York Public Library for the Performing Arts, includes an array of material that reveals Robbins to have been not only an expressive writer by any measure, with a unique voice, but also an avid photographer, watercolorist, and draftsman. Taken together, Robbins's writings and artwork form an extraordinary record of a protean creative life and a time of enormous artistic ferment—a record that is the more extraordinary because so few people, including some he worked with closely, have suspected its existence.

This book aims to construct from that record a chronicle of Robbins's life as it looked from the inside, beginning with his childhood and his struggles as an aspiring but unrealized artist, going on through his glory days as a revolutionary force in American theater and dance, to his latter years, in which he strove to reconcile his conflicts and ensure his legacy. As such it offers a different perspective on this contradictory artist than has been possible in any of the biographical works about him. It is neither objective nor exhaustive—there is no coverage of events or relationships that Robbins didn't write about—nor analytical, at least not in the sense of third-party analysis. It draws on his many journals (including his teenage diary, the work notebooks that lay bare his creative process, and the hundreds of loose sheets of paper on which he jotted thoughts, impressions, and memories); his correspondence; his autobiographical fiction; his occasional essays (published and unpublished); his memoirs of childhood and apprenticeship, drafted for the most part in the 1970s; the script of his autobiographical theater piece, *The Poppa Piece*; and more.

I've arranged these elements to form a selective and impressionistic chronological narrative, one that occasionally groups together material created at different times for what I hope is a richer effect (each selection, however, carries the date of composition). For example, there are few documents from his childhood or early career, but these are the periods he covered most thoroughly in autobiographical writings in later life, so in the first sections of the book I've threaded his retrospective memoirs among his juvenilia. In an effort to avoid repetition or obscurity, and to be as representative and inclusive as possible, I've made cuts in a number of the selections, in particular the memoirs, the creative writing, and to a lesser extent the correspondence and journals. Because this is Robbins's story, told in his own voice, I've chosen not to interpolate editorial commentary between the documents. As he himself wrote to Arthur Laurents about *Jerome*

Robbins' Broadway, "The thing I've tried to avoid . . . is to talk about [the] career, work, etc. and just let the pieces say it for me." But to locate those pieces within the framework of Robbins's life and work, I've prefaced each chronological section with brief contextual commentary; I've provided a chronology of events and work at the back of the book; and I've footnoted references within the text that might be confusing or meaningless to a reader without a detailed knowledge of this book's background.

A different kind of context for Robbins's writings—a visual one—comes from his own photographs and artwork. From his earliest years Robbins was an intensely visual person. ("I have a studio in the basement where I do oil painting and everything," he wrote in high school. "You see, I've gone Greenwich Village.") His childhood journals and juvenilia are illustrated with his own drawings and with montages made from images cut out of books; later he recorded his home and professional life in photographs and other media. Like anyone with an iPhone today, Robbins snapped photos when he was touring with Ballet Theatre—mainly candid snapshots of himself and his fellow dancers*—but he also drew and painted sketches and portraits of his colleagues. In the late 1940s he moved into a duplex apartment in a brownstone on Park Avenue that had belonged to the photographer George Platt Lynes; inspired by some of the darkroom equipment Lynes had left behind, Robbins upped his photographic game, acquiring a Rolleiflex and a Leica with an auto-timer that enabled him to take more ambitious and nuanced photographs, which he developed and printed himself. In the late 1960s and early 1970s he studied painting with the noted landscapist Jane Wilson, and his journals in the next decade became filled with watercolors, particularly of the East End of Long Island and the area around Spoleto, in Umbria, where he spent many happy summers.

In Robbins's writing and artwork, as in his choreography, elements and themes emerge that are both predictable and surprising. One sees, from the first, his drive and ambition; but also his vulnerability and tenderness; his preternatural theatrical sense and his creative anxiety; his humor and his savagery; his fascination with travel and his love of his native New York; his zest for gossip and his

---

* The photographs from the early 1940s that are reproduced here are all from Robbins's personal collection. Most have no negatives or contact sheets, as exist for his images from approximately 1950 on, but since he wrote captions on the versos and research has turned up no other examples of them, they've been presumptively attributed to him.

intellectual and artistic hunger. As a first-generation American, and a gay man, he was often searching for a comfortable and secure place in the world (it's not a coincidence that the phrase "it was home" recurs in his private journals). And he struggled to balance his sometimes lacerating critical sense with acceptance—for himself and for others—a struggle that reached a crisis point in the 1970s.

What saved him, then and always—what ultimately brought him a sense of reconciliation and fulfillment—was the power of art. "When I was a child," Robbins told an interviewer in the 1960s, "art seemed like a tunnel to me. At the end of that tunnel I could see light where the world opened up, waiting."* If for Robbins art was a means of escape, a way *out* of doubt and conflict, for us it can become a way *in* to his personal and creative experience. My hope is that through the words and visual record he left behind, we can enter his world and see it as he did, and in the process understand both art and artist more completely.

---

* Robert Kotlowitz, "Corsets, Corned Beef, and Choreography," *Show: The Magazine of the Arts,* December 1964, 39.

A NOTE ON THE TEXT

Jerome Robbins saved nearly everything he wrote—not just journals, scenarios, and essays, but also letters. Much of his correspondence was typed, even letters from his touring days with Ballet Theatre, and he seemingly made carbon copies of a good deal of that. His copies and drafts—for in writing some letters and virtually all critical or theatrical work, he would compose and edit numerous versions—are supplemented, in his archive, by originals that many of his correspondents returned to him, most during the period in the 1970s and 1980s when he contemplated writing his autobiography and wanted them for reference.

As a result, the New York Public Library's collection of Robbins's papers, both personal and professional, has a nearly complete record of his writings, allowing me to rely extensively on it in compiling this selection. In some cases, such as the correspondence with Leonard Bernstein and Arthur Laurents about *West Side Story,* and with Laurence Olivier and the artistic staff at Britain's National Theatre about a contemplated production of *The Bacchae,* the collections of the Library of Congress and the British Library, respectively, provided valuable supplementary or comparative documentation. Several of Robbins's letters to Tanaquil Le Clercq were handwritten, and to reproduce them, I was fortunate to have access to Le Clercq's papers in the New York City Ballet Archive, where they reside. Other documents came from recipients who shared them with me.

Robbins's multiplicity of drafts presents a special problem in that—as in his choreography—there are often several versions of a given text. Without resorting to variorum-edition-style notation, I've generally opted to preserve the version that in my judgment was the best, which sometimes meant ignoring a penciled edit in favor of the original wording, or choosing between different scene variations in *The Poppa Piece* or the partial memoirs he wrote in preparation for that work.

Robbins was a notoriously erratic speller, and I've left his orthography alone; he also, as an autodidact, had an idiosyncratic way with what some might term malapropisms but that in his hands acquired a kind of eccentric magic. Someone's hair is "astray," thoughts "carouse" in his brain, he is studying something "arduously," a demented Balanchine has "peeks of clarity." Despite the "[*sic*]" that follows them in the text, they're at least as vivid as the "correct" usage would be and I've left them alone too. Major cuts to documents are indicated with ellipsis dots (where Robbins interpolated them himself, that is noted, except in the case of his own—again idiosyncratic—double-dot punctuation); minor cuts, of redundant or extraneous words, phrases, or sentences, have been made silently.

When I first encountered Robbins's enormous archives, they were still in his home office and afterward at the offices of the Robbins Foundation, stored in file boxes with unhelpful names like "Green Cabinet to Left of Fireplace." The move to the New York Public Library and subsequent processing imposed one kind of order on them, but sometimes Robbins's own descriptive titles for documents, such as "Day-to-Day Notes Telling the Story of *Mother Courage,*" were replaced with something else, in this case the generic label "General Notes." Where Robbins gave a title to a document, I've generally retained it.

Finally, this selection from Robbins's writings represents only a portion of what he wrote, and thought, and I would encourage anyone with an interest in his life, work, and times to pursue that interest in his archives. There may be as much to learn from what I haven't included as from what I have.

Jerome Robbins, by Himself

Prelude: 1918–1935

Jerome Robbins was born Jerome (or Gershon) Wilson Rabinowitz in New York City on October 11, 1918. His father, Harry, was an immigrant from the shtetl of Rozhanka in the Jewish Pale of Settlement, in Russia; his mother, Lena Rips, had been born in the United States, the daughter of a garment cutter, and unlike her husband she had not only graduated from high school but also studied for two years at a women's college. In 1923 the Rabinowitzes moved from Manhattan to Jersey City and then Weehawken, New Jersey, with Jerome and his older sister, Sonia, born in 1912. In partnership with his brother-in-law, Harry Rabinowitz ran the Comfort Corset Company in Union City, and the family enjoyed the trappings of prosperity: a Packard car, a private (German) kindergarten for the children, dancing lessons for Sonia, violin and piano lessons for Jerry, trips to concerts in New York City. Although they observed the Sabbath and expected their son to study for and celebrate his bar mitzvah, the Rabinowitzes—like many of their generation—were assimilationist Jews: they celebrated Christmas, with a tree and presents, and Yiddish was rarely spoken in the house except when the parents were trying to keep things from the children.

In the summer of 1924, Lena took both children to Rozhanka, then located in Poland, to visit their grandfather Rabinowitz, an experience that seemed to the nearly six-year-old Jerry like a glimpse of Arcadia, a vision he would return to again and again in his later work. The local public school, which he began attending on his return to America, was the opposite: a terrifying place full of noisy children with WASP names where he tried to be unobtrusive unless there was something he could excel in. Spelling was not one of these things, nor was grammar, but he loved to write and filled notebook after notebook with poems and reflections.

The family suffered in the 1929 crash and ensuing economic depression: the corset factory teetered on the edge of bankruptcy, the family sold the Packard and got a Model T, Lena Rabinowitz went to work in the factory with her husband, and tensions rose between the parents and the children, and between sister and brother. Arguments became physical as well as vocal. Teenage Jerry vacillated between anxiety and anger: ashamed of his Jewishness, resentful of the expectations, and poverty, of his parents. School, surprisingly, offered a refuge. Although his academic performance was erratic, he excelled in writing and in all the arts: he painted, sculpted, made masks, collages, and puppets, even composed music—one piece a setting of an erotic poem ("my sweet old etcetera / aunt lucy") by e. e. cummings. And, following Sonia's lead (she had been a child star with the troupe of Irma Duncan and had recently been appearing with an avant-garde modern ballet company in New York), he began studying dance—modern, "expressive" dance—paying for his lessons with a variety of menial after-school jobs.

His artistic self-expression translated into success: he was vice president of the drama club and had a wide circle of friends, including a girlfriend to whom he dedicated one of his music compositions (not the cummings). But some conflict, some irresolution, nagged at him. In his senior year in high school he wrote a remarkably self-perceptive extended essay, called "My Selves," to which he appended passages from his diary in an attempt, he said, "to express my character as I see it." This seems less adolescent narcissism than confessional honesty, for at seventeen Jerry Rabinowitz already had a terrible need to be honest—a need that would persist throughout his life.

Poppa: Getting to the U.S.A.
July 13, 1976

The sons of my father's father were sent one by one to the New World. The system was not unusual. Most Jewish families endured the same. Enough money would be saved and scrimped to get the eldest son over to the other side. Then he would get to work and as each son got a toehold in America the burden of raising enough money for the next in line eased a bit for the family at home. My father was one of four brothers and one sister—in order: Teddy, Julius, Harry, Sam, Ruth. So he was the third to try to get across. I say try, for there was much danger connected to it. First of all his parents had to buy a grave and a death certificate for him. You see, at a certain age he would be conscripted into the Russian army and the army treated Jewish soldiers about the way our army treated black soldiers. To avoid this his [parents] bought a grave & the attendant burial paper so that when the military authorities come for him they could prove his death, for if he had run off, the Russians would extract a terrible penalty from his family.

Having secured the necessary cover for his escape, for indeed it was a flight, they sewed his money and his boat ticket in the inside lining of his coat. My brain reels when I consider what plotting and risks they must have taken to connive getting the plan that far, for I spent a summer in my father's tiny village when I was six, some twenty-five years after my dad left it, and even then it was a one-dirt-road village, without electricity or plumbing, & many of the homes had packed dirt floors.

He had to travel at night & avoid towns & check points & barriers, & any hostile strangers. He went from western Russia, through Poland [and] Germany, & got to Amsterdam.* He told me how he had met a Russian soldier who was deserting, and how they made the journey traveling together. Oh, he was so handsome, & big, my father said, and evoked his emotional memory [of] a tall man in a heavy army coat as he gestured & puffed up his chest. We had to be careful when we came to the borders where they raked the ground carefully so that footprints would show. We slept in barns & in the haystacks

---

* More likely Rotterdam, which was a seaport.

Weehawken, Robbins once said, was "about three blocks deep and nine wide . . . grubby, ugly, and uninspiring," but drawings he made of it in the late 1930s show that at least some of the houses were more substantial.

& scrounged for food. And once we stopped at a tavern, and there was such a beautiful girl there waiting on the tables. Ai, she was beautiful, he said, as he saw her in his memory. And something in the way he spoke of her and the soldier telegraphed to me the vibrancy of living people in a living plot of relationships.

Dad told me that he made his way to Amsterdam—and that when he got to the pier and realized that the wall rising up beside him was the side of a ship, he burst into tears. For he had never seen anything so enormous, and it was a fearful thing to contemplate being in it & on it.

Family Life
August 24, 1976

My first memories are of living in Jersey City on Booraem Avenue. I have a photograph of me standing on my father's hand, he propping his elbows against his waist to support the weight. I remember my father taking my wrists and ankles in his two hands, swinging me as a package first under his open legs then in an exhilarating arch, up in the air over his head to land piggy back on top of his shoulders with a thump. I remember these intimacies and my father's affectionate embraces and support till the day I asked him to swing me up on his shoulders and he said I can't, you're too big now. And I do believe that we separated at that time.

From then to now, with increasing need and desire and interest, I have tried to track him down, to find my father, who was always present, but never there—a stubborn fortress, an ungiving forest, a book that wouldn't open its pages. I have never broken through to him, or gotten him to break through to me. He is afraid of emotion and even of sentiment, certainly of sentimentality.

To: Harry Rabinowitz
[June] 1924

WHITE STAR LINE[*]

Dear Daddy,

How are you? We are in the middle of the ocean.
I am not sea sick.
Every night we have ice cream.

From Jerry

---

[*] This letter was handwritten in childish cursive on White Star Line stationery: Lena and the children sailed from New York to Southampton, then traveled via London, Berlin, and Warsaw to Rozhanka. Decades later Robbins remembered playing piano in a shipboard concert.

Grandpa

1977

In Rozhanka, in my grandfather's house, I slept under mosquito netting. There was no electricity, no running water—there were kerosene lamps & wells. They told me I spoke Yiddish there, then, and that I played with the children of the shtetl all day in the fields, in the yards.

I bathed in a brook with the women. I peed for them like men do, feet apart, hands on hips. I climbed into haylofts, shopped in the marketplaces, crawled through the abandoned flour mills. I slept in the afternoons, smelled baked bread.

I watched my grandfather stop a drunk from carousing through the town, atop a large farm wagon, lashing his two horses.

A mysterious man was kept locked up behind a heavy door in a dark room. His food was passed to him through a slot in the bottom of the door, at the floor. There was a small shutter we could slide open to look in and see him. Eyes: only eyes.

At night after dinner, by kerosene lamps, songs were sung. I remember apples, embroidery, mud pies, and catching fish in a tin can perforated with holes. So proud was I, keeping them in a wooden pencil case for days before my mother traced the smell to them and I had to give up my prizes. I remember tea, candles, jams and the melodies of voices.

It was all lovely, all lovely. I do not remember one unhappy moment. When we left there, we left at night by hay wagon to travel till dawn to a larger village to the train. The night we left, Itchi Utch (also six), shaven head, friend, ally, landsman, brought me apples in a red bandana, its end tied together in a knot. He handed them to me saying, "Na, Gershen." We got into the small wagon and waved goodbye. As we clopped away into the darkness, I fell asleep.

Reading Chekhov's Autobiography

August 6, 1976

Imagination was always the most fascinating part of growing up, and I loved to use mine. I could go into worlds and believe them. All the prism's colors thrown magically on the wall, on paper, my hand, the table took me on journeys. My mother used to play a game with my sister and me. We had a small children's blackboard easel at home, and we'd take a wet rag and wipe the board haphazardly, then we'd watch it dry and as it dried we'd see faces and figures and landscapes, animals, trees, monsters and all fanciful and real creatures. One summer we had a house at Sea-Girt[*] and every evening we'd watch the sunset from the porch and as the clouds traveled across the horizon we'd point out what fanciful or real things we saw parading across the sky.

Jerry Rabinowitz Poetry & Music Compositions
[1927]

TO MY MOTHER

I offer you this little book
Inside the pages I hope you'll look
For inside of them you'll find
Some little verses I have rhymed.
Pictures of all kinds of stages
Is what you'll find inside these pages.

THE DREAM

I.
Sometimes I dream of funny things
Sometimes I dream I'm dead
Sometimes I dream that I'm so mean
I have to go to bed.

---

* A community on the New Jersey shore.

2.

Sometimes I dream I'm with a ghost
Sometimes I dream I'm not
Sometimes I dream I'm playing marbles
Down in our old lot.

3.

Sometimes I dream of sunshine
Sometimes I dream of rain
Sometimes I dream of a little girl
I know her name's Elaine.

4.

Sometimes I dream that I'm in school
And the teacher gives dictation
And then I'm very very sad
I wish it were vacation.

5.

Then mother comes into my room
And gets me out of bed
And still I am so tired
She calls me sleepyhead.

MOTHER

1.

My mother is the greatest one
Who gives sunshine like the sun
And helps you when her work is done.

2.

She helps you with arithmetic
She calls the doctor when your sick
And gets so nervous very quick.

3.

When some troubles come to you
When your feeling kind of blue
Go to her she'll help you thru.

4.

Your mothers advice is always good
And you promise that you would
Then of course you really should.

5.

There's father sister I'm the brother
But I love best above all other
My most beautiful greatest kindest
Mother.

DANCE

Dance when your merry
Dance when your sad
Dance when your happy
Dance when your glad.

London Journal, 1971
October 27

[A]t the moment she reached the bottom of the stairs and as she started to turn on the landing, with her right hand on the balustrade—she stopped & looked up at me. She was in day dress, a gray woolen jacket trimmed with beige & a pleated skirt that fell to the floor, and her hat like a Tyrolean hunting hat with some tall feathers that was slightly cocked over her left eye. She is as fixed as Sargent's Madame X—stylish, poised & cooling looking up & back.

Mama Mama I was screaming—Don't go—please don't go & leave me—A housemaid—Annie—was holding me fiercely as I struggled to tear myself from her arms; I was crying [in] desperation. [T]he terror of separation & my love for my mother were so intense that my life & security depended on keeping her home—depended on her not forsaking me.

It was these desperate & hysterical cries & physical struggle that made her stop & look back.

And there it is.

Cool. Still. Poised. As if her picture was to be taken—not posing, but still & objective. STAY there it said—you must learn it said—I cannot, I will not turn back. Neither did she smile—wave—blow a kiss say a word—offer consolation or suggest comfort or assurance. She stood and gave me that look and left.

The Factory
September 1, 1976

It was exciting to go to the place where Dad worked—the "*boss*"—and see him in action, directing it. It seemed to me, as a child, a wonderful place of mystery and fascination of machinery. Huge, noisy, it had an old elevator that worked by pulling on a rope to give it a start. I liked the office with its ledgers, ink, typewriters, elastics, clasps, rubber bands, [and] pencils. In "The Shop" itself, as my father referred to it, were four long rows of girls working on sewing machines. My father would heckle and nudge them along—come on girls, no talking no talking—work work that's what I pay you for.

I used to watch fascinatedly as he'd lay out material for cutting. There was a way of folding and refolding the pink patterned material into thick 6–8 inch stacks, holding them down with weights, of stenciling the patterns on them, and then, most terrifying, cutting them out with a rotary blade knife cutter which let out a shrill whine when it hit the cloth. "Be careful of the knife," I was always warned. And I was. And the table where they sewed the stays into the corset—the table where they put in the long laces, the eyelet machine and the most formidable of all, the garter machine, in which the end of the elastic garter was placed with a metal stapler—when you pushed your foot on the pedal, down would crash a heavy hammer-head stamping the staple into the material. Gah! I also loved the enormous cardboard boxes that materials came in or corsets were sent out in. They could become houses, caves, tables, castles, dungeons, forts—what a world was I able to conjure with them. And then there were the heavy cardboard empty spools, [cylinders] with great wheels on either end, perfect for making carts and wagons and scooters.

The floor of the factory was covered by the end of a day with clips and snips and pieces of material cutouts, confetti of satins and elastics. It was fun to take a running start and then slide on the materials, which I did until taking a colossal fall when my feet slipped out beneath me. Later on I used to earn my allowance by sweeping up the factory after work. The materials there would catch in the rough splintery wood floor, or under the foot pedals and legs of the machines themselves. I really hated that job.

In my 15th or 16th year Dad tried to get me to "learn the business." I got as far as handling the big shears, about 16–18″ long, so long that the far end picked up the tip of my finger on the other hand and sliced off a third of an inch of pad. I saw it happen—when I felt the pain and watched the blood rush out, I fainted dead away. (I never can watch my own or others' wounds, cannot watch my blood being taken, or see an X-ray of a friend's broken bone without coming close to or truly passing out). That was the end of my factory career.

Sister—Family Continued
September 1, 1976

It'd start in the kitchen, Sonia and Mother. Pots would be slammed, voices raised: I'll make it myself, my way, your way. Aggravation—that killer disease caused by children of martyred parents; a smell of onions, eggs, and lox frying, challah toasted, a constant going and coming to the table for plates, salt, butter, the meal being eaten piecemeal, the fight going on . . . and on . . . and on . . . until finally hysteria would be reached—my sister my mother, my mother weak-kneed, wobbling, crying to God for help, tears pouring out. And my father erupted, lash[ing] out at us with his Jewish paper. I'll give you a mouth, he'd cry, I'll show you a respectful mouth, he'd blurt out in his guttural inarticulate fury—and we'd scurry for safety and harbor and clear the room as he'd hurl his Yiddish thunderbolts and expand his fury, and we'd all quell and quack after the squall.

Once Sonia and I got into a fight in the middle of an afternoon. Whatever caused it is again a mystery but she slapped me and I called her a bitch. She slammed me again. Bitch, I cried. Slap. Bitch. Slap. Bitch. She had me down on the floor and sitting astride me slapped hard as I refused to give in. *Neither* of us would give in, and her strokes increased in force till a woman who was doing some cleaning for us tried to stop Sonia and failing, telephoned my mother to come help. Our fight went on till she suddenly stopped . . . and instead gathered me into her arms and held me to her. Stop, stop. Don't cry, she said; but I cried and cried and accepted her love and security, crying for both the fight and the acceptance. We were both rocking on the floor when my mother burst in and pulled Sonia away. What have you done, she screamed at her, What did you do, you murderer you—what did you do to him? No, no, mother, I said, it's all right now, I'm all right. Don't hit her. We're OK now. Mother looked in amazement, wild-eyed, hair astray, and said, What's going on in my own house that a servant has to call me out of the factory, drag me away from my work, to come save my son who my daughter is beating up so it will kill him? What? What?

It's all right mama—it's all right now, I said. I was happy in getting Sonia's love again.

Yes, said my mother bitterly, she beat you until she knew I was coming and then she changed her tune. Not to save you—to save herself.

It was true. I knew it. [And] once after having been slapped hard by my sister, I said to her, one day, Sonia I'm going to be bigger than you—I'm going to grow up and be bigger than you and *I'm* going to slap *you*—I'll get even.

And I did.

The Jew Piece
January 1975

I didn't like my father—I didn't like his accent. I didn't like that he couldn't speak English.[*] I didn't like that he seemed drenched in some murky, foul, unclean, unkempt, mysterious filth and dirt, which the whole of the Judaism, as it was

---

[*] What Robbins means is that his father didn't speak English *well:* he had a heavy accent.

practiced, seemed to be—hair shirts and tallises[*] and fringes and beards and drippings and nose-runnings and eyes watering and smells that I didn't know, a language I couldn't understand. It revolted me. And I laid my knife against it.

[I was] training for Bar Mitzvah and an old, old, wizened, decrepit, white-bearded unshaven man came to the house every afternoon to train me to read the Torah. That part of the Torah I had to learn.

I didn't like him and I didn't like what I had to do. One, I didn't understand what it was about. Two, I didn't understand what it was I was saying. Three, it was pounded into my head that from that moment on, after thirteen, all my sins would be on my head. My voice hadn't changed. [I'd] been mother-cuddled all my life. And now I was facing: "Today you are a man."

One afternoon I had been playing on the street with my school friends, hockey tag, whatever we played, and I had to leave to do my lesson with the Tzaddik.[†] I came in and we started. Suddenly there was a rap on the window. I looked up and there were the kids from the block at the three windows that gave into the dining room. They were making faces and imitating him. And he taught me Jewish submissiveness because he understood the baiting and he never looked up.

After a while they opened the windows. They climbed into the room. At this point I summoned up enough courage to say that I was going to call their parents if they didn't get out. That got them out, but the horror and the embarrassment and the shame remained.

Family Life

August 24, 1976

High school seemed to be evenly balanced between learning things from our teachers and learning things from the other boys. How to score a home-run or triple-bagger, not on the playing field, but on sticking your finger down the inside of someone's fly (before zipper time) and seeing how many buttons got undone. A great deal of time was spent learning how to get up and down the

---

[*] Fringed garments worn over or under clothing by religious Jews.
[†] Teacher (from the Hebrew for "righteous one").

staircases ahead of the running mob and not be late for class. The first time I ever had an orgasm was in gym on the climbing rope. I never knew what the ecstatic dizziness was I felt as I twisted myself up, I was too young to really come. But I soon found out that I liked climbing ropes and having that strange thing happen. I did well in English and history. I liked chemistry. I wanted to be a chemist at that time, but I think I made a tactical error by winning a contest. The brother of [Robert Elliott] Burns, author of *I Am a Fugitive from a Georgia Chain Gang*,[*] became a lecturer/preacher/priest and gave a talk on his brother's life at school, ending with telling us whoever wrote him the best letter would receive a book of his poems. I sat down and wrote a poem, and to everyone's surprise and chagrin, I, Jerome Wilson Rabinowitz, won. This did not endear me to Mr. Sarofian, our chemistry teacher.

There were sensitive areas about being Jewish, as most of the population of Weehawken was Christian. Jewish and Christian holidays caused separation. In English class, in having to use a new vocabulary word in a sentence, we were given the word "despise." I came up with the theatrical, "'I *despise* you,' she said." The teacher told me in front of the class that it was plain unchristian to use the word in that sense. I didn't have enough Jewish chutzpah to tell her I wasn't Christian, and it was used all the time in Drama. Instead I sat down and nursed my embarrassment.

. . . I was small for my age and never felt I could compete in sports (though later I became a very fast swimmer and liked basketball). I was a washout at baseball and always hated it at school and camp. At high school I tried out for the cheerleaders—my sister had coached me—but I still didn't make it. I became a vice president of the dramatic club (our male biology teacher took us to see the Princeton Triangle drag show[†] for culture!!!). I made some appearances in school plays and played piano at school assemblies . . .

I liked school. At least it was company. At home my sister was absent—

---

[*] Robert Elliott Burns (1892–1955) was a shell-shocked World War I veteran who had robbed an Atlanta grocery store and been sentenced to six to ten years of hard labor; his book about the experience was made into a 1932 film starring Paul Muni.

[†] The Triangle Club, one of the (then) all-male Princeton University eating clubs, put on a musical comedy show each year, written and performed by undergraduates. Scott Fitzgerald famously performed in one while a student a generation earlier.

working in New York—and my mother and father worked at the factory. My grandmother* had come to live with us . . . a wonderful tiny, amazingly wrinkled little woman, a strict Orthodox Jew who never lit a stove or turned on electricity after sundown on Sabbath eve, kept separate dishes for dairy and meat foods, and was always reading the Talmud. She mostly wore dark clothes with long skirts; she had snow white hair and intense blue eyes and a leathery tiny face.

It was hard when she moved in. I did resent her. I also "despised" her Jewish backward ways. In later years I realized we had a lot in common, she and I: loneliness. We were both always left alone in the evenings. . . . She was the only one who saw my fits of temper—my unhappiness. Alone, often—not wanting to visit relatives in Brooklyn—not wanting to go where my parents went in business—I'd be left home [to] vent my frustration and anger. I'd fall to the floor and beat it and cry and yell and flood the carpet with tears. She'd come up to me—*für vas shreist du, für vas shreist*—concerned and alarmed she'd hover over me. Nothing, I'd fling at her—*lass mir alaine, lass mir.*†

During her lifetime when she lived with us she was a pest to me. Now I miss her, understand her, and know that I must have loved her very much and she me.

Diary, 1934–35

1934 Jan. 7—Rain—Sunday.
Went to N.Y. for a rehearsal for play for reunion of Camp Colony. It doesn't look so hot. Saw lots of people I knew from camp. Went to movies with Seymore Rudges. "Prizefighter & the Lady."‡ Ate at Rudges's house. His sister trying to make me. Everybody so nice to me. 'Specially my grand-ma even if we do argue.

---

* His mother's mother, Ida Rips, came to live with the Rabinowitzes after the death of her husband, Isaac. In order to make room for her, Robbins and six-years-older Sonia had to share a bedroom.
† Robbins's Yiddish is inexact, but roughly this exchange means "What's wrong with you" and "Leave me alone."
‡ A 1933 melodrama about a boxer, a nightclub singer, and a gangster, starring Myrna Loy, Walter Huston, and the real-life boxers Max Baer and Jack Dempsey.

Jan 10, 1934, nice—Wed.

Am sick of Al C. Saw J. Ahearn. He's not such a bad fellow. Saw some inter-class games. Lousy. What'll I do about my gym suit. (It was taken by someone). Worked 2 hours on Chemistry problem, but got it right. Nothing happened today.

Jan 22.

Chemistry exam. Not so easy—might have passed—who knows. Went to movies in afternoon. Saw Four Marks Brothers in "Duck Soup." I laughed my head off.

April 23, 1934

Junior Prom. Went stag. Saw Sylvia there and danced with her. Gee Whiz. Oh Well.

Sept. 11 Tues. 1934

Went out and got my things for school. Got a nice new tie & pin & holder for it. Am prepared for school. Got a haircut too.

January 2 Wed. 1935

School—good to get back. This morning had a terrible quarrel with Sonia. But afterwards I was as sorry as usual. Went to N.Y. to get suit but they said they'd have it Fri. Hope so. Went to gym & met Patty Axelrod, very nice boy I knew from camp. Wish I'd be asked to join a club up at the center*—home, "and so to bed."†

Jan 3 Thursday, 1935

School—but afterwards walked my feet off earning 75¢ selling tax bills.‡ Might make more tomorrow.—Dentist—Oh yes Ruth Abramson, Gladys Roseman,

---

* The Jewish Community Center in Jersey City.
† He had been reading Pepys in English class and here alludes to the diarist's signature sign-off at the end of his entries.
‡ During the Depression, when numerous people defaulted on property taxes or utility bills, the government's lien on an affected property (a "tax bill") might be sold, either at auction to the highest bidder or to anyone willing to meet the government's price.

Rose Adoff, another boy, and myself are planning to go see The Children's Hour.[*] Am picking up in Algebra, but letting down in French.

My Selves: An Attempt to Express My Character as I See It, by Jerry Rabinowitz, English 12

1935

"It's all a question of masks, really: first the painted masks. We all wear them as a form of protection; modern life forces us to. We must have some means of shielding our timid, shrinking souls from the glare of civilization."[†]

I stand before a mirror. Ahead, two dark eyes are looking back at me beneath a shock of black hair. The face is thin, the eyebrows so bushy as to draw the attention toward them as a diamond on velvet.

Slowly, the mask begins to rise, revealing another face. The features of this one are the same but they are distorted into a creation of malignant capability. This also rises leaving me looking at a mask of complete tranquility; but this rises and another one is shown and still another. . . .

Faster and faster they come, spreading over the mirror, the walls, the rooms, the earth. They all look at me with blank vacant eyes where, if they were over my face, my eyes would show through. They are all me, every one.

In school my mask is well known . . . a smile, a giggle, or a laugh. At home I try to be the same, but being a spoilt although not the only child, I am soon arguing with someone. . . . [W]henever I meet a group of boys and girls who are of my age who are totally strange to me, I immediately withdraw to my own reflections and thoughts. My outside mask is still on, but my inside ones are

---

[*] *The Children's Hour,* Lillian Hellman's first play, which concerned false allegations of a lesbian relationship being brought against two schoolteachers, had created a sensation when it opened the previous November; it was later banned in Boston, and could not be considered for the Pulitzer Prize because one of the judges refused to see it. Young Jerry Rabinowitz and his friends had adventurous taste.

[†] Noel Coward's "Design for Living" [JR's own footnote on this composition].

furiously alive, analyzing and sizing up these new persons. When these people begin to talk on a topic of the day, I'm afraid to venture a remark because, I'm afraid that . . . [JR's ellipses] because I have no self confidence. . . .

[But] there is an artistic self. By saying Art I do not mean just drawing. I mean music, drama, literature, dancing, handcrafts, and painting. I believe I have some talent in all of these. I compose and play music for the piano and violin, I have received awards at camps for dramatic ability and handcraft ability, I have written poetry and prose, and have taken a shot at plays, I have had several scholarships in dancing . . . modern and fundamental, and have done much painting, and other drawing skills outside of school. I get the same physical satisfaction out of doing any of these Arts as a man does out of being well fed. I can sit gazing on a line of beauty for hours, memorizing each curve and each arc.

I have tried to give you an accurate picture of myself—my selves. The evil, the good, the bad, the smiling, sneering, artistic, malicious, destructive, benevolent, rapacious, egotistical, sacrificing and selfish are all my selves . . . all me.

Apprenticeship: 1935–1944

Robbins graduated from Woodrow Wilson High School in June 1935 and in the fall began attending New York University as a chemistry major. He'd hoped to study journalism, but his parents insisted he pursue a "useful" degree. Useful didn't mean compatible, however: by the following spring Robbins was failing two courses (mathematics and French) out of five, and his father, struggling financially from the Depression, told him his college days were over.

Robbins wasn't sure what would become of him at this point, but whatever the possibilities, he later recalled, "running the Comfort Corset Company was not among them." He persuaded his parents to give him a year to establish himself, and set out looking for a way into the world he felt he was called to: the world of art. After an unsuccessful attempt to apprentice himself to the art puppeteer Tony Sarg, the Basil Twist of his day, he was accepted (following a rocky first meeting) into the experimental modern ballet troupe of Senya Gluck Sandor, where his colleagues included José Limón and where he attracted the notice of *The New York Times*'s dance critic, John Martin. (It was at this point that, at Sandor's urging, he adopted a string of Anglicized stage names—Robin Gerald, Gerald Robyns, Jerry Robyns—before settling on Jerome Robbins.) He briefly worked backstage making props for the Stanislavski-influenced Group Theatre's production of *Johnny Johnson,* and at the Yiddish Art Theatre he appeared in a near walk-on in I. J. Singer's *Brothers Ashkenazi* ("someone coughed so I missed your line," his aunt told him after she attended a performance). And following Sandor's advice, he began studying ballet—which until then he had considered "false . . . , out of date, and constricting." His first balletic appearance, partnering an older dancer named Lisa Parnova, was an awkward one, but he kept working and parlayed his studies—funded with odd jobs—into paid appearances in ballets by the Russian emigré choreographer Michel Fokine at the World's Fair ground-breaking ceremonies and at Jones Beach's outdoor amphitheater. Finally, after a brief post–Labor Day tryout appearance in 1937, he got a break that would help determine his future path: a ten-week, $200 job as a dancer for the 1938 summer season at a Pennsylvania resort, Camp Tamiment.

In the world of the 1930s, Tamiment was the equivalent of Club Med: the place middle-class singles went in the summer for sun, fun, and the opposite sex—and for the weekly Broadway-style revue directed by the camp entertainment director, Max Liebman. It was a training ground for Broadway (and movie) talent: among Robbins's fellow entertainers were Imogene Coca, Danny Kaye, and Carol Channing, as well as such dance-world figures as Dorothy Bird, Anita Alvarez, and Ruthanna Boris, and under Liebman's often-irascible and temperamental direction all were responsible for performing in, and sometimes creating the material for, the weekly revue. Robbins spent four summers at Tamiment, progressing from ensemble parts to solos, from working out dances anonymously with a small group of intimates to choreographing an entire revue, and his signature performing and choreographic style— fluid, expressive, full of sharply observed details—began to emerge.

But Tamiment was only for the summertime, and he had to make a living, had to pay for the cheap furnished rooms that were the only alternative to living at home with his parents in Weehawken. He dreamed of landing "a job—a job as a *dancer*—a job in a Broadway show—a dream beyond believability." Auditioning ceaselessly, and often fruitlessly, he did manage to get cast in the choruses of *Great Lady* (1938), *Stars in Your Eyes* (1939), and *Keep Off the Grass* (1940)—the first and last of which were choreographed by George Balanchine—and he was a featured performer, and some of his material was used, uncredited, in the Tamiment-originated *Straw Hat Revue* (1939), which made Danny Kaye a star.

While appearing in *Keep Off the Grass,* he heard about an ambitious new venture called Ballet Theatre, a dance company founded by a New England heiress named Lucia Chase, which would employ a permanent roster of principals, soloists, and corps members to present a mixture of classic European ballet and edgier work created by a cadre of contemporary choreographers—including Antony Tudor, Bronislava Nijinska, Agnes de Mille, and Eugene Loring—in regular New York appearances supplemented with national tours. The curtain had barely risen on its first short season at the now-demolished Center Theatre in Rockefeller Center than Robbins began bombarding management with audition requests until he finally won a contract, first as a summer temporary, then as a permanent corps member. At first, dancers' terms of employment were erratic: the company was engaged for two months in the fall of 1940 at the Chicago Lyric Opera, then had a brief season in New York in early 1941, at which point it appeared financing for the venture would dry up. Robbins returned to Tamiment for one last season, as a choreographer, but Ballet Theatre struck a deal with the impresario Sol Hurok that ensured the company's survival, and that fall Robbins went with them to Mexico.

For the next four years Ballet Theatre would be the nursery that brought forth Robbins's mature talent, as a dancer (in such signature roles as Hermes in *Helen of Troy* and the puppet in *Petrouchka*) and eventually as a choreographer, broadening his horizons on tours around the United States and abroad and introducing him to a surrogate family of dancers, choreographers, composers, and other artists that gave him the camaraderie and acceptance he rarely found at home. The support was welcome, for this was a period of considerable conflict and anxiety for Robbins. His first real sexual attraction, to a man, had been followed by an affair with a woman, which had not been sustained; his family had accused him of consorting with "bad company" (code for homosexuals); and his professional ambition, always transparent, had brought him criticism that, in turn, made him doubt his talent and his worth. Traveling the country, he longed for a place to settle and call his own. He found friends, some of whom would be colleagues and companions for years, including the dancers Donald Saddler and Nora Kaye (to whom he would later be briefly engaged to be married), the director Mary Hunter, co-founder of the American Actors Company, and the playwright Horton Foote, with whom he had plans to collaborate on an elaborate danced and acted theater piece based on an African American folk myth. But even among these, he often felt lonely and vulnerable: "made crudely, painted badly," as he described the title character in *Petrouchka,* who he thought was "me in so many ways." He poured out his loneliness and conflicted emotions not only in his journals but in scenarios and fiction that he never sought to have produced or published.

In the end, his vision of a kind of *American* theatrical dance, and his drive to create it, prevailed against his self-doubt. In 1943, tired of dancing in Russian boots and wigs, frustrated from bombarding Ballet Theatre management with scores of overcomplicated scenarios—which featured Cecil B. DeMille–sized casts of thousands—in the hopes of getting a commission, he had an epiphany inspired by watching rehearsals of George Balanchine's nearly minimalist ballet *Apollo.* He realized he could do more with less: a ballet about three sailors on shore leave in the big city and the three girls they meet. Following his usual practice in previous efforts, he outlined all the action in detail and even specified the tone and tempos for the music, leaving very little to management's imagination, and when a work scheduled for the spring 1944 season fell through, Ballet Theatre—nudged by his ally, the company's executive managing director, Charles Payne—gave him the empty slot. He cast two friends, the firecracker Harold Lang as the rowdy, boisterous sailor and the dreamy, sweet-faced John Kriza as the lyrical one, and gave himself the bravura role of their "smouldering" dark companion. Hoping to produce the ballet inexpensively, the company suggested Robbins work with their musical arranger to cobble together a score from existing popular songs, but Robbins had more ambitious ideas. Eventually he persuaded Ballet Theatre to commission the then-unknown Leonard Bernstein to compose the score; since Bernstein was tethered to New York City by his job as assistant conductor of the New York Philharmonic, their collaboration had to be conducted long-distance, but on

April 18, 1944, *Fancy Free,* with a set by Oliver Smith, premiered at the Metropolitan Opera House. It was an immediate, life-changing success. "To come right to the point," said *The New York Times*'s John Martin,

> "Fancy Free" . . . is a smash hit. This [is] young Robbins' first go at choreography, and the only thing he has to worry about in that direction is how in the world he is going to make his second one any better. He has managed to get into this light-hearted little piece of American genre the same quality of humor which has always characterized his personal dancing, the same excellent actor's sense of the theatre, and some first-rate invention to boot. . . . [T]he whole ballet, performance included, is just exactly ten degrees north of terrific.[*]

Overnight, in a stroke that could have come from the Lloyd Bacon/ Busby Berkeley film *42nd Street,* the twenty-five-year-old Robbins had gone from youngster to star. His new life had begun.

How I Almost Did Not Become a Dancer
August 15, 1976

There was no money to allow me to continue college even though I felt I could do much better than the first year, [but] I extracted a promise from my parents that for one year I could try my hand at what I wished. I wasn't at all sure what [things] I did want to do, but running the Comfort Corset Company was not among them.

I had always been fascinated by marionettes and had even constructed a small cardboard theater in the basement of our house and had made a number of marionettes, designed the clothes, painted, built and lit the scenery, etc. I had read some books on puppetry and was most impressed by one [written] by

---

[*] John Martin, "Ballet by Robbins Called Smash Hit," *New York Times,* April 19, 1944.

Tony Sarg.* So I looked up his name in the Manhattan phone book—he lived in Greenwich Village—blindly dressed in my most adult-looking clothes, went to his address and rang his bell. He lived in a rather dark ground floor apartment in a brownstone. I remember a short man, in a dim light, who wanted to know what I wanted.

I said I wanted to be a puppeteer and would he take me on as an apprentice. His answer was a brief "no, he didn't do that"—and I found myself in my best clothes out on the street again.

So then I decided I'd try dancing.

Because my sister had worked with him and because I had watched rehearsals, she arranged an audition and interview with [Senya Gluck] Sandor.† I felt about him then as I do about Balanchine now—he was very much in the limelight, and reviews by Martin‡ were not uncommon. He was the most stimulating creative man that I ever encountered.

He greeted me (he knew me as Sonia's brother) and asked me to change into my dance clothes (bathing trunks and a t-shirt) and then put me through some very elementary movements, running, jumping, rhythmic sequences, etc. Then he asked me to do some improvisations. First he asked me to write large numbers in the air, from 0 to 9 with my arms, then to write different numbers with different dramatic contexts—pleading, anger, as royalty, begging, etc. [T]hen he asked me to do one as Shiva, who both gave and took, blessed and damned. He put one gold spotlight on me and I took off. He said, *very* good—get dressed and we'll talk. After I changed, he invited me for a tea or snack at the bar-restaurant across the street. I was very nervous; being with such a famous creative person, and honored and thrilled to be allowed to dine with him.

We went into the bar-restaurant, seated ourselves in a booth, ordered I don't remember what, sitting opposite each other. Sandor must have sensed my anxiety. Then he said, I have to go to the bathroom—do you want to wash your

---

* Anthony Frederick Sarg (1880–1942) was an art puppeteer—a precursor of masters such as today's Basil Twist, and the mentor of Bil Baird—who presented marionette shows of classic works of theater and ballet and also created the first Macy's Thanksgiving Day Parade balloons.

† Senya Gluck Sandor (1899–1978) was a Bronx-born actor, dancer, choreographer, and teacher whose Dance Center, a modern-dance troupe and studio, was a significant part of the avant-garde dance scene in New York during the 1930s.

‡ John Martin (1893–1985) became dance critic of *The New York Times* in 1927.

hands or anything. I said yes because it seemed more agreeable than saying no, even though I didn't need to wash my hands again. So, with Sandor leading the way we entered the narrow little john consisting of one urinal, one toilet, a sink, mirror and towel rack.

While Sandor relieved himself I washed my hands, using the liquid soap that hung in an inverted jar extended out over the wash basin. You tapped up on the little peg on the bottom of the container jar and it released the soap with that particular certain public toilet odor. As I was drying my hands, in silence, Sandor took his turn at the sink and began washing his hands and then next he leaned forward toward the wash basin to splash some water on his luxurious black long hair before combing it. But as he leaned into the bowl I noticed that his head bobbing up and down was about to hit the short peg of the soap dispenser and I quickly passed my hand under the peg to stop that disaster. But an even more terrible disaster occurred. My hand pressed against the peg and out poured a stream of liquid soap down onto and into the black head of hair of Sandor, who, not knowing what was happening, continued to splash water on his head. A shampoo commercial could not outdo the sudsy foam that ensued. Horror-stricken, I watched as Sandor finally felt something wrong, looked at his hands and lifted his head to see in the mirror what looked like a soapy Harpo Marx. He held still—then wheeled around and stared at me. I don't know what my expression was like. All I know is that I knew for sure that my career as a dancer had come to a calamitous end in the bathroom of that bar-restaurant. Sandor, dearest man, must have seen everything in my face and he read all of it, the accident and my ashen-faced response to it and after a good look, he turned right back to the basin and washed the soap out of his hair as I stood by in complete misery. When he seemed rid of the soap he mopped up with his handkerchief, slicked his hair back with his comb and then we both went back to our booth and never ever to this day talked about what happened in the men's room.

What he did say was something like this: I was, he felt, very talented, but my wanting to be a dancer was to be very discouraged. It was a hard terrible life, one that certainly would never earn [me] enough to protect a future, no less make a present living. Dance was *not* popular in the US, male dancers were thought of as freaks, and the effort needed and the rewards of succeeding were totally out of balance.

But he said, you think it over, and if you want to work with me I'll take you on.

I thought it over then and there for less than a second and said, Yes, I want.

The Story of Hands
August 14, 1976

Across the street from [Sandor's] studio was a bar-restaurant the little company used for occasional meals and drinks, and on one evening when I went there with them someone suggested I have my first real drink. After much discussion it was decided that a Tom Collins was to be my inaugural concoction. Thus it was ordered, toasts were made, and I drank it, and of course got immediately drunk. They decided to return me to the studio and put me to bed on a couch, there to sleep it off, rather than allowing me to try to get home to Weehawken. Four or five people got me on my feet and helped me stagger across to the garage,* up the stairs, and on to the couch, where they undressed me and put me to bed while I sang, laughed and sometimes groaned as the room spun around me. There was one constant that I became aware of. Someone—some *man*—held my hand closely in his through all of this. Someone had my hand warmly in his and held it and me safe from danger and sent through our clasped hands a sensation of love, security and attention.

The next day I awoke and remembered the feeling of my hand in someone else's. I think I must have known who it was, for I went to him and asked, Did you hold my hand last night—and he said yes—and then a shocking thing happened. It was the realization that I was in love—and even more shocking—in love for the first time with a man.

It wasn't that I hadn't had homosexual experiences before—I had, with schoolmates & camp mates—but I never thought of them as being "queer"—only as a way we got secret pleasure while growing up. There was no kissing or anything connected with affection or love—only some mutual masturbation that every male goes through to some degree while maturing.

---

* The Dance Center studios and theater were above a garage in the West Fifties.

But now I understood that my heart had been captured & I completely catapulted into love feelings. It made me unhappy to realize I loved a man, that I was queer; but there was a marked separation between those feelings and the ones I had for Harry, the dancer who held my hand. (Funny—Harry was my father's name.) I confided my sad state to Klarna,* who stroked my hair while my head rested in her lap & who comforted me without approval or disapproval.

And I went after Harry. I watched all his rehearsals, waited for him to arrive each day, & tried to leave with him each evening. He wanted none of the responsibility of bringing me out. I would follow him to the subway & tell him I was going home with him—& he would refuse me & make me go to Jersey. I would dog his footsteps, [noticing] how he talked, laughed, smoked, walked, danced, smiled. But he refused me, nicely, carefully; he would have nothing to do with me physically. I wanted to be with him & hug & kiss him, but settled for whatever crumbs he gave me.

One evening we planned to have dinner together after rehearsal. . . . After everyone left the studio Harry and I sat on the couch. And we embraced & lay down together. And I kissed him so much & held him so tightly & it was such happiness & so blissful to me to be held so lovingly in his arms & be lying next to him.

Then to my surprise his hand slipped down between our bodies & cupped my genitals. I lay still, in shock . . . [JR's ellipses] still, still as I realized oh, that's what it's about, that's part of it, I hadn't thought of that—of sexual activity.

He felt my stillness & recognized what was happening within me. He pushed me away & sat up & smacked his closed fist against his forehead, held it there for a moment with his eyes tight shut & got to his feet. "*Out*," he said, "let's get *out* of here. Come on." And he pulled me to my feet & hurried me down the stairs & out into the street. "I'm going home, & I'm going home alone—& I will not have anything to do with you. You're too young. Go home. That's it."

And that was it. Until years later when I was 22 or 23 and with [Ballet Theatre] and we traveled to Boston where Harry was teaching & living, and I found him, & told him I'm ready now & we slept together. It was good, but too late.

---

* Klarna Pinska (1904–1994) had studied, danced, choreographed, and taught with Ruth St. Denis and Ted Shawn before joining Sandor's troupe.

Training: Yiddish Art Theatre and Classes
August 20, 1976

Sandor was asked to do the dances for "The Brothers Ashkenazi" by Sholem Asch, a huge book developed into a play for Maurice Schwartz[*] of the Yiddish Art Theatre. He picked some of us to work and be paid $10 a week. Nothing for rehearsals. I danced in two scenes of the show, supered in all mob scenes (including one in which we sang the Internationale in Russian), and played the part of the father of the Ashkenazi brothers when he was a little boy.[†] I spoke no Yiddish (it was only used by my parents when they didn't want us to understand what they were saying, i.e. often) and my only line was "Yuh, Tata"—yes, father. I did have to stand on stage in a group of villagers for about 5 minutes and it got to be a game to see how many could pinch my cheek or pat my face playfully before I got off. My family came to opening night[‡] and as my Tante Honey said, "Someone coughed so I missed your line." But I was happy to have a job and thrilled to be working in the theater.

About this time I had decided to take ballet lessons . . . and every evening in the theater I would hold on to the edge of the wash sink in the dressing room and practice barre. For some reason this threw the Yiddish actors into a disgruntled and upset stage. Maybe I counted out loud. Maybe I grunted and groaned. Maybe I was just plain in the way when they wanted to wash their hands.

For beside the 10 or 12 dancers there was a cast of about 20 Yiddish actors and most were over 40. They were fantastic actors and makeup artists. They had to [be]. The action of the play ran over a lifetime of 3 generations and a cast of a hundred would have [been] needed if each actor played one role.

Mr. Schwartz . . . was not well-liked by us. Not only were we deeply underpaid, but he would also force us to rehearse special shows that he would give as benefit performances. So two or three rehearsals would be added to our schedule

---

[*] Maurice Schwartz (1889–1960) founded the Yiddish Art Theatre, which performed works by classic Yiddish, English, and European playwrights, from Sholem Aleichem to Chekhov to Shakespeare, and earned Schwartz the soubriquet "the Yiddish Laurence Olivier."

[†] Robbins was slight and small; at eighteen he could still pass for a child at the movies.

[‡] September 20, 1937.

of nine performances a week. One night when he cut [off] his fake payes[*] he cut his real ear and the story went around the theater with secret smiles. We were being poorly paid because we did not come under Equity.[†] A movement started among the dancers to strike for $15; we all agreed and one dancer was sent to negotiate. Nothing doing. [We] then decided to give an ultimatum: either he'd give us the raise or we wouldn't work that night. Half hour was called . . . 15 minutes. Negotiations, but no give from Mr. S. 10 minutes, 5 minutes, and onstage was called and we didn't move from our rooms. At 5 minutes after the usual curtain time Mr. S capitulated and we got our raise. Sequel. Two weeks later Mr. S. fired 2–7 dancers. Our strike leader tried to rally us again with the fact that in this way Mr. S. cut the cost of us back to what it had been. But he couldn't get us together. *We* didn't want to get fired. And we now had $15 a week. I was the youngest then and I guess I would have gone with the majority—but I also did not want to lose my job, and thus my training. We were all chicken and selfish and I remember thinking if this is the way idealists and causes work, forget it.

Flopping

September 9, 1976

The first notice I ever received was written by Anatole Chujoy.[‡] It was a review of a dancer named Lisa Parnova[§] [who] did a concert of mostly solo dances at The Lexington YMHA. She was a dark beautiful woman, and I have no idea of how much ability she had as a technician. Needing a partner for two dances she'd asked Sandor for help in finding one—and he suggested me. It was [a] mistake, an ill match from every angle. To start with I'd had at that point four classes for

---

* Schwartz's character would cut off the fake side curls of the observant Orthodox Jew in order to assimilate into Russian society.
† Actors' Equity Association, the actors' union.
‡ Anatole Chujoy (1894–1969) was a Latvian-born writer, editor, and critic who in 1936 co-founded *Dance Magazine*.
§ Lisa Parnova was both a ballet and a modern dancer who had performed at the Cologne Opera in the late 1920s and had been a student of Michel Fokine's. This particular concert took place on Saturday, November 20, 1937.

(ABOVE AND OPPOSITE) Dance figure studies from the 1930s,
possibly made as aide-mémoire diagrams to accompany Robbins's
notes from his 1938 ballet lessons.

beginner's ballet. I scarcely knew the terms. I had absolutely no partnering ability. I'd never lifted a woman or protected her pirouettes. And lastly, I was a kid,
still growing, physically smaller than Lisa, and certainly much younger.

We did two dances. The first was to Debussy's "The Snow Is Falling"; it
was full of bourrées & some pirouettes for Lisa. I had no idea how to keep
her on balance as she turned. She was most patient, [but] she felt to me like a
heavy telephone pole, and I never could get her back on center once she started

off. She asked me what steps *I could* do. I liked *sissonnes* & *tour jetés** —so that's what I did when on my own.

The other dance was a Strauss waltz—I had to come on stage as if I had a tryst with someone for whom I'd bought a small bouquet. I wore elegant clothes of the 1870s—including a top hat and white gloves, beige trousers and a fawn coat with tails [and] a starched high collar. The rented costume carried the name of a not-too-well known tap-dancer inked into

its label—and I was thrilled to be sporting his clothes. I got on, running in full of excitement, then realized she wasn't there, looked from side to side, and sat down despondently. Lisa tiptoed in behind me and tapped me lightly and darted away. Finally we waltzed—skinny me in my rented clothes and Lisa in her big hooped skirt. Chujoy put it aptly. "Robin Gerald's partnering hindered more than it helped."

Furnished Room

1939

He sat in his furnished room and looked out the window at the little patch of sky that the buildings didn't block out. A little piece of the heavens, by which he judged the day and decided on his raincoat or bulky winter coat. He sat at

---

* Bourrées (not to be confused with pas de bourrée) are feathery traveling steps performed on pointe; sissonnes are jumps from two feet in which the working leg flashes to a perpendicular position to the front, side, or back; tour jetés are a traveling, turning jump.

the window on the edge of his bed puffing quietly on a cigarette and watching the smoke being pulled out of the window into the busy air of the city . . . air filled with noise and sound and nuance . . . hurrying air and heavy air. The air that pulled at you, at your mind and at your body—that lent no ease. But here in his room, the noises of the cars, the ever-honking horns and police whistles, reached him now faintly and formed the constant dull buzzing background for his city. In his room it was safe, or at least still. It was really an uneasy quiet when he started to think about it. The chair, the bureau, the spring bed, the desk, and the lamp, and the washbasin. So still so motionless and quiet that it frightened him. The furniture all alike.. all alike . . . in every furnished room he lived in, all alike, the only variance being the size and shape of the room.

He lifted his eyes to look out [at] the backs of the old brick brownstones like the one he was in. A few of the windows were lit and he could see into the rooms & watch the people. It was like looking into their lives. Furnished rooms with single people in them. Alone alone. In rooms with crowded walls & the bed chair bureau desk and corner basin, in rooms with the bath in the hall always smelling of faint disinfectant and the inevitable notice pasted on the wall— please leave this bathroom as you would like to find it . . . as you would like to find it—the words struck him—as you would find it find find find . . . oh poor people in poor rooms alone and alone. Can you find what you want—can you find?—Rooms bare and rooms with walls and floors.

Suddenly he realized that the phone was ringing three flights below. He listened to it wondering how long it had been ringing and when it would stop. Where was the land-lady and why did she take so long to answer it? He got up and went to his door and waited. The phone rang on. Why didn't she answer it? It might be for him.

He opened the door and stood in the hall hanging over the bannister trying to see down the three flights through the narrow space between the stairs and the floors. The phone rang on. He knew it would stop any moment now. He wasn't paying six dollars a week to have to run downstairs and answer the phone for everyone else. Why didn't . . .

Then he heard the receiver lifted off and the landlady's voice; he heard her ask [someone] to wait a moment. He stood poised over the stairs ready to run down on cue. He waited for the buzzes. The first one came. He waited. Then the second came. He waited. He waited—how long had he waited? He waited for the third [buzz] for his call. He stood ready. A long time passed. Then he heard her voice saying, No answer, and he went back into his room and closed the door and sat down on the bed.

Tamiment
June 24, 1986

I learned so much at Tamiment.[*] There were ballet dancers, Ruthanna Boris, Nico Charisse; modern dancers, Alice Dudley, Kenneth Bostock, Dorothy Bird, Anita Alvarez. And then there were the comedians, Jules Munshin, a then-unknown Danny Kaye, and a person from [whom] I learned so much of the art of comedy, Imogene Coca. I fell in love with her right away. Tiny, gamin[e] Imogene; her husband then, Big Bob,[†] a 6'2" hunk of the sweetest-natured man; [and] this huge French poodle, who sat in the back seat of their ancient high touring Rolls Royce like a Bostonian Dowager. Coca was wonderful. Her acting was connected and personal, her taste and sensitivities were almost painfully touching. I learned more from her about timing and humor than [from] anyone else. Beau Beyerson[‡] was also on the staff and I enjoyed his songs enormously. I remember staging a very sad bluesy lament, "Where's the Boy I Saved for a Rainy Day," with a very sad and large-eyed singer. She sat on the floor next to a chair with a man's jacket resting on it and touched it longingly and lamenting. I thought it was going to not leave a dry eye in the house. Instead it was the hoot of the evening. The girl singer was Carol Channing.

The biggest problem for the owners of the camp was how to handle the social staff (we entertainers) at meal times. We were getting $10.00 a week, [plus] room and board—but laundry, drinks, Cokes, anything that had to be purchased outside of the dining hall, cost us. If they put us all together, the bus boy

---

[*] After a trial gig at the Pocono resort over Labor Day weekend in 1937, Robbins was hired in advance for the entirety of the 1938 summer season, ten weeks at a salary of $10 plus room and board. It was a significant turning point for him.

[†] Robert Burton (1909–1955) was a performer and later a recording-industry executive who married Coca in 1935 after the failure of a show they were both in called *Fools Rush In*.

[‡] This is a mistranscription by Robbins's secretary (from Robbins's dictation or handwritten draft) of Baldwin Bergersen (ca. 1914–2000), composer, pianist, and arranger. "Where's the Boy I Saved for a Rainy Day?" was later successfully recorded by Polly Bergen, among others.

and waiters would get poor tips, if any, from us, as we were so poorly paid. The alternative was to break us up and sprinkle us around the dining room, a few at each table so that the waiters wouldn't be done out of too much. Neither way worked and all summer they'd try each method.

When they put us together we had such a good time, broke up, made jokes, laughed and carried on with too much hilarity for the rest of the decorum of the room. Once a dancer, who was watching a staffer get ready to blow out the candles on a birthday cake, impulsively seized them and put them bottom side first into her ears and shrilled, "Look, I'm a birthday cake." We looked aghast, as the lit ends of the candle caught at wisps of her fuzzy hair and in one concerted movement, the girl had six glasses of water thrown at her. It made a stir. She said, gasping for air, "What's that burnt smell?"

That made the dining room director separate us again. I found myself at a guests' table (as against a staff table) with one of the dancers whose sense of camp got the better of him. Every few days, particularly Monday, [at] the beginning of a week, or Fridays, the weekend, there'd be a new woman [or two] placed at the table. They'd approach more or less hesitantly in their special clothes bought for the vacation ([hoping to] get a husband maybe) and say, I'm Florence and she's Thelma, and everyone would then say his or her name. [Finally] Richard had had it. [That] day two new women came up. "I'm Ethel and this is Marjorie," said one, pointing at her friend. Richard picked up: "and I'm Frances and she's Helen," he said pointing at me. In silence, the girls nodded puzzled hellos and sat down. Richard and I continued using our new names for the rest of the meal and the next day we were transferred back to the staff tables.

Then there was the time we staffers were all together, and I was describing a costume I was going to wear in some number. I said, "and it has a long feather on the hat," and described in gesture the feather in a swift movement from the side of my head straight upwards with my arm. Crash!—the noise effect was spectacular. I had hit the bottom of a tray a passing waiter held over my head, and platters, cutlery, glasses and tray went spilling all around. In the commotion that followed, the dining director rushed over, his face red with anger. Friday night—and we were trying to cover our laughter. "What happened?" he asked furiously. I caught his attention by saying "It's all my fault. I was telling them about my costume with a hat whose feather like this"—Bonk!—I did it again. The next day, they separated us.

Journal, 1939[*]

October 9, Monday

Today I felt wonderful in class. More strength than I've had in a long time. Of course a poor class does exactly the opposite. 200 percent.

The rehearsal of Pony Boy was thumbs down. Oh, Mr. Andrews.[†] A deep swell of choked guts and rebellion rises in my throat, and any attempt at work is blocked. A heavy terse duel of glances, nuances, silently but densely covers the stage atmospherically. . . .

October 10

I really should call this the 11th because its already fifty-three minutes into that day. And the 11th is my birthday. . . .

Someone said to me tonight—well, you still have 20 years of dancing left—21 gone and how much have I accomplished. Have I still to formulate my ideas of what I want and how to get it. Each day I feel more and more sure of those things. Each day brings more and more resolutions and affirmations. I must declare myself. On this earth, in the dance, with people I meet, with my family, I must be known as positive sure and firm on what is right. I must deal with people better. With friends, relatives, and all I should be able to meet [their expectations] and yet save what I want for my work and my "self"—what I feel is almost holy[,] my deep sincerity of faith in what I'm doing. I must control myself in all ways better. This [is] a resolution I made at least five years ago—the best ever and the best to be kept.

---

[*] This journal is typed on loose sheets of foolscap (and occasionally illustrated with pencil sketches); perhaps because he was typing, and wasn't constrained by bound pages, Robbins felt he could express himself at greater length here than in some diary entries. The date "1940" was inked at some point (by Robbins) on the first page—in error, since internal evidence shows the events described took place in 1939.

[†] After three summers at Tamiment and two winters at the Dance Center, Robbins was at last appearing on Broadway—in the Tamiment-originated *Straw Hat Revue*. However, Jerome Andrews (1908–1992), a student of Martha Graham and of Robbins's own early teacher Alyse Bentley, who had danced on Broadway and at Radio City Music Hall, had been brought in by the producers to coordinate and polish the dance numbers—including some of Robbins's—for which he was given sole choreographic credit. No wonder Robbins called Andrews's own number "Phoney Boy" (see p. 38).

More October 10

. . . Rehearsal again of Phoney Boy the same as usual except I think that Jerome really doesn't want to act the way he does when he directs [but] he can't really help it. . . . If only he weren't afraid of us we wouldn't want to override him and torment him. But his answers are always nasty sharp and smug and without understanding. The number goes in Thursday matinee. . . .

Tonight at performance Balanchine and Zorina[*] were out front and so we did our very best and the Mooche got a very good hand. Their reaction [to] the Zorina Ballet[†] was very interesting to watch: a little bewildered by it all going so fast and trying to see it all, very often laughing and very often serious. . . .

I must be good and take better care of my body if I want to dance.[‡] This is really the last time I will ever say this to me. I can not dance if I am not strong enough to control all my impulses. I will say no more about [this] but that I feel very ashamed and that I will make that resolution good on this point for sure.

October 13

. . . I couldn't write on the 11th because I talked too long with my Mother and Sister. When I got out of the theater that night I found Sonya [*sic*] waiting for me. She had some disconcerting news to say the least. Sylvia[§] had spoken to her and said that the members of the company were worried because I had been kidding with Dick[¶] so much and had been camping very much. First of all I said the hell with all of them, that I refused to give a friend up because people talked and he had a bad reputation. I also felt extremely sick. After thinking it over, though, I came to the conclusion that it was mostly my fault, that I had been

---

[*] Vera Zorina (1917–2003), born Eva Brigitta Hartwig, a Norwegian ballerina and actress, the star of *On Your Toes, I Married an Angel,* and *The Goldwyn Follies,* had married George Balanchine in 1938. They divorced in 1946.

[†] "The Mooche" (to music by Duke Ellington) was a number about strippers; the Zorina Ballet was a takeoff of a dance from the film *The Goldwyn Follies* (choreographed by Balanchine) involving Vera Zorina and a life-sized statue of a horse. Imogene Coca spoofed Zorina in this one.

[‡] Robbins penciled the word "masterbation" [*sic*] next to this sentence.

[§] Sylvia Fine, composer and lyricist, who was engaged to Danny Kaye; she had written music and lyrics for *The Straw Hat Revue* and he was in the cast.

[¶] Richard Reed, a Tamiment colleague and fellow cast mate from *The Straw Hat Revue.*

camping a hell of a lot. I realized that it had been a reaction to the Albia set-to[*] and that I was looking desperately for a friend to turn to quickly. I know that I must be more careful, and can in the way I act at the theater, because talk and gossip go very quickly around.

October 17, Tuesday

Well, here we are again after an absence of a couple of days. Now I am writing and living in N.Y., my new address being 873 7th ave. Apt 6a.[†] Sounds classy, eh? And my goodness by the look of the front of the house you'd think I must be J. P.[‡] himself. It looks like this [there follows a pencil drawing of a large apartment house with a triple-arched porte cochere]. My room is in the interior of this building. It is very comfortable, not large but I have my own bath. The layout of the room is thus [another pencil drawing showing a small bed-sitting room, probably a former maid's room]. And the bathtub is something out of another world—to take a bath you must practically be a contortionist. But it's home.

Last night I went to Dwight's[§] to say goodbye as he is leaving on the road with the Caravan[¶] today. He was very discouraged and disappointed not only with his dancing but with his complete career, all of which has been brought on by his treatment at the Caravan. It is very cruel when a dancer is smart enough to realize he's at the end of his rope. With Dwight it is particularly painful to me as I am aware of his deep sensitivity, and how he has been so open to me in his discussion. . . .

Albia and I have patched up our differences to a degree and now go on with our romance a little sadder, wiser and more carefully. It will not be long I know until the next quarrel, and the making up I think will be easier. I'm very tired so

---

[*] At Tamiment, Robbins had become involved with the dancer Albia Kavan, whom he'd met in the chorus of *Great Lady* in 1938 and who was also in *The Straw Hat Revue;* their relationship was suffering through ups and downs. This was during one of the downs.

[†] Possibly his earnings from *The Straw Hat Revue* permitted him to make this move.

[‡] J. P. Morgan.

[§] Possibly Dwight S. Godwin (d. 1983), who had danced in the chorus of *Stars in Your Eyes* with Robbins; he later became a noted dance photographer and married the Balanchine ballerina Marie-Jeanne.

[¶] Ballet Caravan was a short-lived touring troupe founded in 1936 by Lincoln Kirstein as a platform for American choreographers. It was disbanded in 1941.

no more now. I am going to the studio to practice some Spanish.* I think Anita and I are going to do Frankie and Johnny† for TAC.

October 23, Monday

. . . I was in Jersey Sat[urday] for the dentist and had lunch with Mother. Being with her is more and more difficult because of my watching her and analyzing her and my reactions. I am always terrifically angered at her possessiveness [but] realize that I really do love her and all my irritation is just a reaction [to] that love.

Saturday night Albia and I went to see Jamaica Inn‡ and after we bought breakfast to cook in the morning and I took her home. We had a very lovely time and it was wonderful to feel her lips and body and see her eyes so full. I left about 3 and walked very frightened through the park for home. The next day I went back for breakfast and she sure can cook a mean breakfast. . . .

Martin§ was out front tonight and so of course I danced very badly. Bad from the brains. Which makes me more angry than when my body doesn't function. It's so late and so goodnight.

October 28 4 A.M.

I have found my faith. I am ready to declare myself. At once I have found the purpose and the spine of all I shall do and the regulation of my life. My religion shall become as fanatical as a devout priest's can be, and there shall never pass a day that I will forget at least three prayers to my religion. I am taking on a pledge as important as a vow. My sole purpose is declared. My rising eating living loving sleeping shall all be affected by my faith. I shall be firm straight and

---

* Robbins is probably referring to Spanish dancing, not language, since he needed to go to a studio to do it.

† Robbins had choreographed a number called "He Done Her Wrong," danced by himself and Anita Alvarez, at Tamiment, accompanied by Glen Bacon singing "The Ballad of Frankie and Johnny." It's not clear whether they repeated it for the Theatre Arts Committee (TAC); he and Alvarez *did* dance his "Strange Fruit," originally performed at Tamiment and set to the Abel Meeropol song, for a TAC benefit at the 92nd Street YMHA.

‡ *Jamaica Inn* was a 1939 Alfred Hitchcock adaptation of Daphne du Maurier's romantic thriller set in nineteenth-century Cornwall and starring Maureen O'Hara, Charles Laughton, and Emlyn Williams.

§ The *New York Times* dance critic John Martin, who had seen Robbins dance with Sandor's company and commented favorably on him.

Albia Kavan, Robbins's first girlfriend and
Broadway and Ballet Theatre colleague,
photographed at a whistle-stop on one of Ballet
Theatre's cross-country tours. She's wearing a chic
traveling outfit and fashionable snood, carrying a
somewhat less fashionable paper bag—probably
containing food for the journey, since there were no
dining cars on the trains the dancers traveled on.

even cruel to be faithful. I SHALL DANCE. Yes . . . I shall dance. Say it over
and over and over to infinatum [*sic*]. I shall dance I shall dance. . . . I will live
to dance, eat to dance, sleep to dance. My classes shall be my daily worship and
workshop. Every moment shall be devoted to these purposes. When my rests
come I shall love and live them with as much ecstasy as ever but my most pleasure will come from denying myself for my dancing, and even greater pleasure
will come of the harvesting of my work. I shall wear something around my neck
as Christians wear crosses to always be aware of my religion. I have now the
object of my faith. I have a vessel in which to store my beliefs and which shall
hold them as long as I *know* it will.

Auditions
June 24, 1986

When you are young, ambitious to be in theater, and without work, all auditions appear like rescue ships on the horizon when you are shipwrecked on a deserted island. The ships are not so far off and may come close—close enough to call out to, perhaps rescue you from this unbearable isolation and set you up in the world again.

You have, from the distance, no idea of what kind of ship it is or where it is headed. As it gets closer and you can read some signs your fantasies begin. Yes, your life will change, yes, you will be back in the real world, yes yes yes—*everything* will alter once you have been rescued. One can imagine the food, clothes, comfort, company, but most of all the unbelievable change that will happen in being recognized as a person, an acceptable part of that outside world, no longer an immigrant.

So, as the time draws near, the hopes and anxieties increase. You are to turn up at the Majestic Theatre at 12 noon. What kind of show is it? Who's doing it? The grapevine gossip supplies clues. . . . And off goes your imagination. Do they want tap? How much? You can get through a time step, a Welsh clog, a slim-slam, but it's really a fake. Do they want tall boys? (Tough shit—I'm 5′7.) Do they want ballet dancers? (Hardly ever, but in those days occasionally.) Do you know anyone connected—to give you at least more of a hint about that? How many days away—how many classes can you take—is it so early you won't be able to warm up properly? What to wear? The big question. Pants, tights, shorts, shoes, ballet slippers? Something eye-catching like a red bandanna or a blue belt? Do they want older (wear glasses)? Will you be asked to sing (rare in those days, as there were usually 16 dancers and the same number of singers)? Is it a big show? A period show? And most of all, *please* God, am I good enough, will I appear attractive enough, tall enough, talented enough? And as the day grows nearer the more the fantasies and expectations mount. A job—a job—a job as a *dancer*—a job in a Broadway show—oh dream beyond believability. How the stakes would rise—a breadwinner, able to get free from the anxious nervous economic fears and strictures of the family.

Imagine being free—able to perhaps rent a furnished room, buy your own clothes, pay for classes instead of being a janitor for them, to not watch so closely how much is spent for each mouthful you eat, to be able to take a street-car or a bus instead of having to walk up the palisades, or from the river to 5th Avenue and back. And the part too incredibly exciting to even think about—being a part of the world of theater—a dancer in a show, and being a part of the making of it. Imagine—on Broadway—in a show—legitimate. Oh how the shipwrecked yearns, needs, craves rescue. See me, see me, help me—pick me!!!

It all turns out differently.

That morning you get up early, do a barre, do all the studying you can, do as much jumping as possible in your room, pick your dancing outfit, and pick the street clothes to be seen in, in case they see you dressed. Breakfast is brief—stomach too tight. Gulping your tension down, you walk down the slope of the Palisades, take the ferry across the river. As you glide towards the city it looms bigger and bigger, growing giant-like until the boat unloads you. . . . You walk across 42nd Street to the theater district. . . . When you get to the alley leading to the backstage door of the theater a half hour ahead, the alley is already crammed with aspirants. You do not see anyone you know. Almost all are taller, securer, casually bantering with each other. [But] all eyes anxiously check . . . the closed stage door. All ears strain for mentions of what is thought to be needed—all rumors are put into the anxiety hopper. It's hot, and at 11:30 the sun is beating down into the alley.

Suddenly a stir goes through the crowd. Something's up. Heads swing to the shadowy stage door tucked under a grid of fire escapes. It's too far away to see what's happening but the word spreads. . . . Twenty-five at a time—a stand-up. Which means they just line you up and look at you. If they like you (if you seem to be the kind they need), you'll come back later for the audition. . . . The group moves slowly forward. . . .

Closer. Closer. Finally among those on the steps . . . Closer. You'll be among the next batch. And then push—

You get in. Concrete floor, radiators, dark grey, dusty, brown . . . Through a hall, through a big iron door, and it's suddenly so dark after the down-beating sunlight that you can't tell where you are. But hands are ushering you into a vast dark hole. . . . And you're there. In the line. You can vaguely make out some men in the distance. There is a little pause, and a man passing behind you says,

OK, thank you, and they're ushering you onward and through another dark short hall and through a door where *blast,* you're out on the street, on the other side of the theater, in the harsh daylight.

I can't remember how I passed the rest of those days. . . . I remember how bitter the taste in my mouth was, how hard it was to swallow my pain.

To: Company Management, Ballet Theatre

65 WEST 56TH STREET
April 26 [1940]

Dear Sirs—

Thank you very much for your card informing me of the auditions on the 29th. As you know I am greatly interested in joining the company—but unfortunately I will be out of town at that time for two weeks—returning May 12th, when I will open with "Keep Off the Grass."

However I would gladly leave the show to join and rehearse for the fall season and few summer dates.

I might refer you to Mr. Loring[*]—or Misses Lyon[†] or Konrad,[‡] or any member of your immediate ensemble, if you wish to hear about my work.

And I would be deeply gratefull [*sic*] if an audition could possibly be arranged during the week of the 15th May when the show opens here in town.

Again may I thank you for the card and impress upon you my sincerity in wishing to work with the company. I hope this letter will reach the proper hands with regards to a later audition.

Yours truly,
Jerome Robbins

[*] Eugene Loring (1911–1982), dancer and choreographer, a graduate of Balanchine's School of American Ballet, had been a member of Balanchine's first American company, the American Ballet, and of Lincoln Kirstein's Ballet Caravan before joining Ballet Theatre.
[†] Annabelle Lyon (1916–2011) danced with Ballet Theatre from the beginning and later originated roles in several Robbins ballets.
[‡] Karen Conrad (1919–1976) danced with Ballet Theatre from its inaugural season in 1940.

To: Donald Saddler[*]

[April 1940]

HOTEL LA SALLE, BOSTON
SAT NIGHT

Dear Don—

Just a note. Got here awfully tired & have been rehearsing since.

How's the room[†] working out? Rehearsals? Classes? David[‡] probably told you about the card I got about auditions for Ballet Theatre. If you can speak to Dolin[§] for me—& refer me to *Loring, Lyons, Conrad*. I tackled Pleasant myself on Friday morning.

Tell me what happened at auditions—& spread my regards around (not too generously as I may need them later)—& take care of yourself. If you get a chance, write.

Best regards,

J

Can you possibly send up my pair of blue tights hanging in the kitchen closet? It's gotten mighty cold up here!

---

[*] Donald Saddler (1918–2014) had met Robbins backstage with mutual friends after a performance of *Stars in Your Eyes*. He had already been selected for Ballet Theatre.

[†] Apparently, Saddler was subletting Robbins's furnished room in New York while Robbins was out of town with *Keep Off the Grass*.

[‡] David Nillo (1919–2005), who had danced at Tamiment, was also a new member of Ballet Theatre.

[§] Anton Dolin (1904–1983), born Patrick Healey-Kay, was a British-born ballet star who had danced with Diaghilev and was a founding principal dancer with Ballet Theatre.

Robbins photographed his friend Donald Saddler, whom he would later join in the Ballet Theatre company, on the set for Antony Tudor's ballet *Pillar of Fire* in the early 1940s; the theatrical lighting bleached out the image and gave Saddler the look of a marble faun.

To: Donald Saddler
[May 1940]

HOTEL LA SALLE, BOSTON
TUESDAY MORN.

Hello again—

It's the final dress rehearsal before we open tonight & I have loads of time. We do 1 number in the 1st act and 4 in the second & I know (I've seen to it) that I can't be found. The sets & costumes are very good—in fact wonderful. Karson[*] has done a terrific job & I don't understand why they didn't get him for any of the "ballet theater" things.

The costumes the boys wear are stinky for changes. All stiff shirts & collars [&] padding: all the wrong stuff for a summer show in N.Y. & we're pretty sure it'll run.

How are you getting on in the room? Are you finding it convenient & comfortable? There are plenty of rumors about 2 more weeks in Philly so you don't have to worry about moving if you like my place.

If we stay out on the road, I guess that puts my chances of getting into the company further away—all of which leaves me pretty discouraged. We're all pretty knocked out & tired & I really can't find the strength right now to work & do a bar[re]. We work until daylight—right thru the night. One morning instead of going to bed till noon I walked all around the town—the harbor, etc.—but although I enjoyed it I was too tired & had a hard time getting back to the hotel.

---

[*] Nat Karson (1908–1954) had previously designed the scenery and costumes for *Liliom,* Orson Welles's black *Macbeth,* and *The Hot Mikado,* and was scenic director for Radio City Music Hall.

WEDNESDAY NIGHT

The show opened—got good reviews and we're off. (Whee!) It was good to be performing again, even this stuff, and I am almost getting to like the numbers.

Now I must thank you profusely. First of all—David wrote & said you'd spoken to Dolin for me. Thanks a million-fold for that, Don. I really appreciate & [am] grateful to you.

Next, thanks for sending the tights. Maybe now I'll have more time to use them. (By the way, Marjorie* got a swell notice in one paper & Balanchine was quoted as having said "she was better than his beloved Zorina"!!!! Can you imagine rolling-pins flying chez Balanchine.) (Dirt—spread it, kid, spread it.)

And finally, thanks loads for the telegram.† It was so kind of you & Dave & it made me feel so good inside.

You've really been a hell of a swell friend, Don—& I don't know if it means anything to you—but I think a hell of a lot of you as a friend & person:—glad I met you. (Stuff & stuff—hard to say, but you know what I mean.)

Every night after the show (2 nights) Harriet‡ & I have explored that part of Boston known as "Beacon Hill." It is so charming—Pure American, early Colonial—By the time we get there it's cleared of people & the old street lamps make it look just like a "set."

How are rehearsals & classes. How'd the auditions go. Who was there, etc. How've you been? What's the latest rumors & dirt in the "Ballet Theater."

Well—write me soon, huh—I'd like very much to hear from you—and take care of yourself & dance like mad.

Sincerely,

J

---

* Margery Moore was a featured dancer in *Keep Off the Grass*. Robbins misspelled her name.
† An opening-night congratulations from Saddler and Nillo.
‡ Harriet Clarke played a "Dancing Young Lady" in the show (Robbins was a "Dancing Young Man").

To: Richard Pleasant
[n.d. 1940]

Dear Mr. Pleasant—

I stopped by today to see if I could get some information on the "summer" work I auditioned for Friday.* I am working now, and would have to give my notice in as soon as possible if I want to do the summer dates. I can't proceed to give my job up until I know what performing with your company entails. I'd like particularly to work (classes) with Mr. Tutor [*sic*], Mr. Dolin, & Mr. Loring as it is not for a "job's" sake that I would give up the show. These are some of the questions I wanted to ask.

How soon will rehearsals start?
How soon will I be able to take classes?
How long will the time be between the summer dates and fall rehearsals?
What kind of contract will be offered?

Your secretary told me that a meeting is to be held to discuss those particulars. I wonder if you could find out if I may be considered to be taken in as a regular member of the company—as Mr. Nillo & Mr. Saddler etc. for the rest of summer.

All these questions sound very forward and taking a lot for granted. I apologize. I have been trying to become a member of the company for a long time now & with another job on my hands I want to be careful not to be left with neither.

I hope you will consider my problem.

Sincerely,
Jerry Robbins

I'll stop by again tomorrow P.M.

---

* *Keep Off the Grass* didn't arrive in New York until May 23, a month after the open company auditions, but Robbins managed to be seen and on June 11 signed a two-month, $32.50-a-week contract. Just in time—*Keep Off the Grass* closed on June 29.

Training

July 17, 1976

Fokine staged *Carnaval* for Ballet Theatre just after I'd joined [Ballet Theatre][*] and I was assigned [to be] one of [the] men in the couples to dance the Valse Noble. I was naturally excited about working for the great Fokine.

I was stiff in Fokine's rehearsals. Noble, dressed up romantic gentlemen were definitely not my forte & an awkward embarrassment, the feeling of being a fake (Jewish), prevented me from ever achieving the relaxed gentlemanly attitude. It was that fake "niceness" I disliked about ballet, & I was bad at expressing the desired *élan* Fokine wanted. He stopped me many times to show me how to extend my hand, lift my chin, pull up & at same time relax my body. I felt & looked miserable & I sensed his growing impatience with me. He doesn't like me, I thought—& each rehearsal was approached with apprehension.

---

* In fact *Carnaval* (set to music of Robert Schumann) had premiered at Ballet Theatre in January 1940; possibly Fokine supervised rehearsals with new cast members, of whom Robbins was one, after he became a full corps member in the fall of 1940.

Three Ballet Theatre dancers at the barre, silhouetted against a sunlit window. The circle above the center dancer is a window fan.

To: Harry and Lena Rabinowitz
Monday night [October 1941]

[MEXICO CITY[*]]

Hello fellows . . .

Mother says I must be getting lots of "experience" [here in Mexico]. I don't know what she means, but this stuff that I'm about to give out with is as close as I can come.

[Let me] tell you about the caravan theater we saw in Tasco.[†] They travel around in a sort of small circus tent and the stage is set up on one end of it and they have their own light system, orchestra and microphone. Of course during a performance each of these go on the blink sooner or later and once in a while with a supreme effort they manage to get together and do it all at once. Then the audience which consist[s] completely of natives and Indians breaks into terrific whistles and calls and stamping till it's all fixed. The evening starts with a Drama. And I do mean capital D. The one we saw ran something like this. An Old Man lived in a house with his son who was engaged to a very sweet young girl. The son was the sole support, and although they were poor they were happy. But along came a Woman of the World and with her came tragedy. She enticed the son away from his home and sweet girl, and even went so far as to somehow cause his death . . . (I didn't understand how, but all the people looked very horrified around me). Last act; the Old Man is lame and he is losing his home because he has no money. The Girl must go too because she won't give in to the man who has the mortgage. In a tearing scene the Old Man signs away this deed of the house, and then goes to the garden to pick some flowers. At this point a Priest enters with the Woman of the World. He has gotten her [to] repent for her awful deeds. (I missed the whole dialogue here because the microphone was

---

* After nearly going bankrupt in the spring of 1941, Ballet Theatre had struck a presentation deal with the impresario Sol Hurok, who arranged for the company to travel to Mexico for a two-month residency at the Palacio de Bellas Artes in Mexico City. It was only the second time Robbins had left the United States and he made the most of it.
† "Tasco" is Robbins's transliteration of the scenic silver-mining city of Taxco in the mountains southwest of Mexico City, which he visited with a group of Ballet Theatre mates.

in the center of the proscenium and they played their scene on the side . . . not that I understand too much anyway). The Old Man returns and sees the Woman of the World. He wants to kill her with the stick, but the Priest (with a shaved head of course and an obvious wig) tells him that she has come to Repent. The Woman of the World goes down on her knees and weeps and cries and recites her lines with great elocution lessons.. a touching scene . . . and at the end of it she pulls from her purse almost a million pesos in bills and give[s] it to the old Man. He takes it and forgives her and gives the money to the priest. And as the curtain comes down everybody is on their knees praying like mad. Intermission. A good time to look around and see the audience. They are much more exciting and interesting than the play. Some beautiful Indian women with black hair in long braids . . . some young boys with white flashing teeth . . . numerous mothers with their off-spring collected all around them, on their laps, on their backs, between their knees . . . and there is an Indian mother with her baby on her back in the shawl . . . do you think it will smother. . . . [T]he mother watches the whole show, and her smooth brown cheeks never move and she never laughs or reacts, but watches everything very intently. Lights out and the curtain, which rolled down with a bang, rolls halfway up, gets stuck, jerks, and finally makes it all the way. Now the orchestra plays. This consists of three pieces . . . a piano, a drum, and a sax . . . but the noises that came out of it made it sound like a very old, scratched, and faded Victrola record of about 1919. They are playing some awful old popular U.S. tune, and now appears the soubrette. She is about 34 years old, tall, skinny, and very boney. She does a dance, a routine that looks as if it were picked up from Ann Pennington[*] by a blind chorus girl and transferred to her daughter who did the same to hers and finally evolved in the present form before our eyes. Almost a Charleston or black bottom, but not quite. Her dress was long, but the moment she did a turn and it went up the least bit.. all the young men in the audience screamed, whistled, and punched each other. She got an encore. Curtain bangs down. Lights up. Lights out, all of them. Screams, shouts, whistles, boos, cigarettes thrown, and finally lights on and peace. The curtain rolls up, this time without a hitch, and now comes

---

* Ann Pennington (1893–1971) was an actress and dancer in the *Ziegfeld Follies* and *George White's Scandals*; in the 1926 production of the latter she introduced an African-American-influenced dance, the black bottom, which overtook the Charleston in popularity.

From Robbins's 1942 Mexico sketchbook—
a figure possibly copied from a church
painting or sculpture, or perhaps a character
in a ballet, or an actor in a caravan theater
production.

the part everyone waits for. The comedian. He is always a reproduction, and usually a poor one, of the popular hero and screen idol, Cantinflas. He wears his pants low around his thighs the same way, with the same little hat perched on the top of his head. And he works with a girl and goes on and pulls jokes. They sang a song together, and he gave her a few almost dirty pats in the wrong places and exited. The end. Everybody files out slowly, the women surrounding themselves with squirming babies and the men adjusting their sombreros. They never take them off for such a performance. You see around them.

By the way I went to one of Cantinflas's films. It was called "The Unknown Gendarme." In it he does a "Danzon."* One of my favorite dances, but he does a satire on it.. and it is perfect to even the little frown that you should have if you're really lost in the dance. But it was the first Mexican film I had ever seen and I felt like I was back in the Yiddish Art. The same character actors and actresses with the same patterned parts done in the same patterned style. And the faces looked like it and the voices sounded like it. Only Maurice Shwartz [sic] was missing.

One of [the] things that I take particular delight in is riding the busses to work every day. It's like being a kid again. You can hold on to the running board and hang way out over the street and watch the buildings and people fly past, and nobody says "how childish!" This is all for ten centavos or two cents. If you think that subways in N.Y. are crowded at rush hour, baby you should see what these busses look like all day. You've got to catch them on the fly and get

---

* Robbins would choreograph a *danzon* for his own first ballet, *Fancy Free,* in the variation he made for himself.

off them on the run, and brother, God help you if you don't have both hands free to hold on with. See the bus coming around the corner of the square. On your mark, get set, go. It slows down about 1/2 kilometer and you look to see which door looks the less crowded. People are standing on the outer edge of the running board, the upper part of their bodies hanging way out over the street. But don't let that worry you. You see three spare inches of running board not in use and get your foot on it. "Vamanos" yells the conductor (let's go), and you're off. Now the idea is to get the rest of your weight on the bus while it's already in motion. The conductor takes it for granted you'll make it and never bothers to see if you do or don't. Grab hold of the rail that runs around the window edge if there's nothing else and hold tight. Where do you put the other foot? Oh don't bother about it, just let it hang. If the one you're standing on gets tired, just change feet. As you are flying along, and believe me these cars go like hell, a taxi will pass you with some obvious tourist in it. They will look at you and say, "poor people, ugh, how disgusting, so crowded." To which you smile back and change your feet.

Now I'm going to tell you a little about the food here. One of the happiest experiences with food took place on the road to Puebla. We had been driving way into the afternoon and I was hot, and Charlie* was thirsty, and I wanted something to eat too. At this point we came to a series of stands on the road. I saw a Coca-Cola bottle on one, gave a yell and we stopped. I got out and walked over to the stand. There was a very ancient and withered woman behind a small table about the quarter of the size of a bridge table. It was piled three feet deep with all kinds of meats already cooked. Large hams..veals.. roast of all sorts.. brown chickens.. and lots that I could not even recognize. And next to the stand was the little stove that everyone in Mexico carries with them. It's like a small stone altar or oven and you just stop wherever you're hungry, put some charcoal in the oven and wait till it gets hot. Meanwhile you slap some tortillas together and put them on the stove. You might add an earthen jug filled with what they call soup . . . always red. And there's your lunch. Well anyway.. her stove was going and tortillas were cooking and I smelled them. Well, I said, I'll venture it. Tiene usted tacos de pollo? I asked in my best polite Spanish. (Do you have

* Charles Payne (1909–1994), Ballet Theatre's executive managing director, had become a friend and confidant.

chicken tacos) Ah si, joven, she said. You must permit [me] to explain "joven" now. Joven means youth. It doesn't mean young man, or youngster, or adolescent . . . it means youth. And nothing is nicer than to be addressed by strangers as a "Joven." It kind of takes the bags away from your eyes . . . and life seems so much happier in a way. Well she picked up some tortillas in her cracked shriveled hands and tore some chicken off a breast bone with the same implements and stuck them in the tortillas. Then she turned to a table behind her, just as small as the last. This was covered with brown bowls and in each resided some kind of sauce or other. Green, red, orange . . . even a kind of blue one too. She picked up a little ladle and held it over each bowl. "Esta?" she asked. (This?) Holding my breath and at complete random I picked two of the colors, and she spread some on the "pollo," and then wrapped the whole thing up in another tortilla so it looked like an enormous cigar and handed it to me. Charlie was watching the procedure with what is known as amusement, and he caught my eye as I lifted the concoction to my lips. He seemed to say.. get closer so that I can catch you as you fall. But the moment that I had taken one good bite I ordered three more and consumed them between gulps of Coca Colas. The whole affair cost me 80 centavos or about 15 cents. It was almost the best food I've had in Mexico yet.

Diary, 1942

Monday, January 12, 1942
[NEW YORK]

Today I started rehearsals for Devil in 3 Virgins.* Must work hard. Had to say so long to H.F.† Got suits, & off tonight for Summit, N.J. I can see this tour is going to be an experience. I hope a good one . . . anyway a profitable one.

---

* *Three Virgins and a Devil,* a 1934 ballet in one act by Agnes de Mille, entered the repertory of Ballet Theatre on February 11, 1941. Robbins had played the cameo role of the Youth in the premiere but now was cast in the featured role of the Devil.

† Horton Foote (1916–2009), who would become a Pulitzer Prize– and Academy Award–winning playwright and screenwriter, was a member of the American Actors Company, the group co-founded by Robbins's (and Agnes de Mille's) friend Mary Hunter. He and Robbins were close for a time and collaborated on the scenario for a theater piece based on the African American legend Stag-O-Lee (or Stack-O-Lee).

Today I just was struck with on what thin ice I'd been walking. I didn't realize how close the army was to Horton & myself. He's gotten the chance to go to
Texas before I get back this week—& suddenly I realized I didn't know when I'd
see him again. And all the old feelings of the draft[*] came back.

Thursday, January 15, 1942
WASH[INGTON, D.C.]
LIKE SPRING.

Home at 4 a.m. [but] got up in time to get to rehearsal at 1. At 4 went to the
new Mellon museum.[†] What a real palace of marble. Long halls & rooms with
few paintings. El Greco. Must try a portrait like the Medievals. Very plain. Black
shirt—small white collar—blue or deep red background. *Peter*[‡] was mad on
stage without scenery. My nose fell off!! After went with Nora[§] & Annabelle to
The Troika.[¶] Saw Otto & Meta[**]—so wonderful to see them again. Night club
work is awful—but if I don't get anything done—I'm going to do it . . . & earn
money. I do want a farm, and now with H. it's different. Got his letter today &
it was so wonderful to hear from him.

After dished with Mimi, Mu, Wally,[††] etc. for a while. Waste of time & courage. No more. Alone—but work. Work is better.

---

[*] After the Japanese attack on Pearl Harbor, the previous December, the United States had entered
World War II and had begun conscripting eligible men. Called before the draft board, Robbins had
answered yes to the question "Have you ever had a homosexual experience?" When asked when,
he had said, "Last night." He was classified 4F (unfit for service) because of "constitutional psycho-
pathic deformity" as well as "asthma, bronchial."
[†] The National Gallery of Art, which opened March 17, 1941, was endowed by the financier and
collector Andrew W. Mellon.
[‡] *Peter and the Wolf*, a ballet by Adolph Bolm (1884–1951), in which Robbins played one of the hunt-
ers, and later the title role.
[§] Nora Kaye (1920–1987), a Bronx-born principal with Ballet Theatre, was notable for her roles in
dramatic ballets, particularly those by Antony Tudor.
[¶] The Troika was a Washington nightclub located in a converted mansion on Connecticut Avenue.
[**] Meta Krahn and Otto Ulbricht performed as Mata and Hari and were alumni of Tamiment,
where, Robbins recollected, "they both seduced me one evening. It felt funny."
[††] Mimi Gomber, Muriel Bentley, and Wallace Seibert were all corps de ballet members of Ballet
Theatre.

One of Ballet Theatre's stars, Irina Baronova, who had been
one of the "baby ballerinas" of the Ballet Russe, in her
dressing room putting on her makeup for *Les Sylphides*,
circa 1942.

Wednesday, January 21, 1942
BOSTON

Dorati* likes the ballet!!! Oh god please—I'll be good—I'll work hard—but
please let me do what's right & get to do what I want to do.

* Antal Dorati (1906–1988) was named music director of Ballet Theatre in 1941. Robbins had sub-
mitted a scenario to him.

Tuesday, January 27, 1942

Here we are on the way to Canada & the most wonderful scenery & breathtaking farms are passing. I can't say things as well as Wolfe* but I feel the terrific tug of the earth—and its people's struggles to live on its produce—so very much.

Long mountains—lots of snow—pine trees with snow on the leaves. Farms & country fences. White—clean tall & fragile birches. Gnarled old twisted apple trees. And frozen lakes & rivers.

Monday, February 2, 1942

MONTREAL

HIS MAJESTY'S THEATER.

Up & breakfast at coffee shop. Bought a Tyrolean Hat! Very proud of it. Letter from Horton. No rehearsal of Goya [José Fernandez's *Goyescas*], but will do 1st Virgins instead! Home & lunch with Lucia!† She called me. Dinner with Johnny‡ & to theater. So nice to be in one spot for a week! Dressing room for 4. Quiet. Tried to dance well. After [performance], dinner at Aux Délicieux with

Hurok

Sevastianoff,

Baronova

Markova

Chase

Payne & Robbins!§

Quel day!

---

* Thomas Wolfe's posthumous *You Can't Go Home Again* had been published in 1940.
† An invitation from Lucia Chase, founder, de facto director, and principal backer of Ballet Theatre, was a royal summons.
‡ John Kriza (1919–1975) was one of Robbins's closest friends in Ballet Theatre.
§ His dinner companions were Sol Hurok (the producer), German Sevastianoff (the managing director), Irina Baronova (his wife, a principal), Alicia Markova (another principal), Lucia Chase, and managing director Charles Payne. Young Robbins had definitely Arrived.

Untitled Stories
December 2–20, 1942

Sometimes after a performance he would be in a hectic mood. He would tear into his dressing room & furiously remove his make up, flinging kleenexes to the floor & watching his tanned exactly made up face become a greasy grey color that made him look sick & feverish. And he was. He was torn & thrown by he knew not what. He asked some of the boys what they were doing after. He wanted to go home. He was afraid of going home. He wanted to go out with some of them. He hated them & couldn't stand listening. He wanted to walk for hours alone—no, he wanted to pick up someone & take them to his warm hotel room with the huge soft bed. All this pricked at his mind as he washed his face—packed his make up—dressed himself. He would find himself with three of the boys—a Russian—& French & an American & go with them to eat. They would talk about performance—laugh—flirt—dish—gossip & break each other down—& he would sit there—his hands drumming on the table—or tearing a book of matches apart.

Finally he would take himself home—walking down the cold empty streets—past the corner street lamp—through & beyond its circle of lonely light—& even as he walked—he waited—& wanted it to happen—wanted that magical wonderful thing to happen that would change his life—his spirit—heal his brain & lacerated insides—remake his whole feverish self into a contented sound strong being. He looked at the approaching stranger—peered in the windows of bars—looked thru the deserted lobby of the hotel—watched the elevator boy—waited for a door to open in the long hall of closed doors—expected it in his room as he switched on the light & finally got into bed.

And even on those nights the struggles didn't retreat. Instead as he closed his eyes they swam in on him—exaggerated—caricatured—distorted—till he tossed & got up & opened the window—or put on the light & read—smoked a cigarette—or sighed & paced. And his body would give him no rest either. He would grow excited & think of bodily pleasure & physical sensations—& he damned himself—damned damned himself till toward morning he fell into a forced unnaturally deep sleep from which he awoke—miserably sick & tired.

He was always filled with self doubts & complexes about his homeliness & physical unattractiveness. He was thin—& dark—& he retreated from competition by not shaving & wearing old clothes & sweaters. He played that he ignored the people that came backstage after performance out of curiosity to see the dancers & what they looked like—he played at not caring if they didn't notice him & picked him out—& when they waited for one of the other boys he played at saying well who wants to [go] out with some lech [*sic*] of a balletomane—But under it all—he wanted more than anything to be attractive & desired—& then to be able to reject—And when none of the others were around he played at being important & busy & competent while people hung around the stage door call board. When the boys decided to go out to a night club—he would refuse to go saying to himself—I don't want to go out & mess around & pick up people & be gay & chippy—but under it all he wanted to be that very much—but he wanted to be the most attractive—the most gay & chippy—the center & the happiest. He was afraid of drinking, of getting drunk & becoming unhappy. And he was afraid of the casual gibe & cutting joke. And so he went alone—ate alone—& slept alone, wanting comradeship & joyous company—not knowing if he were superior or inferior because of not getting on with them all.

He would sit in a drugged state—staring out the window as the train rushed on & swayed. He was always fascinated by the endless moving strip of land & honest people that went past him—the hills & plains & fields of withered corn stalks—the unpainted broken down shamble of a house too near the train tracks—the awful lonely cold stoney outskirts & train yards of cities—with black factories & wire grilled fences & old rusted freight cars. It thrilled him to see the names on those cars—Illinois Central—B&O, Ches and O, NYCRR, Southern Pacific, Union Pacific—& his mind flashed across the country, soared over deserts, plains & mountains [following] the trains' routes and back again to the empty barren track-strewed yard.

Often it was necessary to get up before day-break to make a train connection. Although it was agony getting out of bed by dark, & washing, dressing, & packing by electric light—it was at the same time thrilling & refreshing. He always had a special love for early risings & watching day come. It was a period of waiting & expectancy—of searching the sky for the warning greying—of living through a birth of a day through the greyness—& coldness—to the bluing of sky as the sun rose—through the slow increase of tempos of life as the day grew older—He felt that he was stealing something delicious by being up ahead of everyone—that he had something in common with the all-night desk clerk—

taxi driver—train-yard man—factory worker—counterman in the sandwich shop. They were together.

And he loved the nights—the dark—cold empty street nights—& he wanted to prowl—to talk with the soldier walking toward him—to sneak into homes & watch families asleep—to look in their ice boxes—open the closets— read their letters—feel their clothes—know them—know them—

But always he was driven—pushed—tomorrow early train—must sleep—& he would return to his hotel room & crawl into bed feeling [he was] missing something.

Training
July 17, 1976

The next ballet [Fokine] did for us was *Bluebeard* & somehow I was cast as one of the Spanish Lovers. I took off on this troubadour like a sky-rocket. (I had studied Spanish dancing). I ate the material up, did it as fast as he choreographed it—& later on Lucia [told] me how Fokine used to beam & light up as he watched me do this choreographed lover of his.

Then he staged *Petrouchka** for us. I was not selected for Petrouchka; or his alternate, or his understudy, or his understudy's understudy. That stopped me not. As it was a role I loved, had read about, & sworn to do, I went to him and asked him if please could I just study it—he didn't have to spend any time with me, just let me come to rehearsals to watch and learn the role. Very well he said.

I studied everything carefully. I went over it all later many times by myself. I bought all the books I could find about it, studied photographs, and had a recording of the music on constantly. And as rehearsals proceeded F[okine] started to give me a direction or correction here & there. [H]e said something that threw me. "It's not like the Spanish lover" he said, "not inside, real. It's a

---

* *Petrouchka* (or *Petrushka*—Robbins uses both spellings), a one-act ballet to a score by Igor Stravinsky, was first presented by Diaghilev's Ballets Russes in Paris in 1911 with Vaslav Nijinsky in the title role. The plot concerns a misshapen puppet, imprisoned by a magician in a puppet booth and hopelessly in love with another puppet, a ballerina; she spurns him for still another puppet, a blackamoor, who ultimately kills his rival. Ballet Theatre's production would premiere on August 27, 1942, at the Palacio de Bellas Artes in Mexico City.

show, all outside, for show." Now I'd felt just the opposite. The Spanish lover was all show, a caricature capable of few but primary emotions—anger, love, surprise. And Petrouchka, ill-painted, humiliated, struggling for human recognition, dignity, feeling a passion for something beautiful, trying to make sense of his position & emotions, was about as complex an interior as one could imagine. I knew that what F[okine] was trying to tell me was something else—that I had some thinking to do.

[Eventually] I got my chance. I worked so hard on it. I figured out how the joints of the puppet were made, & of what material to justify the movements. I studied Nijinsky's make-up, propped the famous photo on my dressing table & tried to imitate it. I decided because he was the least loved, he'd been made crudely, painted badly—& as one eye was off, so his vision was blurred & cock-eyed. With that I understood all the crazy head positions twisted or cocked on the neck, that Fokine had shown.

Petrouchka was my favorite role. There was a deep instinctive recognition of his plight & wants. In my teens I had a nightmare: I found myself alone in the closed-in backyards of a city's deserted tenements. The empty lots were full of refuse: broken bricks, empty cans, weeds, debris, everything thrown out—discarded—& uncared for. I tried in every way to get out. And could not; for the windows that gave out on the deserted lot were closed with rusty iron shutters & barred; the fences that I pushed at were too high to scale & too well made to push down. I screamed for help. I *had* to get out—I couldn't be left discarded in this dump heap unattended & forgotten. My panic was immense—& there was no release. I knew Petrouchka.

To: Harry and Lena Rabinowitz
July 23, [1942]

Dear folks . . .

I have had something on my mind all day today and want to get it off. I wish you could see your way to come down here.[*] I have saved some money.

---

[*] Ballet Theatre had returned to Mexico City for a second residency during the summer of 1942.

Donald Saddler and Maria Karnilova (later a dressy Tessie Tura in
Gypsy as well as an unflappable Golde in *Fiddler on the Roof*) show off
their Ballet Theatre touring style. "There must be dogs—at least 2,"
Robbins scribbled on the back of this photograph.

I am getting a lot more for directing the dances in the picture.* I get enough
money each week for two people for room and board. So. Now that things at
the factory are slack, I want you and Dad to think of coming down here for a

* Robbins had been engaged to choreograph two dances for a Mexican film, *Yo Bailé con Don
Porfirio.*

month. It would be such a pleasure, to take care of you for the month. I can't do anything about transportation right now I don't think . . . maybe for one of you. But here is your chance to get away for a while, and to get out and see some places you never have before, and here is my chance to [do] something toward repaying you all for bringing me up, such as I am. Honestly folks, I know how much you would enjoy it. And it would give me such a thrill to have you here. Please, please come down. I know how apt you are to say well I might, and talk about it to other people but not really believe in coming . . . but YOU DON'T KNOW WHEN another chance might come up like this again, and I don't know when I'll get another chance to give you a treat like this too. So please, please think about it very seriously. Later on things will be hectic, and what with the war etc. only God knows what will be. Don't muddle over it too much. Decide, pack, and get on a train. I'll love having you. Let me know when you're coming.

Lots and lots of love . . .

J.

To: Harry and Lena Rabinowitz

Saturday eve [late July or early August 1942]

Dearest Folks..

I don't think I can tell you how awfully disappointed I am that you aren't coming down here. This past week has been horribly long only because I have been waiting for your letter. I'm sorry. Perhaps we'll make it a weekend or so in Boston or somewhere else very near to N.Y. when you can find time to tear yourselves away from the factory. Oh, I understand it all right.. why you have to keep the place going, but I hate to see you knocking yourselves out so much, and I thought that this was the ideal time for you to come. I had been planning trips with you and lots of places to go and visit . . . but what's the use of talking about it. Suffice to say I would have been in a little heaven to have had you both here, and I'm sorry you can't see your way clear to come.

Tonight we had a complete run-thru of the Fokine ballet and after working on the classical variation like hell, and getting all worried and upset because I couldn't do it properly, and after almost giving the dam thing up, I did it well enough for Fokine to say that I did it "very well, very well" and I feel that it is something accomplished. I am not a classical dancer really, you see.

By now you have read the story.* I wonder how you liked it. I am working on another one very different in style and subject matter, but I find it very hard going right now. I like to write. You work alone and physically it isn't as hard as dancing. And when you are thru you have your work in front of you, not lost in some performance and once done its gone forever. So there is a lot of satisfaction in writing that there isn't in dancing.

I should like to call you home very soon. But I'm afraid that I would become so homesick on hearing your voices that the remainder of the stay would be too much for me. But perhaps I'll try.

Keep well and happy, please don't wear yourselves out too much at the factory, and write me often.

Love,
J.

Diary, 1942

Saturday, August 8, 1942

Today Horton wrote me a letter resigning.† I sat very well controlled in the lobby reading it till Charles P. came in, saw my face, knew what it said, & asked me if I wanted to get drunk. Then I broke up. "What's the use"—and tried to get to my room. Hysterics all the way & couldn't get the key in the door. Lasted about 15 minutes & then got control. Dinner & movies & then called N.Y. Couldn't speak. To bed.

---

* Possibly a vignette he had written about people he had met in Mexico.
† Reference is unclear. Possibly Foote backed out of collaborating on *Stack-O-Lee,* the folkloric theater piece they had been working on.

But I have control, & that is what is important to me—That is what I've found out. And I'm glad I have it. I don't want to drink—& don't want to sleep around.

Wednesday, August 12, 1942

Last night heard a really tragic story from a 50 year old man. Architect—well set—family wife kids, business—[well-]to-do. When younger fell in love on sight (& only) with a doctor who was husband to a good friend of uncle's. Was frightened by it all & never did anything about it till too late. The doctor died—& all he could do was to suggest putting a flower in his hand as he lay in the coffin.

Saturday, August 22, 1942

Had rehearsal of Petrushka [*sic*] on stage. It seems to get harder & harder for me to do instead of easier!

Today we got news during afternoon rehearsal of Fokine's death. Massine[*] called everyone on stage & we held a 5 minute reverence—& then dismissed for the day. At 6:15 we had a service for him in the church. I think everyone resented the priest mumbling Fokine's name.

We wonder what will happen to his wife. We think, I think he was completed as an artist already—but it finishes so irrevocably a period & era of ballet & dancing. All the afternoon I wonder what Tutor [*sic*] was thinking . . . in Church & on stage.

Tuesday, September 8, 1942

Found wonderful analogy & line to work on. The "different" & strange person—mentally & morally—backed against the "proper" society & conventions. Ballerina must be one you love intensely. Magician & walls are the standards, conventions, & hard uncaring bigotism [*sic*] of the "proper society."

---

[*] Léonide Massine (1896–1979), the Russian choreographer and dancer, had been Diaghilev's ballet master; he was working with Ballet Theatre at the time.

Wednesday, September 9, 1942*

Petrushka—

Was pretty un nervous—& kept that way most of the day. We rehearsed "Helen"† & it kept my mind off Petrushka. Then had lunch with Nora, Don, & Albia‡—& home for 1/2 [hour]'s nap. Got to theater & was thrown in panic because I forgot *make up keys*. Then did Chinese dance in *Coppélia*§ & was very

---

* The night of Robbins's debut—it was his first leading role for the company.

† Fokine's *Helen of Troy*, a comic retelling of the Trojan War, in which Robbins played Hermes.

‡ Robbins's former girlfriend, Albia Kavan, was also a member of Ballet Theatre, and the two had remained close friends if not lovers.

§ The Chinese doll is a small character part in the one-act version of *Coppélia* that Ballet Theatre presented.

Richard Reed in the Ballet Theatre men's dressing room, East Lansing, Michigan, November 23, 1942. "When you first look at this picture," Robbins wrote on the back of the photograph, "you don't see the 5 other people in it because of the confusion."

relaxed. Got made up & dressed for P. just in time. Got into booth[*] early—it was good to do so. Oh God—have never come so close to passing out before in my vie. Tired & knees weak. But got good compliments—Charlie P. gave me a wonderful cigarette case for good luck.

Tuesday, September 15, 1942

Oh god—I'm so happy that Petrushka is working out! It means so much to me. I want to be the very best Petrushka there is. I am & want to be humble & workman like before the part. It has to be good. It is me in so many ways. Please let me be healthy about it—And sincere.

Tuesday, October 13, 1942

PROVIDENCE, R.I.

All right—I'm confused. I've mastered confusion—& getting upset—but I feel I'm putting things away from me—the company—Petruchka [*sic*]—Dancing—I'm pretty mixed up yet—face it. I'm thrown very much. I'd like to do something else—study—work—phyciatry [*sic*]?

Sunday, October 18, 1942

BOSTON

I have stood at nights—in strange cities—under the protecting lone circle of a street lamp—& looked down the darkness & emptiness of strange streets. For the familiar figure which never came. And I have walked through the parks at night of those cities & stood alone, my face up to the dark magnificence of the open wide sky—and asked the question & listened to the silence—: And I have left the paths & walked into the dark foreign shadows & felt my feet on the damp earth—& stood quietly in the black shade of trees waiting for I know not what. And I have grown frightened—& had to leave.

I know—but the knowledge of that truth is torture. I want—& my wants betray me. I love too much but not enough of one. No time—no time.

---

[*] The puppet theater is contained in a curtained booth.

Fancy Free
[1943[*]]

A ONE-ACT BALLET

CHARACTERS: Three Sailors, The Brunette, The Red-Head, The Blonde, (a Bartender)
TIME: The present; a hot summer night
PLACE: New York.

This is the story of three sailors who are out on the town on a Shore Leave. It is a jazz ballet, light in mood, running about 15 minutes. The costumes for the sailors should be the regular dark sailors' uniforms.[†] The girls should wear actual street dresses which permit free movement. The bartender should wear the usual white apron-jacket combination. The set, imaginatively designed, should represent a city street, a bar at center stage so that its interior is visible, and a lamppost stage left. The action takes place at night.

> *Music and Mood*
> *Fast, explosive, jolly, rollicking. A bang-away start.*
> *Transition period to a slower mood.*
> *Slow, relaxed; music should have literal meanings as far as specific action is concerned*

ACTION:

Three sailors explode onto the stage. They are out on shore leave, looking for excitement, women, drink, any kind of fun they can stir up. Right now they are fresh, full of animal exuberance and boisterous spirits, searching for something to do, something to happen. Meanwhile they dance down the street with typical sailor movements—the brassy walk, the inoffensive vulgarity, the quality of

---

* The *Fancy Free* files in the Robbins Papers at NYPL have been cataloged as originating in 1942; it seems unlikely the scenario dates from so early, since as late as January 1943 Robbins was still pursuing other ideas for ballets. This scenario is not dated.
† Dark (navy) uniforms are worn only in winter; by the time the ballet got to the stage, Robbins had realized his sailors had to be in summer whites.

being all steamed up and ready to go. They boldly strut, swagger and kid each other along. This section should serve as an introductory dance as well; bright, fast, gay, happy. One should feel immediately that the three are good friends, used to bumming around together, used to each other's guff . . . that they are in the habit of spending their time as a trio, and that, under all their rough and tumble exterior, there is a real affection for each other, a kind of "my buddy" feeling.

They finally arrive at the lamppost around which they gradually settle as the first impetus and excitement of being on shore dies down. One, with his arm crooked around the pole, swings slowly back and forth; another rocks on his heels; the third leans; and the more seriously they become involved with what to do next, the quieter they become. Finally they decide that a drink is what they need. They saunter toward the bar, enter, and each approaches the bar and places his foot on the rail. They order up three beers which the bartender serves. They pick up their glasses and clink them together in a mutual toast. Simultaneously they lift, drain, and plunk their glasses back on the bar. A moment of satisfaction; a pause of relaxation. They turn front and, as part of their habits, choose to see who pays. Two of them secretly agree on the same amount of fingers, and consequently the odd man pays. He shakes his head (as if this happens all the time, which it does), and pays. The three hitch their pants and move to the door, where they stand looking out at the night and street. One yawns, another stretches, and the third produces a slice of gum, breaks it in three parts and hands a piece to each. Each unwraps it, rolls up the paper, puts the gum in his mouth, and then with a neat kick, deftly flips the wrapper away. They stand in the doorway chewing. A pause of satisfaction, a sigh of "Now what should we do?"*

---

* The entire ballet, a screwball comedy in which the sailors meet two girls, have a fight over them, then race off in pursuit of a third girl, is outlined—and the music described—in the same detail as this first scene. It makes charming reading, but space permits only this brief excerpt.

To: Alden Talbot
[Autumn 1943]

Dear Alden,

Fine!—Swell!—just give me the chance & I'm ready to work like a house on fire. I'm more than anxious to hear Nordoff's* music. I also have two others† to hear when I arrive.‡ I feel it's very important to settle on a musician as soon as possible regardless which season the ballet goes on. Only please, Alden, give me a few days free when we first get in, so that I can hear & contact people. I was pretty hampered out on this coast because I never had time. So unless it's for something very very important—please see if I can manage a few days free as soon as possible after we return—so I can hear, & decide upon a composer. I think you'll agree with me on its importance.

Thanks very much for the note, and the encouragement. I believe myself that it will fit in better with this fall's ballets, by way of variety & style than next seasons. I do hope it can be achieved.

See you soon now—

Jerry

---

* Paul Nordoff, Ballet Theatre's musical arranger. Company management hoped he could concoct a pastiche score for *Fancy Free,* a cheaper option than commissioning a new one, which Robbins wanted them to do.

† Robbins had grand and edgy ambitions for his ballet score: his notes of potential composers list the names of Morton Gould, Marc Blitzstein, Norman Dello Joio, Vincent Persichetti, Lukas Foss, and Elie Siegmeister. Persichetti declined because he didn't do jazz, but he suggested a young unknown who might fill the bill—Leonard Bernstein.

‡ Robbins was writing from the road and intended to meet and audition these composers when he arrived back in New York with the company.

To: Charles Payne[*]

Thursday . . . [late autumn 1943]

THE BILTMORE HOTEL, LOS ANGELES

Dearest Charles . . .

It was so very wonderful to get a letter from you today. Just the thing to make everything feel really fine. For some reason or other I woke up today feeling very healthy and happy (strange, isn't it?) and before breakfast I wandered over to the theater and picked up the mail. It was a delightful epistle indeed, and puts me to shame as now it makes two that I owe you. I think the last I wrote you was after New Orleans, and since then many events have taken place.

The two that seem the most important are these; the premier [*sic*] of that sterling ballet "And Fancy Free"[†] is scheduled for the 18th of April. By the chances of fate it so happens that it falls three years to the day of my rejection from the army. I am trying hard to believe that it is a *good* sign. Because De Mille has wrapped up all the rehearsal time to this day no actual work has been done outside of completing the first dance . . . but *I've got ideas.* As soon as we leave this corrupt city of L.A. I'll dig in like crazy and the poor kids who work for me will not have felt a lash like mine. Outside of occasionally wetting my drawers when I think of opening night at the Met in April, I have pretty good confidence and feel encouraged indeed. When I run into a snag, I'll wire for help. If you chide me and tease me, I'm sure it will make me so mad that I'll plow on right thru any problems that might be disturbing me then. I'm still having trouble with my third sailor. Dick[‡] won't work—(he's back in N.Y. anyway) and Mike[§] is about to be inducted any day now. Which leaves me with either Harold[¶] or

---

[*] Payne had left his post as Ballet Theatre company manager to join the army for the duration of the war and was stationed in Washington, D.C.

[†] The ballet's title derives from the saying "footloose and fancy free." Fortunately, Robbins deleted the "and" before the premiere.

[‡] Richard Reed.

[§] Michael Maule.

[¶] Harold Lang (who ended up doing Sailor No. 1).

Rex,* the problem being one has strength and the other has technique but neither has both. But I think I'll settle on Harold.

And the other exciting news (to me); I've gotten a terrific idea for a new ballet which would startle the hell out of the ballet world and be a really great work if successful. I doubt if you will like it . . . or if as a matter of fact if many people will like it. They will reject it because they might find it frightening or distasteful, in either case the reason being that it is the truth and they won't face it. It would provide a wonderful part for Lucia,† if she *wanted* to do it and *could* do it, would need one set and use a good amount of the company. It is not a closing or opening ballet. It concerns (hold on to your moral hat) the psychological relations between a Mother and her Son and how thru her Mother-love she completely makes a neurotic person out of him. It would all be done much in the manner of psychoanalysis starting with the death of the mother, the sudden feeling of freedom of the Son, and his searching in his past for the reasons for his strange relationship to his mother, and his slow understanding of incidents in his youth etc. that turned and twisted him into a person unable to function normally in regards to his work, society, love, sex, etc. This sounds like a pretty difficult and perhaps dangerous subject to handle in the ballet medium, but I have it figured out pretty clearly, and in a form which would be dramatic and theatrical. I can already hear you sighing a weary sigh and muttering "oh Jerry . . ." But anyway, say it to me so that I know what you think of the business. Have only spoken to Johnny and Nora so far about it . . . they like it very much. I'll have to re-read *Sons and Lovers* again. It's called "I remember, I remember." It would end on a *positive* note. His understanding & being able to enter the world normally.

Because of not being able to rehearse here, and by only being in one or two ballets a night, I have had lots and lots of free time. So I've been quite social here. I have luncheon dates like mad, go to Hollywood at night and day, visit the studios, sip cocktails, and frankly I'm damned tired of the whole business. I want to work. But one party stands out in my mind. It was one that was held in a house on top of Lookout Mountain, in a home [where] an actor

---

* Rex Cooper, who eventually played the Bartender.
† Ballet Theatre's director, Lucia Chase, who had appeared in several of her company's ballets and might be susceptible to the lure of a good part.

Robbins wasn't dancing in this 1942 or 1943 performance of *Aurora's Wedding* (the abbreviated one-act version of *Sleeping Beauty* performed by Ballet Theatre), so he photographed it from one of the side boxes.

named David Bacon was murdered about three months ago. Well, the company (mixed), decided to play "Murder." Do you know the game. By selection of cards one person becomes a murderer and then you put out all the lights (aha!) and if you feel someone put their hands about your neck, you know you are being murdered and scream. Then the idea is to find out who the murderer is.

When you play that in a house with ten rooms that lead from one to another, with closets and staircases, and with everyone very drunk and not really wanting to put their hands on your *neck,* you might understand what a brawl the party turned into. After a while no one gave a damn about being strangled and there was just one large pile of bodies in one room. I quit when in one bout I found someone kneeling on my face. That was going too far I thought. As I said the company was mixed and the only way you knew what you were being groped by was to grope right back. I lost two fingers that way. I got to bed at eight the next morning never having had such a workout in my life. There was one other party fairly interesting. Mitchell Leisen, director of Lady in the Dark, threw us a "Hollywood" party. It was lots of fun. I met Mickey Rooney (he walked over and smiled and said, extending his hand, "My name's Rooney." Get him. I was tempted to ask him what his first name was. Do you think I'll get on well out here?). I danced with Ida Lupino, she's divine. Oh there were others there too . . . but everyone got drunk by the time I was getting sober (I arrived stewed) so I sat glumly and watching the goings on. At one point Agnes danced herself flat on the floor, and Rooney and Markova were jitterbugging. Helmut Dantine* (bore) tried to make all the females, and all the "girls" tried to make him. Johnny K. got really blotto (I fear he's drinking too much again) and Tudor and Lang [*sic*]† sat about with malicious gleams in their eyes. By the way I have had to make my independent stand of Mr. Tudor, and since he had been heckling me and teasing me and being sweetly vicious about my opus, I drew him out in the open and had it out with him. He really is a timid soul, and now although he is very polite to me, hardly speaks to say hello. Funny, it felt just the same when I left home. They were infringing on what I felt was my identity. Now I don't even have an *artistic* father. Well, I really feel better about it. One has to take a stand, and a stand *alone* if they are to do their own work. Tudor has always been a great influence on me, but now that I'm about to do my own work I can't play "son" to him any longer, nor the adoring disciple. I couldn't do my own work then. I'd be always wondering how he would do it, or what he

---

* Helmut Dantine (1918–1982) often played Nazis in American World War II films.
† Hugh Laing (1911–1988) was a principal dancer known for dramatic roles, and Antony Tudor's partner.

would think. Well, I'm still interested in what he will think of my piece, but I'm not inhibited about it any longer. One has to have complete confidence in one's self, and *finally* there will be no one to rely on but me.

We have been having storms and rain for days and days now. This is one of the first clear days we have had. From the window in front of me I can see way out to snow capped mountains. Looks wonderful. By the way, did you know that the company plans to have a four week season here this summer at the bowl,[*] and then two weeks in Mexico. God, how I will miss you if we go to Mexico. But I have had two other offers. One is to do the dances for the musical comedy version of the Taming of the Shrew . . . and the other is to assist at Paramount in choreographing a picture. Both would mean money and some good experience . . . so I'm thinking of them both very seriously.[†]

This is about all . . . (it's enough!) Forgive all the mistakes in typing but when I go fast I make mistakes like mad. Please also forgive my lapse in writing you. Oh yes, Arthur Lawrence [*sic*],[‡] my old frustration, how was he? And by the way—Albia's[§] wedding couldn't have been more sweet . . . she looked divine, and the whole thing almost made me weep. I'm sorry if I didn't get to let you know about it in time. I told her it was all my fault, so blame it all on me when you write her.

Goodbye now . . . again thanks for the letter . . . I loved hearing from you. Do write more and more. Keep well. Have fun . . . and all my love to you as always.

J.

---

[*] The Hollywood Bowl, a large outdoor amphitheater and band shell in the hills north of Hollywood Boulevard.

[†] Neither of these projects appear to have borne fruit. The *Taming of the Shrew* musical does not appear to be Cole Porter's *Kiss Me, Kate,* which arose from a 1947 commission by the Broadway producer Arnold Saint-Subber.

[‡] Robbins had met Arthur Laurents through Nora Kaye, sometime in 1943 or 1944 in New York, where Laurents was stationed in the army.

[§] Albia Kavan had married fellow Ballet Theatre company member Rex Cooper, who would play the nondancing role of the deadpan bartender in *Fancy Free* (see p. 72).

To: Donald Saddler*

[January 1944]

Dear Donushka . . .

First of all I miss you tremendously, Don. Especially here thru Texas and Oklahoma do I think of you. When I go to the Mexican restaurants, I sit and gaze off into space, remembering the meals and fun we had together in Mehiko. Oh all the time, something will remind me of you, and I'll sigh a wall bulging sigh and wish you were with me.

One trip, from Sioux City to Des Moines, about 100 miles, took us 16 hours! We got there at nine, curtain rose at 11:30 . . . and we finished at about 1:15 A.M. And each time we ride all night on a coach, when we rise off the plush seat-beds,† as I reach for my shoes, I hear your ghost voice saying . . . "oooh I'm all puffed up..my feet, my fingers, my face, . . . I'm all puffed up" and I get the giggles.

The first part of tour before Xmas wasn't bad till the last week. We stayed with Charlie in Washington, played the game‡ at the Ritz in Philly. Oh yes, Johnny Kriza, Harold Lang, and myself danced at the stage door canteen while in Philly. We spent two hours discussing whether we should wear full make-up, only pancake, or just false eyelashes. We did the gypsy dance from Lichines§ latest lemon . . . *Fair at Sorochinsk*.¶ When we arrived the sailors et [*sic*] soldiers were jitterbuggin like crazy. They cleared the floor for us and settled quietly and very respectably down. We danced, they applauded. Then they went back to jitterbuggin like crazy. I guess we didn't impress them. The M.P. gave us each a Coca-Cola and a handshake and we went home.

---

* Saddler had left Ballet Theatre to enlist in the army and was stationed in Alaska.
† The dancers created makeshift beds by lowering the backs of the seats in the day coaches they traveled in.
‡ The "army game" was, depending on your point of view, a swindle or a dancers' cost-saving stratagem: on tour, one or two dancers would register for a hotel room, and then a number of others would join them illicitly.
§ David Lichine (1910–1972), a Russian émigré dancer-choreographer, had completed Fokine's work on *Helen of Troy* after the latter's death.
¶ *Fair at Sorochinsk* was a Russian rural folk ballet set to music by Modest Mussorgsky (including the chestnut "Night on Bald Mountain").

The Ballet Theatre principals Nora Kaye and Hugh Laing
vamping, or camping, on the train platform in Columbus,
Mississippi, December 18, 1942.

I flew home for Xmas (my first plane trip and I loved it) . . . saw Carmen
Jones (*wonderful*) and Winged Victory (awfully corny but good). Chicago season was very special, although nothing special about the opera bar afterwards.
By the end of our season there, that bar started to look like Ceruttis on Sat.
night. I met two people whom I liked quite a bit, which surprised me. But you

know how touring is. Someone comes into your life, and for a day or so you are so happy, and then you go out of their life. And it's over except for letters that try so hard to hang on to what you had so briefly. But these days I guess one could be happy for whatever short ideal happiness one can find . . . and be thankful that at least it is experienceable.

Having gotten on this sad philosophical note, I'll close for the evening. This has been written late Friday night in Tulsa, Oklahoma. We played on a stage tonight that would make a sliding-pond look like a pancake. We finished the finale of *Bluebeard* (yes sir, ham and eggs*) in one heap at the footlights the rake was so steep. But Tulsa is a dull town. And it's late, and I'm tired. I'll write more tomorrow on the train. Bye now.

Hello again . . .

Now we're in mad gay Joplin, Mo. It's Sunday afternoon and a deader place there never was. There's one main street that goes from one end to the other with a few movie houses sprinkled on the side with such sterling pictures as "Silver Spurs" and "The Falcon Strikes Back" etc.

This morning I called N.Y. on the company's money. It came to almost seven dollars. I had to speak to Bernstein, my composer, as several problems had come up that could only be settled by talking to him. The music is very wonderful . . . very jazzy and somewhat Copelandish . . . there's a wonderful torchy pas de deux, . . . three short solo variations for the sailors . . . and a rip-snorting syncopated opening dance for the three boys. I wish you were here Don. I could use you, and you'd be wonderful in it, and it's fun so far. Of course I get horribly worried with all the responsibility on my shoulders. At moments I look at the pages and pages of music and shudder, wonder, break out in a cold sweat, gasp, and finally pray. I haven't admitted any nervousness to anyone yet . . . but kid, I'm worried. Its got to be good . . . its got to be . . . or else a lot of faith I have in myself as a person and artist will be shot to hell, and I'll be left ready for the asylum. The few sketches and movements I've done so far please me very much, and the kids like them too which is usually a good sign. But the real work is yet to come. Whenever I think of opening night I wet my pants, so I've given up even thinking about it. Don it will be too exciting . . . I'll take a powder that night and just wake up to read if it's a success or not. Everyone has great confi-

---

* Ballet slang for a mixed bill of short ballets.

George Balanchine rehearses *Apollo*—the stripped-down neoclassical ballet that was one of the inspirations for Robbins's *Fancy Free*—with Ballet Theatre's dancers in 1943.

dence and hope in me . . . and essentially I believe in it being good. I'll let you know how it progresses.

We were in New Orleans for two nights . . . and it was as mad a spree as you can imagine. The first night Johnny Kriza, Nora, Janet[*] and myself went out and got stinking drunk. As we left the bar I got into an argument with Dick[†] out on the sidewalk, and he threw his glass and all in my face. But I was so drunk I didn't know it till Janet started wiping me up. It all blew over cause we were all so drunk . . . but it could have been a real incident. The following day Johnny K., June Morris[‡] and myself went to have our fortunes told by a Madam Gay. She turned out to be an old witch with 2 chins and no teeth . . . and she kept telling

[*] Janet Reed, a soloist with Ballet Theatre, would play the Redhead in *Fancy Free*.
[†] Richard Reed (no relation to Janet) was also a dancer in the company (see p. 71).
[‡] June Morris was a member of the Ballet Theatre corps de ballet.

me about all these *men* in my life . . . and no women. !? Otherwise she was very dull and just kept advising me not to worry about anything, not to worry.

Texas was much colder than Chicago. In Houston I stayed with Alpheus's[*] relatives . . . who were *real* Southerners . . . and who fed us on fried chicken, pork chops, rice and gravy, and who said Grace each meal . . . who hated New Yorkers and Texans (they came from Florida originally). It was all very interesting in a frightening way, and I kept my mouth well shut.

There are probably lots and lots of things I want to tell you that I've forgotten, but then I'll write you more frequently than I have, believe me. It was so good to get your card and I did appreciate the postcard included. Most of all I want to tell you I wish you were here with us . . . I, and everyone else, miss you so much, so much.

Write me when you get the chance . . . take care of yourself and keep well . . . and all my love to you as always . . .

Rosie[†]

There was a picture of me in Cappricio[‡] [*sic*] in a Dallas paper captioned "Robbins, a gypsy from New York."

Spring 1944 Journal

March 3
SEATTLE

Good rehearsal today with boys—1st dance almost complete—feels fine.[§]
I'm trying to dig out the reason for my fear of public knowing of my private life—found 2 influences—my sister's fears for me while I was maturing and my need to hide from her what I felt was guilty and bad—cause she said so. And

---

[*] Alpheus Koon, another company member.
[†] Apparently one of Robbins's nicknames, as the Russified "Donushka" is a nickname for Saddler.
[‡] Robbins and Muriel Bentley often appeared together in Léonide Massine's *Capriccio Espagnol* (music by Nikolai Rimsky-Korsakov).
[§] Robbins had begun the granular work of setting dance steps on his principals for *Fancy Free*.

somehow the shock of being told about José[*]—by a girl—and collapse of an idol—how I couldn't face him—the knowledge that everyone knew about it. Must dig more out about it.

March 29
ATLANTA

6 hours, nothing accomplished. Worked like hell—lifts, etc.—till both so exhausted.
Lennie's concert R&J was *sensational.* Own symphony not as high as R&J.[†]
Home & sleep?
Very depressed.

April 3
[NEW YORK]

Worked A.M. with Janet and Muriel.[‡]
P.M. Sat and worked with Johnny. He's *very* good.
Had dinner with Hugh Franklin.[§] Then to Lennie's. Worked & talked very late, 5 A.M. Stayed there. Got deep into each other's background—family & analysis. Finished my variation.

April 6
[NEW YORK]

A.M. Worked out dance patterns so that focus is clearer. Harold hitting it better.
P.M. Worked with boys on coda of V and whole of 1st dance.
Night. Cleaned up and run-thru. EXHAUSTED.

---

[*] Apparently a reference to José Limón, a former member of Sandor's Dance Center and one of the stars of *Keep Off the Grass.* Limón was homosexual, if not openly so.
[†] Robbins refers to a radio broadcast of a concert by the New York Philharmonic with Bernstein (its assistant conductor) conducting Tchaikovsky's Fantasy Overture from *Romeo and Juliet* and his own Symphony no. 1 (*Jeremiah*).
[‡] Muriel Bentley (1917–1999), who played the Brunette in *Fancy Free,* was a soloist with Ballet Theatre.
[§] Hugh Franklin (1916–1986) was an American actor currently appearing with Helen Hayes in a play about Harriet Beecher Stowe titled *Harriet.*

April 15
[NEW YORK]

Leonard said he was proud to have done music for my choreography. . . . A noble work—cause it makes you like all the people in it—

Interim Years
September 3, 1976

[The] opening night party* of *Fancy Free* was held at Nora's. She lived on 52nd—a sort of railroad flat. We'd been bowled over by the reception at the Met and the backstage furor after it.† We couldn't believe it was happening. . . . We ate, drank, congratulated and kissed each other; the first review came in, read to us over the phone from [John] Martin: "10 Degrees North of Terrific"— wow. We flipped—we got drunk—all of us—I don't remember much except the famous incident of Lennie disappearing in the bathroom with a dancer (an event he repeated at the opening night party at my house for *Watermill*)—and that on the street early in the AM. I realized that now I had enough money to start analysis.

---

* Unfortunately, there's no record of who was on the guest list for this party, but oral accounts mention the cast members, Lucia Chase and other Ballet Theatre figures, Paul and Jane Bowles, Oliver Smith, Betty Comden, Adolph Green, Leonard Bernstein, Agnes de Mille, Sol Hurok, Harry and Lena Rabinowitz, and others.
† The ballet received twenty-two curtain calls, and the cast was mobbed by well-wishers after the curtain finally came down.

3

Breaking Through: 1944–1950

⸻

T wo weeks ago," said Jerome Robbins to a newspaper reporter in May 1944, just after *Fancy Free*'s seismic premiere, "I was just another dancer. Now I'm supposed to be somebody, and I can't get used to it."* And that was before he and Bernstein transformed *Fancy Free* into a musical comedy with the help of the book-and-lyric writers Betty Comden and Adolph Green. Produced by Oliver Smith (the ballet's, and the show's, designer) and Paul Feigay, and directed by the Broadway veteran George Abbott, *On the Town* opened in December 1944 and was proclaimed "the freshest and most engaging musical show to come this way since the golden day of *Oklahoma!*" by *The New York Times*. Suddenly, in addition to being a bright light of the ballet world, Robbins was the Broadway choreographer of the moment at a time when musicals were becoming integrated, book-smart shows, not the song-dance-and-joke pastiches that he'd danced in as a chorus boy, and the dancing in them was increasingly seen as action, not decoration.

During the next few years Robbins made dances for *Billion Dollar Baby* (1945), with book and lyrics by Comden and Green and music by Morton Gould, about a gold-digging flapper's rise and fall in the vertiginous 1920s; *High Button Shoes* (1947), a caper set in 1913 New Jersey, which featured a Keystone Kops ballet as its paradigmatic centerpiece; and two shows with scores by Irving Berlin, *Miss Liberty* (1949), a behind-the-scenes story about the making of the Statue of Liberty, and *Call Me*

* Margaret Lloyd, "Of Human Values," unsourced newspaper clipping, scrapbook, Jerome Robbins Papers.

Madam (1950), a star vehicle for Ethel Merman as a socially connected U.S. ambassador. He also conceived as well as choreographed—and co-directed, with George Abbott—a quasi-autobiographical backstage musical about an ambitious dancer-choreographer in a touring ballet troupe, *Look, Ma, I'm Dancin'!* (1948). The book writers Jerome Lawrence and Robert E. Lee were brought in to flesh out the story provided by Robbins with the collaboration of Arthur Laurents, and they weren't entirely happy to be lectured and hectored by a brash twenty-eight-year-old wunderkind; but *Look, Ma* was a happier experience for Robbins than the show that came immediately after it: his first directorial assignment, a lackluster political fairy tale called *That's the Ticket!* (1948), which closed out of town after a disastrous tryout.

Robbins hadn't abandoned ballet, or even dancing, in his forays on Broadway. He continued (albeit at sharply better terms) to make new dances for Ballet Theatre: ballets that gave the classical vocabulary a modern vernacular inflection, such as the jazzy *Interplay* (1945) and the angst-filled *Facsimile* (1946). In 1948, smarting from the failure of *That's the Ticket!* and looking for fresh inspiration, he left Ballet Theatre for George Balanchine's newly formed New York City Ballet. At City Ballet he began making ballets (*The Guests,* in 1949, and *Age of Anxiety,* in 1950) that featured his special theatrical sensibility while also appearing in numerous dramatic and character roles, including the lead in *Prodigal Son* and one of the principals, opposite the long-limbed nineteen-year-old ballerina Tanaquil Le Clercq, in *Bourrée Fantasque.* In 1949, Balanchine appointed him associate artistic director.

It's perhaps ironic that during this time of success Robbins was also involved, if seemingly peripherally, in the American Communist Party. He'd joined the party toward the end of 1943 or the beginning of 1944, believing that it was "an organization which was very much for minorities and for advancing their causes."[*] His activities were confined to attending the occasional meeting (basically an ideological kaffee-

---

[*] JR, "Testimony of Jerome Robbins," *Communist Activities in the New York Area* (report of the House Un-American Activities Committee), 1320.

klatsch), signing petitions, and going to the odd public event, and by 1949, disillusioned with an *apparat* in which artists "would be accused of writing . . . formalistic . . . and bourgeois [material and] hav[e] to repent publicly, and then get a benediction to move on,"* he withdrew, or resigned. But markers of his involvement are visible in at least one of his ballets from these years, *The Guests,* with its theme of inclusion and exclusion, and in his populist ideas about dance, expressed in a *New York Times* article he wrote in 1945.

Other examples of Robbins's work during these years reflected themes from his personal life, and vice versa. While working on *On the Town,* he'd met a beautiful dark-haired actress named Lois Wheeler, who like Robbins was active in Communist Party circles, and they had begun an affair. At the same time, in late fall of 1945, Robbins also became romantically involved with the rising young actor Montgomery Clift—an attachment that had to be kept secret because of the harm exposure would do to Clift's growing fame as a brooding matinee idol. The tensions of this triangulated affair can be felt in *Facsimile,* and they certainly contributed to the failure of Robbins's relationship with Wheeler, which ended in the spring of 1947. (She went on to marry the renowned journalist and Sinologist Edgar Snow.) Another romance with a woman, Rose Tobias, also foundered because of Clift, but shortly afterward, in the spring of 1948, with his film career exploding into supernova stardom, Clift broke off the relationship with Robbins and moved to Los Angeles. And shortly afterward, when Robbins joined New York City Ballet, he began a different kind of love affair: an intense intimacy—which might or might not have ever been physical but was romantic, intellectual, and professional—with Tanaquil Le Clercq, whom he cast as an understudy in *The Guests* and to whom he gave a central role in *Age of Anxiety.* She was unlike anyone he'd ever met, a witty, poised, precocious child of the intelligentsia whose interests were as wide-ranging as his; they gossiped and teased each other, played word games, and took pictures of each other. She would become his muse,

* Ibid., 1319.

and much more. "All the ballets I ever did for the company," Robbins would later tell an interviewer, "it was always for Tanny."*

During this turbulent transitional period—in which both work and relationships were under stress—Robbins found some security in the surrogate family of friends he had begun to assemble around him: his *On the Town* mates Bernstein, Smith, Comden, and Green; the composer (and later writer) Paul Bowles and his wife, Jane; the duo pianists Robert Fizdale (whom he'd met through Bowles) and his partner Arthur Gold; the critic Edwin Denby; the playwright Arthur Laurents; and several Ballet Theatre and New York City Ballet colleagues. Increasingly, as he and they traveled in response to the demands of their careers, these friendships were carried on by letter, accounting for a richer correspondence record than is available for Robbins's earlier years.

If friendships were an anchor at this time, his compass was psychoanalysis—for in 1944, after years of feeling "thrown" and "confused" by his sexual orientation as well as his professional anxieties and his complicated feelings about his family and heritage, Robbins had begun seeing a therapist, a kind, compassionate woman named Frances Arkin. The founder of the first psychoanalytic training program at New York Medical College, where she was also on the faculty, she seemed to want to help Robbins relieve his repressions, not be governed by them. Certainly if productivity and achievement are any measure, she was successful: in 1950, when they agreed to terminate his therapy, Robbins won the *Dance Magazine* award for his performance in *Prodigal Son* and for his choreography for *Age of Anxiety;* New York City Ballet, embarking on its first foreign tour, to London, took a full complement of Robbins ballets with them; *Look, Ma, I'm Dancin'!* had been optioned for the movies; and *Call Me Madam* was a hit. As Robbins's surrogate, Jake Whitby, would say years later in the autobiographical *Poppa Piece,* "I'm taking off and I'm making my fortune and my future."

---

* JR, transcript of a taped interview with Clive Barnes, marked 1973 by Robbins but filed in the Robbins Papers as dating from 1969.

Interim Years
September 3, 1976

I had started analysis in 44 and it's probable that took all [the] energy and attention that was left out of my non-working hours. . . . [T]here was another thing which took some of my energy. The party. And my affairs. . . . Both were very bumpy experiences. I was lovers with men and women, and I went to meetings. Both seemed to be conducted under water—my feelings were not felt directly by me. I did [these things] . . . and now I can't remember feeling much of anything.

When I lived on 11th St. [in] 45–46, our street boasted a good sampling of the arts. I lived at #24, top floor; at #28, one house away, lived Oliver Smith and Paul and Jane Bowles; at #32, one house in between again (top floor) lived Lenny Bernstein. There was a lot of traffic over the roofs to each others' apartments. Jane and Paul and Oliver lived in between Lenny and me and so Jane's apartment* became the rendezvous place. Jane was a source of delight; warm, fun, witty and hilariously complicated. I relished each visit. Sometimes she'd get a bit high with us and get up on a table and sing some Mexican street song and swing her skirt to and fro. "Come on Jane, get down, we've seen that before," Oliver would say with a great loving grin. We'd sometimes eat together. I always hoped it'd be a Chinese restaurant for there Jane's inability to decide on anything came to the fore with the most hilarious scenes. What are you going to have, she'd ask each of us at least 4 times. In most cases we always lost the waiter who—tired of attending Jane's decision and our laughter—disappeared to take other orders, and who would check in every 10 minutes to see if Jane had arrived at a decision. Most often she'd give the whole thing up and say I'll just have some of each of yours. Oh God, she'd moan and then laugh at herself. She was a very touching soul. My favorite times were the occasions on which we'd gather at Jane's late at night—not planned—but we'd all drift in: Oliver, Jane, Victor Kraft (a photographer then), Paul, Lenny and myself. Somehow we'd all be lying on Jane's huge bed like at a picnic or on the beach. And we'd talk—I don't remember even about what—and someone would tell a story or play some music. Those evenings I felt as if Jane's bed became some special raft on which we all floated off together, lolling, resting, talking, being silent, but so easily comfortable in each others' presence.

---

* The Bowleses maintained separate apartments in the same building.

The best Jane story I remember: somehow she'd been talked into the idea of visiting a psychiatrist by some friend who had convinced her that her problems were getting in her way. Jane agreed to a visit. The first thing she had to do to get to him was walk uptown. We lived on 11th and the shrink was in the upper 80's. Jane walked, because having claustrophobia she could not be forced into a subway or bus. Taxis were too expensive, so getting an early start she hiked uptown, getting there in enough time to find he lived on the 12th floor of the building, and because she couldn't get herself into any elevator, climbed the 12 flights—arriving in time to plunk herself down exhausted in the chair opposite the doctor and gasp—well, I don't know why I'm here, there's nothing wrong with me!

Paul was much different. He seemed to sit back, puffing on his pipe, guarding his—privacy and solitude are the wrong words—his separateness. His mood was gentle, humored, tasteful. He seemed to me to be the most glamorously exotic man I'd met. Snake skins on the wall, the paraphernalia to make his own perfume, African musical instruments, drums, native masks from all over. His apartment seemed more sunlit and North African somehow. I was sold on his music, as Oliver and Lenny both praised it so highly. He was I believe a very strong influence on both of them and to his surprise (a) found Lenny surpassing him in acclaim and accomplishment and (b) found himself writing more and more instead of composing and thus surpassing Jane in output and reviews.

My City
[1940s]

My city lies between two rivers—on a small island—My beautiful city is set on rock between two flowing paths of water that run to the sea. My city is tall and jagged—with gold & slated towers. My city is honey combed with worm tunnels of roads. My city is cut and slashed by hard car-filled streets.

My city chokes on its breath, and sparkles with its false lights—and sleeps restlessly at night. My city is a lone man walking at night down an empty street watching his shadow grow longer as he passes the last lamppost, seeing no comfort in the blank dark windows, and hearing his footsteps echo against the buildings & fade away—.

My city presents a face of brick & glass to its people. Blank & empty. Hard & cold.

Hear the noises of my city—hear the city noises. Do you know rain on pavements—or cars shifting gears late at night—do you know traffic jams—or a dull sob of a boat in dock at night—listen to my city—the whistle—the horn,—the drill—the train—the undistinguishable [*sic*] buzz & soft thunder under it all. Have you heard the voice of my city—the poor voice, the lost voice—the voice of people selling—& swearing—cursing & vulgar, the shrill & the tough—wail and complaint and the defiance—have you heard the voice of my city, fighting & hitting & hurt.

To: Leonard Bernstein
[May 13, 1945]

Dear Lenny,

It was rather nice seeing you the other night at Al and Dick's.* What with your letter and our chance meeting, I thought that maybe (as you said) we could get "that old show out of our heads" and do some work. However I have just finished reading the interviews in *Dance Magazine*.† Have you seen them? Well, in yours, you talk about the trilogy idea based on Fancy Free, even mentioning "Bye Bye Jackie" by name and describing the material. And somehow Leonard it all sounds like your idea, and to boot my name isn't even connected with my own registered play.‡

---

* Al and Dick's was a music-industry steak house popular with the *On the Town* cast, on Fifty-Fourth Street just east of Seventh Avenue.
† Francis A. Coleman, "Composer Teams with Choreographer," *Dance Magazine,* May 1945, 12–13. In the article, Coleman says, "For some time, Leonard Bernstein has considered the composition of a trilogy of ballets to be built around *Fancy Free*. . . . The opening work, to be called Bye, Bye Jackie, is to furnish a picture of adolescence, in a Brooklyn setting."
‡ In the wake of *Fancy Free's* success Robbins had written a full script, with dialogue and action, for a short play—"a braiding of . . . dance, music and voice"—called *Bye Bye Jackie,* about a group of young people in Brooklyn, one of whom enlists in the navy. He had registered the copyright to it and hoped to interest Bernstein in pursuing the project, but Bernstein hadn't followed up on it. No wonder Robbins felt—and was—snippy.

Now it all might be the fault of the interviewer, and if it is, too bad, because it makes you appear to be dishonest. But if it is something you did yourself, it is a low, dirty trick—and I wouldn't try it again. Fortunately the majority of people in the dance world already know about "Bye Bye Jackie" and the Theatre Guild and others have read it, so that if and when it's done, it won't seem that you have supplied my material and ideas.

I don't like writing a letter like this. But I thought it best we get straightened out on things like this. We are well suited to work together as far [as] talents are concerned, and it would be good if we could manage to do some more ballets. But this kind of business is not a good gesture either as a friend or business associate. So let's have no more of it.

Sincerely,
Jerry

The Ballet Puts On Dungarees[*]
October 14, 1945

Twice each year, in the fall and again in the spring, the Metropolitan Opera's box-office people face a lobbyful of ballet fans and answer such questions as: "Is Markova dancing 'Giselle' two weeks from Sunday night?" and "When do the murder ballet and the sailor ballet come together?"

Twelve years ago, when Mr. Hurok first brought ballet back to America,[†] not only the Metropolitan's box-office men but a whole generation of ballet fans, who remembered Pavlova and Nijinsky, would have been demolished by that last question. The idea that a murder ballet and a sailor ballet came at all, let alone together, on a ballet program at the Opera House would have sent them into the night moaning softly for their smelling salts.

---

[*] This article, illustrated with photos of *Fancy Free,* was published in *The New York Times* on October 14, 1945, with the subheading "A choreographer describes how ballet has emerged from the hothouse and become in America a people's entertainment."
[†] Sol Hurok presented both Serge Denham's Ballet Russe de Monte Carlo and its rival, Colonel W. de Basil's Original Ballet Russe, in the 1930s, before taking over Ballet Theatre in 1942.

But in twelve years a good deal has happened to the ballet. I feel that such ballets as "Rodeo," "Billy the Kid," "Undertow" and "Fancy Free" are only a few of many signposts. . . .

What has happened is that ballet, that orchidaceous pet of the Czars, has come out of the hothouse and become a people's entertainment in our energetic land. A democratic people's mark on the ballet is directly evidenced in its subject matter, its dancers, and the kind of audiences that attend it.

One discovers, on tour with Ballet Theatre, that all across the country, the people of towns like Waco, Tex., and Joplin, Mo., no less than New York, Boston, Chicago and San Francisco, have been welcoming the ballet's arrival with capacity houses. Broadway, quick to adapt itself to the new enthusiasm, made haste to abandon tap-dancing chorus routines, so that one weary drama critic has already sighed that it would be a relief to see a musical without a ballet. Hollywood is learning to translate dancing to the celluloid techniques through the efforts of first-rate young dancers like Gene Kelly and Jack Cole. . . .

The ballet revolution came about gradually, so gradually that one must stop and remember what the first ballet company was like, stepping off the boat from Paris just twelve years ago. The America which received that company had not seen ballet since Pavlova made her final farewell appearance in 1925–26. Faint shreds of memory carried back to Diaghilev's plush-covered ballet seasons in 1917 and 1918, when the customers paid $25 a seat and Otto H. Kahn paid a bill of a quarter of a million dollars at the end of the season. Serge Diaghilev knew his ballet, but his ideas of cost-accounting and double-entry bookkeeping dated from the days when a ballerina was a Grand Duke's mistress as a matter of course, and the gilded youth of St. Petersburg inherited their stalls at the Marinsky [sic] Theatre along with their titles and their lands.

In 1933 Diaghilev had died, Pavlova was a name on an urn of ashes at Golder's Green,* and Nijinsky was a patient in a Swiss asylum. Ballet, however, was showing signs of reincarnation in a company gathered by René Blum (brother of Léon, who later became French Premier), and an ex-cavalry officer of Old Rus-

---

* Golders Green Crematorium and Mausoleum was the first such facility to be opened in London, in 1902, and besides Pavlova such eminences as Sigmund and Anna Freud, Bram Stoker, and the playwright Joe Orton were cremated there.

sia. Its members were the "baby ballerinas," children of émigré Russian nobility trained in the Paris studios of the former Imperial Ballet stars. Most of them were under 20; two of the four primas, Toumanova and Baronova, were actually 14 years old.

The company which stepped off the boat that December day in 1933 looked more like a not very fashionable school than a ballet company. Four mamas and two papas accompanied the children. The girls wore black cotton stockings and cheap flat-heeled shoes. Their thin cloth coats were shabby; their heads were bare or topped by berets; their little noses gleamed in utter innocence of make-up, and they reacted to the ship-news photographers' requests for crossed leg poses with a cascade of giggles. Only one among them looked like a ballerina: Danilova wore her furs and her jewels in the grand manner.

Hurok welcomed them on the pier with the Russian ceremony of bread and salt. At the opening night party Mr. Kahn drank champagne out of a ballet slipper especially made for the occasion by one of the city's expensive bootmakers.

The very next year saw the beginning of the transformation of the ballet girls. With their American earnings they had all bought fur coats. They wore their lipstick and their chic little Paris hats with an accustomed air, and automatically crossed silk-stockinged knees when the cameras appeared.

On the stage, too, change was in the air. Ballets began to be paced with an American tempo. American dancers were being auditioned in every city and town, while the Continentals were learning the mysteries of the five-and-ten and "coca-cola-vidout-ice."

American composers and scene designers were being enlisted. There were fewer and fewer "Scheherazades" and "Prince Igors" on the programs. Archibald MacLeish wrote a ballet about the building of the Union Pacific Railroad, for which Albert Johnson designed the settings. Richard Rodgers composed the music for a ballet about a gold-mining town and conducted its premiere at the Metropolitan. And these ballets enticed a new audience who cared less for champagne out of a ballet slipper than for a good cold beer between ballets.

Today our culture has infiltrated the ballet from topknot to toe-slipper. The Ballet Theatre company numbers but a handful of Europeans. The rest are American boys and girls, who learned their sautés and entrechats in the cities of America. A list of their home towns reads like a railroad timetable of a coast-to-coast journey. . . . Americans no longer feel they need a trip abroad or at least a dictionary of ballet terms to help them understand the ballet. They may not spot the difference between an entrechat-six and an entrechat-dix (very few can) but they can enjoy a hiking up of dungarees, the flipping of a chewing-gum paper between thumb and forefinger, without any help from experts, while a dash of juke-box jive is a natural accent in the new ballet picture. This is not to say that the ghost maidens and enchanted princesses of classic ballet have been discarded—no program in a big or little city can be without its "white ballet" or the customers feel cheated. . . . But the audience's happy reaction to ballets it can understand, about people it can recognize, is an augury of the ballet's future in a democracy.

A choreographer can justifiably look to the ballet as a medium in which he can say pertinent things about ourselves and our world, no less than a playwright or a novelist or a movie scenarist. For its part, the audience will come to expect as much of ballet as it does of a play, a novel or a film. And as the ballet and the theatre draw closer to each other, an exciting prospect opens in which not only musicals, but theatre pieces with vital ideals, will combine drama, dance and music, to the benefit of all three.

To: Leonard Bernstein
Late Monday night [January 21, 1946]

Len,

It was a really wonderful concert tonight.* I'd never heard you really play anything but Fancy & Town—& the Bach was quite an exciting experience. Then the Stravinsky was new to me—& god! what an experience. 3 Bravos for that alone. I rode along on the Don Juan nicely anticipating the Variations—& then I sat & chuckled & gurgled & beamed & nodded & emphasized & had a

---

* On January 21, 1946, Bernstein conducted the City Symphony Orchestra in a concert at City Center that included Stravinsky's *Symphony of Psalms,* Bach's Brandenburg Concerto no. 5, Strauss's *Don Juan,* and the conductor's own *Three Variations from "Fancy Free."* In addition to conducting, Bernstein played the harpsichord part in the Bach.

wonderful time. They sounded marvelously—& the only complaint was a little something on the encore of Harold's dance,[*] trying to picture him keeping up with it. But it sounded wonderfully unsaddled by dancers.

So thank you for a very special evening of music.

Good luck & continuous success.

Jerry

To: Donald Saddler
March 25, 1946

Dearest Charmane,[†]

I am sorry I have not written you over these number of years.[‡] So many things have been happening and at such a furious pace that it's been hard for me to keep up with them no less keeping my friends posted. The distance seemed to grow too fast and I did not know what to say. Believe me when I say that I thought of you often and wished you were here and wished there was some way of us having one of those heart to heart talks. I suppose when we do meet we will undoubtedly go through the "how much has he changed" business. I feel I've changed a lot—I guess I've had to what with the responsibilities involved. And besides, living the kind of life physically and emotionally and even mentally that we lived in the ballet was something I wanted to get away from. So now I am settled in New York, pretty comfortable with an apartment, girl friend, and some normal kind of social life—and work. I have lost a lot more hair and even find a couple of grey ones in what's left. Of course I haven't gotten any taller and not having danced for almost a year I've gotten a little wider. I sound like S. Hurok, don't I—but don't worry I still have my points.

---

[*] Harold Lang had danced the First Sailor's variation in the ballet, a bravura allegro part full of jumps and turns.

[†] Another nickname for Saddler, derivation unknown.

[‡] After Saddler was demobilized, he had returned to his native California for a time, and he and Robbins—busy choreographing new ballets for Ballet Theatre and shows, including the December 1945 *Billion Dollar Baby,* for Broadway—had fallen out of touch.

I still see the kids from the ballet* about every half year when they come into town. Even in their mad way they seem to be getting a little older and settled. You're right about Johnny† and it is a little sad and I, too, cannot understand how they manage to exist that way year after year. That is why I have hesitations about going to England with them this summer. As much as I love them all I don't know how happy I would be having to live with them again.

Donald, if you come here and have no place to stay you are certainly welcome to live with me until you get settled. Housing situation being what it is I even have no guarantee of how long I will be here, but you can count on this place when you get off the train. I only wish you were coming sooner.

I guess this is all I can say not having written for so long. Let me hear from you again, will you. My love to your mother and all your sisters.

Keep well, be happy,

Love
Jerry

John Kriza, who had originated the role of the lyrical Second Sailor in *Fancy Free*. He and Robbins were close in their Ballet Theatre touring days in the early 1940s, when this photograph was taken, but Kriza's vulnerability and wistfulness always made Robbins feel "a little sad."

---

* Robbins now had a guest artist contract with Ballet Theatre that granted it rights to his ballets on a license-only basis and permitted him to choose when (or whether) to dance in them.
† John Kriza had developed a drinking problem.

To: Donald Saddler
August 19, 1946

Dear Don:

This is the first day I have been home since I have come back and the first moment to drop you a note. The trip back was wonderful. I guess I would have thought so even if I left by aquaplane and it would take me 23 days—anything that moved away from the UK.[*]

I spent two weeks in Nantucket resting and making up for lost time and stuffing my face with anything that didn't smell like lamb or cabbage. I went to Stockbridge and worked for a week with Bernstein on the score for my new ballet.[†] I think the music is wonderful and I think the choreography will be just what I want it to be, but whether the whole thing will satisfy the critics and the public is a moot question.

New York never ever looked more beautiful or seemed more exciting, or sounded more busy, or teemed with more wonderful healthy looking people before. If it appears this way to me now, it will really look like a city of gold when you get back. Honestly, there is no place like home.

From the looks of things my show goes into rehearsal about the 15th of November.[‡] I get the first version of the book early next week and will have more definite news about it. I have not seen Oliver[§] long enough to ask about you but I have a hunch that if you want to leave B.T. it will work out. At what price I can't say yet—plans are not anywhere near that stage.

How is the season going? How did Fancy Free and Interplay get on? What is the morale of the company? When are you all returning? Please write me a long newsy letter.

---

[*] Robbins had accompanied Ballet Theatre on the first half of its first London tour during the summer of 1946. The city was still littered with bomb ruins and suffering under rationing, and conditions were difficult.

[†] *Facsimile,* which would premiere on October 24, 1946.

[‡] This projection was wildly off the mark. The show was *Look, Ma, I'm Dancin'!,* and it took another two years for all its elements to come together for production.

[§] Oliver Smith was the original producer for *Look, Ma;* in the end George Abbott, who also directed, replaced him.

I miss you very much—especially across the stewed rhubarb. I also miss the chambermaid walking in while I had no clothes on. It is so damn quiet here—no boots—no valet—no tea—no fish—no sausages—and especially, no bronco.* I am getting soft at the bottom.

See you soon,

Love,

Jer

To: Jerome Lawrence and Robert E. Lee
Sept. 10, 1946

Dear Boys:—

I don't know if my cards inspired you to write any brilliant scenes but I do know that my plane trip back† inspired me not to travel for a long while—24 hours—WOW! However my trip to the coast was a very happy one, thanks to you, your work and your hospitality. Mucho gratias [*sic*], Amigos.

This is kind of a strange letter—its purpose is to try and save us all time. Having worked with you out on the coast and feeling that we understand each other I want to get right to the core of issues. This is the whole point: on no account do I want the show postponed or delayed, and having studied the script and talked with you, I am sure you can and will write a really terrific show. On the basis of this confidence I want you to please try to incorporate as many of the suggestions that I gave you on the coast as you can. Please understand me when I say this is no criticism of what you have done so far. I just want to get to production as soon as possible and I know that unless we take a direct route,

---

* "Boots" is the British term for a hotel bootblack, who picked up shoes left outside the door every night, polished them, and returned them in the morning; Bronco was the brand name of British rolled toilet paper—notorious for many years—rough on one side and shiny on the other, seemingly nonabsorbent, and advertised with the slogan "Bronco, for the bigger wipe."
† Robbins had flown to Los Angeles (where the writers lived) to confer with them, and also to see Montgomery Clift in between location shoots in Arizona for Howard Hawks's *Red River*.

any time spent in rewriting will put us in a hell of a hole. Please do accept my experience in the theatre and have confidence in my judgment. I know it is easy to rationalize any given moment in the show as it stands now, but believe me, certain things will not play and do not make for a concise direct dramatic script. Oliver and Dick* had to admit that they pulled you off the track in a lot of places and I feel that even the original scenario was given too much emphasis in certain places. My fault.

Do not feel you have to keep every person's suggestions or ideas [for] the show, especially when they are unrelated to the core story. Please be bold in this respect and put the blame on Robbins, boys. Please let me know what your reactions are. I am most anxious to be of any help I can. Call if necessary. Dick and Oliver and of course myself are steamed up to the hilt and excited as hell about the whole show. We have lots of casting ideas, Oliver has lots of wonderful scenic ideas and Hugh† is arriving tomorrow. We are all dying to hear the music which we know will be great. No one is depressed about anything. Au contraire, enthusiasm runs sky-high and we are all foaming at the mouth to get started—so finish the script and hurry up back so we can pull our telepathy act on Dorso and Smith.

Keep well, work well and my best to you as always,

Sincerely—
Jerry

Flopping
September 9, 1976

[*That's the Ticket!*] was my first directorial job. Joe Kipness, one of the producers of *High Button Shoes*, had offered it to me, and I debated for some time and then said no, I wasn't ready. He looked me in the eye and said, I won't

---

* Oliver Smith and Richard Dorso, Robbins's agent.
† Hugh Martin (1914–2011), who had written the score for the MGM musical *Meet Me in St. Louis*, composed the songs for *Look, Ma*. Owing to producer turnover, the show didn't open until January 1948—after *High Button Shoes*, which Robbins didn't begin working on until the winter of 1947.

take no for an answer. So I did it.* Written by Julius and Philip J. [*sic*] Epstein,† it had a witty and entertaining plot‡ and a good score by Harold Rome.§ I wasn't ready or mature enough to see the thing correctly. I made mistakes about the style of the show, and the sets, some poor casting and worse performances that I couldn't strengthen; and, to boot, I assigned the choreography elsewhere (as I knew I couldn't do both in four weeks' rehearsals) and it didn't score. The two leading ladies seemed to have some bond going, for if I cut [one's] lines or scenes, the other would become recalcitrant. The whole venture was a mistake and it closed out of town in Philly in ten days. I was numb and relieved both.

Robbins often documented his friendships with visits to photo booths—as he did in this late 1940s image showing, clockwise from top left, Todd Bolender (a dancer, later choreographer, with New York City Ballet), unidentified man (possibly the City Ballet dancer Robert Barnett), Robbins, and John Kriza.

* A burly former garbageman, cloak-and-suiter, and restaurateur, Kipness was reputed to have mob connections. No wonder Robbins said yes.
† Although they had no Broadway credits, Julius and Philip G.—not J—Epstein had written the screenplays for *Arsenic and Old Lace, The Man Who Came to Dinner,* and, most memorably, the already-legendary *Casablanca.*
‡ *That's the Ticket!* was an election-year satire involving a frog who is kissed by a young woman and magically returned to his native form as a medieval knight; he becomes the presidential candidate of the conservative, even reactionary Feudal Party.
§ Harold Rome (1908–1993) had written songs for *Pins and Needles* and *Call Me Mister;* later he would have big successes with *Fanny* and *I Can Get It for You Wholesale.*

To: Frances Arkin
[Spring 1949]

Dear Dr. Arkin,

I hate to complain—but I don't seem to be able to break thru my ice enough to work.* I don't know what it is exactly—No ideas bear fruition—nothing seems to excite the dancers—I guess I feel like a *flop* & this hurts again. Maybe I'm already anticipating a "Ticket" deal—& all my thoughts fly to getting finished & thru as soon as possible—& trying to get out of the show as quickly as I can.

Am I afraid that after this show, if it's NG [no good], I'll be stuck out on a limb of failure again & cut off. No one will want me. So now the truth of my dependency on success [as a] raison d'etre & substitute [for] friends is apparent.

To: Mary Martin and Richard Halliday (Excerpt)†
April 13, 1955

. . . When I was doing *Miss Liberty* I was working [for the first time] with Irving Berlin and Moss Hart. After I had been in rehearsal only five days they came one afternoon and I had to show them my work. Naturally I felt it was terribly unfair and premature because in those days I usually threw out everything I did in the first few days. I had finished two dances and had begun two others. They saw all this work and raved and flipped over everything. That was on Friday. On Monday morning Moss called me and asked if I would have lunch with him between rehearsals, which I did. He spent the first hour and a half talking about

---

* Robbins had been hired as the choreographer for the high-profile Irving Berlin musical *Miss Liberty* and would shortly be named associate artistic director of New York City Ballet, which he'd joined barely two weeks after *That's the Ticket!*'s ignominious closing, but that show's failure still haunted him. This letter is a draft, probably written while *Miss Liberty* was in out-of-town tryouts (which would account for Robbins writing to Arkin rather than telling her this in one of their sessions); it's not clear whether another version was ever sent.

† This paragraph was deleted and not included in the final draft of the letter it was written for.

how he had used his shows psychotherapeutically to help him over problems, and about the benefits that he was able to derive from applying his analysis to his shows and vice versa. I sat in complete bewilderment. In the next half hour he pussy-footed around some more concerning how difficult it was for him to find an approach to work with me as we had never collaborated before. The last half-hour he finally got around to telling me that they didn't like what I had done so far. In the last five minutes, I set him straight and told him that the best way to work with me was to let me work, and when I had finished show them what I had done, and then I would accept any criticism, and as for collaborating with me, the only way I could work with him was if they were completely direct with me and straightforward

George Balanchine, whom Robbins had idolized from a distance and who from 1948 on would be the most important person in Robbins's professional life, photographed in 1950 or 1951.

about anything they had to tell me. I've always found that circumvention and cottoning of opinions has so put me off that often it has turned me against the validity of those opinions.

To: Robert Fizdale[*]

Sunday night, June 25th [1950]

Dearest Bobby—

I wrote you a fairly long letter just two weeks ago & didn't send it off because I was waiting to determine whether I'd be in Florence in August or Sept—I had my letters of credit, typhoid shots, international license for driving, the apt sub-

* Sometime after they were introduced by Paul Bowles in the late 1940s, Robbins and Fizdale had had a brief affair, but it had cooled (or ripened) into a close friendship by this point—a friendship in which the often-guarded Robbins felt able to speak of matters close to his heart.

The pianist Robert Fizdale, with whom Robbins had a brief romantic relationship followed by a lifelong friendship; in Snedens Landing, circa 1950.

let & all. I didn't want to mail the letter until I knew exact dates. Since then, (as a matter of fact on Tuesday) I was offered the Ethel Merman show,[*] Lindsay & Crouse book, Berlin score, Abbott direction, Robbins choreography—at a nice fee & percentage; and so having to face the practical things in life—like money—I took it. It's been hard getting adjusted to the change of plans—& as I said O.K. to my agent—I could also hear Arthur G.[†] saying—"I knew he'd never get here." But I will, I *will*. This will leave me free to do what I want when I want it—& it has been a poor year financially although I've had a fine time spiritually.

I have finished my analysis. I told the Doc I thought I'd had enough & she completely agreed with me—which surprised the hell out of me. You all were right about my expecting too much from it—but I feel I was very right to stick with it till I felt that I knew & felt enough to stop. It's a strange feeling to know

[*] *Call Me Madam.*
[†] Arthur Gold, Fizdale's performing (and eventually life) partner.

it's over. I have changed so much since I began 6 years ago that I cannot remember not being on the couch. So—having finished that I felt it'd be good to set myself up with an income—& then see the world next year—I'll get to the seat of culture yet.

I've missed you all very much—& I cast doleful looks at 16 West whenever I pass. Have you been happy? Please Bobby do write me. I love you very much—& now that I'm not going to see you, I need words from you badly. How is Edwin?* Do give him my very best. Tell him if he can, to come to London for the opening. We are doing Serenade, Anxiety, & Bizet, & then Jinx, Firebird, Bourrée.† The company really looks terrific. We have eight new members & greatly strengthened corps & soloists. I've gotten to be closer with George & love him very much. N.Y. now is terribly hot & nicely empty. My soul & conscience seem to be at some kind of peace—but again I can't wait to get free of N.Y. I will be in London from the 4th till the 13th & then I'm flying to Paris for Bastille Day & 2 more. Then home. Keep well—& write soon. C/o NYC Ballet, Royal Opera House, Covent Garden, London City.

Jerry

To: Frances Arkin
Sunday night [June 1950]

Dear Dr. Arkin—

It has taken me all of the weekend getting over walking out of your office. The most terrible depression hit me as I stepped out onto Park Ave & realized it was the last time. Sort of a relapse I guess.

You know, I didn't say the things I wanted to at all the last day. And mostly my words of "thank you very much" were so awful in my ears. The truth of

---

* Edwin Denby (1903–1983), a poet and influential dance critic, was a friend introduced to Robbins by Fizdale.

† The ballets were *Serenade* (Balanchine/Tchaikovsky), *Age of Anxiety* (Robbins/Bernstein), *Symphony in C* (Balanchine/Bizet), *Jinx* (Lew Christensen/Britten), *Firebird* (Balanchine/Stravinsky), and *Bourrée Fantasque* (Balanchine/Chabrier).

the matter is that I am unable to tell you how really very grateful I am for all the time & energy & patience you have given me. I don't think words can be summoned up which try to equalize [*sic*] 6 years of the interest & friendship & understanding I've had. And maybe I don't feel it is the end of the relationship. I hope now I will be able to return some of the friendship to you. One thing I do want you to know though. You said my art was demonstrable while yours wasn't. Please Dr. Arkin—take the pleasure & take the credit in the success & demonstration of my art—because you are so very responsible for it. I do hope you realize this for it is so—& if there are more times when you sit out front & the work is good & is applauded, listen & be proud—as it is for you too they applaud.

Have a wonderful wonderful summer. I'll let you know how everything's going when you get back—but I'm so interested to hear how & what you've seen and done.

Keep well & again—my deepest & sincerest thanks—

Yours—
Jerry

To: Robert Fizdale
[postmarked July 13, 1950]

SAVOY HOTEL, LONDON

Dearest Bobby—

Well, this just about winds up the London season[*] for me. It's been very strange—& in a way I hate to leave. We have just finished doing 4 consecutive "Anxieties"[†] which improved as they went on & Melissa[‡] was just wonderful in

---

[*] In the summer of 1950, New York City Ballet had made its first foreign tour, to London.
[†] Robbins's *Age of Anxiety,* to Leonard Bernstein's score, loosely based on W. H. Auden's poem.
[‡] Melissa Hayden (1923–2006), a Canadian-born dramatic classicist who had danced with Ballet Theatre from 1945 to 1947, had joined City Ballet in 1948.

Robert Fizdale (right) with his performing partner, Arthur Gold, in their New York apartment in the early fifties.

it in Tanny's role. The ballet has had success with public if not with the critics, Edwin included. No doubt he'll tell you all—& everything he said, although very disturbing, was also very stimulating to me & will have its results in future works I guess. He always makes me feel so very inadequate as a choreographer, besides his constant baiting, which isn't as disturbing. It's been wonderful to see him & speak with him as well as it's been exhausting. I guess if I didn't think so much of him, this wouldn't be—but the combination of that sensitive face—learned & intuitive words—plus the irritating quality of being someone who sits outside life & finds amusement in everyone else's struggles with it (not malicious amusement—but god-like "beyond-&above-it" amusement)—this all gets frightening & overpowering, like too strong drink & values & importances change & shift about, leaving one wondering & angry. I feel better about him having written this out.

I hate, *hate* the idea of returning to the States. What with all the news as it is,[*] & how I felt before, it seems idiotic to return. But why do I, then? Maybe just to disprove [*sic*] to myself that it all can't be as bad as I believe, & as dismal an outlook as I see it. Does it all enter the air there in Florence? Or doesn't it get a chance, between practice, living, loving, & badminton. How I long to see you.

I better stop. I suppose I'm a little depressed, because I hurt my ankle, can't dance well—& won't be here to do Prodigal,[†] etc. Oh, well, can't have everything:—& *that,* Edwin says, is my trouble. True, too.

Write me in N.Y. do.

My love to all & most to you.

Jerry

To: Robert Fizdale
Tuesday, August 22, 1950

Dearest Bobby—

It was so good to get your letter—it made me very happy & picked me up out of the dullness of facing another day inside a dirty theater under a work light.[‡] I do so wish I were there with you for a while—rains or not. The closest I've come is to go down to Little Italy Sunday night for dinner, & to walk around street festivals going on. They look so beautiful with the arches of different colored light bulbs spanning the streets. The air was wonderful—not at all like N.Y. or American air—but like Europe or Mexico, because the sidewalks were lined with little stands in which fat Italian mamas cooked sausages over charcoals or slapped dough into pastries & fried them in deep grease—or sold candies &

---

* On June 25, North Korea invaded South Korea, and on July 4 UN forces had engaged North Korean forces for the first time. It appeared that an extended conflict was inevitable. In addition, Congress was currently debating the McCarran Act, which would require registration of all Communist organizations. And Julius Rosenberg and his brother-in-law David Greenglass had just been arrested for nuclear espionage. For someone with Communist associations, however much behind him, this was an ominous time.

† Balanchine's 1929 ballet *Prodigal Son,* to Prokofiev, which the choreographer had revived for Robbins and which had become one of the latter's signature roles.

‡ Robbins was choreographing Irving Berlin's *Call Me Madam,* starring Ethel Merman.

fruits & nuts—or parasols, tambourines & fans. Although it was August the first fall breezes moved the paper decorations & carried the marvelous mixed smells all around. A huge paper-flowered Madonna had a special stand surrounded by light bulbs, candles, & contributed dollars. Opposite on a wooden platform, a six-piece band blared Italian waltzes over a mike that seemed to prefer the clarinet to the other instruments. Occasionally someone sang a selection (after passing her music to musicians) & the whole thing was topped by a lottery conducted completely in Italian, with the populace yelling fraud because the owner of the largest grocery store on that corner won the prize. All in all it was like being *not* in the states—which is a great relief & pleasure to experience. I don't know if you are at all aware of the concentrated drive to full out atomic war that's being conducted here. Every day the Tribune has articles about what to do for and in case of atomic explosions—best places to hide—how to treat burns—etc. etc. In other words they are completely preparing us to accept the idea of N.Y. & other cities being destroyed—& suddenly the conscious belief we each have in our own immortality & invulnerableness shatters & drops away—& we see ourselves as part of the rubble after the disaster. And so what. (After rereading the above I don't know if it's depressing or funny!)

As for the show—well I haven't been going through that great turmoil & anxiety I usually have with a show—but on the other hand I don't feel I've turned up with anything special either. There is very little dancing in the show all in all, what there is has been very confined & watched by Berlin. This has really been a whore's job: doing it for money. And although I always felt I could do good work even in a dull situation, I'm afraid my lack of empathy with the opus shows in what I've done. What *has* been fun is staging Merman's numbers & working with her. She always sings full out & it's a real treat for me. I have to give her each movement—& she stands behind me & imitates—but then the way she does it is so her own & hilarious.

Friday Aug[ust] 25th
Got caught up in work—& depressions about it. Took a look at what I had done & didn't like it very much. I go through this with every work—& hope this is just *that* stage—Only sometime (maybe this) it won't look good to me & won't look good later to others. Oh well.

I'm being pursued by Hollywood again—but I want to come to Europe in

Robbins clowning in the mirror in the early 1950s with the Rolleiflex he
was then using. His apartment, which had belonged to the photographer
George Platt Lynes, had a small darkroom, enabling him to develop and
print his own contact sheets and photos.

Oct[ober]. I couldn't quite understand where you'd be. I again have that great
desire to get the hell out of N.Y. If not Europe—maybe I'll motor to Mexico
which I've been dying to get to since 42. I guess this is the time I say to *you*—
come along—it's so beautiful & such a center of culture. Well write anyway &
let me know how & where you will be.

After again rereading this letter I'm afraid I've misled [you]. The show looks very good & very funny & will be a hit.[*] Merman is just wonderful & you will adore her. Just don't enjoy my own work—but then—etc.

I've been going to the movies like mad, mostly out of loneliness—& reading a good deal, mostly junk—& hardly seeing anyone or getting into good talks with them. Oliver has been very busy although Jane's play[†] was postponed & I haven't heard yet what the next step on it will be. Got a brief note full of the usual from Lenny from Tanglewood—& saw Marc Blitzstein[‡] who is directing Britten's "Let's Make an Opera," doing a score for "King Lear"—& working on his own opus "Reuben Reuben." The only other cultural incident in my life [is] that I was introduced at Sardi's to Jeannette McDonald & Margaret Truman (sitting together!!). With this last, I leave you. My bests to all & my love to you as always. Do write.

Miss you!!
Jerry

Collecting (from *The Poppa Piece*)[§]

October 21, 1990

POP

What are you doing?

JAKE

Collecting it.

---

[*] It was: it ran for 644 performances, and Robbins's choreography as well as Berlin's score was especially praised by critics.

[†] Jane Bowles's play, *In the Summer House,* which Robbins admired intensely and would have liked to direct, was being produced by Oliver Smith. It would finally get a Broadway production, directed by José Quintero, in 1953.

[‡] Marc Blitzstein (1905–1964), whose pro-union *The Cradle Will Rock* had been locked out by the WPA in 1937, was one of the composers Robbins had considered for *Fancy Free.*

[§] In some versions of Robbins's unproduced autobiographical theater piece, his alter ego was named Jay or Jake Whitby, formerly Yakov Vitkowitz.

POP

What's "it"?

JAKE

Everything.

POP

Everything? Everything?

JAKE

Yes, Pop. Everything I can get. Fame, publicity, money, friends, awards, articles—and books, records, paintings, clothes, lovers, and most of all *attention*! Attention, and love—yes, and power, control; control over others and control over myself. I've got so much rage inside me that I can't control it—it will explode out and over everything and everybody—I can kill the world. I want all those things—and more. I want good food, and a good apartment, and I want to travel. I want to see places, foreign places—magic astonishing lands and people; and I want to go to all the plays and hear music and see paintings—I want to catch up and learn and read books and study things and ask questions. Pop, I've got wants, needs, wishes, terrific appetites. I want, I want, I want— and I'm starting to collect it all. Now I can. I'm in. I do good work—I want to do more—try everything. Watch me, Pop—I'm taking off and I'm making my fortune and my future.

POP
(after a pause)

You're making yourself meshugana.*

---

* Alternate spelling, *meshugenah:* Yiddish for mad, crazy, stupid.

The World

The world is a bubbel a giant blew
With thousands of people and
     even you.
The world is babblea giant   blew
With skys and seas and animals   too.
The world is a bubbel a gaint   blew
That even floats thru the air
And if that gaint came   to this earth
Guess whon he would
     scare.

The Greeness of the grass

The blueness of the sky
The greenness of the grass
The world is like a picture
What more is there to ask.

A page from the poetry collection that nine-year-old Jerry Rabinowitz made as a Christmas present for his mother, illustrated with artwork scissored out of an anthology of Greek myths called *Enchantment Tales for Children*. "I offer you this little book," reads his handwritten dedication, "Inside the pages I hope you'll look . . ."

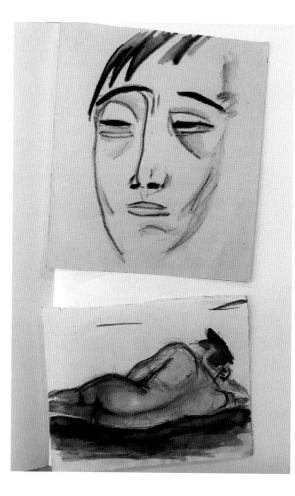

Two sketches, possibly of dancers with Gluck Sandor's Dance Center company, that Robbins made in the 1930s.

Man on the street, Mexico City, 1942. "Everybody seems so busy down here," Robbins wrote to his parents, "and nothing seems to get done."

Self-portrait from the 1940s.

"Petrouchka was my favorite role," Robbins said. He made this costume sketch when he first danced it in 1942.

"My city is a lone man walking at night down an empty street watching his shadow grow longer as he passes the last lamppost." The watercolor, by Robbins, is from the late 1940s.

4

Rising and Falling: 1950–1964

Over the next fourteen years Robbins seemed to be playing a game of high-stakes bridge, cross-ruffing between Broadway and ballet (and, in his personal life, between relationships with women and relationships with men), winning ever-greater sums, with ever-greater risks of failure—or worse. Although it was an extraordinarily productive period for him, it seems not to have permitted him (or he didn't permit himself) any real time for introspection: almost no journals from these years survive.

In the spring of 1950, before he started work on *Call Me Madam*, he'd had an unsettling encounter (described in a recently discovered memorandum written for his personal files) with the popular newspaper columnist and television host Ed Sullivan. Anti-Communist hysteria was on the rise because of the Korean War and the Rosenberg case, and Sullivan—whom FBI files reveal to have been a facilitator (if not an informant) for the Bureau—told Robbins he'd become aware of his Communist connections and hinted he might expose him unless he gave information on others to the authorities. According to reliable contemporary witnesses, Sullivan also suggested—possibly in a follow-up conversation—that he might make an issue of Robbins's homosexuality. The former allegation could cause Robbins to lose his citizenship, according to a provision in the new McCarran Act, and the latter could get him a prison sentence. Both could threaten his career—the career that had lifted him from poverty and obscurity and given him the life he had scarcely dared to dream of.

In an effort to forestall a public unmasking, Robbins had met with the FBI, telling them of his own party activities but nothing else. "It was obvious to the interviewing agents," wrote one of them to FBI director J. Edgar Hoover, that Robbins "had no interest in furnishing any information to the FBI of value . . . [and] there was absolutely no indication from the conversation that ROBBINS is no longer a Communist." However, though they gave him no reassurances ("the FBI does not clear anyone," said the examining agent), the G-men seemed ready to let the matter rest—for the moment.[*]

But Robbins was unmoored, and it didn't help that things were unsettled in his new home at City Ballet. George Balanchine, having separated from his wife, the ballerina Maria Tallchief, was courting Tanaquil Le Clercq, disrupting the rapport Robbins felt with her. (Balanchine and Le Clercq would marry on the last day of 1952.) Feeling subjected and rejected—"Petrouchka in contemporary terms," as he described it—he went to Paris as soon as *Call Me Madam* opened to oversee Ballet Theatre's presentations of his ballets on their European tour. He and Nora Kaye renewed their old intimacy; when they returned to New York, they were engaged, and she joined City Ballet, where Robbins created one of his signature ballets, *The Cage*—a macabre fable about a female insect who turns her mate into prey—for her. At the same time he was working on Broadway, acting as show doctor (for George Abbott) on *A Tree Grows in Brooklyn,* and choreographing *The King and I,* by Richard Rodgers and Oscar Hammerstein, with its central ballet, "The Small House of Uncle Thomas"—the story of a runaway being chased by a powerful bully. He had been hired for that show shortly before fleeing to Paris in the fall, and it was in part the promise that work held out to him that lured him back to New York despite his anxiety over his interview with the FBI.

The King and I was a hit and won Robbins his third Donaldson Award (a precursor to the Tonys); its success led to a movie offer, for the choreographer as well as the show. But a week before the show opened,

---

* Robbins's meetings with the FBI are documented in a confidential memo from Special Agent Edward Scheidt to J. Edgar Hoover, April 27, 1950, obtained by Robbins under the Freedom of Information Act and filed in the Robbins archives. Information about Sullivan's threats came from interviews with contemporary family witnesses George Cullinen and Robert Silverman.

Ed Sullivan, reneging on the promise of confidentiality he had made to Robbins, published a front-page column in *The Philadelphia Inquirer* urging the just-reconvened House Un-American Activities Committee to subpoena Robbins for "backstage glimpses of the musical shows which have been jammed with performers sympathetic to the Commie cause."[*] Robbins's lawyers managed to keep the column out of the other news outlets, and it didn't get wide currency, but he was justifiably afraid of a HUAC summons. At the same time he and Nora Kaye had postponed their marriage plans (permanently, as it turned out), and now Robbins left the country again, supposedly for six months, although he wondered if he might have to stay indefinitely, out of the reach of HUAC.

His flight yielded unexpected rewards: he went to Israel for the first time, an experience that made him "proud to be a Jew"; he traveled through Brittany, Italy, and Greece, his first real exposure to the European countryside, soaking up impressions of landscapes and paintings and people, with which he regaled Tanaquil Le Clercq; and he met two people who would be important to him in the short and long terms: the composer Ned Rorem and the dancer Buzz Miller, with whom (after a halting start) he began his first sustained liaison, which would last nearly five years. But the trip badly frayed the relationship with Le Clercq, who—unaware of his troubles with the FBI—could not understand his absence, nor his reluctance to return, and let him know it. Return he eventually did, however: to dance the lead in Balanchine's *Tyl Ulenspiegel,* which had been created for him; to choreograph the jazzy *Pied Piper,* the haunting *Ballade,* the comic pageant *Fanfare,* and the poetic duet *Afternoon of a Faun* for City Ballet—all but *Fanfare* featuring Tanaquil Le Clercq, who remained his muse despite her marriage to Balanchine on New Year's Eve 1952; and to stage musical numbers for a Broadway revue called *Two's Company,* starring Bette Davis, as well as his past and current lovers Nora Kaye and Buzz Miller. He also directed the dance sequences for the film of *The King and I;* staged *The Ford 50th Anniversary Show,* a television special; and acted as show doctor for the Bernstein/

---

[*] Ed Sullivan, *Philadelphia Inquirer,* March 24, 1951.

Comden/Green musical *Wonderful Town*. And on May 5, 1953, after three years of threats from the FBI, and having refused a Paramount movie contract that his lawyer assured him would buy him immunity from prosecution, Robbins testified in front of a New York hearing of the House Un-American Activities Committee and named the names of eight people who had been his associates during his Communist Party days.

His testimony was denounced by many, including members of his family. Others sympathized, or approved, and even friends who disapproved of his actions, such as Arthur Laurents, soon rationalized or got past them somehow. His agreement to testify haunted Robbins himself, however. Though he almost never spoke of it, in later years he would revisit it continually in his private journals, and he placed it at the center of his autobiographical drama, *The Poppa Piece,* in a surreal scene that eerily reproduces much of the actual hearing transcript and portrays his naming of former colleagues as a patricidal betrayal of his Jewish heritage.

After the HUAC hearing, perhaps to distract himself from introspection, Robbins threw himself into professional hyperactivity, co-directing *The Pajama Game* (1954); doctoring Cole Porter's *Silk Stockings* (1955); directing his first opera, Aaron Copland's *Tender Land* (1954), as well as the musicals *Peter Pan* (1954)—which he also staged for television (1955)—and *Bells Are Ringing* (1956). He was also still making dances for City Ballet, including his comic masterpiece *The Concert* (1956), but he had stopped performing, and increasingly he felt ambivalent about working in Balanchine's shadow, or having his creative choices questioned or rejected by Balanchine and Lincoln Kirstein—as when, for example, they declined to pursue a ballet adaptation of S. Anski's mystical Yiddish play, *The Dybbuk*.

Amid all this activity he, Leonard Bernstein, Arthur Laurents—and eventually the young Stephen Sondheim—had been working intermittently on a project Robbins had first mooted in the late 1940s: a danced-through musical adaptation of *Romeo and Juliet,* updated to a modern urban setting. Robbins pushed this endeavor with single-minded tenacity despite the conflicting demands of his and his collaborators' crowded schedules and the discouraging response of the marketplace, which decreed that a musical about teenage gangs was dead on arrival (virtually every producer they tried to interest in it turned it down). And his relentlessness, his drive to control every aspect of the production—not to mention his insistence on the credit "based on a conception by Jerome Robbins" in a box on all marketing materials—put his relationships with his collaborators to the test. When *West Side Story* opened in 1957, it was recognized at once as a game-changing musical, but the bulk of the credit for its success—in critics' appraisals and in awards recognition—went to Robbins, something that strained his relationships with his collaborators even further but did help secure him the right to co-direct the film version, which MGM planned to start shooting in 1960.

In the meantime his personal life was once again fraught. Lena Robbins, whose hold over him he had both sought and rejected, died suddenly of cancer on April 12, 1954, just before the opening of *Pajama Game* and the start of rehearsals for *Peter Pan,* a musical about lost boys who want a mother. He was with her at the end and kept his feelings about his loss close, hinting at them only in a letter to his frequent correspondent Robert Fizdale, but years later he revisited them—with a candor made possible by perspective—in dialogue in *The Poppa Piece.* His relationship with Buzz Miller ended in 1956, in part because of Miller's restiveness and in part because of Robbins's attentions to Nancy "Slim" Hayward, the glamorous wife of the agent and producer Leland Hayward, whom he'd met during rehearsals for *Call Me Madam* in 1950 and who was deeply attracted to him. To make things more complicated, during the spring of 1956 Balanchine and Tanaquil Le Clercq decided to separate. That summer she and Robbins became close again; she came to stay with him on Fire Island, and when City Ballet left on a European tour in August, she wrote to him almost daily, letters full of gossip and affection. "Darling," began one, "I'm going to miss you like crazy."[*] Then tragedy struck: on tour with City Ballet in Europe (Robbins stayed in the United States to direct *Bells Are Ringing* and to

[*] Le Clercq to Robbins, n.d. [1956], Jerome Robbins Personal Papers, NYPL.

cast *West Side Story*), Le Clercq contracted polio and became paralyzed. Robbins was shattered. He wrote to her nearly every day during her hospitalization in Denmark—she kept his letters on her pillow in the iron lung so she could read them over and over—and she reciprocated, although she had to dictate her correspondence to her mother, Edith, who had flown to Copenhagen to be with her. When she returned to the United States, Robbins visited her, first in New York and then in Warm Springs, Georgia, where she was undergoing rehabilitation treatment, and when he couldn't get to her, he telephoned. "I will think about the two days in the sun when I go to sleep so I can dream them,"* she wrote to him after his Georgia visit, but she had a new life to adjust to—without him and *with* her formerly estranged husband, who had at least temporarily abandoned plans to leave the marriage—and her relationship with Robbins entered a prickly phase in which she tried to reinforce the boundaries between them. For Robbins, her absence transformed New York City Ballet's home at City Center into a haunted place, and—he said decades later—after *West Side Story* opened, he "couldn't go back to it."

Instead he threw himself into other endeavors: a new musical, *Gypsy* (1959), based on the memoirs of the stripper Gypsy Rose Lee, with Laurents, Jule Styne (composer of *High Button Shoes*), and Stephen Sondheim; dances for his very own pickup modern ballet company, Ballets: U.S.A., which was featured at the Spoleto Festival (1958–1960), toured Europe for the State Department, and appeared on Broadway (1958 and 1961) and at the Kennedy White House (1962); and the motion picture incarnation of *West Side Story*. In this last venture his perfectionism and relentlessness ran afoul of the Hollywood budgetary process: after he had filmed all but two of the dance sequences, the "Dance at the Gym" and the final fight in which the hero, Tony, is killed, he was fired from the production for taking too much time and costing too much money. But he insisted on screening, and offering suggestions on, the rough cut of the picture, and in the end won two Academy Awards for it, one

---

* Le Clercq to Robbins, undated but postmarked October 8, 1957, Jerome Robbins Personal Papers, NYPL.

for choreography and one (shared with co-director Robert Wise) for direction.

As the 1960s began, Robbins explored new frontiers, some personal, some professional. With the poet and novelist Robert Graves he was one of the first to experiment with hallucinogenic mushrooms; soon thereafter he ventured into the world of straight plays, directing Arthur Kopit's offbeat "pseudo-tragifarce" *Oh Dad, Poor Dad, Mamma's Hung You in the Closet and I'm Feelin' So Sad,* and then Bertolt Brecht's *Mother Courage,* a work he was initially ambivalent about, in a production that—in the end—failed to fulfill his visions for it. This process, which he chronicled in a journal of the production, added to a growing sense of disillusion about the workings of the commercial theater. It didn't help that at the same time as he had been working on *Oh Dad* and *Mother Courage,* he had also been involved with two musicals, *A Funny Thing Happened on the Way to the Forum* (1962) and *Funny Girl* (1964), and had contentiously withdrawn from each because neither appeared to be ready for production, then was persuaded to rejoin both, reshaping them substantially, when they were foundering during pre-Broadway tryouts.

But whatever sense of dissatisfaction he had with the theater, it was seemingly overcome by a project that first presented itself to him while he was still struggling with *Funny Girl:* a musical adaptation of the stories of Sholem Aleichem about Tevye, the shtetl milkman, his wife, Golde, and their five daughters, to be written by Joseph Stein (book), Jerry Bock (music), and Sheldon Harnick (lyrics). Seeking to put as much distance as he could between himself and the "horror and shame" he had felt when his Gentile playmates had mocked the old tzaddik who was teaching him Torah, Robbins had avoided overtly Jewish material all his professional life, but now, with a shelf full of awards and a White House appearance on his résumé, he could afford to be "proud to be a Jew" and to revisit the world he had known in childhood that was "all lovely." And so he signed on as director for *Fiddler on the Roof.*

Ed Sullivan, 1950[*]

[early 1951]

In January, 1950, Ed Sullivan contacted my agent, Harold Hoyt, about my appearance on TOAST OF THE TOWN,[†] to do "Fancy Free." A date was set and contracts were in the process of being drawn up. I was supposed to appear on the program in the middle of March, but about ten days before this my agent called and told me that Sullivan had decided not to use me because my name was linked with communist activities. He accused me of being a communist and told my agent that if I wanted to straighten it out with him all I had to do was come to his office and talk with him. I believed, at the time, I was just dealing with a newspaperman who had heard some talk or had been tipped off by someone about some past activities, and that my going to Sullivan in his office would clear myself in his eyes.

We met in his office at the Delmonico Hotel, 59th Street and Park Avenue. Mr. Sullivan said that he had been very anxious to have me on his program but that as the deal was about to go through someone told him that he had seen my name announced for making an appearance at an ASP cabaret[‡] to be held the following weekend at the Capitol Hotel. . . . [H]e felt he had better check further into my background, and said he had seen a huge dossier on me from the FBI files which listed all the organizations cited as communist front[s] that my name had been associated with, and that I was also down as a communist.

I asked him whether he himself had seen these files and he said "yes." I said "FBI files?" and he said "yes."[§]

---

[*] This undated memorandum was written by Robbins to himself a bit more than a year after the events it describes. He dug it out to use as background for *The Poppa Piece,* probably in the 1980s, and it was later filed with scripts of the trial scene and forgotten, until I uncovered it in compiling this book. The document runs to nine typed, unparagraphed pages, and is full of repetitions; I have cut it for space reasons and also inserted paragraph breaks for clarity.

[†] Since 1948, Sullivan had been the host of a television variety program called *Toast of the Town,* which was broadcast nationally on CBS; in 1955 its name was changed to *The Ed Sullivan Show.*

[‡] A benefit for the National Council of Arts, Sciences, and Professions, a group formed to combat attacks on free speech and academic freedom; the anti-Communist newsletter *Counterattack* called it "Moscow's top culture destroying agency in the U.S."

[§] Robbins seems to have suspected that it was highly irregular if not illegal for a private citizen such as Sullivan to have access to FBI material.

I told him that I could not deny that I had been connected with Left Wing organizations but that was in the past, [and] that I had quite often given my name or appeared on programs [for] which a large number of outstanding Broadway people had done the same thing. I told him that my early activities had been a part of an emotional and unstable period of my life, and [they] represented my identification with the underdog and fighting anti-minority issues. At that period of my life I had sought the help of a psychiatrist to aid me in the confusion and neurotic state I found myself to be in at that time. I told Mr. Sullivan that the sudden success of "Fancy Free" and the ensuing attention and acclaim had thrown me very much, and I was seized upon, as a celebrity, to endorse and give my name to many many things, and I was always proud, in my new-found fame, to be asked to appear with other great names. I told him that at this period of my life I didn't know which end was up, and probably would have given my name to the Mickey Mouse Club.

Mr. Sullivan said he felt it was important that I not be associated with these organizations, as I was a very influential person as far as young people were concerned. He was particularly distressed because of his young daughter, who, he said, was a particular fan of mine. He said he felt convinced about my honesty, but that if I really wanted to clear myself he would introduce me to Kirkpatrick,[*] a friend of his, and the four of us would have a friendly meeting and talk the whole thing over. He said "Jerry, I'll never publish this, but I'm glad you came to me because someone else might." Sullivan told me that Counterattack's [editors] were former FBI men who had access to the files and knew what they were talking about. The specific impression that Mr. Sullivan gave me was that talking to them and clearing myself with them was as good as any official clearance.

The meeting with Mr. Kirkpatrick occurred a few days later at the same place. Present were my agent, Mr. Kirkpatrick and Mr. Sullivan. Mr. Sullivan reiterated that this was all confidential and that this little talk would clean things up. I went over the same ground with Kirkpatrick that I had with Sullivan. At one point Kirkpatrick asked me directly if I had been a member of the Party. I

---

[*] Theodore C. Kirkpatrick, who along with two fellow former FBI agents had founded *Counterattack: The Newsletter of Facts on Communism*, in 1947. He was the newsletter's managing editor and spokesman.

directly answered yes, I had been but it was over with, that I had no connection whatsoever with the Party for the past three years, that I had joined the Party for the reasons mentioned earlier and had left when I decided it was an unorganized mess of people with whom I had no common interest. I was asked if I were called before the Senate Committee would I testify, and I said yes. Asked if I would volunteer to give names I said I would, but I didn't want to be responsible for smearing people whose activities I had no knowledge of for the past three to six years.

Sullivan asked me if it wasn't true that [the Party] had promised me work and jobs and quick advancement. I had to laugh at this idea, as my success had been established before I had attended any meetings, and if it were true the Party would be more popular than MCA.* Sullivan wanted to know if he could have a printed statement from me which he would run in his column for his own purposes. I objected because I felt there was no reason for me to publicize these facts and stir up attention which would harm me. Kirkpatrick said supposing Russia attacks the United States, would you be willing to fight and make statements? I answered yes. Kirkpatrick then felt the next step to be taken was for him to write this up and asked me to sign the statement and they would use as little or as much as they felt was necessary for their magazine "Counterattack." My agent and I both objected to the line of new demands and requests. I thought the whole meeting was to be confidential [and] began to have fears of putting into the hands of private people, matters which were the business of the government. The whole thing smelt badly to me.

After we left, my agent and I decided we needed some legal advice, and consulted with Paul Williams, of the firm of Cahill, Gordon, Zachry and Reindel, who represented my agent. They pointed out that "Counterattack" had no right to any signed statement from me about anything. They felt I should immediately take the whole matter to the FBI; I agreed, and Jerry Doyle,† former assistant to

---

* Founded in the 1920s as a music-booking agency, MCA (Music Corporation of America) was by 1950 the largest talent agency in the world, representing preeminent artists and directors of film, theater, television, and the recording industry, and had just launched a television production company.
† Doyle has an interesting role in McCarthy-era history: he was one of two Cahill Gordon attorneys who declined to represent Alger Hiss, because of an unspecified conflict of interest, in his second hearing before HUAC in August 1948.

J. Edgar Hoover, and now associated with the firm of Cahill, Gordon, took us to the FBI in the Federal Courthouse Building in Foley Square. I reported to them, completely, the two conferences [with] Kirkpatrick and Sullivan. I reported my own activities as far as the Party was concerned. I refused the name of the girl who had recruited me, on the grounds that I had been very intimate with her, that she had been influential in getting me some aid psychiatrically, that I had not seen her in many years, had no idea whether she was still a member of the Party, and did not want to involve her.

The meeting lasted about one and one-half hours. When asked why I had given my name to the organizations on which it appeared, I answered that it was not solely because of the other people's names, but also because the supposed premise and issues seemed to be tolerant and liberal causes. The man looked at me and said, "Do right but don't write."

Journal, 1950
Monday November 13th 6PM

Somewhere along the way I have already died. At 32 I feel this way & it doesn't matter what the answer when asked how old. Something has passed me & I feel it's all too late too late for so many things. And how strange that it all comes out of me still. Will it I wonder? Will it still come out now after that confession & giving up is over with. When will I find myself & what I believe in again. When can the "I" join the "me" & be whole to work together again. I guess I've had it & been had too. . . . Petrouchka in contemporary terms.

Wednesday Nov. 15
Nora is staying with me.[*] I like it. I like the companionship & like the sex. I guess yes it's like we have been married for 10 years & some of the excitement of a younger & more passionate kind of love (& not just sexually passionate)

---

[*] After City Ballet's fall season Robbins went to Paris to supervise Ballet Theatre's staging of some of his ballets on a European tour. He and Nora Kaye were staying in the Hotel du Quai Voltaire, which would become his favorite Paris haunt in the 1950s.

is missing . . . a be all–end all feeling about it. Nor do I at all think it a negative thing to say we get on well. It's more than that, but that is plenty. Nor am I putting myself on any test basis. What is, is, & what will be, will be—& I no longer expect perfection or disaster from myself. I'll indulge I guess sometime elsewhere & otherwise sexually, I think—but now this with Nora feels like home, & I think we both want it to be enough—(no, more than want it enough, much more positively) for it to work out & to be home. Maybe the splits & seams in me are coming together again—maybe it's all coming together & I'll not be afraid to look at people and feel fraud. Where does the talent come from I wonder, when I have felt such a hoax.

I feel like the racer, who after leaving the envious & admiring pack long behind, turns a corner & sits to rest a moment, laughing—"Ha—not me!" There musing over his conquests & successes, & with self admiration of being still untouched & after a while he peeks back to see how far off they are—.

The street is empty.

They have not even now followed him—& the chase is in another direction—after someone else—down some other boulevard.

Nora Kaye Memorial, Notes

1988

[Nora] hated to fly. She'd always told me so, but not having experienced it myself, I found it hard to take it seriously. But in 1951, I was with Ballet Theatre and they were going to fly into Berlin for a week's run. I asked Lucia if I could tag along and she said yes, so the next day we got on the plane. I'm a cheerful traveler and somewhat talkative. Nora got into a window seat and I sat down next to her—I talked to whoever was across the aisle for a minute and then turned to Nora. She was lettuce-leaf green and wet with an ice-cold sweat. Her eyes were glazed with fear and she could hardly talk. I covered her hand with mine, put my arm around her. All she could manage to get out to me was, "Don't talk."

To: Oscar Hammerstein II[*]

November 11, 1950

PARIS

Hello, Mr. Hammerstein, first of all I want to tell you how really very, very excited I am about the show. The bad part of it is I haven't gotten it out of my head since I've gotten here and it keeps obsessing all my time [*sic*]. Last night I went to see some Indonesian dancing at the legation here [and] saw some wonderful things which started me thinking of how they could be used in the show. One thing I was particularly impressed by was a dance between a man and a woman in which

[*] Oscar Hammerstein had written both the book and the lyrics to *The King and I;* he and composer Richard Rodgers were also sole producers and had hired Robbins to choreograph an act 2 ballet retelling the story of *Uncle Tom's Cabin* in the style of Thai court dancing. This letter was recorded on a Dictaphone—not written and revised—and enclosed in a longer Dictaphone message to Hammerstein from Leland Hayward, who had co-produced Rodgers and Hammerstein's *South Pacific* and had been corresponding with Hammerstein about a London transfer of that show. "Jerry Robbins is with me," Hayward told Hammerstein, and "I thought perhaps he could talk to you a few minutes on this record. . . . [H]e is full of good ideas and hot notions about the whole project, so wait a minute and I'll introduce you to Jerry Robbins."

The Bois de Boulogne, Paris, 1950s. "They have not even now followed him—& the chase is in another direction—after someone else."

the woman did very, very little. Most of the time she just stood there with her eyes cast down and sort of presented herself to the man, who was standing across on the other side of the stage, watching her. The music was very exciting, not loud, but rhythmic and pulsating, and he, while he was watching her, would only very slowly move his head, somewhat birdlike, somewhat snakelike. It was terrifically sexy. It was almost as if he had been touching her all over, and the distance between them pointed this up all the more, and I was immediately struck by the parallel between this dance and the story of "Anna and the King of Siam"—that there was no contact between them but that this thing was going on all the time. . . .

I have a lot of thoughts about the dancing in this show. From what I have seen the tone of it should be very quiet. It should not be balletic in any sense at all. It should be based completely on native material. I don't think it should be large or extravagant [but] jewel-like, and performed with great dignity and great elegance, and that the humor should come out of the juxtaposition of what they are dancing about and the manner they dance it with, rather than any broad or farcical elements. Perhaps Anna has given them [the Siamese court dancers] ideas about theater in the Western civilization rather than the Eastern. What I think would be very lovely and very beautiful is if she had rigged up this fake paper snow to come down at one point, which would float gently down and which the dancers would move through.

The next thing I tell you is not because of any particular ambitions I have concerning the show. I am completely pleased to do just the ballet, but in reading the script over and over I felt very much that all the movement should be a particular style, and maybe by this time you have arrived at this same idea yourself. I think that the entrances of the servants and the entrances of the children and the deportment around the court should all be of one style which should really be connected to the ballet [so] that it is all of one piece.[*] I'm very excited about the script. I think it's a wonderful script. It kind of crept up on me slowly. When first I read it, I was very tired and didn't want to think of work, and then over the days I slowly haunted Leland about it.

---

[*] Although originally engaged only to choreograph the ballet, Robbins was ultimately asked to stage the entrances of the King's children, for which special music was written, and also to create other dances, such as "Getting to Know You," a number for Anna and the King's wives and children, and "Shall We Dance?"—which incorporated some of this letter's ideas about Eastern and Western traditions, and about distance and sexual connection.

. . . The music interests me as to what will be used there, because the [Southeast Asian] music that I have heard here plays a very important part. The percussion quality, the nasal singing quality, and all that is indicated in the script, but I did not know how far you were planning to go on this. I'd be very interested to hear what your view is on this subject.* I can't think of anything else right now. If I do I'll jot it down and try to make a lot of notes and ask Leland to do this for me again. I'm very, very flattered and honored that I have been asked to do this, and very happy to be working with you all on it.

To: Tanaquil Le Clercq
July 4 [1951]

PERROS-GUIREC

Dearest Tany,†

Here I am in a small & delightful little Breton village on the north coast of Brittany.‡ The car broke down here while I was touring about, & the enforced stay has turned out just wonderfully. But I'll go back and start from the beginning. I got to Paris, & was given the same room as I had when here last which was so wonderful & nostalgic too. And then after a few days there I got terribly depressed and decided to get out of Paris. The last night before the trip I was invited to the Lido (night club) by the owner who wants me to do some work

---

* The ballet music for *The King and I* would be written by Trude Rittman, a German émigré composer who had created dance arrangements and underscoring (and sometimes all-new compositions) for Rodgers and Hammerstein's *Oklahoma!*, *Carousel*, and *South Pacific* and had worked with Robbins on *Billion Dollar Baby*, *Look, Ma, I'm Dancin'!*, and *Miss Liberty*.

† Although Le Clercq always used two *n*'s in her nickname, in the beginning of their relationship Robbins used only one.

‡ Robbins had had an eventful spring: after returning from Europe in December 1950, he and Nora Kaye had become engaged, then semi-un-engaged, and he had worked on two Broadway musicals—doctoring *A Tree Grows in Brooklyn* and choreographing *The King and I*—as well as creating his ballet *The Cage*. When he was asked by a nonprofit group to report on the state of dance in Israel, he'd decided to combine a visit there with a summer traveling in Europe. All this before Ed Sullivan broke his vow of confidentiality by publishing a column about Robbins's Communist affiliations—making a trip abroad as much refuge as relaxation.

for him. It was great show & after it I went out with some of the kids performing it & their friends. I stayed up till 7 A.M. (not difficult in Paris) & then while
driving people home, two of them decided they should go with me, if I started
immediately. So I packed, & off we went. Arrived in Chartres at 10 A.M. The city
& cathedral were so beautiful & we were so tired that we all cried while inside.
After lunch one of the boys got on a train back to Paris, the other* is still here
with me, & I've never had so much fun & enjoyed life so much. I am very lucky,
as he is a wonderful person & marvelous to travel with. We've been to Vitré, a
wonderful walled city, Mont St. Michel—where we walked way out onto the
sands & [it] felt like you were in a strange world of no horizon & weird light
& what an atmosphere to dance in!!—what colors & clouds & mists. Then St.
Malo. Then Guincamp where that night they held a procession carrying lighted
candles & banners & the Virgin thru the streets singing Breton songs, & then
lighting huge bonfires in the square at midnight & holding mass afterwards. I
walked with my candle clutched tightly in hand, singing Ave Maria & trying
desperately to look French. Then the car broke down (1st time) & we decided
to sleep in it. Damned if the thing didn't start off [next morning]—so we went
to Lannion, then here, where a French mechanic stuck his hand in the engine,
pulled out half its guts, then threw them on the floor & said Mal, mal. And it's
been mal ever since, four days now. I love it here, though. There's a huge sandy
beach; wild paths through huge boulders that look like a giant's been diddling
in clay; cliffs & fishing ports & superb food. Either I speak with a Breton accent
or my French is improving, cause they understand me very well here. Maybe is
Jewish French? I'm off to Israel the 17th of July for 2 weeks. I don't expect to be
back before October 20th. Nora sent me all the reviews of the ballet.† Scary, ain't
it? I kinda was shocked myself when I saw it opening night.

Do write me—I miss you.

Love,

J

---

* This was Buzz Miller (1923–1999), then a film and nightclub dancer, who at that point had never
heard of Jerome Robbins.
† *The Cage,* which Robbins had made for Nora Kaye after she joined New York City Ballet that
spring, had premiered on June 10 to great acclaim and some discomfort: the *Herald Tribune*'s Walter
Terry thought it "startling, unpleasant, but thoroughly absorbing," and Kaye's performance "frighteningly inhuman, provocative, and glitteringly feral" (*New York Herald Tribune,* June 15, 1951).

Tanaquil Le Clercq, who would become Robbins's muse, after a rehearsal. Of *Age of Anxiety,* the first ballet he made expressly on her, Le Clercq remarked that it was "Bernstein and Robbins and sweat."

To: Tanaquil Le Clercq
Undated [July 1951]

Dearest Tany,

Hi yourself.* Back in Paris. The trip was wonderful—full of such unexpected loveliness & unexpected force—or unexpected breakdowns!—but in any case *always* exciting. . . . The things we saw and did were so very good. All the churches, the little ones [in the] villages, are so marvelous—entering each is like meeting a new personality. They are all a strange combination of something extremely crude & gauche, strong & forceful, with an almost pagan intensity. The "calvaires"† too were something. Such drama & theatricality—I loved them & would like someday to do a ballet based on the passion. Tonight or tomorrow night I'm going to see my first passion play. They're doing one every night in front of Notre Dame with thousands of people in it. . . .

We went to Point de Raz [*sic*], the last bit of Europe stretching to [the] U.S. Against my better judgment a guide took us over the paths. Because I felt we didn't need him, *he* took us over *the* most dangerous places. You should have seen me, white & green & shaking, holding on to tiny holes in the rocks as we climbed up and down, trying to look casual and take pictures. I can't wait to see what comes out of that roll! You'll be very pleased to know that so far not a *single* picture has come out.

At Carnac are the aliments‡—rows & rows of upright stones dating prehistorically—something like 2000–25 B.C. Very eerie and scary somehow, you have to wonder why, how & what for—& no one seems to know. They average above head level and stretch for miles, almost like a graveyard. . . .

Back in Paris I found your letters & cards & was oh so very happy to have them. You write so wonderfully—it's like being with you, & you've inspired me

---

* Le Clercq frequently began letters "Hy—."

† Granite sculptural groups dating from the fifteenth to sixteenth century depicting figures from the Passion.

‡ A misspelling or mishearing of *alignements,* the French term for the Neolithic menhirs found at Carnac and elsewhere in Brittany.

The twenty-eight-year-old dancer Buzz Miller—"a wonderful person, and marvelous to travel with"—at Pointe du Raz, Brittany, July 1951, at the beginning of his and Robbins's five-year relationship.

to write you all *this*! Nora, Hugh, & Di[*] arrived & we spend most of the time wishing so very much you were here with us—& we all talked about how lucky we are to be in the company & working with George[†] & the marvelous people of the co. . . .

My love to George & Nicky,[‡] take care of yourself, & think of me.

Love & kisses,

J

* Diana Adams (1926–1993) was a principal dancer at New York City Ballet, currently entangled in a romance with Hugh Laing, whom she briefly married. She, Laing, and Kaye, like Robbins, had all migrated to NYCB from Ballet Theatre.
† George Balanchine.
‡ Nicholas Magallanes (1922–1977), a principal with City Ballet, had danced one of the lead roles in Robbins's first work for the company, *The Guests*.

To: Lincoln Kirstein[*]
August 18 [1951]

TEL AVIV

Dear Lincoln,

. . . Please do write & tell me what is the *very* latest possible date I can return & still do Tyl.[†] . . . I have to tell you that I dread returning to NY in spite of my deep love for the company & working with you all. Because of that stinking newspaper story[‡] I expect any day for a blow to fall, & find myself put in the "do-not-hire" class that so many artists have found themselves in along with very unsavory publicity. So I have considered the possibility of sitting the winter out in Europe & seeing what happens in the US. I would appreciate your advice on this. I am being urged, quite insistently, by my lawyer to accept a movie contract which he would make unbreakable in case of any investigations; he feels I should safeguard myself economically this way. It all sounds perfectly ghastly. The *only* reason I want to come back to the States is to work with the company—. That's not quite true. In spite of everything, my roots are in the US & it is my *home*, & my land & country & people, & I *feel* that very strongly. What a dilema [*sic*]. . . .

[*] Lincoln Kirstein (1907–1996), poet, critic, and arts impresario, had co-founded the School of American Ballet and New York City Ballet and was the de facto executive director of the company. He and Robbins had a close but complicated relationship.
[†] Balanchine's planned ballet to Strauss's *Till Eulenspiegel's Merry Pranks*—in which Robbins was to dance the lead—was set in the Spanish-occupied Netherlands during the sixteenth century, and the main character's name was therefore given the Dutch spelling, Tyl Ulenspiegel.
[‡] Ed Sullivan, "Tip to Red Probers: Subpena Jerome Robbins," *Philadelphia Inquirer,* March 24, 1951, 1.

To: Tanaquil Le Clercq

August 24th [1951]

Dearest Tany,

. . . I came back to Israel to attend a folk dance festival held in a natural ampitheatre in the hills. It was quite an experience. As a matter of fact, the whole stay in Israel was a truly wonderful experience & affected me very deeply. I didn't want to leave. It felt like home, and made me very proud to be a Jew, something I always negated, and rejected. The people there are fabulous, the young people particularly. They are the most beautiful people I've seen. Healthy, blonde, red-headed, with marvelous bodies. And the Yemenites are dark, lovely people, full of dance & happiness. There is so much work for dancing to be done here. And I want to help.

And strangely, enough, in the middle of all these feelings, I was terribly

Yemenite folk dancers—"full of dance and happiness"—in Israel, August 1951.

homesick too. Maybe it was a letter or cable from Lincoln, or your pictures, but suddenly I *missed* people so.* You know, I really love the company, & working with it. I feel so lucky & happy & proud to be working with George, & I love you all (the dancers) very much. (I can hear you throwing these words back at me at some moment when I am low & *hate* everything.) But I feel I have friends there—& I like that feeling.

We are now flying over the Greek Islands. Did I write you how much I adored Greece & what a wonderful time I had there living in a fishing settlement? It was a streak of pure luck—but I was picked up by a Greek family while I was bumming around the country—& they kept me with them for 3 days or so. Such generous gracious people. And the fishermen danced with me, & for me, & I had to get drunk with them, & eat octopus & walk barefooted thru paths filled with donkey shit. And I sailed with them, swam with them, & so instead of seeing a lot of columns, I got to know a few people & village life well—& loved it. . . .

Then Italy, which so far has left me with mixed feelings. The art in the churches is just too rich & too overpowering. There is just too damn much to see in *one* church, & it's like being at a 7 ring circus . . . with everything painted up on the ceilings or high walls. Venice is so beautiful that it took me 2 days out of the 4 I was there to get used to it. The Piazza San Marco is *made* for dancing. There is something about the space & dimensions of it that calls for movement to cut thru it. . . .

Everything inside of me seems to be going thru a great reshuffling—which is always upsetting. I don't know quite what the matter is, or what the results will be—. I just feel I'd like to be in Nantucket, where it's quiet, & do some thinking. Usually *some* good comes out of these periods, but life seems so strange to me now—& what has happened to me, & what to do next all seems both wonderful & helter-skelter. . . . I wish you were in Rome—so we could talk, & walk; tease each other, eat together, & try to outdo each other taking pictures. By the time you get this you'll be deep in rehearsals & the season will be on. Please please write me. I may come home earlier than planned or I may never come home. Give

---

* It probably didn't help that Buzz Miller, afraid of what he was getting into, had fled to the United States in a funk. He and Robbins wouldn't connect again until midwinter.

my love to George, Lincoln, & the kids—& to Bobby & Arthur. Give them the news & prepare a huge picnic for my return.

Love & kisses,

J

I miss you.

Same day—much later.

. . . There is a story that you and G are wed. I thought you'd have written it if so. You know how stories are, anyway—I've heard that

Balanchine and Tanaquil Le Clercq, early 1950s: "Who stands where, and with who?"

L. Bernstein has lost his mind, that Nicky & Maria are carrying on to spite George.* And when I hear those stories *here* I can only imagine what's being said about me *there*.

. . . I've gotten the strangest collection of letters from people about *Cage*. One from a man who thought that as death was inevitable, he'd just as soon die *that* way. I'm so curious to see it again. I was very thrown by it opening night. You know, it seemed to be no part of me—& in a way I don't want to see it too. I was surprised that the love or communion between Nora & Nicky† didn't come across—& it also seems as if the point of Nora's conflicts is not apparent to [the] audience. Well, it's done, & everyone seems to think it's my most artful & forceful work. Send me the clips, will you? I wrote Lincoln I'd like to do *Jeux*‡ for you & Nora & Maria. I guess by now you are over your complex about your

* Maria Tallchief and Balanchine had been separated since City Ballet's 1950 London tour.
† Nora Kaye played the Novice, the pubescent insect being trained in the murderous rites of her insect tribe, and Nicholas Magallanes played the Intruder, the male with whom she dances an erotic pas de deux and whom she then kills by garroting him with her legs, on orders from the tribe matriarch.
‡ *Jeux* had been originally choreographed by Nijinsky, to music by Debussy, in 1912.

dancing & Maria's. Do you remember what I told you during *Guest* rehearsals?*
If not—well, I feel you are such a really marvelous dancer with even greater
potential. And I feel & have always felt that too about you as a person. So pull
yourself together & get to class. Write me, do you hear!!! My love to G and Nick
and MA & all. & to you as always.

J.

To: Tanaquil Le Clercq
September 17th 1951

ROME

Dearest Tany—

I got back to Rome yesterday, flew to American Express, & found 3 letters
& 1 postcard from you. I kiss you on each cheek & in between. Your face, that
is. Oh, it was so good to hear from you. I always get depressed in Rome, & this
is no exception, so your letters have been life savers. I'm sitting at an outdoor
café having ginger ale. I just made the mistake of talking to a Peke that looks a
little like Snuff,† & now his mistress, an aging florid redhead with huge sagging
breasts, is winking like mad and making all sorts of invitations with two of the
crookedest eyebrows I've ever seen. Do you suppose I'll have to move? As it is I
can't lift my eyes from the paper without her going into the act. Oh, well, let's
sit tight. . . .

I have seen more than I can take in. Once, somewhere, I woke up one morning and had to go to the window to look out before I could remember what town
I was in. I will get to Paris as quickly as possible, & wait for my boat on the 16th.
In Paris I'll do my first pliés. Maybe it's too late to ever try again. At any rate I've
several ideas for ballets, the most exciting being one based on the "Villa dei Mis-

---

* Robbins had cast Le Clercq as Tallchief's understudy in *The Guests,* and when she goofed off in
rehearsals, he scolded her, saying, "You'd better learn this role, because you're going to dance it."
† Snuff was Robbins's by-now-aged dog, who in his photographs looks more like an affenpinscher
or Brussels griffon than a Pekingese.

teri" in Pompeii. My God, they're loaded with atmosphere and drama and dance. I've bought several huge books on them, all in Italian, so why *don't* you study Italian? Also some fabulous reproductions of the frescoes. Wait till you see them. . . .

When I get back let's really have a picnic. I know a wonderful place in NJ, north, where there is a beautiful state park where the brook tumbles down a mountainside thru pine trees. There are campsites there, & you can stay overnight. Let's do that. We'll rough it, & do everything wrong & laugh & be cold all night. But we'll make wonderful food. . . .

I miss you—& am glad you dreamed about me. I will be so happy to see you, Tany.

Love,

J.

To: Tanaquil Le Clercq
September 25th, 1951

FLORENCE

Dearest, dearest Tany,

I got your letters today—& one postcard from Tahoe, Calif. Dated July 28th!!! It's so strange getting everything in the wrong order. . . . These were all warm & affectionate & I loved them. But how are you NOW? Your foot then was still pretty bad, but how is it NOW. You seemed to miss me more then, but do you NOW? Well I miss YOU—. We're strange aren't we. Well let's not talk about it thru letters. Only that today I realized how much you're in my thoughts—cause I bought something here in Florence, something perfectly useless—but while I was looking at it I thought of what fun it would be to show you & how much YOU would enjoy it & get the same kick out of it I would. As a matter of fact so many of the things I see, I picture you in them, on them, or looking at them too. And not too consciously—just that I can imagine you seeing them & almost hearing what you'd say. So you see, I miss you. And I look forward tremendously to seeing you again—& to next year being in Europe with you. . . .

This is one time I can't say it feels like I've only been away a few weeks. It's been months—& it feels like months. I wonder how the whole trip is going to come out in me. I know something has happened to me—I can't tell what, but I know something big has taken place inside. It's a change (not due to traveling but to being away) but I honestly can't tell if it's a good one. . . .

I'm talking to N.Y. tomorrow & I'll find out if Lincoln & George will please please wait for me to get back to N.Y. for Tyl. . . . I got a letter from Lincoln which excited the hell out of me. In trying to tell him how much I was out of condition, he got the impression I didn't *want* to dance. I want to work *very* hard this year so I can dance well in Europe. . . . With the knives of Hugh and Frank in my back, I would like to dance Prodigal in Paris, & do Bourrée with you,[*] and Tyl.

Florence is lovely & too full of things to see . . . it all *looks* like a 14th century drawing. I'm replacing my Leica here and will probably lose it again before returning. I've missed it, but also I haven't had to worry about it. If I carry that philosophy far enough I'll end as St. Francis.

Well—to bed, to bed. It's 2:30 A.M. here which means 9:30 where you are & I wonder what you're doing. Try to remember. And tell me when I get back.

With my love,
J

To: Tanaquil Le Clercq
Undated [October 1951]

PARIS

Dearest Tany . . .

The thing that surprised me most about your letter was the real lack of understanding. I did believe that when I was unable to return to NY when

---

[*] City Ballet had planned a 1952 European tour, for which Robbins hoped to reprise his New York success in *Prodigal Son* (Laing and Francisco Moncion were his alternates in the role) and to repeat his partnership with Le Clercq in Balanchine's *Bourrée Fantasque*.

planned that a lot of people would jump on the "fuck Robbins" kick and I'd be pretty blasted all around. But I also thought that a few people I love and that I've written to would understand there was a deeper reason for not returning, one which I couldn't write and couldn't talk about.* No one was more excited and looking forward to the return than I was, and everything was packed and ready to go in six hours. And then came some news and I was not able to leave. I am not angry at you. I love you . . . [JR's ellipses] but *have* some understanding and *think* deeper about me. I have been here sort of stranded in Paris, like between stations—not knowing what would happen next or if I'd ever be able to return. And no letters, and how I looked forward to getting one from you. Tanny will understand that it isn't caprice. And I think you *do* . . . or *would* if you stopped for a minute. Was it because of George that you were so angry with me . . . or was it you, because of you. And where do I stand anywhere, anyways, with you.†

Please tell George it wasn't my decision to stay here and not return. It was forced on me thru circumstances. I love the company and wanted to work the whole winter with it. I'm to leave here now the twenty-sixth of October and arrive in N.Y. November first. The last I heard, George will save Till [*sic*] for me. I hope so, not so much because I am selfish about it as it would be a gesture of confidence & understanding. Doesn't anyone know what's happening to me? Please write me Tanny. I'm not angry at all, and I don't think you wrote me in order to cut off our relationship. . . . Do write dearest.

Love again,

J

---

* Robbins had been told by his lawyer to stay out of the United States until after subpoenas were served on people for a fall HUAC hearing, but he wanted to keep the reason confidential.

† In response Le Clercq wrote to him, "I knew we would get around to the who stands where? and with who. I just don't know—anyway, I'm staying with [George]—Can't we be friends? like they say in the movies—"

Later

Dearest Tanny. . . . [JR's ellipses]

Your next letter* arrived this afternoon and I was afraid to open it. I just couldn't take any more blastings, waranted [*sic*] or not. I don't want to write about it (the reason I stayed for a few more weeks) and I may not even talk about it when I get back. But I am sure that you would have understood, and others would, too, if I could have communicated it all to you. . . .

I have always felt that when I had to make choices between the company and other work that it was always a shakey [*sic*] prospect to choose the company as the next season was never *set,* or there was never much *money* or enough. In spite of this I often turned down jobs that were very commercial. [But] I don't want to do *only* ballets and work with ballet companies. I *like* doing shows when I get one to do, and [it] always gives me a much better perspective on ballets when I do do them. . . . I never want to feel (or exist) as I did when I was in Ballet Theater. More than that, I even want to do ballets here in Europe for European companies and I want to make some sort of life and career for myself here. If my output is small, you mustn't judge by George who is older, works differently, and has other talents and approaches. In seven years I have done 7 ballets, all of which are being performed, seven shows in which I did work I am proud of, danced myself, worked in Hollywood, done five minor works, traveled a lot and got to know myself which was most important. George is your ideal, good. But don't be a little girl about it and expect everyone else to be like him. He is my ideal too. I adore him as a person and he is my God as an artist. . . . [But] your feelings around him must affect your feelings to me. More than anything I've always looked toward your letters and you in them this summer. And I have changed Tanny . . . [JR's ellipses] I don't know how, maybe terribly . . . but all sorts of things have swirled around inside and now things that mattered so much before don't seem to at all. Maybe all I need is to get to work. I will. I have a wonderful idea of a romantic ballet for you . . . [JR's ellipses] about a moonsprite, a capricious night fairy who invades a party where she can't be seen

---

* Another scolding: Le Clercq complained that he was the best young choreographer but never choreographed, a wonderful dancer but didn't dance, that he neglected City Ballet for his own projects, and more besides. Robbins attempted to answer her.

by mortals and frolics with them, till she sees a human she loves. When he plays blindman's buff he can feel her, but when he takes the handkerchief away he can't see her. Thru his desire however he tears her wings off, and at the end of the ballet when he is reunited with his earthful love, and goes off, she must remain in the ballroom, an unseen phantom, unable to fly away.. [JR's ellipses] sitting in the ballroom chair near the window in the dark. . . .*

Well, I feel better having written all of this. I felt terrible all day today, shaking and nervous. Paris is having the most wonderful weather, clear, cool, and leaves showering down on you. I watched a puppet show in the tuilleries [*sic*] and I'll take some pictures of them before leaving. . . .

Do write me. Nice things. My wounds still hurt.

Love,

J.

* This image would acquire a haunting resonance with Le Clercq's illness in 1956. Robbins never choreographed the ballet but in 1985 briefly flirted with the idea of doing so and went so far as to cast it provisionally: the theme of Love, or Art, as both creator and destroyer was always potent for him.

The Pont Neuf from the Quai des Grands-Augustins, Paris, 1950s.

To: Ned Rorem*
[1951]

OCTOBER 31 AND HAPPY HALLOWEEN.

First of all I'm a god awful typist, and you will find more mistakes in English than you ever did in my French.

It's six P.M. and all of N.Y. traffic is crawling up Park Avenue. It's really a nice time of day and the sky is a deep deep blue, almost night. I haven't really *looked* at the city yet. I just don't want to. I'm deep deep in rehearsal of Tyl and everything seems exactly the same as when I left except for the glass wall between me and everything that seems the same. The apartment has rain stained ceilings, peeling walls and torn carpets, like it's all crumbling from every direction at once. I'm about to have dinner now and get back to rehearsal again. The body aches and rebels at each breath I take, my dog follows me afraid that I'll disappear again, three months' letters are piled unopened on the desk and today I think of Paris and Marie-Laure† on her birthday, and wonder what it is in your mind that makes you not write. I'm really not here, you know, in spite of all the hectic activity I'm plunged in. I am much more in Paris walking down Grands Augustins toward your hotel to take a bath, talk with you, eat with you, argue with you etc. I am much more opening the door of your room and seeing you at the piano than I am here writing this now. . . .

I had a long talk with Lincoln today. He is wildly excited about the ballet you're doing.‡ He says yes we can bring you over here for doing it, and give you *something* to boot but that it couldn't be very much. . . . For this season I may do either Paul Bowles double piano concerto (with Bobby and Arthur playing it) or else Aaron's Clarinet Concerto for Benny Goodman (god knows who would

---

* Shortly before he sailed home to New York, Robbins had met Rorem (b. 1923), a dazzlingly handsome young composer, at Le Boeuf sur le Toit, the nightclub founded in the 1920s by another composer, Darius Milhaud.

† Marie-Laure de Noailles (1902–1970) was a noted French *saloniste,* patron of the arts, and muse to Jean Cocteau, Man Ray, Salvador Dalí, and others. Robbins had been introduced to her by Rorem in Paris.

‡ Robbins had proposed that Rorem compose a score for the "moonsprite" ballet he'd described to Le Clercq.

play it).* Then next season I would do one large work (yours if all works out well). . . .

Tyl is a very strange ballet . . . really a montage nightmare impressionistic affair . . . like a Bosch (ask Marie Laure). For me it is nothing but a seventeen minute obstacle race, changing clothes, handling props, climbing scenery etc. I figured out that over the whole length of it, there is only 30 seconds where I am prop free and can dance. I don't expect at all to be very good in it until after four weeks of performances and then I'll be able to tell what I am doing.

Sunday Night, Nov. 5th . . . a week after I've arrived.
Your very nice letter came during the period in which I couldn't get around to finishing the one I started to you. I'm so sorry to hear you are ill. I hope by now you are well again, but I hope to Christ you are not boozing it up again. Of all the stupid behaviors yours is the corniest and silliest of them all. Saying you were on the wagon when I met you sounded terribly young, but watching the way you drink, and even more the reason *why* you drink that way is real high school. . . . This is strong, but that's because I *care* about you and feel close enough to you to put it straight.

Even if you are sick you're still not thinner than I am, as I've lost seven pounds in running around in Tyl. The ballet has shaped up even more, and I do think it will be a big success. I'll get away with it because it's so flashy, but I haven't yet conquered the actor's problems in it, not to mention the juggling of props, etc. But his conception and invention is fantastic, I think it will be a big hit. I'll send you the reviews. [. . .]

Well, goodbye now. What is my "nuque" and "concitoyen." It sounds dirty, and I don't dare ask Tany. . . . Do write me about what you're doing unless you don't like it yourself. Except if you're getting drunk. I lose pieces of *you* when I hear about it. Bobby and Arthur send their love. Keep well, stay thin, think of me . . .

With my love
J.

---

* Robbins did indeed choreograph a ballet, *Pied Piper,* to Aaron Copland's Clarinet Concerto (see p. 113), which the composer had written for Benny Goodman.

To: Ned Rorem
[November 1951]

Dear Ned . . .

A letter from you arrived today with one cent's postage due. I thought it was somehow either typical or significant. . . .

After two weeks in N.Y., a reaction has set in. I feel absolutely choked here . . . there's no air, there's no light, there's no beauty, there's certainly no life here. I miss Paris even more than I did when I first got back, and every time I walk on the street I think of how very beautiful it must be there. I don't know if I love you but I do miss you. I don't see people at all. From ten in the morning till eleven at night I'm dancing, rehearsing or choreographing . . . and all I see is the inside of the studio and my apartment. . . . The season opens tonight and Tyl tomorrow night. Still haven't seen a costume or a prop, but what the hell, this is Theater (hmph). As a matter of fact all this life seems very strange, I mean this dancers life. And I'm not at all sure it's for me. First of all it's not living . . . no time to enjoy everything or anything, people, food, love, hate anything. All your energy goes into work and stops there. At night you crawl home and fall into bed and think of how nice it would be to be with someone, if you had the energy to do so. And furthermore I'm also not at all sure that all of this effort sweat and sacrifice is really worth it. I just can't seem to take a bunch of ballet dancers seriously. I do think Balanchine is a genius, and it's a truly great experience working with him. And I love the kids in the company etc. etc., but these days I'm in the is-this-really-what-I-want-to-do stage. Well time will tell. . . .

The Bowles piece is out because they couldn't get two pianos into the orchestra pit, and they couldn't afford to put the rest of the orchestra on stage. So now I am deep in work on Aaron's clarinet concerto, and it's turning out to be lots of fun and somewhat of a camp. The humor is coming out in this work, and I'm sure that all of N.Y. will find it a relief after Cage.

I have received a fabulous offer to go to Hollywood, one picture deal at three thousand dollars a week for about twenty weeks.[*] And I'm turning it down and

---

[*] This was an offer from Paramount that his lawyer had negotiated for him, claiming it would protect him from having to testify to HUAC; the properties involved were a film version of *Look, Ma;*

Diary entries for July–August 1973.

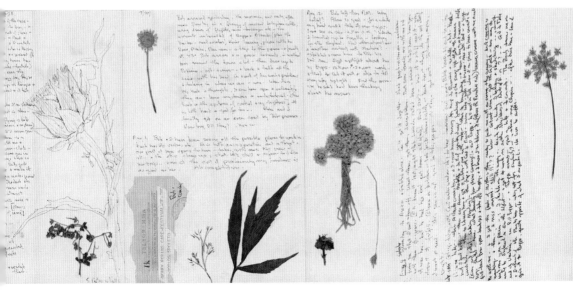

(ABOVE AND OPPOSITE) "The theater of my life"—journal for March 3–6, 1976.

Robbins then . . .

. . . and now.

1600 PENNSYLVANIA AVENUE

Collage page from one volume of Robbins's journals. He had been instrumental in persuading Balanchine to bring Baryshnikov (RIGHT) to New York City Ballet.

feel like an idiot. I should really take it, work hard, save the dough, and then go off and paint like I say I want to, for a year or so.

Right this minute I suddenly thought of St. Germain and the Rue du Bac and other places. I thought of that place we ate in where you took my beret off and we went into a mad conversation.

So do write me my sweet Ned. I miss you, and wonder about you. I kiss you too in all those French places like you say.

Love . . .

To: Unknown [Buzz Miller?]*
[early 1950s?]

Hello dearest—

Late—only late late at night do I come to any peace with myself & the world. At some moment in the dark—when the whole of the city has quiet and the only sound of an occasionally passing car sounds friendly instead of hostile—at some moment there is a sudden release, & I am free & the puff of the cigarette smells good rather than choking & the world and myself toe the same mark—sit opposite each other at breakfast—give each other hello-nods.

Somewhere in that—you figure—the slight indelible thought of you—working its way around the unpressured part of my brain—this slight thought steps on the scales of my conflicts and weights things even. And the up & down tussle suddenly eases. Off.

---

another musical based on the life of Mack Sennett; a new Bing Crosby picture, *Mr. Famous;* and an adaptation of Louisa May Alcott's *Eight Cousins.*

* This note is handwritten in pencil on two small pieces of paper, like something one would leave for someone sharing the same living space, and the handwriting is consistent with Robbins's in the early 1950s. It's not clear whom it was intended for, but Miller and Robbins reconnected in January 1952 and Miller moved into Robbins's flat.

Buzz Miller with his and Robbins's "errant son," the affenpinscher Otis, at Bradley Beach, the Jersey Shore community where Robbins's parents had a house, early 1950s.

To: Buzz Miller

Wednesday, April 29th [1952]

Dear [Buzz],*

Today is Independence day in Israel—4 years old!! And for the first time I have a day free. I'm spending it in a kibutz [*sic*] (collective farm) in the country which is so beautiful—lovely long rolling hills, treeless, blue blue sky & nice large fluffy clouds & a good warm breeze. This morning I slept till 11. Every

---

* Miller was dancing in *Pal Joey* on Broadway and had stayed behind in New York while Robbins went to Israel to act as a dance adviser for the American Fund for Israel Institutions, and to Europe with City Ballet. For unexplained reasons, letters received by Miller have had his name either erased or scissored out of the salutation. The letters were returned to Robbins at some point, possibly in the 1970s, when Robbins contemplated writing his autobiography; it's not clear who did the redaction or why. But Miller's name appears in Robbins's file copies.

other day I've had to be up at 7:30 or 8. I teach or rehearse about 6–9 hours a day—and I've never been so tired in my life.

I'm so anxious to hear about your dance—.* I am also anxious that it goes well. Just now, thinking about it, and remembering the steps you showed me, I wonder, (or rather hope) that it doesn't get too full, or too tricky, & too effective. The little bits of the material you showed will look 3 times as effective if occasionally played against very easy steps. But of course again it's really silly of me to offer any suggestions where I know nothing about the work really. It was just a thought in passing. At any rate, work hard, keep your head, and lots of luck—my fingers are crossed.

How has the rest of life been going? Several times, at strange moments I half expected you to walk in thru a door & nod a casual hello & sit quietly & watch me work. Just wishful thinking I guess.

What is the news—& what have been the repercussions of Kazan's statement?† . . . [W]hat other show biz gossip is there?

Last week I visited a Druze village. The Druze are like Arabs except they have very light & translucent blue, green or gray eyes, and are the Arabs' enemies. They are exceedingly hospitable, and gave me strong, sweet coffee which I *had* to drink, and then sang & danced for me. Ah!!

Well—evening is slowly coming on. I'm off for a walk up in them hills. Today, because the work has cleaned off my mind, *you* have been around more than ever. Forgive me again for not writing sooner. And write me in Paris, 19 Quai Voltaire. It takes a week or sometimes two, for a letter to get here.

Keep well, work hard—& think of me.

Love,

J.

* A piece Miller had choreographed, possibly for a nightclub act he was developing; details are unknown.

† This was hardly idle gossip. On April 10, 1952, Elia Kazan, a prominent film and theater director who had been a member of the Group Theatre, testified before the House Un-American Activities Committee, admitting to membership in the Communist Party and naming eight actors who he said had also been members—an act that would darken his reputation as long as he lived. Given his own HUAC troubles, Robbins must have been both anxious and curious.

To: Buzz Miller
Tuesday, May 27, 1952

FLORENCE

Dearest [Buzz] . . .

It was so good and also so frustrating to talk to you the other night. You sounded as if you were at the wrong end of a bad phonograph record, and it must have been equally difficult for you to talk from the theater. Nevertheless, because of my own feelings of the need to speak with you, it was comforting.

I'm so pleased about your success. I can't tell you how happy it made me, and I'm equally pleased because I know how much good it is going to do for you. Of course now you have to work very very hard, and be twice as patient as you were before and keep your eyes on the final goal and not get thrown off by unimportant immediate difficulties. You catch the flies with honey, remember? I want so for you to make good and do well, as it means as much to me as it does to you. It is going to help you as a person so much, and will also help us too. I think you know how. So, if there is any advice I can give you or any help or suggestions on the numbers (even from here) please let me know. Write it all out if you have an idea or are stuck, and maybe from here I can be of some help. With music, be sure you check the orchestrations with whatever record you rehearse with so that you are not choreographing things which won't appear in the final version (like licks and drums etc. etc. and dynamics). If possible keep simple, and above all always keep it clear to the audience *what* the dance is about, and *why* everything or anything is happening. I hope all continues well. Don't get discouraged if suddenly you dry up, or if all the sudden excitement about you dies away. Broadway is like that. Try if possible to get some immediate engagement right away so that you are in the light even if it's not the best one. Don't worry now about credit or attention for yourself. . . .

I realize of course this all spoils the plans for summer, and I'm terribly disappointed that we aren't going to spend time together. It got to be real painful being in all the places we were at together and for a while I couldn't wait until you got here. But now I've sort of adjusted to the fact that you probably won't come, and for very important reasons too. So the excitement of that is all gone now. I'm not sure what I will do now. Maybe stick with the company longer. I don't want to go driving off with George #2* alone but maybe even those feelings will change by the time Paris comes around.

I'll write from Switzerland. Please do write me long & often. Keep well, work hard—

With my love—
J.

To: Robert Fizdale
Undated [June 1952]

Dearest Bobby,

Forgive me. I was *going* to write each day & each day went past without doing it. I'm having a hard time pulling myself together—& I'm not sure of the reasons. First of all, in Israel I worked harder than I have anywhere else—& there just wasn't enough energy to write anyone. Then came the terrible shock of rejoining the company—& suddenly I felt like I was back in Ballet Theatre struggling for recognition & attention. I resented the whole thing & felt it completely degrading to stand in line for money, pick up & return shoe bags & costumes, get assigned a dressing room that was poor etc. etc. As a matter of fact I've so hated dancing that I've spoken to George & am coming out of Bourree and Piper & will only dance Tyl as there is no replacement for me—& Anxiety. I also couldn't stand the complete lack of attention given to me prior to the opening in Paris—all attention given to George. The girls of the company were also in a tizzy because of Tany acting like a queen bee & George favoring her more than he ever did anyone. Well—there were surprises. The rage of the first season in Paris was Piper, with Cage a close second. The papers carried huge headlines

---

* George—named after Balanchine—was Robert Fizdale and Arthur Gold's car, which they left in Europe and which Robbins was using while they were in the United States (and borrowing *his* car).

about them & long articles were written. Now in Paris for next season my name is right under George's. . . .

If you sense some competitive feeling in all of this you're damn right. . . . This whole sense of competition has permeated the company. Now we are assigned dressing rooms according to rank—& if someone's name appears over anyone else's, quel scandal! I'm disappointed in Tany. I don't see much of her as George dictates everything—even that she should not learn Nora's role in Cage. . . .

I've been in quite a state since rejoining the company. I've missed Buzz terribly & my whole insides seem to have gone crazy—but nothing makes his absence less painful, nor does any other fling seem to take the place. He's made a good success for himself in N.Y. with the act he's begun & I know how very important that is for him, so he probably won't come to Europe. I'm resigned to that *now,* but terribly disappointed. I have much struggle to pull myself together. The success has been good for me so now more than ever I want to do another ballet, & more, & more. Time now seems enormously precious to me. And energy too. Leonidoff* says he can arrange a year of choreography for me here in Europe. If only I had more courage. Maybe I should do it now as the events in Europe & Asia don't seem to guarantee any lasting peace. . . .

Suddenly I feel like I've been away from the States for years, & that everything between us has changed—. In a way it's true—& I don't think it was just Buzz although that played a part. I love you very much—you know that I think. I don't like it, it scares me, when something which has been so valuable suddenly seems less so. Or is it only in me, did you not feel anything different. Do write me about you. Come to think of it, you have never really *talked* to me about you. Are you afraid . . . [JR's ellipses] of me or of you. Or is it just my egocentricity which doesn't give you a chance. . . .

I met Nadia Boulanger† at a reception for Stravinsky. She's wonderful. And *Igor* now calls me *Jerry*!! At the reception for him he looked around, saw me, came over, put his hands on my waist & rocked me gently, saying, "Jerry, come

---

* The impresario Leon Leonidoff, who arranged City Ballet's European tours.
† Nadia Boulanger (1887–1979), a pianist, composer, and teacher, taught many of the twentieth century's leading musicians and composers, among them Marc Blitzstein, Elliott Carter, Aaron Copland, Philip Glass, Dinu Lipatti, Gian Carlo Menotti, Yehudi Menuhin, and Virgil Thomson.

to my rehearsal tomorrow yes, & rest well for tomorrow's performances You have great success here, I am so happy." I felt like Christ had looked over the crowd, picked me out, & blessed me. . . .

All writ out. Write me a *long* letter.

My love, as always,
J

To: Robert Fizdale
Undated [late June 1952?]

SUNDAY IN PARIS

Dearest Bobby,

I sit in the Quai Voltaire on a hot Paris Sunday afternoon, and do so wish we were all here together having fun. . . . While being the rage here I've been quite social with dinners at Maxim's luncheons at Versailles etc. etc. with the Duchess of Windsor and Aly Khan,[*] but now I've had it . . . [JR's ellipses] and now I'm deep in ideas for ballets again, and starting it I feel whole and myself again. All the craziness hasn't left yet, and the constant needling by the thoughts of waste of time and energy keep my nerves popping. Do you feel that way ever. Oh Christ I feel helpless and scared when I think of how I have the gift to choreograph, and how time is passing and I'm not working, and seem to be carousing and drinking and whoring. "Live it up" seems to be my motto for a while, while the other Jerry stands aghast and white being raped, destroyed, defiled and maligned. And like a merry go round out of control, the days pass one two, one two, day night day night till the result is just a blurr [*sic*].

[Remainder of letter missing.]

---

[*] The former Wallis Simpson, Duchess of Windsor, and Aly Khan, a millionaire playboy and (just) former husband of the actress Rita Hayworth, were fixtures in society gossip columns. Robbins certainly was "the rage."

Nora Kaye Memorial, Notes
1987

[In 1952] Nora & I did a show which starred Bette Davis.* It was a mess. It had some good moments—Bette could be astonishing at times—[and] there were some good dances—& some bad ones. And when we opened in Detroit, it was clear there was a lot of work to do, & a lot of backstage fire, flood, & mayhem to get thru if we wanted to save the show. So there in July in Detroit Nora & I found ourselves onstage at two a.m. one night after the [performance] working under one bare stage light-bulb trying to fix a dance for Nora for the next day's matinee. We were both wet, cold, tired, dirty, and depressed, & found ourselves sitting on the stage floor, out of breath, out of ideas, even out of talk. After a while Nora said, "Well, look at it this way—here we are, [the way] we always wanted, just like Warner Baxter and Ruby Keeler in *42nd Street*."†

To: Buzz Miller
[Undated, early 1950s]

Dearest [Buzz]

It's six thirty. . . . I've been working all afternoon. Couldn't sleep last night after talking to you and finally had to take the pill bit about five thirty this a.m. I'm going up to Bobby and Arthur W. for dinner and then back here for more work.

It was so very very good to talk to you last night. The conversation meant a lot to me and gave me the kind of security I need to be able to go on working

---

* On Robbins's return from Europe he signed on to stage musical numbers for a revue, *Two's Company*, with sketches written by Charles Sherman and Peter De Vries (and additional material by Horton Foote), lyrics by Ogden Nash and Sammy Cahn (with an assist from a later Robbins collaborator, Sheldon Harnick); the nonmusical sketches were directed by Jules Dassin. Nora Kaye, and also Buzz Miller, were in the cast.

† *Two's Company* opened on Broadway on December 15, 1952; the *Herald Tribune*'s Walter Kerr was acerbic about Bette Davis's performance ("like hearing the Fifth Symphony played on a comb"), but Robbins won his fourth Donaldson Award for his choreography. The show closed March 8 when Davis withdrew for medical reasons.

and living as if there was something really worth while that it was all for. I think sometimes, being on opposite sides of the continent,[*] we start to doubt and worry about the future . . . lets not. I love you dearly. And my love for you and yours for me is the most important thing as far as I am concerned. I want you to know this and remember it and repeat it each day you wake up and think about it each night before going to sleep. Wear it for a sweater when you're cold, and use it as a booster when you're blue. Must run. Keep well and think of me often and I'll feel it. Write, and keep happy in the warmth of my love and respect and admiration.

XO

J.

To: Buzz Miller
April 22, 1953

Dear Buzz,

It's late, I've just had a bath, I've been playing the score of the Britten piece[†] for the 90th time, Otis[‡] is out in the hall because he won't let me type without chewing on the paper, I'm hungry and when I finish this I'm going to make me something gorgeous, and most of all, I miss your not being here. Last night I had a dream . . . something about my coming to Cleveland[§] and getting mixed up in a dress rehearsal because I happened to be back stage. Your show in my dream was a backstage story about the circus. I got mixed up with some ropes and before I knew it I was being swung out on stage and toward the front row. I jumped nimbly off, did a big bow and asked Bob Alton[¶] who was sitting down

---

[*] Miller had an uncredited dancing role in the 1954 film *There's No Business Like Show Business,* and he might have been in California filming that or on tour with Kay Thompson, in whose act he frequently performed. Robbins was in New York (as the reference to "Bobby and Arthur W." shows).

[†] *The Young Person's Guide to the Orchestra,* which Robbins was using for his ballet *Fanfare.*

[‡] Otis was Robbins's (and Miller's) dog; Snuff had died sometime before.

[§] Miller was in the chorus of Rodgers and Hammerstein's *Me and Juliet,* which was having out-of-town tryouts in Cleveland. (See p. 166.)

[¶] Robert Alton (1906–1957), the choreographer of *Me and Juliet,* as well as *Anything Goes, Pal Joey,* and other musicals, also staged the nightclub act *Kay Thompson and the Williams Brothers.*

Tanaquil Le Clercq "had a terrific sexuality, underneath—the possibility of that— which was much more interesting than the obviousness of it," Robbins said.

front if he needed any extra dancers. But you were there in the dream and that was nice.

I feel real good tonight about the Britten piece. . . . If the damn thing pulls together I may have a good work, and that makes me very happy and delighted that the talent hasn't dried up yet. You know talent is really a gift from nowhere, alighting on some poor slob in spite of himself; and anyone who thinks that he had something to do with it himself is nuts. Sure, if you've got it doesn't mean it will come out and be clear. That takes work, and effort, and technique (and on my part a hell of a lot of agony). But the nice thing with me is that the older I grow the more I appreciate what I manage to do and that gives me great happiness in this world. I've redone the beginning of Faune[*] for the 9th time (actually!) and yesterday I seemed to break some of the ice around it. God I hope so. I had to address and be asked questions by the N.Y. Ballet Club on Sunday and boy were they ever curious about Faune. So is everyone. So am I.

The news about the company[†] is distressing and I made a list tonight of about twenty five people I'm going to put the bite on for money. I can't really tell how serious it is, but I'll be furious if we don't have a season. Otis has just pushed the door open, jumped up and has given the paper chewing up to work on my fingers instead. I just popped him in the nose so he stopped chewing and is backing his ass into the typewriter for revenge. The bell went off and scared him. Quel chien. Now he's trying to put his paws on the keys and write himself. This summer I'm going to take this machine with me and work out some large

---

[*] *Afternoon of a Faun,* to Debussy's *L'Après-midi d'un Faune* (Robbins ended up using the plain-English title), featured Tanaquil Le Clercq and Francisco Moncion and would premiere on May 14, 1953. He had set it on Le Clercq immediately after her return from her honeymoon with Balanchine; "she had a terrific sexuality, underneath—the possibility of that," he told an interviewer later, "which was much more interesting than the obviousness of it."

[†] A financial crisis at City Ballet would force cancellation of the upcoming fall season.

ideas I have about a ballet. Also I'd like to do some painting. You know what I *will* be doing, don't you. Putting up screens, painting the walls, hammering my thumbs, all sorts of joyous bits.

Try to work out something about getting home if you can between stops. But don't try to push time . . . it doesn't work. Be patient . . . there's plenty time left and this will be over soon.

I'm a better choreographer than I am a dancer or typist, nest ce pas [*sic*]. Keep well work hard and take care of yourself.

Love,

J.

Trial Scene (from *The Poppa Piece*)[*]
February 18, 1991

A long table. Sitting in the middle, THREE INVESTIGATORS with microphones and papers. JAKE at one end . . . POPPA at the other end . . . American flag on one side.

INVESTIGATOR

What is your name?

JAKE   POPPA

Jay Whitby.   Jacov Vitkovitz.

---

[*] Robbins testified before the House Un-American Activities Committee on May 5, 1953. His appearance is unmentioned in *all* of his contemporaneous correspondence (including the preceding letter) but was by his own account one of the definitive events of his life. His experience of it provides the core of *The Poppa Piece*, a work that went through a multitude of drafts, some handwritten, some typed (often with handwritten revisions), including one "final" script from the Lincoln Center Theater workshop production, which reflects unspecified editorial contributions from Gerald Freedman. In this version Robbins changed the name of his protagonist from Gershon Rabinowitz/Jerome Robbins to Jacov Vitkowitz/Jay "Jake" Whitby. The text here largely follows the Lincoln Center version, although in a few places (such as in references to the Communist Party, which Robbins changed to the American Protest Party for the workshop, and in a section where the typist appears to have put some material out of order) I've silently returned to an earlier iteration.

INVESTIGATOR

How do you spell your last name?

JAKE

W-h-i-t-b-y.

POPPA

V-i-t-k-o-w-i-t-z.

INVESTIGATOR

Where do you live?

JAKE

429 Park Avenue

POPPA

In a hole, hidden.

INVESTIGATOR

Are you accompanied by counsel?

JAKE

Yes, I am.

POPPA

His father.

JAKE

My lawyer.

POPPA

Tata!*

JAKE

(Points)

Robert Sternberg.†

---

* "Tata" is Yiddish for "Daddy." But also, perhaps, "Ta-*dah!*"
† Robbins's lawyer for the HUAC hearing was R. Lawrence Siegel.

INVESTIGATOR

Now, where and when were you born?

JAKE

New York.

POPPA

New York.

JAKE

1918.

POPPA

He was a draft excuse.*

INVESTIGATOR

What is your profession?

POPPA

A Jew . . .

JAKE

I am a choreographer . . .

POPPA

. . . but he plays at passing.

JAKE

. . . and a dancer.

INVESTIGATOR

Will you tell the Committee your education, preparation for your profession.

JAKE

I attended grammar school and high school in New Jersey.

---

* The U.S. Army had instituted a draft after the United States entered World War I in 1917, but men with dependent children could be exempted.

POPPA

Well, we sent him to all kinds of Jewish schools . . .

JAKE

I graduated there . . .

POPPA

. . . schlepped him to shul on holidays, made him fast, sent him to cheder.*

JAKE

. . . and then I attended NYU.

POPPA

We Bar Mitzvahed him.

JAKE

I was a dancer in 1937 . . .

POPPA

And then "genius"! He stopped, and turned his back on us.

INVESTIGATOR

Will you give the Committee, please, a better understanding of the nature, type, etc. of your profession?

JAKE

Choreography?

POPPA

Jew?

JAKE

Well, choreography is the technical term for creating dances, the same way as one would write the script or create music for a show. I conceive the ideas for the dances, create the steps and instruct the dancers how to perform them, and direct the performers.

* School for children's religious instruction in Judaism.

POPPA

Now listen to this drek. Write, conceive, choreograph, instruct, direct . . . whoo hah! We tried to teach him to be Jewish.

INVESTIGATOR

Your credits?

JAKE

Many—here's the list.

(Hands typed papers.)

POPPA

Nothing—after a botched Bar Mitzvah.[*]

INVESTIGATOR

Now, the investigation shows that you had an association with the Communist Party. Is that information correct?

POPPA

Here we go.

JAKE

Yes, it is.

INVESTIGATOR

Have you ever been a member of it?

JAKE

Yes, I have been. I am not now.

---

* The teenage Robbins's voice had cracked when he had to chant his prepared Torah portion at the ceremony, a humiliation that caused him to burst into tears and is depicted elsewhere in *The Poppa Piece.*

INVESTIGATOR

Can you tell us why you joined it?

JAKE

I joined because it seemed to me to be the only organization committed
to fighting for the rights of minorities. I had, prior to joining, many
severe and painful instances of minority prejudice. The fighting against
discrimination interested me very much.

INVESTIGATOR

And if you had not had those experiences, you might not have gone to
the Communist Party?

JAKE

Perhaps not. It was also fighting fascism. Fascism and anti-Semitism . . .

INVESTIGATOR

Were synonymous?

JAKE

. . . were synonymous to *me*.

INVESTIGATOR

Do you still believe that the Communist Party is opposed to anti-Semitism?

JAKE

May I answer it this way? . . . In the light of the recent purges and waves of
anti-Semitism, no, I do not believe—

INVESTIGATOR

Would you say today, as other witnesses have said, that the Communist
Party is as anti-Semitic as the Nazi Party ever was?

JAKE
(Pauses)

It appears to be that way.

POPPA

Jacov!

(THEY look at each other.)

JAKE

I'm scared, Pop.

*(The THREE INVESTIGATORS confer. Then, while TWO of them continue,
ONE turns to JAKE and speaks personally and quietly.)*

INVESTIGATOR

Look, we're coming after you—we know who you are, Whitby, behind
those energetic, funny dances—we are ready to unmask you if
you don't give us what we want. You thought you'd built enough of
a name to be safe. OK. Now give us what we want or we'll take it
all away—your position—your safety—your security. We can
make it vanish like that, and there you'll be—that naked shriveled
impotent old Jew.

(Open from conference)

I will ask you a few more brief questions. How many persons were
members of this group at the time you joined?

JAKE

The personnel shifted constantly, sir. It would vary anywhere between ten
to thirty.

POPPA

Careful, Jake.

INVESTIGATOR

How many meetings in all do you think you attended?

JAKE

I think I attended twenty meetings.

POPPA

Watch it now.

JAKE

I was busy with my work—going in and out of town.

INVESTIGATOR

Who recruited you into the party?

POPPA

Jake, don't.

JAKE

I'm scared, Pop. I'm scared shitless.

POPPA

Jake—

JAKE

They'll take it all away.

INVESTIGATOR

Will you give me the names of the other persons who were in this group whom you can identify?

POPPA

Jake, don't—you'll be sorry. Don't, boychik, don't.

INVESTIGATOR

Will you?

JAKE

(breaking down)

I can't—I can't.

POPPA

Oy, Jake . . .

INVESTIGATOR

Well?

JAKE

(In anguish—stands and points at POPPA)

Take *him*. Take *him*.

POPPA

Jake!

(The INVESTIGATORS turn and look at POPPA. Flashes,
photographers, everything aimed at POPPA who gets
covered up in a melee of NEWS MEN.)

INVESTIGATOR

(Stands. To JAKE)

The witness is excused. We want to thank you for your Americanism.
Keep up your good work.

COURT SERGEANT

Whereupon at 4:36 the hearing is recessed, to reconvene at
10:00 AM tomorrow.

Thoughts on Choreography[*]
[March 1954]

I don't think I have any set theories about choreography. I think there is too
much theorizing among dancers anyway. I believe in work. In creating a ballet,
I say what I have to say in the way I feel it.

   Having started out as a modern dancer, I am somewhat influenced by [that]

---

[*] This seemingly never-published essay exists only as a much-edited draft of a piece bylined "Jerome
Robbins, as told to Selma Jeanne Cohen," the New York correspondent for the English publication
Dancing Times and a frequent contributor to *Dance Magazine, The New York Times,* and other pub-
lications. It's dated by references in correspondence between Robbins and Cohen.

approach to dancing though I work within the ballet idiom. In each work that I have done I've tried to solve a particular theatrical problem. . . .

[In] *Afternoon of a Faun** . . . I aimed to re-use the original idea of the composition. . . . I always work in rehearsal toward a key movement to establish the mood, or gender, of a whole work. Then I build from that. . . . Every ballet, I believe, is individual. It sets up its own world, its own society and mores; it has its own life. The approach, therefore, must be specific in each case. . . .

I can't *sit* and direct a ballet. I have to get the feeling of the movement; then I can tell where it ought to go. Only a dancer can choreograph. One has to feel, physically and emotionally, the rightness of a movement. . . . [S]ome will belong to the classic vocabulary; others, though stemming from the same source, will seem closer to the modern idiom. To choreograph in this way I need flexible dancers with whom to work. I find that those with ballet training are best for my purposes. That is not to say that they are without faults. I often feel that the mirrors should be taken away from the ballet dancers & given to the modern dancers to the advantage of both; the former are too conscious of externals; the latter not conscious enough. But I believe ballet dancers are more adaptable. I teach a sequence to the dancers; let them try it; then see if it has the quality I want. Unprejudiced dancers (and I find that ballet dancers are less prejudiced than modern) allow me greater scope in creation.

My starting point in composition is that of the modern choreographer— the feeling to be portrayed. I would not limit the kinds of feelings expressible by dance. Each choreographer to his own taste. A ballet is a ritual which makes a rite out of any subject matter. My aim is, through form, to give to each ballet idea its own life, its own fulfillment.

---

* *Afternoon of a Faun* had opened on May 14, 1953, to puzzlingly mixed reviews given the classic it has become. *The New York Times*'s John Martin was ambivalent about it, but the *Herald Tribune*'s Walter Terry thought it "a major creation" (*New York Herald Tribune*, May 24, 1953).

To: Edwin Lester[*]

March 18, 1954

421 PARK AVENUE, NEW YORK

Dear Edwin:

Just a note to let you know how things are going from this end. I'm enormously pleased with what Moose and Carolyn[†] are turning out. Some of it couldn't be better. The only possible problem that we may face is the tendency of Carolyn's to always write towards the hit record rather than toward the situation of the show. She shies away from using Peter and Wendy's names or specifics that might make the song unusable in general context. However, I keep hitting her on the head and I just hope I'm not hurting my fingers to no avail. I'm going to try to have a session with her this weekend and pump her full of my feelings about the show. I have a slight hunch (and perhaps unwarranted) that she doesn't "get it." But this may be due to her lack of experience. Moose's music continues to delight us and we are seeing them both tomorrow night at which time Leland and Mary Hunter[‡] will also hear what they have accomplished so far.

In spite of all the ghastly horrors that seem to be mounting around me while working on the opera[§] I find time to turn to PETER PAN and become terribly excited and impatient with all that stands between my getting to work on it. So I look forward to this summer and to working with you on this proj-

---

[*] Edwin Lester (1895–1990) was president of the Los Angeles Civic Light Opera and one of the producers—with its star Mary Martin, her husband, Richard Halliday, and the former talent agent Leland Hayward—of *Peter Pan*. The production had been Lester's idea, and bringing Robbins on board had been Martin's.

[†] Mark "Moose" Charlap (1928–1974) and Carolyn Leigh (1926–1983) were the original composer and lyricist for *Peter Pan*. Both were novice songwriters, though Leigh had had a hit with a single ballad, "Young at Heart," in 1953.

[‡] Mary Hunter, one of the founders of the American Actors Company and Robbins's friend since his Ballet Theatre days, was working as his assistant director on the show.

[§] Aaron Copland's *Tender Land,* directed by Robbins, concerned the aborted romance of a midwestern farm girl with a drifter falsely accused of molestation; it had its premiere on April 1, 1954, at New York City Center.

ect. Thank you for all the co-operation that you have given me so far and all the support and co-operation I'm sure you will continue to give me from here on out.

Sincerely,
Jerry

To: George Abbott
March 26, 1954

Dear George,

This is re the run-through[*] last night.

I honestly think it's going to be a very successful show. There were, I felt, things that must be fixed, but I'm sure you sensed them as much as I did.

There are too many characters to follow, too many old men, too many people who parallel each other. The[y] conflict and rob each other of effect by spreading material too thin over too many people.

It seems that the premise, the spine of the show, is a conflict between Capital and Labor presented in light, humorous, zany, musical-comedy terms. All the characters fall on one side or the other, and the love story breaks and recovers on this issue. Although the possibility—and finally the actuality—of a strike runs throughout, its import as the thread of the show doesn't seem either dramatized or effective. There doesn't seem to be any real pressure by the workers [for] the strike and consequent increase of distress, stubbornness and defiance by [the company owner].

. . . I felt very big jars [*sic*] when we moved into each musical number. The

---

[*] *The Pajama Game,* a musical about a romance between a shop steward in a pajama factory and her manager, which is complicated by the threat of a strike (among many other things), was about to leave New York for out-of-town tryouts. The show was written by George Abbott and Richard Bissell (book) with a score by Richard Adler and Jerry Ross; co-directed by Abbott and Robbins; and choreographed by Bob Fosse. Robbins's complete notes, made after a run-through just before the production's departure for New Haven, go into great length and granular detail, and they have been much cut down here.

majority were not prepared enough, so quite often I felt them to be out of place. . . .

Of course, so much of the show will work much better when we get under-scoring, but one thing that disturbs me is the feeling that the boys extended all their songs too long [with] interludes, arrangements, and general playing around. Don't let them pull the show around for songs which are slightly out of kilter or completely out of place. It's easier for them to re-write than to re-do book production, choreography, etc.

Well, these are my *brief*—?—thoughts on the show. Just let me restate that I really do feel we have a good and successful show here[*] and I look forward to pitching in with all the help I can give.

Yours,
Jerry

To: Arthur Laurents
March 29, 1954

Dear Who-Can-Keep-Up-With-You-To-Write:

The letter came on the first day of real spring in New York and did it ever make me want to go down to the boats and get on and get off on the other side.[†] You must be having a wonderful time and I envy it very much. If you go to Positano keep going a little further to Amalfi, and then right above Amalfi is Ravello, my idea of heaven. It's a perfect place to do any writing. Stay at one of the hotels that look down on Amalfi and the Mediterranean and give it all my love.

The opera opens Thursday. The whole thing has been one of the worst experiences I have ever had in the theatre—somewhat akin to a nightmarish dream of slowly sinking in quick-sand while everyone is standing around asking if everything is under control. No wonder opera looks the way it does.

---

[*] They did: *The Pajama Game* would open on Broadway on May 13, 1954, to sparkling reviews and a robust box office.
[†] Laurents was traveling in Europe and had arrived in Italy.

There was a run-through of PAJAMA GAME the other night—the first run-through—and I think it's going to be a wonderful show. Janice [*sic*] Paige is touching and sexy; Carol Haney will be sensational; and John Raitt is John Raitt. Will go out of town with it next week, then off to Boston and I hope at least to have a yocky time after this drudgery I've been through. What I'm most excited about, though, is PETER PAN for the summer. If it comes up anyway near to what my dreams and ideas are for it, I'll be happy and in a way the horrors of the opera have been very good experience for me.

After that, if we don't bring PETER to New York*—and it looks like we may very well do that—a month's rest; after that, *Ninotchka,* as choreographer; or THE SKIN OF OUR TEETH for television, as director.† Now that I'm directing a few things everybody wants me to direct for them, but nobody has yet seen whether I can do it or not. I'm not sure myself, though anything that requires a certain amount of technique, which comes through experience, must be a shifting of what I already know into other terms. Well, we'll see.

Nora Kaye has been very busy doing nothing except getting her new apartment ready and looking beautiful in her old mink coat, and taking many classes by day. Buzz is in PAJAMA GAME and has taken a new lease on life by just not being in ME AND JULIET.‡

Otherwise, things in New York are much the same, but to my eyes getting a little out of hand, and I won't be surprised when one scandal blows the whole thing sky-high.

Now don't say I don't write. Give my love to Paris, Chez Genevieve,§ Italy, etc. etc. By the way, Bob told me yesterday that they have started building your

---

* Because the Los Angeles (and San Francisco) Civic Light Opera companies were producers, the plan was to open *Peter Pan* in San Francisco, then take it to Los Angeles.
† Robbins didn't take on either of these projects—neither choreographing the Cole Porter musical *Silk Stockings* (an adaptation of Ernst Lubitsch's 1939 film, *Ninotchka*), nor directing the Thornton Wilder play. Eugene Loring did *Silk Stockings,* and Vincent J. Donehue—who would later direct the 1960 telecast of Robbins's *Peter Pan*—directed *The Skin of Our Teeth.*
‡ *Me and Juliet* was a backstage musical about the cast and crew of a musical called *Me and Juliet:* its baroque but uninvolving plot was no match for the actual production's behind-the-scenes soap opera, which involved nepotism, adultery, and near-fatal mayhem. Even its composer hated it.
§ A Montmartre restaurant whose owner, Ginette Auger (Geneviève), not only did the cooking but entertained her clientele with her singing.

house. Can't wait to give you a jibby[*] for it. Have fun, take care, work hard and keep well.

With all my love,
Jerry

A Last Conversation (*The Poppa Piece*)
December 12, 1980

There was a time I did a ballet, an opera, and a musical[†] in one period of time, each overlapping the end of the other. It was at the opening of the opera, the middle work, that I saw my mother for the first time in a long time, and it became shocking [*sic*] clear that she was *very* ill, seriously, to die. I called her doctor the next day and he told me how sick she was, and even then I couldn't take it in and went on with my work, the musical, and I was in New Haven when the doctor called and advised me to return to N[ew] Y[ork] immediately. She died in a few days.[‡] . . .

There, in the hospital, before she died, I saw [my parents] embrace for the first time, and a shocking discovery it was. I knew they loved each other. I knew she loved him. I had lost. I had lost.

To: Buzz Miller
[September 1954]

CHATEAU MARMONT, LOS ANGELES

Dear Buzz,

Here is my first letter I've written to anyone in months on a typewriter I haven't used yet.

---

[*] Jibby, or gibby, was Robbins slang for an antique knickknack.
[†] *Quartet, The Tender Land,* and *The Pajama Game.*
[‡] Lena Rabinowitz (or Robbins, as she ordered carved on her tombstone) died on April 12, 1954, at Beth Israel Hospital, with Robbins at her side (Sonia and Harry had both gone home, exhausted).

It's the end of a very hot long and tiring day. I just went down to the pool and jumped in to refresh myself but at six in the evening the pool seems to be filled with fat floating aged men who puff and make the water level higher. The past few days have been clear and brilliant and very hot; I feel cheated by having to work* during the day when I know I could get very dark and attractive by just sitting around the beach and water. Oh well I'll have money instead. Last night I had a dream in which I was shirking working this job, and in the dream you suddenly voiced your disapproval of my attitude, and I was so shocked and worried and surprised. When I woke up and thought about it, it occurred to me that you never have expressed approval or disapproval about the way I work. Here I've given you many lectures about doing the job fully if you've taken it on and not complaining etc. etc. and trying to advise you, and the dream made me wonder if you ever have had unexpressed reservations or criticisms about the way I work. I guess the whole thing is provoked by some inner feeling which I recognize I have about not concentrating and giving the time to the job that I should. But isn't it strange that I bring you into it and make you my conscience.

The new number for Mary and Cyril† is going well, and Cyril will be wonderful in it. It's all done except for putting Mary into it and we start on that tomorrow. Occasionally someone comes up with an idea for a big production number and everything inside me gets worried and cold because I don't think that at this point I could work up enough steps and ideas to fulfill anything very large. Betty and Adolph are working well and it's fun to have someone professional on the job. Dick H.‡ is still floating around in his camel hair coat and drinking and groping and looking evil, but oh well, only a couple more months of this and then BOOM!

I'm sitting here eating those little tomatoes dipped in salt and pepper. Watching me is the Japanese tiger with the feathered nose, and now and then

---

* *Peter Pan* had run into trouble in San Francisco: the score had serious holes in it, and Mary Martin was having understandable difficulty mastering the aerial choreography she had originally been so excited by. Now, during the show's run in Los Angeles, Robbins's old collaborators Betty Comden and Adolph Green (lyrics) and Jule Styne (music) had been brought in to create new material, and Robbins had to stage it and rehearse it.

† Mary Martin and Cyril Ritchard, as Peter Pan and Captain Hook, respectively. This number was the duet "Oh, My Mysterious Lady."

‡ Richard Halliday, Mary Martin's husband and a co-producer.

he either nods or shakes his head. Tonight after show I'll probably go swimming again, and I wish you were here, natch. After show, coming home is always the loneliest time. If you were here I'd probably sit up and work like I should but because you're not, I miss you, and feel uncomfortable in this large apartment and rattle around something fierce. . . .

I have to go eat now and then sit thru the show again. Why I don't know. Maybe I won't. But then I'll have bad dreams again. Well, I'll see. At any rate, take care of yourself. Take care of that cold. Take a good hot drink and a good hot bath and a good hot friend and get into bed and sweat it out. If your cold isn't too bad I've been told you can leave out the drink and bath. But no tricks now.

Write me again. Tell me about the house on the Island* and what else I should look for. I feel a buying spell coming over me, I haven't

Buzz Miller (left) and Robert Fizdale: lovers old and new.

bought anything personal since that mad bathrobe which I'll never use. What's going on at Vesture, Casual Aire and Mark Xs.† If you get a chance stop in at the last and buy me another of those long sleeved tee shirts with the straight neck and not quite to the wrist sleeve. In Black with a pink stripe medium size. Mail. Thanks.

---

* Miller had bought land on Fire Island and was building a house.
† Vestiaire, Casual Aire, and Mark Cross were upscale retailers for clothing and other goods.

And if you get a chance go look at our errant son Otis and see how he is. Give him a kiss for me.

I'm writ out. Help. Goodbye.

Love
J.

I showered—washed out socks—am going to eat & then to a movie. So there.

J.

To: Lincoln Kirstein
November 11, 1954

Dear Lincoln,

Thank you so much for your letter and forgive my delay in answering it.

Frankly, I was shocked and surprised by George's reaction to the Dybbuk.[*] His reasons for not wanting it are really dismaying, and I can't figure out whether it's through a lack of sympathy and tolerance for the material and subject or his lack of belief in my talent. His suggestion that I do it for Inbal[†] is about as valid as my suggestion that he do Apollo for the Greek Folk Dancers that were over here or Western Symphony[‡] for a group of cowboys. And what discourages me more seems to be his apparent distrust in my ability to convert the material into dance terms suitable to our company. Then it occurs to me that at least four bal-

---

[*] Almost immediately after *Peter Pan*'s successful Broadway opening on October 20, Robbins had proposed a new ballet to Balanchine and Kirstein, an adaptation of S. Anski's Yiddish drama of star-crossed love and spectral possession in a Russian shtetl, which would have a score by Leonard Bernstein. Kirstein, writing for Balanchine and himself on October 31, 1954, declared *The Dybbuk* unsuitable for City Ballet's world of "elegance, clarity, balance and good manners" and said Bernstein "doesn't give a fuck for anyone living or dead, and . . . prays for success on any and every level."

[†] Inbal Dance Theatre, a modern dance troupe, was founded in 1949 by Sara Levi-Tanai; Robbins had worked with them on his 1952 visit to Israel and again in December 1953.

[‡] *Apollo* (1929) was one of Balanchine's first modernist masterpieces. *Western Symphony,* to a folk-song suite by the American orchestrator and composer Hershy Kay, is what might be described as a classical horse-opera-house ballet.

lets which I have suggested over the past couple of years have been turned down, criticized, or dismissed for one reason or another. This gets to be a little insecure making, especially if one has such high regard for George as a choreographer.

I'd like to make my own mistakes, I guess. . . . This is not to say that I don't have doubts and I certainly welcome any advice about possible pitfalls of the work, but I want to do the Dybbuk, and if Leonard can manage to do the score this winter,[*] I would like to offer it to Ballet Theater for Nora.[†] . . .

Don't worry about the things you said about Leonard and psychoanalysis. I know what you were driving at and the only wincing I do is in trying to consider and apply, relate or compare our two experiences. Anything that makes you think is good, and you always make me think. . . .

Let me hear from you. Meanwhile, happy winter!

Love,
Jerry

To: Heller Halliday[‡]
June 10, 1955

Dear Heller,

Thank you for your note. Smell this paper and see how you like it.[§]
Here are your misspelled words:

terable—terrible
wounderful—wonderful
drector—director

---

[*] Bernstein didn't, of course, manage to do the score of *Dybbuk* that winter; it took another two decades for the project to develop.
[†] Nora Kaye had recently returned to Ballet Theatre, whose repertory she felt was more compatible with her dancing.
[‡] Halliday, the thirteen-year-old daughter of Richard Halliday and Mary Martin, had played the Cockney maid Liza in *Peter Pan* and was now appearing in Thornton Wilder's *The Skin of Our Teeth*, starring her mother and George Abbott. The production was directed by Alan Schneider.
[§] Halliday had sent Robbins a note on scented paper.

Thank you for the gold coin. I ought to have included half the coffee beans you spilled in my car in this letter, but I used them to make coffee.

Glad you are happy with your role and that you get on so well with the director (ha ha). I will probably come to see a run through on Tuesday night, so you better have a few bar[re] exercises before.

Love,
Jerry

To: Arthur Laurents
October 6, 1955

[LOS ANGELES]

Dear Arthur,

I am sending this via Tommy[*] because I think it will get there faster. I will sure be sorry to see him leave here,[†] but as he says, what a wonderful Christmas we are all[‡] going to have together in New York and I do look forward to the fact that both of you will make New York a happier place to be in.

[Now about ROMEO.[§] First of all, let's get a couple of things out of the way. It's a tricky thing, trying to arrange a schedule for three people as busy as we are. What bothers me most is the constant confronting we do to each other about each other's work—the business about Lenny doing a television show, or my doing a movie, or CLEARING IN THE WOODS,[¶] or CANDIDE, or

---

[*] Tom Hatcher, who became Laurents's life partner.

[†] While working on the *King and I* film, Robbins had rented a three-bedroom house in the Hollywood Hills for himself, his secretary, Edith Weissman, and (occasionally) Buzz Miller.

[‡] Laurents, Hatcher, Robbins, and Buzz Miller.

[§] The long-deferred *Romeo and Juliet* musical—still referred to as "Romeo" by the participants—was finally getting under way, and Robbins was trying to get a workable schedule from his collaborators. The following paragraph was deleted, by pen, from the document sent to Laurents; Robbins wrote "unimportant" next to the material in brackets, but left those sentences visible. Everything from the end of the brackets to the end of the paragraph was impenetrably crossed out; it's reconstructed here from the original carbon in Robbins's files.

[¶] Laurents had proposed that Robbins direct his play *A Clearing in the Woods,* about a woman's attempt to come to terms with her past.

Betty and Adolph's show. Underneath all of this lies a bad kind of competition which can really be injurious and I think we ought to drop it once and for all.] Each of us is in great demand for any number of projects and it's really too easy a way to make for arguments when the going gets tough. It isn't true that anyone has been idle while others have been working; you have been working on a movie script and Lenny had to do Tanglewood, so the whole summer went past: I already made my film commitment: Lenny was supposed to have done CANDIDE and instead it has been postponed until the time we were supposed to do this show; CLEARING was waiting for a star, and so we can go around in circles forever—so let's drop all that.

The thing I *do* agree about is getting this show on, but getting it on *properly*. [My thinking is this;]* I had an idea seven years ago, I have been waiting that long to get it on, and unless we have the time to do it properly and with the most and best kind of collaboration, I don't want to do it. The time element in aiming for Spring bothers the hell out of me. If the script and the score were already written I could be brooding over it now as I did with PETER PAN while working on PAJAMA GAME. [This show is important and]† the collaboration is important; it's extremely important that the *three* of us aid, help, influence and stimulate each other's talents and contributions. According to the schedule that's now laid out there *is* the possibility of your not being available in January when I'm free, if a production of CLEARING IN THE WOODS comes up. And honestly, Arthur, for the sake of the show I don't want to do it under those conditions. I don't think you would like it if CLEARING were planned for a March first rehearsal and I was to direct it (my first straight play) and between January and March (when we would be casting and getting everything ready and doing last minute changes etc.) I were to take on a television spectacular or a ballet. Even CLEARING would be easier than ROMEO under those circumstances, as you and I have spent so much time on the script and I already feel I have a grasp on it. ROMEO isn't even on paper yet, and with all real deep appreciation and enormous respect I have for your talent, this will be *your* first musical and there will be things that will be problems that you don't know about.

* Another crossed out phrase.
† More crossed-out material.

[You see I feel][*] you and Lenny are the best possible people ever to write this show. I have felt that for seven years and have waited that long. When you and Lenny got entangled with the SERENADE[†] producers and then wanted out, I allowed you to substitute ROMEO for it, although I had reservations about the producers; when you and Lenny want to try the lyrics I agree, even, again, with reservations (which are doubled because of new time problems). Now, when you and Lenny say you want to shoot for a Spring production I have enormous reservations [about the practical side of there being the real collaboration this show should have. In spite of these reservations][‡] I will go along with you both, because of my respect and knowledge of your talents,

* And more.
† *Serenade* was Laurents's adaptation—which was to have music by Bernstein—of a James M. Cain novel about an opera singer who discovers his homosexuality. They had hoped to interest Robbins in choreographing and directing it.
‡ In the sent draft Robbins deleted this material and replaced it with "But."

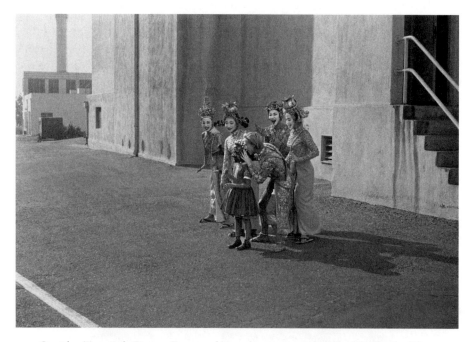

Outside a Twentieth Century Fox soundstage, dancers in costume for *The King and I*'s "Small House of Uncle Thomas" ballet try one of the masks on a young admirer.

Monday Aug 16 - Beach.

I'm writing more — & liking it. Such associative memories arise. I'm not afraid of it at this point. Don't know when it will stop or where it will go.

Sunshine today. Finally. Weekend with Bills Didion & fog & rain. Nice — but damp. Now sand & ...

Aug 18th. 76

Robbins's beach house in Bridgehampton was a refuge where he wrote, sketched, and thought—about choreography, theater, and life.

Jesse Gerstein in Umbria. When he contracted AIDS in the late 1980s,
he and Robbins reconciled and Robbins cared for him until his death.

A flowering thistle from one of Robbins's sketchbooks.

A series of pages from Robbins's 1977 journal. City Ballet's musicians had gone on strike in December 1976 and *The New York Times* prematurely reported the cancellation of the winter season before last-minute negotiations put everyone back to work. Robbins's stress level and ambivalence found their way onto the page.

"Life at the beach is very calm," Robbins wrote to a friend, "quiet and frighteningly inactive in every way." Perhaps that's why he made calendars for his weeks there, crossing off each day in succession.

though to me, it's cutting the margins pretty slim. But I do *have* to say No at the point where there's the possibility that even *that* kind of collaboration is not certain from January on. I understand how you feel about CLEARING [and with my knowledge of that understanding I have to say No to a Spring production, unless you would promise that if we *all* give things up you would give that up also].* There's no way of knowing what life time dream may be offered to any of us next week, but if we want to get ROMEO on this Spring we all have to guarantee clearing the boards completely. I also don't mean to be completely rigid, because if ROMEO was written very fast and very well and then the possibility of a production of your play came up in the next month or two, we could all sit down and look at the situation and come to some decision. But finally Arthur, at a certain point [I don't think]† there should be any turning back, and the decision for you to reach is whether you want to gamble a possible production of CLEARING against a full speed ahead sign on ROMEO. All that stands in my way of saying Yes is the question of Time, which you can tip the balance on.

Now about CLEARING itself, I'd like to get a little bit off my chest about it. You know how I feel about the play, how much I love it and am moved by it, and how much I feel I can contribute to making it what you want. I want you to understand my feelings of *not* counting on it in light of developments around it. You selected Oliver‡ to produce it. Oliver talked with me, said he had reservations about my doing it and finally, would certainly not want me to do it if they could get a name star who might want another director. This as much as tells me that if I wanted to wait around for the *possibility* of directing it, I should keep my schedule clear. Frankly, you have never said anything to the contrary, except at the times when the pressure of ROMEO brings the subject up. I no longer feel that you or Oliver have given me any sense of a commitment on CLEARING. I also felt surprised and very upset by the fact that you decided on producers without any word to me. And I think that if you had

---

* Another deletion.
† And another.
‡ Oliver Smith, who in addition to his work as a designer had co-produced *On the Town* and *Billion Dollar Baby,* as well as Jane Bowles's *In the Summer House* (another play Robbins had wanted to direct—see below).

Costume designer Irene Sharaff silhouetted against the lights during filming for
The King and I.

really considered me as a director I would have been consulted about it. I think
Oliver has fine taste. But, *I* have been the one who has had him as producer
on a couple of shows, and I have also seen the other shows he has produced,
and, outside of IN THE SUMMERHOUSE I don't hold much for the taste
or production of any of his shows. I think that even SUMMERHOUSE was
produced weakly. I also feel that what I have produced and directed has been
much more tasteful and not a quarter as compromising in final production.
In spite of all this I would go ahead with Oliver because of our deep mutual
respect and long friendship, and we would get along; but you gave me the very
strong sense of dropping me and taking up with Oliver, and the thing that
bothered me most about it was that I felt you did it because I was pushing you
for changes (and maybe using poor methods to get them). I rely on you, for
the sake of everyone's long associations, to keep this completely to yourself.

When the time comes I will express this to Oliver myself. Let me hear from you about all this.

Buzz stayed over rather than taking the train to Houston, and a very good thing, as he became violently sick that very night and I had to call a doctor and a surgeon in, fearing either appendicitis or hepatitis, both of which he had every symptom of. It turns out to be food poisoning, and the only thing I can guess is that Raymond[*] put it in the wrong portion. We have solved any future occurrences by going into the kitchen saying, gee, that smells good, and making him taste it.

All goes well with the picture.[†] I've been working with Deborah Kerr and Walter Lang on staging the numbers. He is really a nice guy but has absolutely no imagination whatsoever and has no wish to attempt anything inventive or unusual. I'm starting to get fidgety and nervous with the time growing shorter. There's a big production conference Friday night on the ballet. Something tells me the ax will fall on either minutes, dancers, costumes, orchestra or spangles. I suggested today that if it were all too expensive, to scrap the whole thing and instead I could do a hot two and one half minute number called "Sunup in Siam" which they could later cut down to one minute. I got a sour laugh out of Lang.

Write me bubby and tell me all. I envy you the Fall in New York, the life in Quogue, but I am happy for all the happiness that you will be having.

With all my love,

P.S. By the way, get a copy of Jo Sinclair's book "The Changelings." It's about the undercurrent background of gangwar on a street which is inhabited mostly by Jewish people but is slowly being taken over by Negroes. Somewhat apropos.

---

[*] Apparently the chef.
[†] Robbins was directing the dance sequences for the Twentieth Century Fox film of *The King and I*, directed by Walter Lang and starring Deborah Kerr as Anna.

To: Arthur Laurents and Leonard Bernstein
October 18, 1955

[LOS ANGELES]

Dear Arthur and Lenny,

I'm dictating this in 15 minutes I have free during lunch, so I'll get right to it. Excuse the directness, but it's the only way I can get this off to you.

It concerns the outline, but before I tell you my objections I want you to know that I think it's a hell of a good job and very much on the right track, and that these differences are incidental to the larger wonderful job you are both doing.

I don't agree with the 3 act division. I feel very strongly that this negates the time pressure connected with the whole show and mitigates against [*sic*] the tenseness of the story being crammed into 2 or 3 days. Moreover, there's not sufficient material in Act II or III to stand up by themselves. And it's a serious mistake to let the audience out of our grip for 2 intermissions.

Act I, Scene 2. Would like to suggest that the meeting between Romeo and Juliet be more abrupt rather than an observing of each other from distance at first. In general, suddenness of action is something we should strive for, beginning with the tempo key in which we establish Scene 1. Its violence and excitement should cue us for all our dramatic moments; i.e. the suddenness and horror of the murders at the end of the rumble, the discovery of love, etc. etc.

Act I, Scene 5. You are away off the track with the whole character of Anita.[*] She is the typical downbeat blues torch-bearing 2nd character (Julie of SHOW-BOAT, etc.) and falls into a terrible cliché. The audience will know that somewhere a "my man done left me" blues is coming up for her. Furthermore, if she's "an-older-girl-kicked-by-love-before-experiencing-the-worst" (and I'm quoting you) she's much too experienced for the gang, or else is sick, sick, sick to be so attached emotionally and sexually to a younger boy.

Act III, Scene 5. There are a couple of things I can't adjust here. The boys

---

* In his autobiography, *Original Story By,* Laurents admits that he modeled the character on an older singer he knew and admired, Anita Ellis.

are jitterbugging to avert suspicion from the police—but what has happened about the death of their beloved Mercutio?[*] In other words, how do you make compatible the effect of the murders on the boys with what you have written? I think this *can* be done, but isn't indicated at all in the outline.

Act III, Scene 6. From the outline I'm inclined to feel that it's all a little too goofy.[†] Juliet becomes Ophelia with the reeds and flowers and is playing a "crazy" scene. I had to read the whole thing a couple of times to find out why Romeo died and I also think it's too right on the head placing it back in the bridal shop.

As for the all-over picture, we're dead unless the audience feels that all the tragedy can and could be averted, that there's *hope* and a wish for escape from the tragedy, and a tension built on that desire. We must always hold out the tantalizing chance of a positive ending. Romeo and Juliet particularly must feel this and be sure of it. It's another reason why I dislike qvetchy Anita so much. Let's not have anyone in the show feel sorry for themselves.

About the dancing. It will never be well incorporated into the show unless some of the principals are dancers. I can see, easily, why Romeo and Juliet must be singers, but Mercutio has to be a dancer, maybe Anita, and for sure some of the prominent gang members, otherwise, if any of the dance sequences do take over the stage, your principals will move to the side and a terrible separation happens. Practically, it's easier to rehearse with separate units, but with all the experience I've had it's by far the most beneficial to the unity of the show to have the principals do everything. It's a sorry sight and a back-breaking effort, and usually an unsuccessful one, to build the numbers around some half-assed movements of a principal who can't move. Think it over.

I'm sending this off as fast as possible, so please excuse the abruptness. Let me hear from you both.

Love,
Jerry

---

[*] Shakespeare's Mercutio becomes Riff in Laurents's adaptation. Difficulties over the contrast between the song "Gee, Officer Krupke" and its context persisted throughout the development of *West Side Story;* and in the movie version the song was moved.

[†] Although he would deny this in his autobiography, Laurents had, in initial treatments, intended Maria/Juliet to kill herself, in the bridal shop, after the death of Tony/Romeo.

Arthur Laurents (left) and Stephen Sondheim, who wrote the book and lyrics, respectively, for *West Side Story* and *Gypsy,* photographed in a rehearsal studio in 1959.

To: Arthur Laurents
November 16, 1955

Dear Arthur,

I keep writing to you and I hope you keep Lenny and Steven [*sic*] informed about my reactions out here.

I like Scene 4 very much, almost the best. I like best the sections in which you have gone on your own path, writing in your own style with your own characters and imagination. Least successful are the sections in which I sense the intimidation of Shakespeare standing behind you. You have to rid yourself completely of any sense of writing either competitively or in the pseudo style of Shakespeare. Perhaps it isn't apparent to you; for instance Riff, in the opening scene, seems a parody and shell of Shakespeare's Mercutio—the braggart, Queen-Mab-speecher, Lothario etc. In contrast, as you continue writing, he becomes someone created by you and is so much more convincing. I hope I am putting this constructively because you know how much I think of your talent and I trust *it* and want it much more than I want a rewritten Shakespeare.

Now about what I meant about the difference in tempo and intensity of the dialog. All your scenes of action without dialog (and almost each scene begins that way) have a great dramatic intensity, vigor, concentration and force. In contrast the dialog tends to not be as concise and terse and does not concern itself with *only* the essentials. You establish a style which is exactly right at the beginning of the show and at the beginning of each scene and you key the audience to a certain pace and tempo which couldn't be better. Then when you start to talk you relax into a legit play tempo rather than a lyric drama tempo, which is different than life-like or straight-play tempo. You would sense this immediately were it put upon the stage. The larger-than-life approach, the balletic approach which you have captured at times is exactly right and you must keep it in mind all the time. If you keep each scene down to strict story points (outside of Romeo and Juliet themselves) you will be writing perfectly for this type of show. Not that the characters should lack dimension or that you should be artful in making your points, but the more concentrated everything is the better show we will have.

I'm dying to hear some music and lyrics. Betty Bogart[*] feels the same way as Nora. Quote—you three characters will never get on together—unquote.

I think I'll be home in the next two or three weeks. The shooting is over and the scars and bullet holes are scarcely visible. Most of the ballet I'm enormously pleased with, some not. I'll be editing this week, but the terrible part is that I'm already starting not to care as it's all over with. If all goes well with PETER PAN I hope I'll have enough time to work with you during rehearsals.[†] They seem to be getting most of the original cast back. If I can just get a week's rest between this job and PETER I'll be happy.

Give my love to Nora. I can't wait to see her. And of course to Tommy. I'd love to spend Christmas with all of you, or at least as much of it that I can squeeze in between rehearsals of PETER PAN. Got a couple of letters from the

---

[*] Lauren Bacall.

[†] After a live broadcast in March 1955, *Peter Pan* was slated for a second live presentation in January 1956. Robbins was to supervise the staging.

Buzzer. Doesn't sound too happy, wishes he were home. Natch. Saw THE BIG KNIFE* which I loved after a lousy start. Real scary . . .

The weather has been like New York Fall, clear, crisp, snappy and sunny, and the tugs to get back have started. I'm giving a party for the gypsies tomorrow night.

This is all for now cooky, take care, keep well, work hard and have fun. With all my love,

Your gypsy,

J

Working with Lenny
August 7, 1978†

There are few moments that compare with the experience of having a composer play you his newest piece of music for a show. I'd arrive at Lenny's for a meeting and be greeted by, "I've got something." He'd lead me over to a piano covered with scribbled music sheets, lyrics, pencils and erasers in various destroyed states, and the several inevitable overflowing ashtrays. He'd sit down and open with, "I can't play this myself, there are so many voices." Or "This won't sound like it will in the orchestra." Then he'd postpone playing by giving a ten-minute analytic lecture on the composition. It was, of course, his delaying tactic (common to many composers) to cover his anxiety about it.

When he'd finally get to it he'd *make* it sound like an entire orchestra! His feet would stamp out the chords and percussion, threatening the ceiling of the apartment below. His prodigious piano technique allowed him to produce the

---

* Based on a 1949 play by Clifford Odets about a movie star blackmailed into accepting a role he doesn't want, *The Big Knife* was directed by Robert Aldrich and starred Jack Palance, Ida Lupino, and Rod Steiger.

† This tribute was written for Leonard Bernstein's sixtieth birthday celebration, but it perfectly evokes the rapport that existed between composer and choreographer at its best. "I remember all my collaborations with Jerry in terms of one bodily feeling," said Bernstein, "which is his hands on my shoulders, composing with his hands on my shoulders" (*Dramatists Guild Quarterly* [Fall 1985]).

second and third voices of the piece, and his voice, singing in several ranges, doubled back and forth over octaves demonstrating orchestral parts, choruses, duets and solos. Sometimes (oh, happy moment) he'd have me play a single constant piano figure while he showed me what the other voices were doing. His excitement was contagious and in no time at all I'd be on my feet showing him the type of movement, gesture, action that the music evoked. He'd take fire. And the give and take would fly back and forth. Sections might be repeated, enlarged, or cut; each of us added ideas. The deepest satisfaction was the knowledge that it all locked in on the target, so right that I couldn't wait to get to rehearsal to start on it, finish it, and show it to him.

To: Nancy "Slim" Hayward[*]
[April 1956]

Dearest Pearl,[†]

How is Leland?[‡] I'm terribly worried. Please write me right away. It's terrible to be so far from those you love and I love you both so much, and I want to be of help if I can, and being way over here is just frustrating now. So get out that little poisonous pen of yours and scribble me a nice long letter telling the-one-whose-shoulder-is-the-mostest[§] all about it.

So here I am half way around the world in little ole Copenhagen typing on a Danish typewriter. And ever so often I ask myself what the hell I'm here

---

[*] Nancy Gross Hawks Hayward (1917–1990), while married to her first husband, the director Howard Hawks, had "discovered" Lauren Bacall; she'd met Robbins when her second husband, Leland Hayward, produced *Call Me Madam,* and sometime in the mid-1950s they appear to have begun an intermittent affair.

[†] Because she loved pearls (and had legendary ropes of them), "Pearl" was Robbins's nickname for the woman everyone else called Slim; hers for him was "Gypsy"—a reference, perhaps, to his chorus-boy, show-gypsy past as much as to his dark coloring.

[‡] It's not clear what Hayward's health problem was.

[§] A reference to the song "The Hostess with the Mostes' on the Ball" from *Call Me Madam* (which Leland Hayward had produced and during which Robbins and Slim had met).

Francisco Moncion, the City Ballet principal whom Robbins paired with Tanaquil Le
Clercq in *Afternoon of a Faun,* photographed in the garden of Robbins's brownstone
apartment, July 4, 1956.

for.* So I'm working for the King, so I'm increasing my international reputation, so I'm being somewhat stimulated by new dancers, so what. On the other
hand I'm doing an old work, and spending a lot of my diminishing strength
and youth and time, and life seems to be like working a crossword puzzle to
pass the time and keep busy. The other day I was walking down the street and
suddenly I felt heavy in the knees and numb in the calves at the loneliness of
it all. And honestly I don't blame anyone. It's the life I've made and the decisions I've made and the results are mine. And the older I get and the better
I know myself the less I like it and understand what it's all about. On one
hand I can adjust to it and say well that's it boy, face it and go on, and then

* Because his *West Side Story* collaborators were otherwise occupied (Bernstein with his musical
Candide and Laurents with the film *Anastasia*), Robbins was staging *Fanfare* for the Royal Danish
Ballet—the first time a foreign company had performed one of his works.

I say Oh what the hell dump it all, give it up and don't struggle. About Life I feel that way, which is scary. And I know I should accept the challenge of doing new things trying new ballets, extending myself further with each effort, and ever since I've been sick,* I feel like playing it safe, repeating what I've done and not risking the position I've gained for myself. But even writing this now, I know that I *have* to go on, that I *must* try further, that I must risk new things. I suppose behind it all is such doubt about myself as a director which I'm moving toward, and equal doubt about contributing anything further as a choreographer which I'm moving away from and perhaps won't be able to get back to. (Just think, I'm able to tell you all this, dear doctor, and it doesn't cost twenty-five an hour either). So this makes me get to *work* again, which I suppose *is* my life, and that's that. Voila, as I'd say in French. Anyway thanks for *your* shoulder Pearl.

Now about this place. I arrived on Easter week, which here means everything is closed up. Then at the same time there was a general strike. So between no shopping, no cinemas, no theatre, no museums, no newspapers, no buses, no boats, and no friends it was a little like an evil jail. The Royal Theatre itself was shut for five days so no work either. My dear I just slept and slept. I took short walks at evening, when I got up, came home, ate, bathed, looked at the mirror and took my sleeping pill and off again to no man's land. Charming, huh?

Then work began. And it's been work. The Theatre is marvelous. The whole system's just too good for dancers to be true. Every year out of about three hundred applicants, they select about ten students. They are seven or eight at most. These children are given classes in dancing and also regular school classes and appear on the stage in some production at least once a week. The class rooms are so beautiful (I mean the ballet rooms). Very old and decorated so tastefully with the old ballet masters of the 1700's and 1800's looking down. Big French windows beautiful wood floors and such a wonderful atmosphere. The children themselves look like a roomful of trolls and elves. They all wear the uniform of royal blue wool tights and sweaters, most a little baggy at the knees. They are beautifully behaved and dance already quite well. They do their entrechat sixes

---

* Robbins had been hospitalized, at Slim Hayward's insistence, with a life-threatening bout of hepatitis in the winter of 1954–1955.

already and the girls are bouréeing on point. The girls always dip into a little curtsey when they enter or leave or pass you, and the boys bow. They are delicious angels all. . . .

The town is charming, and seems to be one big Bonnier's.* . . . There is a truly wonderful Theatre museum, which is located in a theatre that was built in 1766 as a private court theatre. It's fantastic to visit the dressing rooms, see the make-up tables, read the notices, and also they have a large ballet collection including Pavlova's costumes and toe shoes. Even more fascinating is to see drawings of the scenery and sketches and later photos of ballets that were created in 1846 etc. that are still in the current repertory of the Royal Theatre and are danced exactly the same today!!! You can see pictures of four generations of the cast of La Sylphide or Napoli both of which will be danced in N.Y. this Fall. The theatre itself is a delight with little boxes and a raked stage the old candle chandeliers, etc. You'd flip I know. There is also a pretty good collection of French impressionists here and a very good collection of Roman and Greek and Egyptian sculpture all housed in a large museum built and collected by the man who started what is now the leading beer company of Denmark. And believe me that must be plenty beer. Wow they drink it all the time with everything. Mostly with fish. Herrings. The food is very good here without being exceptional in any way. They have real inventive open sandwiches . . . things like very rare roast beef, topped with a curry mayonnaise that has French fried onions mixed in it. They can sometimes even top this with a poached egg and an anchovy, all on that good thin pumpernickel. The coffee is good but mostly I am taken by the fact that women over forty like to puff at a good cigar after dinner. Yep, the most elegant. This makes the atmosphere somewhat smelly and more than butch, but when in Denmark you better do as the Romans do. Lie down and throw up. I've also learned a lot of Danish words. All the food, natch, all the everyday greetings, all the directions for dancing etc. and a couple of things like how about shacking up ce soir kid? But I've really been a good boy, as much out of tiredness as out of no ambitions. . . .

---

* Bonniers (the firm didn't use an apostrophe) was a furniture and housewares retailer specializing in modern Scandinavian design; the company had an outlet in New York.

What else. I have seen no pearls, dear girl. My ballet opens the twenty eighth and the King and Queen are to be there. No [curtain] calls are allowed after any performance, but I am allowed a solo call. I will feel like Ethel Merman in the presentation scene from CALL ME MADAM. I have re read three Shakespeare plays and finally feel I've reached the age of true enjoyment. Also have read The Story of a Year–1848, pretty interesting, Trial and the Blackboard Jungle (for teen age background*), three books on the Danish ballet and three books on Kjobenhavn as they call it here. . . .

Now the least you can do is write me. Or publish this.

I love you, and I think of you often.

As we sang in Peter Pan . . . "send up a flare, and I'll be there."

[J].

* Robbins was doing background research for *West Side Story*.

The "delicious angels" of the Royal Danish Ballet School in Copenhagen, April 1956.

To: Nancy Hayward
April 26, 1956

Dearest Pearl,

Thank you for your good long letter. I do hope Leland is feeling better. I know how dreadful the whole thing must be. It is so hard for us to have patience, especially you and me. We like to have the fruit of our pleasure very soon. You are even more impatient with time than I am, but, you know, you needn't be. I'm not handing you a line. I like you like you are and each time I see you I like the looks of you even better, and something wonderful is happening to you each time I see you. So stop qvetching (you and me), try to last it out, and it will get better. . . .

I thought of you so much on Sunday last. I went to a museum that had rooms and rooms of the most exquisite porcelains. Little boxes, dishes, statues, and everything that reminded me of you. I could picture you looking at them and maybe worrying your thumbnail and saying God, I'd give my life for that. I also went to a huge store [that] sells every hand craft and art designed thing made in Denmark, with fabulous cheap prices on things that make Bonnier's and Georg Jensen's look sick. I sent to you three little dolls, one for you and one [each] for Kitty and Bridget.* . . .

What else? Nothing much. The ballet opens Sunday. Tivoli, an amusement park in town, opens May 1st and I'll stay for that. After that I'm not sure. I'd like to go to Italy for a few weeks, but hate the thought of doing it alone. Any chance of your coming to Italy? We could have two weeks of sightseeing love and arguments.

I'm very distressed to hear about Bogey.† Please give them my love. Yes, I've read Out of Africa‡ and loved it. Have just finished "Island in the Sun"§ which I found fascinating not because of the quality of the writing but because of its insight into Caribbean island life in relationship to blacks and whites. . . .

---

* Kitty Hawks and Bridget Hayward were two of Slim Hayward's daughters.
† The actor Humphrey Bogart (1899–1957), whom Robbins had met through the Haywards, had just had surgery for cancer of the esophagus; he died the following January.
‡ *Out of Africa* by Isak Dinesen.
§ A novel by Alec Waugh about the postcolonial West Indies.

My personal life? "Niente" as they say in Italy. Seem to be somewhat asleep inside, or again recovering from les upheavals,* but at any rate nothing happens and only my little message to you at the beginning of this letter keeps me from being a nudnick† on the subject. I want to run somewhere and come alive, but where and how. I'm tired of Danish open sandwiches and Danish open faces. There really isn't anything large or grand or stirring in this country. Give me Rome with its brutal statues and oversized monuments and flaring architecture. Or even Paris with its slightly snobbish elegance and rapier-like people and taste. Or New York with its energy and vulgarity and variety. Listen. There has to be good things in Store for us. I know it. Don't worry.

So write me, Pearl. I'll be here another week at least, so get the letter off now. Keep well. I love you, and miss you and wish we were together to talk or walk or read or listen or watch together.

My love to Leel. Please let me know how he is.

My love to you—always.

J

To: Tanaquil Le Clercq
September 17, 1956

MORNING.

Dear Tanny,

Thank you so very very much for all your letters and notes, your reviews and postcards. It's been a pleasure receiving them every morning and makes facing the day a lot easier. I haven't written before because of the rehearsal schedule I'm on.‡ It starts early in the morning and goes on until after midnight.

You must know the glassy-eyed mood I'm in. I can't wait for it all to be over at the end of November and to go away for a couple of weeks. It's always at

---

* Robbins and Buzz Miller had parted, first tentatively, then definitively, and Miller was in Paris dancing with Jean Babilée's company.

† Yiddish for boring pest.

‡ Robbins had just begun rehearsals in New York for *Bells Are Ringing;* New York City Ballet was on a European tour, which Robbins, due to his show schedule, could not join.

points like this I wonder why I ever got into this business and how nice it would be to own a book store or record shop or restaurant. I haven't seen any movies but have read a couple of Willa Cather stories that I loved. That's about it.

I'll try to write again but I don't know when I'll be able to manage it; however don't stop sending your letters as they mean too much to me. The summer was a lovely one and a great deal was due to the fact that you were part of it.* Now the Diavolo† and the kites and the Tambourelli‡ are all put away. I have gotten all the sand out of my clothes and the bathing suits are back in moth balls. Only a few stones, seashells and some nice memories are left but still I figure we're ahead of the game.

Please write again. All my love to all the kiddies and take care of yourself.

Love,

J.

Now it's 2:30 A.M.—& tomorrow I start again. I've been terribly rude by *not* being able to go to the Danish Ballet, or even see or send them greetings. It's also a big moon tonight—and I'd love to walk with you in the park—or on the beach. I'd like to see you—tease you—have you make fun of me, or *ignore* me like you do. I think of you.§

Yours

J.

Adolph Green in a rehearsal room in New Haven during out-of-town tryouts for *Bells Are Ringing*, December 1956.

* Le Clercq and Balanchine had decided to separate after NYCB's European tour, and she had spent part of the summer with Robbins on Fire Island.
† A dice game where players compete for tiny devil or jewel tokens.
‡ A court game like badminton played with a shuttlecock and tambourine-shaped rackets.
§ And she was thinking of him. "Darling," she wrote in an undated letter just before her departure, "I'm going to miss you like crazy . . . it seems so long till I see you, better perhaps, all the way round."

To: Tanaquil Le Clercq
October 8, 1956

Dearest Tanny,

Thank you so very very very much for all the letters. It's the most perfect way to start the day but unfortunately, you have spoiled me with them. . . . When I don't get one something seems missing. Now that I'm leaving for New Haven, Boston, and Philadelphia (not Pittsburgh) I'll miss them terribly.

I have been terribly busy, the show is a strain and . . . I wish I could have been on tour with you the whole time, as the places sound wonderful, but on the other hand, I have such an aversion to traveling in groups by train. . . . I think I really was given a trauma by the five years of touring with Ballet Theatre, scrambling for taxi cabs, hotel rooms, dressing rooms, makeup boxes, etc. The one European trip I had with NYCB was much nicer, but I guess I just hate being regimented.

Betty Comden and Adolph Green wrote the book and lyrics for four Robbins musicals; here they watch a rehearsal for *Bells Are Ringing* at New Haven's Shubert Theatre in December 1956.

The show seems to be in fairly good shape for opening out of town, but I'm sure that next week (after we open in New Haven) we'll find many holes and flaws in it. You would have been real proud of me, never lost my temper and the company all is in good happy spirits and I get on well with them much to everyone's and my surprise. However I really prefer dancers to actors, dancers are a much hardier and tougher bunch and I mean that in the good sense of the word. . . .

I haven't seen any movies at all. I have been reading Thomas Wolfe's letters, some of Shakespeare's plays, and the New Yorker for relaxation. Social life niente. The weather is real fall, but I see so little of daylight and daytime that I can't be sure what's happening. . . . The World Series is on, the election speeches are being made all over the place, the segregation down South is a mess . . .

Please take care of yourself and write me some more.

All my love,
Jerry

X X X not sedate[*]

To: George Balanchine
November 9, 1956

Dear George,

Needless to say I was completely shocked at the news[†] and all my prayers and sympathies and best wishes are with you and Tanny as you must know. I am happy to hear that she is out of danger and has started treatments. The reason I am writing is that I want you to know that if there is anything at all that I can do, or any way that I can help please let me know. I'd be so grateful if you'd allow me to be of some assistance. . . .

---

[*] Robbins and Le Clercq had begun ending letters to each other with fanciful *X*s for kisses, sometimes labeled (as here)—rather like an emoticon.
[†] Robbins had just heard that Tanaquil Le Clercq had been stricken with polio in Copenhagen and was in an iron lung in the hospital. It wasn't yet clear (or he hadn't been told) what her prognosis was.

To: Tanaquil Le Clercq[*]
November 9, 1956

Dearest Tanny,

The grapevine has it that the news is good and you are on the road to recovery. How happy we all are for you. You'd have been shocked at the speed with which I hustled off to the nearest church to pray when I heard the first news. Even a bouree at twice the tempo held no candle to the path I cut. I sure wish I could be there to see you, joke with you, bring you a happy happy. I have considered flying over to visit you. Would you like me to do this? Just say the word.

What's new here? Nothing much. The show seems to be successful although I don't care for it too much myself. Somehow it seems very unimportant. I can't tell whether this is because of the world situation or that I'm just growing past the Broadway stage. If the latter is true what the hell will I turn to? Maybe I'll just put all the junk I've been collecting all these years in the window of some dirty little store on Third Avenue, get myself a rocking chair and a dog, have a back room full of dirty magazines and nip at a bottle all the time. . . .

In Boston I saw *Candide* (book by Lillian Hellman, music by Leonard Bernstein, sets and costumes by Oliver Smith and Irene Sharaff, direction by Tyrone Guthrie) and it was a real bore. I sat there not knowing what it was about or what the point of view was or anything. The sets are beautiful and some of the score is lovely but there's a terrible air of snobbishness about the whole shebang and the odor of a large egg hangs over everything. While I was watching it I thought of you seeing it and how loudly you would fuss and fume at the whole thing. I also saw the O'Neill play[†] there which I loved. It's true it went on for hours and hours but the characters are so marvelous, a dope fiend mother pretending not to be one, a bragging pinchpenny father, two sons, one a dipso and

---

[*] Over the next six months Robbins wrote to Le Clercq almost daily, except when she returned to New York and he was able to visit her in person. These letters are excerpted and run in here as a continuous document, though the excerpts are dated.

[†] *Long Day's Journey into Night* was first produced in America in October 1956 at the Wilbur theater in Boston prior to its Broadway premiere on November 7.

the other a consumptive makes for a really happy evening. I also saw GIANT* which I just loved. It's a wonderful picture with the greatest visual beauty. . . . When you come back we'll see this one together. . . .

Well this is all for now. Be of good cheer Tanny, so many people love you and care about you and are grateful for your existence and so happy for your recovery. So much that happens doesn't make sense but you must know of my love for you and my deep concern of all that happens to you.

December 3, 1956

. . . The show seems to be a big hit even though the reviews are not all completely favorable. . . . Opening night started at 7:30 and I spent most of the show pacing up and down in the back of the theatre, walking around in Shubert Alley and trying to look encouraging when I went backstage. Can't you just see that tight grin. Afterwards there was a party at the Hampshire House to which all the Broadway names were invited, and there was a rather unconscious competitive fashion display by all the women in a fairly small room. . . .

I'm reading a badly written but fascinating book called "The Great Migrations." It's about the extinctual [*sic*] accuracy of the migration of birds, fish and animals. . . . If there were any way of converting this material into a ballet it would be terrific but I don't see how. . . .

Do you want me to send you "the Great Migrations" and the Capote book† or do you have them. Soft woolly animals are on their way. I am very worried about the word that you are holding me to. I keep looking at the letter and trying to figure the word out, I have made it into practically everything except mink. . . .

I miss you Tanny and think about you constantly. I don't at all look forward to rehearsing the company because I know I won't see you. However time is going by and you are getting better and before you know it there will be one dark balding gypsy waiting for you at the end of a gangplank or airport. Your

---

* *Giant*, a film adaptation of Edna Ferber's novel about the conflict between Texas ranchers and oilmen, was directed by George Stevens and starred Rock Hudson, Elizabeth Taylor, and James Dean.
† Probably *The Muses Are Heard*, an account (first published in two installments in *The New Yorker*) of the U.S.S.R. tour of the Everyman Opera company production of George and Ira Gershwin's *Porgy and Bess*.

handwriting is improving, I love each word of each postscript and can't wait until you write more yourself.* I love you very much.

December 12, 1956

I wish you'd stop hitting yourself in the head with cries of not being brave or strong. What you have gone through has been terrific and is a severe test for anyone and you are passing it with more than flying colors. I know that you must be terribly impatient but one thing you must *not* be, and that is self-damning and then guilty. Certainly you are more than entitled to momentary slumps and depressions. I wish you would come home where friends who love you so very much could be with you and give what help they could give. . . . But most of all, and maybe selfishly, you would be where I could be with you and talk to you. Think all of this over and if it upsets you throw the page away or put it away and think about it later.

. . . I [went] over to Brooklyn the other night to confer with Oliver Smith about the new show.† He lives in Brooklyn Heights and has a marvellous old house with a circular winding staircase. Truman and Jack‡ live in the cellar and some strange people who edit films live in the garrett [*sic*]. The house is quite beautiful but has a faint air of refined poverty about it. . . . [W]hile I was there I saw the truly marvellous vista of downtown Manhattan all lit up and the bay with a half moon shining across it and the Statue of Liberty farther away and the dark silhouettes of tugs sneaking around in the night. . . .

I've been rehearsing our company. Mostly "Interplay" and "Fanfare." They seem in good shape and for the most part work very hard . . . all those new little corps de ballet girls' faces look pale, harried, and full of counts.§

I took some pictures of rehearsals and back stage while I was with my show and now my publicity agent tells me that "Life" is interested in them. This

---

* Initially, paralysis had affected all Le Clercq's muscle function, and with the exception of short postscripts she had been dictating letters to her mother, Edith, who had flown to Copenhagen to be with her. Edith also read her daughter's incoming correspondence.

† *West Side Story,* for which Smith was designing the scenery.

‡ Truman Capote and Jack Dunphy (1914–1992), a novelist, playwright, and former dancer who was Capote's off-and-on companion for thirty-five years.

§ Dancers move on counts, or numbered beats, in the music: the novices are trying hard to remember what to do when.

means I am spending more than two weeks in the darkroom printing them up as my nails turn browner and my eyes redder and I *know* that they won't be interested in them because I think they're rather dull myself. The ones that I like (portraits and other strange negatives) are exactly what they can't use because they don't feature "Judy Holliday in action." What a bore . . .

At Bobby [Fizdale]'s the other night we played eight-handed piano on two pianos. There were Fizdale, Gold, Barber[*] and Robbins and we were all a little drunk and "did" Gershwin, Berlin and Cole Porter. How Bobby and Arthur manage to keep their lease I don't know.

This is all for now. I miss you very very much and I love you very very much.

January 28, 1957

. . . The other night the Arthurs[†] and Bobby and I met at Chuck Turner's to hear the score for Frank's ballet.[‡] It's quite a lovely score with some very sweet lyric moments in it and I liked the serious way Chuck played it. I also like to watch people when they're working and concentrated on something, not being animated socially or trying to impress or talk to someone else. Suddenly you can "see" their faces. . . .

After hearing the score Chuck took us to a cocktail party on Gramercy Square.[§] It was in a lovely lovely old house, on the top floor, [and] given by two architects. The apartment was painted completely white with hardly any furniture at all. In one room there were two cane back sofas facing each other, a big ancient cupboard, and that was all, and in the other room there were two black canvas chairs and a low long cocktail table which had once been a carved door. . . . I thought it was quite wonderful and suddenly my place at home seemed like a real junk shop. . . . The cocktail party itself was very funny, all new faces: lots of architects, UN people, IBM people, a priest out of his habit or whatever it is. I grabbed a gin and tonic and just waded in. When the party

---

[*] Samuel Barber (1910–1981) was a notable American composer of piano, orchestral, choral, operatic, and other music.

[†] The designer Arthur Weinstein was romantically involved with Fizdale and was also close to Fizdale's professional partner, Arthur Gold.

[‡] Charles Turner (1921–2003), a violinist and composer, was a friend of Samuel Barber, Gian Carlo Menotti, and others. Lincoln Kirstein had commissioned him to compose a score for a ballet by the NYCB principal dancer Francisco Moncion, *Dark Pastorale*.

[§] Actually Gramercy Park.

broke up we went to have a Chinese dinner . . . and as we all separated and started home, I found myself accompanied by a man who said he didn't feel well. He walked uptown with me, feeling worse by the moment, and when he got in front of my house threw up. Naturally I couldn't leave him standing there so asked him in to clean up and get a glass of water etc. and I spent the whole night holding his head, feeding him aspirin, taking his temperature which went up to 102 and trying to ignore the grunts and sighs emanating from the guest room and his john. He really had me cornered as he lived way out in Jersey and I couldn't send him in that condition out into the night. The next day (whose dawn I saw come up) I told him I had an appointment, thinking this would get him going. He said "just run along, I'll be all right" so I ran along to the Philharmonic concert and when I came back he was gone. The house really was a mess. New faces indeed, give me the old ones.

The Concert was at the Philharmonic and I really went to hear Glenn

In the star dressing room at the Shubert during *Bells Are Ringing*'s New Haven tryout. From left, stage manager Ruth Mitchell, Judy Holliday (Ella), Betty Comden (kneeling, reflected in the mirror), photographer (and director and choreographer) Jerome Robbins, Sydney Chaplin (Jeff).

Gould, the young Canadian pianist, play the Beethoven Second Piano Concerto. I wanted to see what would happen when Lenny Bernstein, who dances up a storm on the podium, locked horns with a new protégée [sic] at the keyboard. From the very beginning it was the pianist's match and Leonard wisely retreated behind the piano to conduct the orchestra. The pianist marched out downstage, sat at the piano, crossed his legs, rested his chin on one hand and watched Lenny conduct the opening section. He let his arms dangle, then shook them as if they had been asleep, then took out a handkerchief and mopped his head, his hands, his mouth; then crossed his legs again, then sang and conducted with Lenny for a while, then stretched and shook his hands out again, dangling them from his shoulders, and began to play. He sang each note as he played it and when he had a hand free would make movements as if he were playing a violin with lots of bravado [sic]. All in all it was rather a lewd exhibition and I had a hard time making myself not watch so I could hear the music.

My landlady* . . . came to see the "All Robbins Night" last night as she had never seen any of my work. She was polite about it for a while and then offhandedly asked "and how long ago did you do 'The Cage'?" She followed this up by asking me the choreographical order of the [evening's] ballets. I told her "Age," "Cage," "Pied Piper," "Fanfare." She looked thoughtful for a while and then said "well at least they get happier."

January 31, 1957
. . . The Museum† I sent you the clippings about is absolutely ghastly. I have never seen a room make the people within it more uncomfortable or self-conscious. Everyone acts like men in New York act when they wear Bermuda shorts on the street in the summer. I backed away from walls that bulged out at me and instinctively lowered my head whenever the ceilings billowed down.

---

* Robbins lived in a garden duplex in a brownstone on East Seventy-Fifth Street owned by Muriel Resnik, who would later write the successful comedy *Any Wednesday* (1964).
† World House, a gallery (not an actual museum) designed by the surrealist Frederick Kiesler, chief of scenic design at the Juilliard School, on two floors of the Carlyle Hotel on Madison Avenue between Seventy-Sixth and Seventy-Seventh Streets, had continuous curvilinear surfaces instead of conventional walls, as well as "floating" cantilevered staircases. The gallery opened officially on January 23, 1957, with a loan exhibition *Struggle for a New Form*.

One of three contact sheets of photographs Robbins took of Tanaquil Le Clercq in her wheelchair on the sun roof of Lenox Hill Hospital in New York, March or April 1957.

There were lots of little pools and fountains dripping or sprinkling and the only effect it had on me was to make me want to go to the bathroom. The show itself was quite lovely, ranging from the Impressionists who seem so sweet and good-natured and life-loving compared to the contemporary non-subject painters who seem to hate everything, are terribly defiant and throw temper tantrums at their canvases. . . .

You get special special points for your music kiss and for your one-sided kiss.[*] Besides worrying about the word "fickle" would you please worry for a while about the following words because I'm too busy: ILK, FUNK METTLE, FETTLE, COUTH and GAMBIT. Let me know what you *think* about these words.

I love you very much.[†]

February 5, 1957

MAYA DEREN'S DOWNFALL[‡]

Sneered a lady well versed in voodoo
I bet I can better what you do
But she'd boasted too far
And found out her faux pas
When a nun made her shrink where quite few do.

---

[*] *X*s with musical notes at the ends, and half *X*s (<). Other letters from her concluded with "Roman" kisses (Roman numeral *X*s), "fer forgé kisses from New Orleans" (curlicued like wrought iron), croquet kisses (wickets, crossed mallets), German kisses (swastikas), and tropical ones (covered with flowers).

[†] His letter concludes with a page of kiss drawings: crossed exclamation points (surprised kisses), crossed question marks (questioning kisses), crossed cigarettes (filtered kisses), a trail of arrow-tipped *X*s ending with a circle (kisses leading to nothing), and so on.

[‡] Maya Deren (1917–1961) was an important experimental filmmaker and folklorist whose book on vodou ritual, *Divine Horsemen: The Living Gods of Haiti,* had been published in 1953. Through ironic symmetry, her third husband, the Japanese composer Teiji Ito, who completed Deren's unfinished film of the book, would be the composer of the score for Robbins's 1972 ritual ballet *Watermill.* Both these limericks are illustrated with comic line drawings.

THE PONDERING

Mused a lady returning from tea
Is the matter I wonder just me?
Not a soul said a word
When they served the fried turd
And I know what I drank was hot pee.

February 6, 1957

. . . I'm starting lessons with an acting studio this week.* I don't have any ambitions at all to become an actor but I do want to learn more about their problems and how they work because Lord knows it's certainly different from dancers. . . .

Sunday I gave a brunch which went very well. First I fed everyone Bloody Marys and while they were getting drunk I slaved away in the kitchen over a hot stove trying to make eggs, bacon, toasted rolls and coffee all come out at the same time. They did, along with three dozen dirty plates. While everyone was eating I was serving. After that a hot game of Parchesi [*sic*] started with what guests remained and being the perfect host and the extra person I just absented myself back to the kitchen and did the dishes. Two hours later as I emerged and they were just finishing, it seemed that tea was in order. So I made tea and served it with cookies and cake while they finished discussing the various plays of the Parchesi game. Then they left and it was 5 p.m. Dear Abby,† do you think I should continue with these brunches? I know it does make people happy to be here but does it really make me happy? I would appreciate hearing from you about this. Signed Dishpan Hands.

I'm glad you like my poem. Dear Abby, I think I have poetic talent but everyone laughs at me. Things just come out of me. I don't seem to have any control. Sometimes I even think of French words. What do you advise? Signed Edna St. Vincent Schwartz.

. . . What happened to all those kisses you were sending me and why

---

* Robbins had enrolled in Stella Adler's legendary script analysis class, whose alumni included Marlon Brando, Karl Malden, Eva Marie Saint, and Elaine Stritch. In the late 1940s he had also been a member of The Actors Studio.

† "Dear Abby" was the name of a syndicated advice column by the pseudonymous Abigail Van Buren that began running in numerous newspapers in 1956.

did you stop and why suddenly "platonically yours"? Signed Perplexed. . . .
[I]s it just that you're getting so much better that you occasionally Put me in
my Place? . . . I laughed and laughed at the way you started your paragraph so
gently and knowingly and how you manage[d] to work yourself into a real state
by the time you were finished. I love you so for just that quality which really is
very honest and always makes me blink and laugh at its directness and acuteness.
I just looked out of the window and a funny short lady is marching belligerently
down the street. She is wearing bright red shoes a dark green coat and a dark
green and gold hat turban like something out of an Italian painting of the 3 Wise
Men. Well this is all for now.

I miss you and love you and will write you more poems as soon as I get the
right sujet. Love and more love.

February 13, 1957

The weekend was really hectic, Larry Osgood* from Boston visited me and I
took him on a round of theatre and parties that I usually never indulge in. Friday
night we went to see "Clearing in the Woods" (my third time around). The narcissism was more apparent this time [but] what really was more exciting about
the evening was the obvious feud going on between Onslow Stevens, the male
lead, and everyone else in the cast: exits were jumped, lines covered [and] things
reached such a crise that night that offstage one actress kicked Stevens who hit
her back. . . . I thought the whole thing terribly unprofessional. . . .

Saturday had a few of Larry's friends over for a drink. Creepy. The most fascinating was Ted Gorey† who wrote "Listing Attic" and "The Unstrung Harp."
At first all you can see of him is his beard and mustache, then you start to see
his eyes and teeth and some of his expressions; then you notice all the rings he
wears and finally the fact that although he wears a rather elegant fur-lined coat
his feet are shod in worn out sneakers. As an added fillip you perceive that the
skin between his socks and the cuffs of his pants is very white and crowded with
black and blue marks. Dear Abby what do you think? . . . After that we went to

---

* Larry Osgood is a poet, novelist, and playwright who was a Harvard contemporary of Frank
O'Hara's.
† Edward Gorey (1925–2000), author and artist, was the creator of numerous enigmatic and
unsettling books illustrated with quasi-Victorian drawings and the designer of book covers for the
Doubleday Anchor series of literary paperbacks.

a party at Leo Lerman's* for Nora Kaye. His house makes mine feel like a bare modern one almost austere in comparison.

Sunday evening to the Ballet Theater. What a truly dismal evening . . . The company could be marvelous but there's no one to tell anyone what to do or how to act on stage and what to work for. . . . The star of the evening, for my money, was one little corps de ballet boy in "Graduation Ball" who believed in everything he did and seemed to be enjoying himself for dance's sake. . . .

February 14 [postmark], 1957

THE UNCONSCIOUS DISARMING BOMB

There's a lady whose looks are so vile
She can shatter thick glass with her smile,
While still more alarming,
When she thinks she's charming
The fallout is felt for a mile.

EPILOGUE

I think that I spend too much time
In searching for words that will rhyme.
I find it quite rough
On the brain. It's so tough
That I'm giving up and going

to bed

[signed with a heart pierced with an arrow] J

February 20, 1957
You're right, something has happened but I don't know what the hell it is or where it began or quite how to get out of it all. It's a little like our relationship

* Leo Lerman (1914–1994), writer and editor, lived with his partner Gray Foy in an East Side town house crammed with antiques and bibelots. When they later relocated to the Osborne, an apartment house on West Fifty-Seventh, it took three days for the moving vans to transport their belongings.

generally: all of a sudden in some area an irritation begins, never spoken about but only felt by both of us and then we get a little mean and tease each other. . . . Well anyway I do love you and am so concerned over you as I have always been and always will be and I miss you terribly terribly and still wish I could be there or you here [here Robbins penciled in six *X*'s in circles, his symbol for a hug and a kiss, in a row, with the words, "for real"]. . . .

Stella Adler's acting classes are both crazy and wonderful. She makes what hair I have stand on end. We don't pretend and do things. It's more class in script analyzation [*sic*] and the actor attempting to find all the possible things he can do with a role in a show. Stella has great immediate intuition and insight into what everyone is like and what they're feeling so sometimes the class becomes a terrible exposure. . . .

Yesterday afternoon I went to the Dance Magazine Awards cocktail party. Agnes [de Mille] and Martha Graham were both given awards, Agnes for her Omnibus shows* and Martha for her world tour. The whole thing was a camp, filled mostly with the lousy kind of balletomanes, a spattering of modern dancers, and about three ballet dancers, the three being Diana, Mary Ellen† and myself. Diana wore a dress which turned out to be the same color and pattern as the carpet we were standing on which was both puzzling and dizzy-making. I sat in the back [and] the long table they were all seated behind made it look like the Last Supper and there seemed to be an unconscious competition between Agnes and Martha over who looked the holiest. Martha won hands down of course with that bony white face and black velvet dress. Agnes only looked like she had been drinking for three days and was trying to look saintly. But for a while it was nip and tuck as to which one was going to rise to heaven first.

Last night I went to Carnegie Hall to hear Verdi's "Requiem." I found myself in a box with five old Jewish ladies who kept fussing with their hats, glasses, jewelry, fur stoles, and girdles. . . . [W]hen someone hit a good high note they would turn toward each other and nod approvingly. Something very strange happened though. Attached to the front chair in the box was a very

---

* *Omnibus* was a live ninety-minute CBS television program devoted to arts, literature, history, and entertainment, which was hosted by Alistair Cooke and ran from 1952 to 1961. It featured such figures as Benny Goodman, Orson Welles, and James Agee; Agnes de Mille did two specials for it titled "The Art of Ballet" and "The Art of Choreography."
† Diana Adams and Mary Ellen Moylan, who had been one of Balanchine's ballerinas since the 1940s.

thin nylon black thread which disappeared up above the box . . . into a box above that tier. I tugged at it a couple of times and after a few minutes there was an answering tug back. Later when all the Jewish ladies came in and sat down, a particularly myopic lady sat in that chair and got her hat in the thread. She didn't seem to see it but instead kept fixing her glasses and her veil. Finally at one of the most quiet and lyrical moments of the music she discovered it and the rest of the "Requiem" was filled with a long and elaborate pantomime in which each lady showed the next lady the string, pointed upward, made gestures of tugging it, looking at it, shrugging and nudging. It really was

Tanaquil Le Clercq at Lenox Hill. "I love you very much," Robbins wrote to her, "and nothing can change that."

hilarious and somewhat like a crazy ballet although I must say it didn't help Verdi at all. . . .

I didn't send you a Valentine or ask you to be mine because you ARE and let's not have any back talk on that one. . . .

Love, love, love—[followed by an ascending line of circled X's, captioned "kisses gaining altitude before taking off"]

February 25, 1957

. . . Hurray. That's a cheer not so loud that it frightens you but loud enough to express my joy that you're coming home. I do think you can be helped better in America. And there's nothing I would like better than taking you for walks in the park, speaking to you on the telephone, having you cut me up with your remarks when I visit you, planning surprises for you and knowing you are just around the corner at Lenox Hill.* . . . What fun it will be to be with you and I already

---

* Lenox Hill Hospital was between Seventy-Sixth and Seventy-Seventh Streets on Lexington Avenue, a block and a half from Robbins's apartment on Seventy-Fifth.

have visions of our going to the park together. I'll have my camera and you'll keep telling me what a terrible thing I'm photographing. Or we could go down and watch the little boys sail their little boats right near 72 street, or I could take you to the Metropolitan Museum which I've been slowly examining and find just marvelous. I could show you all the card tricks I've learned (3), ask you to translate the French I don't understand, have you read technical books on photography on things I'm not up on, bring my plants over to you for advice. . . .

[On Saturday] night I went up to the Puerto Rican Harlem section to watch a dance given at a school.* It was absolutely like going into a foreign country. I got into a long conversation with a 19 year old Puerto Rican boy who used to be a member of one of the most notorious gangs in the section. Great background material for my show. The dancers themselves were from age 13 to 19. They do dances that I've never seen before anywhere, evolving their own style and approach. In one dance, after starting with your partner for about 2 bars, you leave and separate and never touch or make any contact again for the rest of the whole dance. When you look at the floor each person seems to be having a ball of their own but I'm told that the partners know damn well who they're dancing with. All the boys wore their overcoats and this is because if a fight breaks out they're well padded. There's a huge sign that says NO GRINDING. This refers to slow pelvic movements pushed against each other. . . . [S]ome day I'll take you up there if you'd like to see it. . . .

I do think of the beach, and often.† I think of the porch with the white paint that came off and the dunes and the night. I can relive it all very easily. . . .

Last night when I got in bed and closed my eyes I began thinking about the old apartment on 55 Street. Do you know what happened? I was able to walk into the apartment and slowly turn and *see* everything and recognize things I'd forgotten. I could tell where each picture was on the wall, what was on each table, where the rug was frayed, what books were on each shelf and a thousand details which go to make the thing real. In actuality it's no longer in existence and is really in the past but just by closing my eyes and thinking about it a little I can make it as real as if I'm still there. How strange.

---

* Robbins's trip to Harlem was field research for *West Side Story*.
† In a letter postmarked February 20, Le Clercq had written, "I like to close my eyes and think of the beach—and you go with it—XXXXXX T."

March 1, 1957

I'm so very happy that you are coming back. I'll see you much more often than I write you. You may even get to dread my visits. Please let's not get into any tizzy and state about seeing the other one. I love you very much and nothing can change that except a great big character change on your part which can't possibly happen, because if you're only one-half as wonderful as I think you are I wouldn't feel any different. If necessary I'll call you an hour before I'm coming to see you and we can both get good and plastered. Thus we can get over our first day's nerves.

March 1

LATER

Oh, oh, oh, so many complaints. I felt like you went through my whole letter and took everything apart. You don't like the word relationship.* . . . Well, I

---

* "I love you, I really do—no matter what," she wrote, in an undated, unpostmarked letter, "but I think our 'relationship' (your word, not mine) stinks."

The gang fight, or rumble, in *West Side Story,* which Robbins photographed from a catwalk above the stage, 1957.

Chita Rivera (Anita) and the other Shark girls singing "America" in *West Side Story,* photographed by Robbins from the wings, 1957.

love you, I really do—no matter what. RELATIONSHIP—kinship; affinity; a state of affairs existing between people a connection by way of relation. That's Webster's definition. I feel much more about it than that. Love, experiences in common special experiences which maybe we don't even understand, times of pleasure in being together, times of antipathy at rehearsals, times of looking at each other and understanding, and so much more that can't be put into words. You and I understand. [O]ur "relationship" has had its ups and downs. But basically I feel there has been a steady love at the root.

. . . Please write me. Please write me nice letters. I do love you so very much and I miss you terribly and can't wait till we meet again.*

---

* Edith Le Clercq and Balanchine kept the details of Tanaquil's return to New York secret so Robbins was unable to meet her at the airport as he had hoped, but they did get to spend time together at Lenox Hill Hospital—including an afternoon when he photographed her, in her wheelchair, taking the air on the hospital terrace—before she was sent to the Warm Springs Institute for Rehabilitation in Georgia.

To: Robert Fizdale
November 15, 1957

Dear Bobby,

I'm at Trunk Bay, St. John, Virgin Islands.[*] The place I'm staying is as remote from civilization as you can be. Two planes, a boat trip, and a half-hour by jeep over bulldozed trails thru the virgin jungles and thru mud (it's the rainy season in the hills) and you get to this paradise. The house is on a slight bluff overlooking the most beautiful cove beach you've ever seen. The whitest finest sand, turquoise water, coconut palms, etc. There is no electricity, or telephone, and even the wireless they used to have is out of commission. The food is native grown or caught and marvelously prepared. But the best part is that the house (which at its most can accommodate ten) has no one in it but me! . . . You sleep under netting (very glamorous if one were to see you) get to bed by ten at the latest and up at eight or nine. I'm reading like a fiend, thinking like a fiend, and haven't yet found any of it lonely. This scares me, too. I think of friends, lovers, would be and has beens, find myself a year from forty and wonder still what the hell it's all about. This would be the perfect place to spend [time] with someone, I know. What happened with Lee?[†] Turned out, *she* had the problems, not me, and so furiously did they emerge I never had the chance to act up and twist about myself. It is a shame because I really dug her in a big way and felt that perhaps everything was going to fall into place AND HIGH TIME. At any rate she took to spinning like a top, till I grabbed at her and shook her and tried to get to her. Impossible at this point. She doesn't feel good enough for me!? she says. How about that. Isn't that the switch of all time. Maybe when I get back she'll have calmed down a bit. I think of her here. Also, unfortunately, of Buzz. He was down here with me twice,[‡] but that isn't why. I guess I come back to

---

[*] After *West Side Story*'s triumphant opening on September 26—"The radioactive fallout from 'West Side Story' must still be descending on Broadway this morning," said the *Tribune*'s Walter Kerr—Robbins departed for his customary vacation in the Caribbean, after first making a trip to Warm Springs to take Tanaquil Le Clercq out for a picnic.

[†] Lee Becker, who played the tomboy waif Anybodys in *West Side Story,* had become involved with Robbins during the out-of-town run of that show and had told friends that they were engaged.

[‡] Seemingly Robbins is referring to his memories of previous stays with Miller in St. John, not to this one.

him in thoughts whenever I'm strung up and alone. I know he does the same thing. Isn't it crazy. When I see him, I always see why it couldn't work, but when I haven't seen him in a long time I build up the whole picture again of the good times, and forget the evil ones. Que faire?

I started the ballet with N.Y.C.C.* It was hard getting going. The change of atmosphere and response of the dancers was tough. I did two rehearsals and found that I was so tired that I was settling for really poor stuff just to keep going and get the damn thing on. Then I did what I have never done before but felt it was time to be able to indulge myself. I said I didn't want to go thru all that shtuss to make another little work. So I hied myself off here where I'm resting like a fiend (I said that didn't I), getting very dark and contemplating my navel. Tell Arthur G to stop laughing.

. . . I'm writing this up on the terrace of the house above the beach. Pelicans

* NYCC is City Center, that is, New York City Ballet. The ballet in question was to Stravinsky's *Concertino,* a chamber work he finally did make a ballet to in 1982.

Robbins and Tanaquil Le Clercq picnicking at Warm Springs, Georgia—a reprieve from what she described as the "limbo" of her rehabilitation hospital. (Robbins used an auto-timer to shoot the photograph.)

are sailing by and occasionally diving after fish down below. Far out the damn Caribbean spreads like Cinemascope across the entire horizon and a parade of huge assorted clouds travels by. Rain squalls can be seen pouring teapots down on one little area and native boats toss their way to Tortolla, a British island a few miles away. Yesterday we had turtle! Turtle! Did you ever eat it, it's delicious, like wonderful turkey. We also had fish chowder, etc. You'd be very proud the way I eat the potcheese and avocado. There was even brown sugar and I pensed à toi.

Tanaquil Le Clercq in the convertible Robbins rented to take her out in Georgia, October 1957. "I will think about the two days in the sun when I go to sleep so I can dream them," she wrote to him afterward.

I'm glad the tour[*] is successful. No matter how good [it] is you *must* be back by the twenty-fourth. I don't trust the twenty-fifth and Xmas won't be Xmas if you aren't here. And that's that and let's have no words about it. Today I got a card from a creep named Arthur Todd[†] who said that Tanny was coming to N.Y the 25th of November.[‡] I heard from her a few days ago and she didn't say anything about it. I may get a letter in a day or so. We'll have her for sure for Xmas, don't worry.

I'm reading Dinesen's Last Tales. Also the plays of Plautus. I bet I'm one up on you with that last one. Arthur Laurents wrote a nasty petulant article for the

---

[*] Gold and Fizdale were performing in Europe.
[†] Arthur Todd (d. 1978) was a dance critic and photographer with a wide net of acquaintances in the dance world, from Frederick Ashton to Mary Wigman.
[‡] According to Le Clercq, when a social worker had told the visiting Balanchine that she might be able to come home in September, he had said, "No, *much* too soon . . . Please tell them to keep my wife as long as possible." Wrote Le Clercq to Robbins, "It was very funny. HA."

Times[*] that really burned me. I didn't want to make a public fuss in papers so let it go and now I'm sorry although I know I did right. Oh well. C'est la lousey [*sic*] vie.

Ill close now; I feel like I've been rattling on here like crazy. Forgive the mistakes. Ima [*sic*] terrible typist, speller, and this little Olivetti[†] jumps like Ive goosed it every time I touch a letter.

Keep well, have fun, work hard and take care of yourself. I do miss you very much, and I hearby [*sic*] ask you for a *date,* just you and me when I get back and we'll talk way into the night.

My love to you
And my love to A,
J

To: Leonard Bernstein
13 February 1958

154 EAST 74TH STREET, NEW YORK, NY

Dear Lenny,

. . . Enclosed are two interviews[‡] which struck me with as much force and excitement as anything I've read in many, many years. The potential of using this first interview as a basis of an examination of the Beat Generation and their search, pain, drives, ecstasies, depressions and astonished puzzlement could make

---

[*] "Musical Adventure," by Arthur Laurents, *New York Times,* November 3, 1957, dealt with the travails of the playwright in musical theater. While conceding that musicals are "essentially a collaborative medium" and in the case of *West Side Story* "an exciting, stimulating one," Laurents complained about "the emphasis placed on polishing a pirouette rather than a scene"—a comment certain to get under Robbins's thin skin.

[†] Olivetti typewriters were the last word in elegant design; they had been the subject of an exhibit at the Museum of Modern Art in 1952. Robbins seems to have taken an Olivetti Lettera (the ultra-portable, ultra-lightweight model) with him to St. John.

[‡] One of these clippings seems to have been an interview by Mike Wallace with Jack Kerouac, published in the *New York Post* on January 21, 1958; the other is unidentified but was possibly with another of the Beat writers.

a wonderful theatre piece. My instinct is to use a protagonist who would answer the questions, but open up all the "meanings" and possibilities of those answers. I'm sure you'll see the immediate places such as "visions," "motorcycle rides," "jazz," "dope," "Paradise," "Heaven," "tremendous," "empty phantoms" and most of all the very very painful last line. I can visualize a lot of these things being episodic experiences which well up and take over the protagonist and leave him with everything inside him and a cool, knowing exterior. In a way these are our W[est] S[ide] S[tory] kids a little older. Do you know any of these Beat people? They're scary, and what's most frightening is that it isn't an act or an adopted attitude and façade to deal with life, but a real living thing.

I'd appreciate hearing from you on this as soon as possible. Drop me a note and give me at least your immediate reaction, and if you are interested, when do you think you will be able to have a talk on it.*

All the best,
Jerry

Robbins's "Beat generation" ballet, *N.Y. Export: Opus Jazz,* which premiered at the 1958 Spoleto Festival. Despite the jivey music and hipster costumes, Lincoln Kirstein called it "classic."

---

* Bernstein seems not to have picked up this cue. At the time Robbins was in the process of forming his company Ballets: U.S.A. (see p. 214), and some of these ideas found their way into the work he made for them, *N.Y. Export: Opus Jazz;* the score was written by the young composer Robert Prince (1929–2007).

To: Leland Hayward
May 25, 1958

Dear Leland,

Off today to what you call Spalate.* Looks like hell out, but things have to get better.† I'm writing this mainly to tell you how excited I was by Steve Sondheim's songs for the Roman Comedy.‡ I was truly impressed and got a big boot

---

* Robbins had accepted an invitation from the Italian composer Gian Carlo Menotti to participate, with a small company of handpicked dancers, Ballets: U.S.A., in a three-week summer arts festival in the Umbrian hill town of Spoleto.

† In the event, bad weather forced the cancellation of the company's charter flight to Rome; they took a train to Philadelphia and boarded a hastily arranged charter there.

‡ Stephen Sondheim, Burt Shevelove, and Larry Gelbart had been developing, with Robbins's encouragement, a musical based on the comedies of the second century B.C. Latin playwright Titus Maccius Plautus—which four years later would become *A Funny Thing Happened on the Way to the Forum*. Robbins hoped eventually to direct and wanted Hayward to produce it.

N.Y. Export: Opus Jazz photographed from the wings.

An orchestra rehearsal for *Gypsy* during the April 1959 Philadelphia tryout, with (from left) music director Milton Rosenstock, Jack Klugman (Herbie), Sandra Church (Louise), and a skeptical Ethel Merman (Mama Rose).

out of it. Listen to them as soon as you can and have Steve explain the ideas I have. Maybe he would be a good idea for "Gypsy,"* but first listen to them yourself and see what you think.

I miss you and your wife already. . . .

Love—

Jer or Gyps!

---

* Robbins had been signed to direct the musical adaptation of the stripper Gypsy Rose Lee's memoirs even before *West Side Story* opened; originally the book and lyrics were to have been written by Betty Comden and Adolph Green, and the music by Jule Styne, but all had developed other commitments. Robbins had brought in Arthur Laurents to write the book, but the show—to be co-produced by Hayward and David Merrick—needed someone to compose the score, and Robbins had suggested Sondheim.

To: Leland Hayward
June 4, 1958

SPOLETO

Dear Leland:

It took a few days to straighten out your letter. I couldn't tell (and still can't) what you are for or against.

1. How do *you* like Steve's songs?
2. Steve will do *anything* to do Gypsy but in spite of all his desire he *has* a contract on Jet* and a real moral commitment on "Roman Comedy" (as *we* do too).
3. I'm tired of Merrick trying to push "Roman" out of the way. Tell him to knock off.
4. Steve cannot do 2 shows at once. Who can?
5. It looks like you and I must decide which show comes first—and not let it so much to chance. Roman looks further along doesn't it? . . .

Steve is ambitious, hardworking, but a little greedy and scared too. No matter how practical he sounds don't let him mislead you into thinking he can finish both shows. One will take, and should take, *all* his concentration. . . . [D]on't let Arthur with his dogmatic pronunciations railroad you into or out of any decisions or personal beliefs. He's very good at doing that. With Arthur you'll find someone is either perfect or dead, and not much tolerated in between.†

---

* *The Jet-Propelled Couch* was a proposed musical about a psychiatrist based on *The Fifty-Minute Hour,* by Robert Mitchell Lindner. It was never produced, although Sondheim wrote a handful of songs for it.

† In the end, the Roman project wasn't ready, and *Gypsy* was, but Ethel Merman (*Gypsy*'s star) balked at singing a novice composer's songs; Jule Styne was persuaded to rejoin the team, and Sondheim was engaged to write lyrics only.

Slim Hayward (later Keith) in Spoleto, June 1959, after the breakup of her marriage to Leland Hayward. "I love you darling dearest Gyps," she had written to Robbins then, and he responded, "Move over, Lady Brett. Why don't you come and be with me?"

June 10
Leland—

First chance I've gotten to write since I started the other page. The last few days got really hectic & tiring. The ballets opened and were a smash such as I've never had. I feel I could put Italy in my pocket.

Now we are being deluged with offers. Hurok, Columbia concerts both want to try to tour us in Russia. Hurok offers us 2 weeks Jan 12th, Bway & tour U.S. in fall 59. That's too long to hold a company together. I'd like *you* to do it in N.Y. but you ought to be aware of problems. 1. The sets by Shahn and

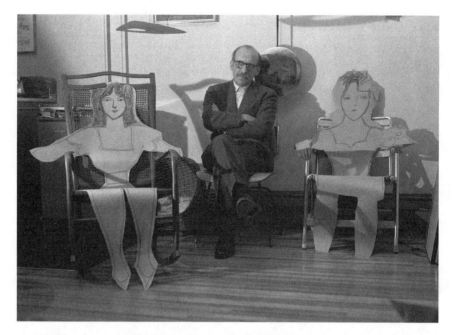

Saul Steinberg, who had designed scenery for Ballets: U.S.A.'s production of *The Concert*, at home in New York with two of his creations, 1958.

Steinberg[*] are a *must*. Which means you must pay a double union fee to someone. 2. Orchestra for whole program now about *60*. It can be cut down some but not to 24 or 30 and still do all 4 ballets unless someone is willing to take expense of re-orchestrating and recopying parts—and only with musicians and my approval. 3. I will not consider any TV offer unless it guarantees as much rehearsal & more importantly CAMERA *rehearsals* as "Peter Pan"—"Cinderella" etc.[†] Dance on TV needs more time than anything else. OK? OK.

. . . Life here is the best ever. Honestly—wasn't kidding that I'd rather make this my headquarters than be in N.Y. Here everything is in good balance between what you give out with & what you absorb.

[*] Ben Shahn (1898–1969), a Lithuanian American artist whose work encompassed both social realism and artistic expressionism, had designed the scenery for *N.Y. Export: Opus Jazz;* Saul Steinberg (1914–1999), a Romanian American cartoonist and illustrator, had designed the drop curtain for the Ballets: U.S.A. production of *The Concert*.

[†] Ironically, Ballets: U.S.A. would make its television appearance (several of them, in fact) on *The Ed Sullivan Show*.

Did I tell you I'm living in a villa on a hill high over the whole Assisi valley & that dawn comes up at 3:30 so beautifully that I haven't been to bed early once!! Please wire reply pronto.

All love

J

To: Robert Fizdale
September 25, 1958

Dearest Bobby,

I just don't seem to be able to write these days at all and I'm not going into why, because I don't know why. Thank you so much for your letter—the big long one you sent. Oh everything seems so hard—when I read it and I go back and think how it must have been with you all and how it has been in my own life.* Isn't it fantastic the meshes and thicknesses of the crisscrossing of defenses, sensitivities and reactions, retractions, nuances and cadences that separate us and prevent us from exposing our real feelings and accepting someone else's directly. I guess no one likes to get hurt, it's that simple but oh so many times it would be so good if you would just say, tell me how you feel, tell me do you love me, tell me do you hate me. The cocoons, that we don't know we live in, get doubly thick afterward when any wound appears, because of guilt and that's the worst part. Wrong, all wrong to feel the guilt, and how we blame ourselves and say, but if and if, or maybe if I had or someone else had etc etc. You know what I mean. One can't go back to a plane trip anymore than a telephone call, a meal. Accumulation of those little threads and layers of hurts and dissensions are unravelable [*sic*]. Oi vey, oi vey, it's too much, and why I ever feel I want to get back into it again I don't know. You're dead with it, you're dead without it huh, so what's to do? I'll come back to all of this later.

---

* While Robbins was in Europe with Ballets: U.S.A., Fizdale had suffered a painful breakup with Arthur Weinstein (a designer, not his performing partner, Arthur Gold), and Robbins had written a long and awkwardly affectionate letter asking him if it would help if they renewed their own long-ago relationship; apparently, Fizdale—just as awkwardly and affectionately—demurred.

About "Ballets: U.S.A." It's been a terrific success, particularly the jazz piece and the "Concert." ... 3 x 3* I can't tell about at all. I loved it during rehearsal—it seemed clean, fresh and inventive but as soon as it got into harlequinade costumes the whole thing took on a completely other color and I hate it now, and the critics are correct when they call it cute and coy. I've had this happen to a number of ballets, one was "Ballade" and the other one was "Quartet." It seemed to be one thing in rehearsal and then when it got into costume the effect of it was changed. ... "Faun" they dance beautifully. Of course no one will ever make it like it was made originally† so I really don't watch it myself. I talked to our girl Tanny today. It's her birthday October 2 and she's decided to cook for me or have someone cook for me and we'll have a joint party. I wish you were here for it.

---

* *3 x 3* was a short ballet to a woodwind trio by Georges Auric: the musicians sat onstage, in tailcoats, on high stepladders, and the set consisted of balloons.
† When Tanaquil Le Clercq danced it.

Dancers from Ballets: U.S.A. relaxing in a café during their 1959 European tour. "Life here is the best ever," Robbins said.

I had dinner at Saul Steinberg's the other night. Wow what a brilliant mind that man has. I thought of him as somewhat of a negative shlep [*sic*] but he makes George Balanchine, Robert Oppenheimer[*] and Ben Shahn dwarfs. He is just fantastic and I have never been so stimulated in all my life in anyone's company. Along with this fantastic intelligence is naturally his humor and Jewish warmth. It happened to be Yom Kippur so we all had a ball. . . .

My life. Strange. Uneventful and eventful. Sudden gusts of experiences that look like they may lead to something and then the eddying [*sic*] out, showing me they led nowhere. I'm not unhappy though and everyone seems to think I'm in very good shape, but you know what, I could easily slip into being an alcoholic. I have discovered that Vodka slips down me without any effects. Dear Doctor, what should I do? Don't drink. But seriously something's been happening inside of me but I don't stop to try to poke around at it. I just know that, first of all, New York doesn't have for me what it used to have, I know that the streets, the sights, the smells and people don't hook me the way they used to hook me, and I find myself looking at it the way I used to look at Pittsburgh when I was touring. Secondly I have just decided to enjoy what happens as it happens, to enjoy each day for what is in it. God here comes Aimee Semple McPherson.[†] . . .

[L]ast night at a party that Oliver gave for Nora Kaye, I came late and walked into it and suddenly felt like I was frozen in a Hirschfeld cartoon, and if I looked down and matched numbers I could tell who everybody was. You know, Dietrich, Lena Horne, Ruth Ford—oh on and on, but ever so often there were very crazy exaggerated faces that you didn't know and you wanted to refer to the listing to see who they belonged to.

I gotta stop now, I just can't go on.

Please give my love to Arthur and all my love to you. You know how I miss you. Please write. Much affection, much heart.

Love—

J.

---

[*] J. Robert Oppenheimer (1904–1967), a theoretical physicist, was the technical director of the Manhattan Project, which developed the atomic bomb.
[†] Aimee Semple McPherson (1890–1944) was a celebrity Pentecostal preacher and radio evangelist whose philosophy of optimism won her an enormous following in the 1920s and 30s.

To: Robert Fizdale
Undated [October 3, 1958]

Dearest Bobby,

. . . It's late at night . . . [JR's ellipses] and this may be another late telephone call. I loved your letter. And I want so that you come live here if you want
to. . . . This little snuggly guest room has been waiting for someone and it's so
right that it's you. . . . You'd be so nice to come home to, and you can have as
much company as you like. It would make a great big difference in my life if you
would, and I think I could be helpful to you.

Last night I went over to Tanny's for her birthday. It's the first time I've
seen her in a long long time.* There were others there and so she was her usual
spiteful nasty self to me. It seemed more than ever. I can't tell if she has turned
on me because I didn't see her in so long a time or whether it was just drink
and stimulation that brings out the worst in her over me. Diana† was there, and
Nickie, Natasha, Edith‡ and George. I couldn't get with it very much but then
she didn't let me. George talks a huge huge streak these days, more than ever,
and Tanny is hooked on cooking. She tells with wonderful details the ups and
downs of making a Bavarian cream etc. She looks wonderful, her hair is short
and bobbed and poofed, her breasts seem very large now, and George says that
she is starting to have a few very slight but evident minute abilities to feel or
tense tiny muscles she didn't before.

I finally figured out why its been so hard for me to write you till now. It's
because I couldn't even start to feel the tiniest identification without it opening
up all the things I felt around Buzz's behavior again, and my realization that
there really wasn't anything that I could say to help outside of the complete
capitulation of my heart to yours. Do you understand. I'd always been able to
say something to people who had a death in their family until *my* mother died

---

* Robbins had been absent in Europe from May to September with Ballets: U.S.A.
† Diana Adams, now divorced from Hugh Laing, had become Balanchine's current muse, and likely
more.
‡ Nicholas Magallanes; Natasha Molostwoff, general administrator at the School of American Ballet
and a friend of Le Clercq's; and Edith Le Clercq, who had been so insistent that Robbins not fly to
visit her daughter in the hospital in Copenhagen.

and then I realized that no one could say anything, anything at all, and all that did get to me was certain peoples affection. The only similarity is in the area of loss. Believe me I know what goes on within you. Only one thing you must accept no matter what happens and it is this: you will *always* feel something around A.W. and be thankful because it is the measure of the love you gave to him and got back and no matter what happens, *that* won't change. Don't expect it to ever fade away and don't expect not to feel anything. Even when you understand it all some time, and even when your affections are based elsewhere, you won't erase the time when you were together or what it meant. How can one ever forget family? The rise that the mention of Buzz's name gets out of me no longer startles me. I loved him. I was deeply hurt by his rejection of me (even though I had had it) but even this knowledge doesn't ease the movement within when I see him or talk of him. It's unfinished business that unfortunately plays right into all the neurotic sense of rejection I felt by Momma and Poppa and

September 1958. "What do you know," mused Robbins to Robert Fizdale, "I have my own company with just four ballets."

there it is. I'm glad I feel something about him still, otherwise I would feel those years were really wasted. I know they weren't.

. . . I'm going tomorrow to see the last night of Ballet Theater. I'll write all. I saw only one performance so far. You would not believe how dreadful it was. They had new costumes for Theme and Variations[*] and George said [they] made every girl look like the Queen of England. He clutched one hand around his throat imitating a choker, and spewed [sic] another up from his forehead like a tiara and made a dowager face. Can't you see it.

Must hang up. Goodbye. Hang up! Count three and then we'll hang up, OK?

one

two

three!

To: Bernard Perlin[†]
Undated [1959/1961?]

Dear Bernard,

I've been thinking about some of the questions you asked me and thought maybe I could make them a little clearer. Regarding the kind of movement that is in my jazz ballet[‡] (and I guess for that matter that's in *Fancy Free* and all my ballets), the basic technique that I depend on and insist upon from all dancers is a ballet technique. I don't think that jazz dancers could do it without ballet training (I occasionally use completely balletic movements), nor do I think that dancers trained strictly and preventively in only ballet technique could do it

---

[*] Balanchine had choreographed *Theme and Variations* (to Tchaikovsky) for Ballet Theatre in 1947, before the founding of New York City Ballet, and it remained in their repertory.
[†] Bernard Perlin (1918–2014) was a genre-defying American artist who shared many connections with Robbins: George Platt Lynes, Lincoln Kirstein, Leonard Bernstein, and others. Although this letter (which exists on a dictation tape, not in paper form) has been tentatively dated 1961 by the Robbins estate, it refers to events of 1959 in immediate terms, which may place it a few years earlier.
[‡] *N.Y. Export: Opus Jazz.*

(as I use references and movement derived from contemporary dancing as well as influence of the freedom of the body as used in the modern dance). I don't consider it "personal" in the sense that I criticize a lot of the jazz dancers of their classes and technique as being a representation of the only way that they can move.

As to having to show the movements, this is not an individual thing. Every choreographer has to do this even if he's working in a strictly classic ballet because unless there is invention within it—and the invention must come out of the choreographer—it is lifeless and dull. Balanchine always showed me what he wanted when he choreographed for me *Tyl Ulenspiegel* or *Bourrée Fantasque* or when he revived *Prodigal Son* for me. Even Fokine had to show movements. Every choreographer *has* to do this, and although the movements may be closer or further from the strictly classic ballet technique, the vocabulary of the strictly classic ballet technique can be used as a frame of reference which I think you found even at my audition. When Balanchine showed Maria Tallchief the role of Swan Queen in his version of *Swan Lake,* Maria said, "If only I could do the port de bras and dance it the way that you do."

I think that all choreography has to be shown to a dancer and the dancer eventually picks up the "style" that the choreographer is aiming at. Of course, unconsciously, every dancer picks up a lot of personal stylistic approaches of the choreographer. A Graham dancer will use her hands and head in a certain way. The same with a Tudor dancer, a Balanchine dancer, a de Mille dancer, and I suppose even a Robbins dancer. I'm the least aware and worst person to understand or realize what if any influence my dancing has had here in America. . . . I don't think I have a school of dance as much as an approach to theater and the presence on stage and what it is I want to evoke on the stage and in the audience. I know a lot of people feel I am a jack-of-all-trades what with my success on Broadway, in ballet, in television, and (I hope) in movies. But George ran the whole gamut also and at one point was the reigning choreographer of Broadway, knocked off a couple of films—one of which, *Goldwyn Follies,* is still a classic as far as ballet is concerned—and now happens to be settled more or less strictly in the ballet field. I would think that not only is this because of his growth as an artist and his need for that specific outlet but, from my own experience have found that, the less money involved and at stake in a project, the more freedom there is. . . . For myself, I know that my ballet *Moves: A Ballet in Silence,* must have in some way come out of the stuss and storm [*sic*] of *Gypsy*. I did *Moves* immediately after *Gypsy*. In that show, I was involved with an author, a composer, a lyricist, two producers, a scene designer, a costume designer, a star, and the horde of hanger-on-ers and would-be helpers and advisers. And as a matter of fact, even before the show came into town, I was already starting to work on *Moves* where I worked with just the dancers and myself and space. What a pleasure it was and how quickly the work evolved, faster than any other ballet I'd done before and I finished almost thirty minutes of it in three weeks. My usual rate of speed is about five minutes a week. George's, I imagine, about a ballet every ten days or two weeks. I'm not as fast as he is and I realize this, which is always somewhat inhibiting when I start to work with the New York City Ballet group. His craft, skill, and facility make the dancer used to his particular kind of speed, and in comparison everybody else seems rather a blunderer and fumbler. George seems to go directly toward what he wants either through intuition, skill, or what have you. I have to work through many layers of what I don't want until I start to get toward what I do want. Once I hit that vein or key, I work rather rapidly. But generally I would say for most every ballet that I've done, I must have at least a half of one left over that I haven't used. . . .

I don't think it's terribly hard just to do "choreography." I have never felt it's been difficult to fill up a certain amount of time with a certain amount of music. What I find is the challenge and what I strive for constantly is to say what I have to say as freshly as possible. . . . Sometimes when I start a ballet, I'm not always sure what the subject is, although I have a feeling toward it. It's rather like searching in the fog for something you know is there or modeling with clay, and only by work and stripping off layer after layer do I finally get to the key and essence of what it's about. What I've just described is one way of work. Another way (and that which is most common to Broadway and occasionally to ballet) is to know specifically the characters' situation, atmosphere, story, the moment of what is about to happen on stage, and to tell what you have to tell as succinctly and directly but always inventively as possible. *Fancy Free*, my first ballet, had a very detailed scenario, and the final ballet hardly varied from it at all. I don't write scenarios out anymore for a number of reasons. One, I don't have to in order to convince people that I've got a story. But more importantly, I feel that what I am striving for in ballets has altered and that the "story" ballet is not quite as interesting and fascinating to me as is the nuance, ritual, and saying something in movement which evokes a whole atmosphere, life, and relationship which cannot be said in words but which is understood through movement and gesture by the audience.

Of course, all of this is theory and no one has said it better than Stravinsky, who, when asked what theory was, said, "usually hindsight." . . . But I will say the foregoing is in a general way what my thinking is at this time. . . . I do believe in the ballet as a ritual. Most ballets celebrate something or another. The most fascinating part to me is that each ballet creates a total world of its own with a morality and behavior particular only to it. Good choreographers convince the audience of this world and its behavior and its relationships immediately. The audience feels safe and secure that what they are seeing on stage is fact and they can believe in it. Poor choreographers fumble, twist, are embarrassed, or struggle bombastically to convince you. Hardly ever do you see a Balanchine ballet or a Graham ballet without knowing that a master hand has been behind this and that one feels absolutely secure and can believe what is happening on stage.

All best wishes as always.

Sincerely,

To: Robert Graves
[February 1960]*

Dear Robert,

Thank you for the letters—for the poem—for the mushrooms—& for the too-brief times we spent together. Slivers of the mushroom dreams still hang

---

* Robbins had been introduced to the British poet Robert Graves (1895–1985) by the poet's daughter Jenny Nicholson Crosse, who had handled press for Ballets: U.S.A. in Spoleto. According to both Robbins's date book and Robert Graves's diary, the two men took psilocybin together on January 31, 1960, at the New York home of Robert Gordon Wasson, a banker turned ethnographer who was studying the effects of hallucinogenic fungi.

about—& during the night's sleep-wanderings come back & take me on other journeys. The wall opposite my bed & I took off slow motion train speed traveling where?—somewhere to do with water & sea. . . .

Having taken the mushroom pills (word gets about) makes one an "in" person. Having taken them with you is cemented "in." I had a light drunk & heavy hangover for 3 days it seemed. Sleeping is still strange—but maybe it's other things. I found the other volume of the Villa di M.* the next day & sent it over to Wasson to peruse. The plates are fine & I look forward to your seeing them. . . .

[Signature missing]

To: Robert Fizdale

June 5, 1960

916 NORTH FOOTHILL ROAD†
BEVERLY HILLS, CALIFORNIA

Dear Bobby,

It's Sunday, grey, 3:30 in the afternoon and I'm sitting home out on the patio looking at the pool all alone and very happy to be this quiet restful and at ease. Please do forgive me for not writing myself sooner but it's been pretty hectic. The hours are fantastic and the time and energy is demanding and I don't think I have quite adjusted to all the strangeness of the place. I found a couple of things were wrong with my method of work. One thing that was disturbing was the amount of space I had to work in, which was so huge that nothing I did seemed

---

* Presumably the Villa dei Misteri book he had written to Tanaquil Le Clercq about in 1951.
† After strenuous negotiations a deal had been struck to have Robbins co-direct the film of *West Side Story* with Robert Wise, a studio veteran with a background in film editing. After the Prologue footage for the *West Side Story* film had been shot on location in New York, shooting had moved to the Goldwyn Studios lot in Hollywood, and Robbins had rented a house in Beverly Hills for the duration of production.

to fill it and, on the other hand, I felt that I *had* to fill it. I had the dancers tear-assing all the hell over the huge studio thinking that one thing the camera can do is give you the different locales, and I struggled this way for 4 days before I limited my space to about what I had it on the stage and found that everything was much better this way. The other thing is that I somehow seemed to have no deadline that I was working toward. It wasn't like I was going to open out of town in 4, 6 or 8 weeks. My concentration wasn't as good because I found that I was thinking that I had no need to hurry as we weren't going to shoot this episode that I was rehearsing until sometime in September and here it is the early part of June. I gave myself a lecture over the weekend and next week hope to be better at it.

. . . I've gone to a couple of parties and I think, for the sake of namedropping and for Arthur's[*] sake (so he knows just what I'm doing) here's a list of thems what I met. Starting with the writers it's Nabokov, Isherwood, Romain Gary, Tennessee Williams, Gore Vidal; with the movin' picture stars it's Mary Pickford, Marilyn Monroe, Merle Oberon (Scott Burton[†] says that it sounds like The Three Fates), Yves Montand, Agnes Moorehead, Jimmy Stewart, Gina Lollobrigida, Jennifer Jones and surrounding personalities such as David Selznick, Arthur Freed and a host of the young starlings and starlets, all of whom grin at you and make with the eyes. As a matter of fact everyone is on the show and on the make. It's so funny here when people ask you how do you like Hollywood: they're not asking about a place, like how do you like New York or how do you like Paris or how do you like London—they're really asking very self-consciously, how do you like *us,* because there's *no* place, there's just people all of whom are here for phony show reasons. It's corny and a cliché but honest to God the values here are so way out and different and if I do get used to them I'll worry about myself.

Tuesday night I'm going to hear a concert of Stravinsky conducting "Les Noces" and one other work. So much for culture. Your recordings sound wonderful and I wish to hell I could hear you practice and prepare them. The other day I was driving to the Studio and had the radio on and there was a piano piece

---

[*] Arthur Gold, Fizdale's performing partner.
[†] Scott Burton (1939–1989) was an American art critic and sculptor.

being played which I was certain was Chopin but it turned out to be a Mozart rondo, K511 or 517 I think. Have you ever heard it? It's really lovely. Try to get a copy of it and play it.

The work with Robert Wise still continues to be as good and sensitive as always and now we're starting to get into the fields of how to do certain musical numbers so that they'll be more than just realistically shot. Lord help us. I'm more at ease on the sound stage with the cameramen: don't feel so far out about what I don't know. What I really need is a Berlitz course in Hollywood language, because it's full of such things as gaffa, mos and laptrap and thousands of initials which mean nothing to me and have to be translated all the time.

I guess I haven't written Tanny because I just felt that she didn't care to answer, etc. Last year when I went away she didn't write at all and I wasn't upset by it but just felt that it was one less obligation for her. I'll try to write to her this week if I can and I'll certainly try also to call her.

Otherwise nothing new. A friend from St. Thomas came and spent the week here and I, unfortunately, have to confess I was relieved when he left. I got a letter from Robert Graves who is now on to Jewish legends and also a history of Paradise. My God he is fantastic, isn't he? I wonder how he manages to be so interested in so many things. I'm always *interested* but I never see anything through. I also received an outline of Alastair Reid's (breakdown rather than outline) concerning THE WHITE GODDESS and it really sounds exciting.* I'm going to try to write them today.

My concentration isn't very good so I'm going to close now. Please continue to write me. I do get upset when your notes sound somewhat low and wish so fervently that I could be there or you here. . . . I miss you and our talks and our evenings together. Stay well, be happy and all my love as always.

XXX
J.

---

* Alastair Reid (1926–2014) was a Scottish poet, translator, and scholar of Latin American literature. He and Graves wanted to interest Robbins in collaborating on a film of Graves's *White Goddess,* a discursive meditation on matriarchal myth.

To: Leonard Bernstein
June 15, 1960

Dear Lenny,

If this is *your* version of what happened about "Somewhere"*—it's news to me. Sure, we differed on it—but nothing was played by any orchestra ever that you did not know of. Nor would I ever be destructive to your music—I have too much respect and admiration for your taste and talent. If it *is* your version (which I doubt) you owe me an apology I think. . . . I don't think Lenny—if I *am* to be accused of fang and claw—that I ever used them on you. I fought *for* "Somewhere"—over Arthur's and occasionally Steve's objections. Maybe I'm jumping the gun—and if so forgive me. I value our collaboration and friendship. In spite of difficulties we have when working (I'm sure both have moments of wanting to brain the other) I find it always the most stimulating and valuable of all I've ever had anywhere. . . .

Signed—like in Dear Abby—
"Upset"
Jerry†

---

* Robbins enclosed an article about *West Side Story* that Bernstein, in his conciliatory reply, said he did not cooperate with. The article—which Bernstein suggested was based on information from either Laurents or Sondheim—described Robbins's ordering *West Side Story*'s music director, prior to the Washington, D.C., opening, to change a passage in Bernstein's orchestration that he considered too "Hollywood." Bernstein was present and could have objected but didn't; possibly he knew better than to try. Instead, according to Stephen Sondheim, he silently went to a bar across the street and ordered a line of neat Scotches.
† Although the copy of this letter that Bernstein received was handwritten in ballpoint on Robbins's Foothill Drive stationery, it appears to have been dictated to Robbins's secretary, Edith Weissman, then typed (the version conserved in the Robbins archives), and *then* hand copied by Robbins. Seemingly he wished it to appear spontaneous, but also wished to leave no phrase to chance.

To: Robert Wise*
April 12, 1961

NOTES ON "WEST SIDE STORY" FILM

The main problem of the picture is to fix the Dance Hall† sequence. It isn't a question of the dancing or the choreography; what's lost is the tense *action* of plot and story leading to a highly emotional meeting of the lovers. The most important aspect of the whole Dance Hall [scene] is that each gang is desperately *rivaling* [sic] with each other and aggressively *taking* the dance floor away from each other. In its present cutting this story point is lost and it looks like "general dance enthusiasm." The Sharks (in a shot including the Jets) should be seen to withdraw and then take over the dance hall; then the Jets (in a shot including the Sharks) should be seen gathering and taking it back. . . . When Riff and Graziella are dancing competitively against Bernardo and Anita, the *total* picture, including both couples, isn't seen until the last moment. One doesn't get the impression that this is a highly pitched and desperate gang fight for supremacy. It is of utmost importance because Tony and Maria must meet at the *fiercest* moments of the gangs' crescendoing competitive dancing.

When the group starts upstage away from the camera, *stay* on the long shot (even if it means additional music) because you can't see Tony and Maria see each other. I cannot express strongly enough how disappointing is the meeting of the two lovers. This was one of the most effective moments on the stage and in the film becomes prosaic, untouching and insensitive. Next, when Tony and Maria meet and start to dance, some softening and added opticals should be used to enhance it. Finally, when they start their dialogue, the close shots work best and I suggest using or making additional closer separate shots of Tony's and

---

* Robbins was fired from *West Side Story* the day that "Dance at the Gym" was to be shot. Afterward he asked for and was given permission to see the rough cut of the entire film. Some of the changes he suggested were incorporated, but with Robbins gone, Robert Wise had not shot enough film coverage to make many alterations to that scene.

† What Robbins refers to as a "dance hall" is really a high school gymnasium where teenagers from rival gangs, the Sharks (Puerto Ricans) and Jets (Anglos), are attending a supposedly conciliatory dance, presided over by a do-gooder social-worker, at which Maria, the Puerto Rican heroine, meets Tony, a Jet. Bernardo is Maria's brother, Anita is his girlfriend, Graziella is one of the Jet girls, and Riff is the Jets' leader.

Maria's heads and eyes (as close as you can get) as they are speaking their lines. Don't worry about the people in the back or the choreography in the back.

Let me stress something about all the sequences. The point is I don't care about the *choreography* or the steps themselves. But I feel forcibly insistent that the story and emotions be saved. . . .

. . . There are many places where I'm just overjoyed with what has been done and I write this letter only to call attention to the places that I feel can be helped.

I would like to hear your reaction to this letter.

All best,
Jerome Robbins

To: Richard Buckle[*]
May 30, 1962

Dear Richard Cleopatra Buckle,

. . . Now let's see; April was the cruelest month coming and going, with Oscars and Presidents showered upon me. I found it difficult to take so I flew off to Washington to help on a show called A FUNNY THING HAPPENED TO ME ON THE WAY TO THE FORUM [*sic*]. It was a flop before Robbins put his magic little finger to it and now it's a great big hit, bringing glory and fame to everyone but me because I refused credit.[†] Got to know Tony Walton and Julie Andrews through it and I like them both immensely. They're probably in London now on their way to some little island off the coast of Brittany.

Before the President we danced AFTERNOON OF A FAUN and OPUS JAZZ. No one mentioned FAUN in the reviews, it was not wild enough I guess. . . . The Queen of Iran is beautiful, Mrs. Kennedy is charming, Mr. Ken-

---

[*] Richard Buckle (1916–2001) was ballet critic for the London *Observer* and founder of the magazine *Ballet*. He and Robbins had become friends when Ballets: U.S.A. appeared in London in 1961.
[†] According to its producer, Harold Prince, half the audience was walking out of the show in Washington before Robbins ordered a new opening number and concocted a comic pantomime to go with it, restaged songs, even altered the set; in the end it ran for two years.

nedy makes you feel like he's your old pal from somewhere or other and the Shah and I just eyed each other suspiciously.

The Oscar night* was the wild crazy way to treat Hollywood. I came in the night before and had a huge bash thrown for me at Romanoff's (The Place) to which all of the big wig celebrities, names, faces and VIP's were invited. I took Mrs. Hayward with me. We arrived 15 minutes before the party, both got plastered, both went home, both got up the next day, fixed ourselves in the various barbers and beauty salons, went to the Oscars, collected two of them,† went to two more parties that night, got on a plane the next morning and came home. Wow, quel [*sic*] vie! The Oscars themselves I think are rather trashy looking, with no faces, no fingers, no asses, no balls, no nothing. They're bland like Hollywood, they're gold and glued over. Forget it. There's a new hip expression here—the word "later." If you want to get rid of somebody you just say to them "later." If someone makes you angry and you've had enough you just say "later." It means sort of "forget it" or "get lost" or all those things rolled into one and it's great.

. . . I'll be doing FANNY BRICE first.‡ Perhaps with Anne Bancroft. When I get through with that I hope to do either a ballet or an off-Broadway production in the spring, and to follow that with MOTHER COURAGE the following fall. My house in the country§ is starting to be repaired both inside and out and I can't wait to get into it. It really is lovely and you would be so at home there, which, by the way, it is anytime you want to come and use it.

I've been feeling very un-ballet these days. I don't exactly know what it is except maybe the whole experience of BALLETS: U.S.A.'s last tour and Martin slapping it¶ and many other things have combined to put me off from trying

---

* *West Side Story*, which had taken in $40 million at the box office, had been nominated for eleven Academy Awards.
† Robbins won Oscars for Best Director and—in a special award—for Choreography.
‡ Buckle had asked him what his future work schedule was; at this point the plan was for Robbins to direct a musical being developed by the producer Ray Stark about the comedienne Fanny Brice (Stark's mother-in-law) and then to take on Brecht's *Mother Courage*.
§ Robbins had signed a long lease on an old white clapboard house on the Hudson River in the village of Snedens Landing, about half an hour's drive north of New York; the house had previously been lived in by Aaron Copland and Robert Fizdale and Arthur Gold.
¶ In a Sunday think piece in *The New York Times* on September 28, Martin had characterized the work of Ballets: U.S.A. as "grubbing around in a depressing cul-de-sac . . . an abstract classicism of the vulgar." Their first American tour, in 1958, had been truncated by a lack of audiences in the Midwest, and their 1959 European tour for the State Department had been grueling.

for a while. I have had some good ideas but they all seem to convert themselves into plays. I guess it's just temporary, or age creeping up on me. Whatever it is, it feels odd not to want to do one. I usually do have one lurking around in the back of my mind.

. . . What are your plans, where are you, where will you be flying off to, when are you coming over here, when shall we meet again? How deep is the ocean, how high is the sky, how can I tell you how much I love you. Write me a nice big, good juicy letter and take care. I'm having dinner with Chita[*] tomorrow night and I'll give her your love, meanwhile all mine.

Yours devotedly,
Sir Ike

To: Isobel Lennart[†] (Telegram)
July 28, 1962

DEAR ISOBEL IF YOU ARE NEEDLING AND DEFENSIVE ITS BECAUSE
I'M THE LONE CRITICAL STINKER IN THE FACE OF EVERYONE'S
PRAISE AND HOW COULD YOU REACT. YOU MUST KNOW HOW DEEPLY
FOND OF YOU I AM AND HOW VERY ENTHUSIASTICALLY I AM LOOK-
ING FORWARD TO THE SHOW AND WORKING ON ITS PROBLEMS WITH
YOU. LOVE JERRY

---

[*] Chita Rivera had played Anita in *West Side Story* both on Broadway and in London.
[†] Isobel Lennart, a screenwriter with no Broadway experience, had been hired by producer Ray Stark to write the book for *Fanny Brice*, eventually titled *Funny Girl*; script problems with the show would cause Robbins to withdraw from the production in September, with the proviso that he would return if and when they were solved. Amazingly, considering that it was Lennart's script that was sabotaging the show, Robbins felt undiminished affection for her, which was reciprocated. "STOP THIEF," Stark had wired Robbins in April, "YOU HAVE STOLEN THE HEART OF MY WRITER AND I AM HUNG IN THE CLOSET." (He was riffing on the title of the Arthur Kopit play Robbins had directed the previous winter.)

Day-to-Day Notes Telling the Story of *Mother Courage*
November 26, 1962

Cheryl Crawford[*] offered me [*Mother Courage*] as far back as August, 1961. I didn't see the riches it contained [and] I was a little intimidated by this great work being offered to me and wondered whether I could come up to its stature and reputation. . . . [But after I] decided to pull out of *Fanny Brice,* Cheryl called and said she wanted to go into rehearsal with *Mother Courage* for this year and have it open in early spring. Gerry Page[†] was very interested in doing it. . . . I decided not to hesitate but to accept the challenge of preparing the show and getting it ready.

I had one meeting with Gerry Page in Cheryl's office. I was shocked at her voice, which was high and babyish and singsongy. I couldn't possibly see, while talking to her, where she had gotten a voice to use in *Sweet Bird of Youth,* nor could I find any inkling in her of anything that I hoped to find for *Mother Courage*. However, she told me how, when she was in London, playing in one theatre, next door or across the street was the Berliner Ensemble, and she used to sneak over to see part of their show because she knew sometime she was going to play that role. And with that her voice took that deep plunge down to bass and she rubbed her hands, and the ferocious wish and determination were so frightening in comparison to the little light girlish voice that had been singing away a moment before, that I immediately realized that as a sure sign of what was to happen.

I decided to fly out to the coast to see Gerry again. When I got to her hotel at 7:30 she wasn't there but arrived with Rip Torn about 15 minutes later. They [had] both just come in from a Mexican hunting trip, with bags and birds, and they were prepared to make dinner for me. I went up with them to their apartment where they cooked and we drank. I managed to talk with her a good deal

---

* Cheryl Crawford (1902–1986), a co-founder of the Group Theatre and The Actors Studio, was a prominent theatrical producer whose Broadway credits included four Tennessee Williams plays as well as the Lerner and Loewe musicals *Paint Your Wagon* and *Brigadoon;* she had been the original producer of *West Side Story* but bowed out because of creative differences with the writers and director.
† Geraldine Page (1924–1987), a noted film, stage, and television actress, had recently starred in Tennessee Williams's *Sweet Bird of Youth* on Broadway and was about to film Lillian Hellman's *Toys in the Attic* in Hollywood. She was married to Rip Torn (b. 1931), a fellow member of The Actors Studio, whom she'd met when he had a small role, then replaced Paul Newman in the lead, in *Sweet Bird.*

about the play and she grasp[ed] the meaning immediately. I got her to sing for me. I said "fine" and she said "fine"—as far as she was concerned it was settled and all she had to do was tell another show she wasn't going to do *it*.

When I got back to New York, on October 22nd, Cheryl told me that by this time Annie Bancroft [had] read the play and seemed very hot to do it. . . . I said to Cheryl that, at that moment, with what I knew about Annie, Gerry was better agewise, and there was an exchange of telegrams and letters with Gerry's agent and Cheryl about how excited [Gerry] was, how glad she was it was all settled, how she looked forward to the work, how she would be back December 12, how we would all get going, what her ideas were for costume, makeup. She asked me a few questions: I called her and [gave] her some hints that I found in research, and everything was jolly except that I had to tell Annie Bancroft that we had made a decision. She was heartbroken and angry and I was sick that I had to tell such a talented girl that we had to make a decision elsewhere. . . .

The next Monday Cheryl said that she had some bad news: Gerry didn't want to do this play, she wanted to do *Strange Interlude* instead, with the Actors Studio, and Anne Bancroft would do [*Mother Courage*]. . . . I thought the hell with this, I wasn't going to accept it: I wanted Gerry Page and she had made a commitment to me. I called [her] and told her that, and she, with a high little voice, said, "Oh, dear, can't we postpone it" and oh my she didn't know it had been so involved, etc. . . . I told her that we had a moral and legal contract. [But] Bill Fitelson[*] pointed out that a contract with an actor is not legal unless it was signed by Equity. . . .

After thinking it over I decided to take the bull by the horns and go ahead [with Anne Bancroft]. One thing Annie has in her favor is her tenaciousness and what she feels is her knowledge that she can do this show. I'll buy that because I trust her. . . .

Tuesday November 27

. . . Most of the afternoon was spent reading people.[†] I found that during the readings so much of the play became illuminated to me. It really isn't an anti-

---

* William Fitelson (1905–1994) was Robbins's entertainment lawyer. A member of the original Actors Studio board of directors, he was also counsel to the Theatre Guild; his clients, in addition to Robbins, included James Baldwin, Elia Kazan, and Gypsy Rose Lee.
† That is, auditioning actors.

war play, it's an anti-"business-as-usual" play, and the people in the play seem unaware of their responsibility to each other. If anyone is crushed it can't be you, it must be the person next to you. . . .

. . . In the evening Eric Bentley[*] came and we worked on Scene 6. We work very slowly on the translations to try and pull them together. I find it's hard to roll them out and make it smooth, due to the fact that Brecht used both ancient and colloquial language and made a language of his own, but I don't think Bentley has yet accomplished this. . . .

Thursday, November 29

I met with Cheryl in the morning and we got into some discussion about the musicians' union. It seems that if there's more than 25 minutes of music it doesn't become a dramatic show but a musical. In which case 7 musicians, which is what we want, will not be sanctioned by the union. We will have to have at least 16, and if we have 16, that also means our ticket price will have to go up to cover the expense. When it came to publicity for the show I felt very strongly that it was necessary for us to create an image that was not tragic, morbid, and depressing: we should announce that it's going to have 10 songs and feature my name because it's connected with musicals. But Cheryl was afraid of this because if the musicians' union saw it we [would have] already labeled [it] as a musical. . . .

Friday November 30

. . . I had to meet Annie Bancroft at six o'clock. We had a very good talk and we both felt very excited about it. In her intensity I could see the woman and I was thrilled by that. She said that when she thought she hadn't gotten the part because Gerry Page was supposed to have it, she felt so desperate she would have done anything to get it, including screwing Cheryl.[†] I must have looked for a moment askance, as they say, because after a short pause she said "of course I

---

[*] Eric Bentley (b. 1916), a prolific critic, playwright, and translator known for his scholarship on Brecht, not only had translated the text Robbins was using but also had been given, by the Brecht estate, the right to approve certain production decisions, such as casting. This was a recipe for friction with Robbins (see p. 239).

[†] Crawford was an essentially out lesbian, at least in the theater community. She lived with the cookbook author Ruth Norman, co-founder of James Beard's cooking school.

wouldn't"—but she would have. I gave her a book of pictures about the [Hundred Years'] war and a book of Breughel for her to work on. . . .

Monday December 3rd

. . . I've been very depressed because it seems to me that working in the theatre, for the creative people, is like being a terrible work-horse who slogs his way or plods his way to get to a certain point. Thrown over him are the nets and luggage of everyone making money on his effort because when you come right down to it, the only thing that really keeps theatre going is that work-horse. . . . In between the need to create [the work] and the need to see it, is a whole vast intricate merciless industry and business and I now feel it's a business just like in Hollywood which is a business. I suppose up to now I've been unaware of it or blind to it. . . . [I]n a way it really is like *Mother Courage*. . . . I find a growing sickness in my stomach at the enormity, the complexity and barbarity of it all. . . .

To: Eric Bentley
January 22, 1962

Dear Eric:

I do apologize for "laying about me."* It was indeed inconsiderate, and my temper and anger was uncalled for and I ask forgiveness. I realize that, as usual, what I meant and what I said or what you understood didn't come out the same.

I have *no* pretenses or illusions of being a lyricist. I wish I were, in which case I'd be more helpful to you. I think you're completely mistaken about my implications about crowing over my own talent. I must have upset you terribly to have you think it, I know.

I do object and react violently (unfortunately) when I find, as in "Capitula-

---

* Apparently, Robbins, frustrated by the intractability of the German lyrics and music for the play, had lost his temper during a work session with Bentley, who retaliated with a fierce letter (dated January 19), to which this was a response. Asserting that "Brecht lyrics are rather my specialty," Bentley told Robbins that "*Mother Courage* cannot be put on in America without my approval and collaboration, as I proved in a two-year-long lawsuit."

tion" or any song—a meaning unclear, unfocused, or ill-defined,—or even more so—unsingable and unactable. I feel very strongly that most of the lyrics are very literate and clear on paper—but not always so when sung and acted. On this I trust *my* experience over yours. I "come at you" with the German in hand purely for my own enlightenment and sometimes to check with you to enhance a point that I feel is right for the song or the play along the lines I am directing it. And because the lyrics of Mother Courage are attached to a highly complicated, weak and dated score, they must be doubly and forcibly strong and clear as there is no tune or safe musical structure and sound to hold the audience's focus.

I am also as avid a researcher as I can be, and if there are still any other translations of Mother Courage available, I not only will read them, but if I find anything clearer or pertinent, I will fight to get the clarity into the script or lyrics *in your* terms. I won't kid you. My demands are high (not just on you, but on Annie, Cheryl, Ming*—and most of all *on myself*). There are many lyrics I feel *very* happy and secure with—and others I am not . . . and these I'll keep trying to get better. However I am sorry for my insensitive outburst. I guess my patience is running low as time gets shorter, and I ask you to forgive my expressions of frustration which arise from wanting not to have to deal with anything but the direction of the play.

I understand your letter, or rather your hurt and justified upset. What I don't understand is any of the talk about your lawsuits and litigation. I don't see what that has to do with what is on the stage, or the actors playing it, Cheryl and I producing it, or my directing it or how your having engaged in lawsuits make[s] the play any better.

I hope you accept this letter as an honest expression of my feelings. I very much want you to be proud of every moment on the stage—and hope that I can make you so by my efforts. The problem of the score and lyrics in Mother Courage is a sticky one—and I guess I've gotten stuck in its messiness. Let's get to work—I'll try not to attack and goad and insult, which is *not* my method of work, but a faulty obstacle to it.

All best. See you this evening.

Jerry

---

* Ming Cho Lee (b. 1930) is a notable American designer who trained with Jo Mielziner and went on to create more than thirty sets for Joseph Papp's Public Theater, including *Hair*.

To: Isobel Lennart[*]
April 17, 1963

Dear Issie,

. . . Thank you for your sweet words and also your encouragement. Brecht, it seems, is like the weather; you know everyone talks about it but nobody does anything and it never seems to please everybody.[†] The thing I am most proud of is the work I managed to accomplish all on my own, from the time we opened for previews to the time we opened for the critics. Cutting, editing, cleaning, changing, re-directing without any help was a new experience, not that I liked it, as I love collaboration, but it didn't panic me into a booby trap as I always felt it would, and I managed to improve the show enormously.

I'm up in the country staring at my growing bulbs and wondering whether to manure them or not. I've been reading scripts and so far laugh a little and long a little but don't take off. I'm going to Europe for a couple of months: Sicily, Rome, and Spoleto where I'll do some experimental work with amateurs. Good luck. I'll be back in July, I believe.

Meanwhile, take care, don't worry, and as always, all my love,
Jerry

---

[*] Lennart was still working on *Funny Girl,* and Robbins was intending to sign on as director—if the script met with his approval.

[†] *Mother Courage* opened on March 28, after a two-week preview period in New York (undertaken, instead of an out-of-town tryout, as an economy measure) and in the middle of a newspaper strike, which meant that the all-important review coverage only reached its audience via television or radio. Although those reviews were favorable and the play and production were nominated for Tony Awards, the show failed to recoup its investment.

Barbra: Some Notes[*]
[1965?]

The kook's looks are ravishing. Her beauty astounds, composed of impossibly unconventional features. Her movements are wildly bizarre and completely elegant. Her body is full of gawky angles and sensuous curves. It scrunches, elongates, and turns on in spotlights. Her El Greco hands have studied Siamese dancing and observed the antennae of insects. . . .

At rehearsals she often arrives late, haphazardly dressed in no nonsense clothes, her hair shoved up under a cap. She accepts the 12 pages of new material to go in that evening's performance and pours [sic] over them while schnorring part of your sandwich and someone else's Coke. She reads, and like an instantaneous translator she calculates how all the myriad changes will affect the emotional and physical patterns, blocking, costumes, exits and entrances, etc. When she finishes reading her reactions are immediate and violent—loving or hating them—and she will not change her mind. Not that day. During the rehearsal, in her wildly exploratory fashion, she goes way out, never afraid to let herself go anywhere or try anything. . . . That night on stage, in place of the messy grubby girl, a sorceress sails through every change without hesitation, leaving wallowing fellow-players in her wake. . . . When she sings she is as honest and frighteningly direct with her feelings as if one time she was, is, or will be in bed with you.

---

[*] After *Funny Girl* resumed preproduction in the spring of 1963, Robbins insisted, against producer Ray Stark's objections, on casting the little-known twenty-year-old Barbra Streisand in the star-making role of Fanny Brice. Shortly afterward, dismayed by persistent script problems, he quit the production definitively. This appreciation of Streisand was drafted a few years later for Roddy McDowall's *Double Exposure,* a book of photographic portraits.

To: Garson Kanin
February 18, 1964

BARCLAY HOTEL

PHILADELPHIA

Dear Gar[*]—

I want you to know that I consider "Funny Girl" your show. I was hoping to work on it with you, but Ray, in deciding to take advantage of the little time left out of town, felt it could only proceed this way. I am very sorry indeed, believe me. I just hope I fulfill the very wonderful job you've already done.

To: Ruth Mitchell[†]
August 29, 1963

DEAR RUTHIE I'M GOING TO DO A MUSICAL OF SHOLEM ALEICHEM STORIES WITH HARNICK AND BOCK[‡] STOP I'M IN LOVE WITH IT IT'S OUR PEOPLE STOP LOVE JERRY

---

[*] Garson Kanin (1912–1999) was a successful playwright/screenwriter and director of film and theater, often of works adapted from his own material. After Robbins withdrew (again) from *Funny Girl,* he was succeeded, first by Bob Fosse, who left after a couple of weeks, then by Sidney Lumet, who lasted about the same amount of time, and finally by Kanin. The show was running three and a half hours when Barbra Streisand insisted Robbins be sent for and he took over as "production supervisor."

[†] Ruth Mitchell had been stage manager for *The King and I, West Side Story, Bells Are Ringing, Gypsy, A Funny Thing Happened on the Way to the Forum,* and *She Loves Me.* Robbins hoped to enlist her in this new venture.

[‡] Sheldon Harnick (b. 1924), lyricist, and Jerry Bock (1928–2010), composer, had won the Pulitzer Prize for *Fiorello!* (1959); their most recent musical, *She Loves Me,* had opened in April 1963. When they approached Robbins about the project, in August 1963, *Mother Courage* had closed, and he had just withdrawn the second time from *Funny Girl;* initially skeptical, he was disarmed when the authors auditioned their material for him. Although he committed to the show, there was a long delay while the script and score were developed, enabling Robbins to come to *Funny Girl*'s rescue in February 1964 (the show opened on March 26 to reviews that prompted producer Stark to wire Robbins, "THE KEY TO THE VAULT FOR MY MONEY BELT IS UNDER THE RUG IN THE BATHROOM").

5

Changing Course: 1964–1983

Robbins's singular vision of, and fiercely protective love for, the world of *Fiddler on the Roof* shone through all his work on the show, and it was rewarded by the kind of enormous success— warm reviews, a battalion of Tonys, and a record-breaking eight-year Broadway run—that he had sought and mostly achieved throughout the previous two decades. But the musical, which he would describe as "a glory for my father," marked a change for him, a turn toward something he'd been avoiding engagement with all his life yet had longed deeply for: his Jewishness, his sense of community, including the community of dance and theater, and his identity.

It was also a turning *away*—away from the commercial musical theater he had dominated for two decades. In the months after *Fiddler's* opening, he explored and then abandoned an attempt to collaborate with Leonard Bernstein, Betty Comden, and Adolph Green on a musical adaptation of Thornton Wilder's *Skin of Our Teeth;* he flirted with returning to Ballet Theatre (now American Ballet Theatre) in an advisory role and with directing Euripides's *Bacchae* for Britain's National Theatre; he choreographed Stravinsky's sprawling *Les Noces* for ABT and directed María Irene Fornés's whimsical experimental farce *The Office* Off-Broadway—the latter to the first critical and commercial raspberries he'd received since the failure of *That's the Ticket!* Then in 1966 he received one of the inaugural grants of the newly formed National Endowment for the Arts to form a studio company—eventually named the American Theatre Lab—to explore, in a rehearsal setting and not for performance, techniques of theatrical presentation that incorporated dance, voice, and drama: an apotheosis of the integrated theater he had pursued from his earliest days.

Robbins's work with ATL continued for two years; although its designed inconclusiveness deprived him of the focus and closure he experienced in performance, it liberated him to try things he might not have, such as a quasi-Noh* play based on the life of the fifteenth-century Japanese Zeami Motokiyo, a married homosexual and actor-playwright whose advice to players is still read today, and to investigate ideas about masks and identity that had perennially fascinated him. When ATL closed—although he considered directing George Tabori's surreal anti-Nazi play *The Cannibals,* and would later attempt to adapt Brecht's *The Exception and the Rule* with Bernstein, Sondheim, and the rising playwright John Guare—he didn't immediately fasten onto a new project. He found his life slowing down so he could experience it and analyze it in ways he hadn't done while careening from show to show. He wondered about the nature and permanence of his (and his colleagues') art. As he had not done since his early days with Ballet Theatre, he began keeping detailed and introspective journals. And the old questions about who he was and what he wanted, what the knots were in his own tangled family story, came increasingly to the fore.

He was nourished and stimulated by a new (and old) group of friends: Gold and Fizdale; Tanaquil Le Clercq—who, impelled by Balanchine's obsession with his newest muse, Suzanne Farrell, separated from her husband in 1965; the London critic Richard Buckle; Grover Dale (from the cast of *West Side Story*) and his then partner, Tony Perkins; Stephen Sondheim; the young artist/director Robert Wilson, whom he'd met at ATL; the artist and actor Allen Midgette; his Snedens Landing neighbor the psychoanalyst Daniel Stern; and others. But he wanted something deeper and more enduring than friendship or the fleeting affairs, with both men and women, that had been filling the void in his "niente" personal life. At the house of friends in Water Mill he met a twenty-

---

* Noh is a form of dance-based music-drama developed by the Japanese actor Kan'ami Kiyotsugu and his son Zeami Motokiyo in the fourteenth century; it uses masks and props to tell stories often derived from traditional folk literature.

something aspiring writer and producer named Christine Conrad; following a two-year on-again, off-again courtship he became involved with her—and shortly thereafter, unbeknownst to her, with a bisexual young actor, Edward Davis.* One result of this triangulated relationship might have been his interest in developing a motion picture based on the recently published diaries of the bisexual and schizophrenic ballet legend Vaslav Nijinsky (the dancer and choreographer who had been Diaghilev's original Petrouchka)—a project he pursued intermittently for several years before it fell apart. But more directly and fruitfully, his feelings of romantic fulfillment and personal balance, and his desire for simplicity, as one or another complicated potential venture collapsed on him, expressed themselves in a ballet.

This was the groundbreaking *Dances at a Gathering,* a work whose huge success surprised him—enough so that he made a rare attempt to examine and analyze the creative process that led to it—and brought him back into the City Ballet family at a significant moment in the company's history. For the premiere of *Dances* also marked the departure from City Ballet of Balanchine's latest muse, Suzanne Farrell—an event that threw Balanchine into a personal and creative depression. It was Robbins who stepped into the momentary void, creating a trio of wildly different ballets: the moonlit *In the Night* (1970), to Chopin nocturnes; *Goldberg Variations* (1971), an intricate piece of classical ballet architecture set to Bach; and the Noh-inflected *Watermill* (1972), which translated ideas about ritual and autobiography he'd originally intended to explore in *Zeami.* Balanchine returned to full creative force, however, with the extraordinary display of City Ballet's 1972 Stravinsky Festival, an eight-day extravaganza featuring twenty-two new Balanchine ballets plus works by six other choreographers (including Robbins) and showings of repertory ballets by himself and Robbins, conceived as a memorial to the composer, who had died on April 6, 1971. And while Robbins professed himself happy to continue on at City Ballet in Balanchine's shadow, it proved difficult for him to accustom himself to being—for the first time in years—in second place.

---

* Not his real name.

It was while struggling to integrate himself, once more, into the fabric and aesthetic of City Ballet that he read a book called *The Ordeal of Civility,* a critical exploration of the accommodations forced on assimilated Jews by European and American society, and—as he described it—the lid blew off his own conflicted feelings about Judaism. At the same time, his father's health was declining, which forced Robbins into a reckoning with their relationship and with the details of his life, details he would begin to set down in random autobiographical sketches, miscellaneous journals, and a set of diaries kept in accordion-folded Japanese notebooks. His own health was fragile: he ruptured his Achilles tendon in the fall of 1969; while in London in 1970 he came down with both strep and hepatitis, combined with a bad reaction to cortisone prescribed to cure them, and was hospitalized on his return to New York; and he underwent treatment, including surgery, for diverticulitis in 1977. Like virtually everyone he knew in the 1970s, he experimented, in his case gingerly, with recreational drugs, which played havoc with his psychic sense of balance. His and Conrad's relationship had foundered over his involvement with Davis, but then Davis had left him, and he'd begun a series of frequently concurrent short-term affairs, this time exclusively with men (although he would still find himself attracted to certain women, such as the novelist Edna O'Brien, the dancers Natalia Makarova and—in the 1980s—Sylvie Guillem, and the choreographer Twyla Tharp). These were the years immediately after the Stonewall riots, when homosexuality came out of the closet and into the streets, and Robbins should have felt relief at being able to be open about his sexual preferences, but instead he was anxious and ambivalent—possibly because it wasn't so much sex he was after as love. "When I am . . . 'in love,'" he wrote in his journal, "I am also turned on to work."

And work was proving difficult. After finally getting Balanchine and Kirstein to commit to his long-cherished dream of a ballet based on S. Anski's *Dybbuk,* he found himself at frequent odds with his collaborator, Leonard Bernstein, on both scheduling and conception, and when the ballet finally made its way to the stage, it failed to realize his ambitions for it. In addition, a cluster of dances produced on assignment from Balanchine for City Ballet's 1975 Ravel Festival, which gave him

"*O of C* [*Ordeal of Civility*] dreams" and seemed "not my cup of tea," were indifferently received by critics, who used the occasion to make slighting comparisons of his work to Balanchine's. And although during the past few summers he had rediscovered the Umbrian hill country around Spoleto that he'd first visited with Ballets: U.S.A. and luxuriated in its landscape and its extraordinary art, he lost another refuge closer to home when his landlords in Snedens Landing turned down his offer to buy his house there. Struggling with feelings of conflict and rejection, he suffered an episode of suicidal depression and in July 1975 checked himself into McLean Hospital, a Massachusetts mental institution whose alumni included Robert Lowell and Sylvia Plath.

He stayed less than a month, but the respite helped, and over the next months he began patching himself together again. He found inspiration in the work of new choreographers, composers, directors, actors; he revisited Chopin, an old love, to make a new ballet commissioned for ABT, *Other Dances* (1976); he turned down an appeal by Bernstein and Alan Jay Lerner to help rescue their Broadway-bound musical, *1600 Pennsylvania Avenue,* which he found too "messed up" for intervention; he began tinkering with an autobiographical theater piece based on the memoir sketches he had been writing; and in the fall of 1977 he began a relationship with a much younger photographer, Jesse Gerstein, that sustained him when his father died that December. Shortly afterward his "other" father figure, Balanchine—who had seemed in full creative spate—began to suffer from ill health, and Robbins had to pick up slack at City Ballet, helping to finish ballets Balanchine could not deliver (*Tricolore, Le Bourgeois Gentilhomme*) and choreographing such diverse new works as the exuberant *Four Seasons,* to Verdi, and the moody *Opus 19/The Dreamer,* to Prokofiev, the latter as a vehicle for Mikhail Baryshnikov, newly arrived, through Robbins's intervention, at City Ballet.

In 1981, Robbins made three ballets for City Ballet's Tchaikovsky Festival, and that fall he was named a recipient of the Kennedy Center Honors. He took a small company of dancers to China and traveled to Egypt with Jesse Gerstein. His emotional equilibrium was still uncertain—a negative review or a rehearsal frustration could throw him into depression—but he was working productively, creating new dances for City Ballet, and discussing with Philip Glass plans to direct the world premiere of his opera *Akhnaten*. And then came loss: the end of his six-year relationship with Jesse Gerstein, the death of his much-loved longtime assistant, Edith Weissman, who had been the silent continuo in his life since 1944, and on April 30, 1983—after months of a progressive brain disease and a bruising last-minute succession scuffle at City Ballet—that of George Balanchine. As Robbins had noted at the loss of Fokine forty years previously, "It finishes so irrevocably a period & era of ballet & dancing." Suddenly Robbins was alone onstage.

To: Patricia Zipprodt*

[1963]

Don't romanticize the characters [in *Fiddler on the Roof*]: they are tough, working, resiliant [*sic*], tenacious; they fiercely live and hang on to their existence; *they* have the word, everyone else is wrong; we are not to see them thru the misty nostalgia of time past, but thru the everyday hard struggle to keep alive and keep their beliefs.

They are not "Characters" but laborers, workmen, artisans, and the effect of their work on their clothes and bodies must be apparent.

This is a rural *unsophisticated* area . . . no newspapers, or any communication with the rest of the country around them. *It is poverty stricken.* Everyone just about ekes out an existence. The honey mists of time do not make life beautiful for them. All that is beautiful is their continued efforts to and tenaciousness to hold on to what they believe in.

LOCATE TEVYE'S FAMILY:

socially

economically

geographically

---

* Patricia Zipprodt (1925–1999), a Tony Award–winning designer for theater, ballet, and opera, had designed costumes for *Oh Dad, Poor Dad,* and Robbins hired her to do the same for *Fiddler*. She saved this memo and later used it as a teaching tool for her class in costume design at Brandeis University.

This is a *country* community . . . [JR's ellipses] a little group of houses in the middle of sprawling Russian countryside. The Jewish community is kept apart, separate, huddled together, isolated and then told to keep alive. To do so they work hard and fight for existence.

FARM not *CITY*
RURAL not *URBAN*
PRACTICAL not *ROMANTIC*
TOUGH not *PICTURESQUE*

To: Jerry Bock and Sheldon Harnick
April 4, 1964

Dear Boys,

I've been sick for a week which has given me time to examine where we stand and to put down on paper my reactions to the reading; what has to be done by the end of this month if we don't want to find ourselves in another, and this time, much more lengthy postponement.[*] . . . I can't come to London,[†] so please wire when you are returning here.

Best,
Jerry

GENERAL NOTES:

The score is wonderful but it did not fuse with the show the way it should on the basis of our reading. One reason is the over length of the book[‡] which prevented musical continuity. You must find the places to play things in song . . . vital places and not just divertissement.

---

[*] The casting process alone had taken ten months, contract negotiations for Robbins's first choice as Tevye, Zero Mostel, took nearly as long, and during all of this the original producer, Fred Coe, had dropped out, to be replaced by Harold Prince.
[†] Bock and Harnick were in London preparing to open *She Loves Me* in the West End.
[‡] The book was by Joseph Stein (1912–2010), who had also written *Enter Laughing* (1963) and the libretto for *Take Me Along* (1959). He wasn't in London, because he hadn't been involved with *She Loves Me*.

The score itself is too one dimensional. There is an insistent repetitiveness of a Russian Jewish song to such extent that its beauty becomes a whine. Though most of the songs are charming even the charm wears thin. Missing in the show is the toughness, tenaciousness, robustness, virility and hard-core resilience of the people. It's too easy and sentimental to comment on them romantically as an all-over approach to the show. If every song is sweet, sentimental, sad, touching and nostalgic, all will come off as Second Avenue.

Tevye has only one fully realized musical moment—his first song. In all the other songs he is but an unimportant participant.

Golde has no musical moments of her own, and Golde and Tevye, our leading characters, have none between them.

Tevye's soliloquies are the missing essence of the show.

I'm being very tough and cold hearted because a good strong clear look is necessary at this point. Although new songs have come into the show, a basic trouble has not altered; too ethnic and too one-note Jewish. I keep sending everyone to see the Russian Sholem Aleichem film because the guts and toughness of the people, environment, actions are remarkable and therefore admirable. We err in "begging" for love for our "kindness," "sweetness," "gentleness," "understanding," "patience," "pixie humor," and boy scout virtues. What we should be asking for is admiration for our tenacity, effort, frailties, vigor and not holier than thou qualities.

Poppa Piece (Personal Notes)
August 11, 1976

I don't think Pop understood most of my ballets. He appreciated the fun shows (from *On the Town* on out) and the most popular-easy of the ballets—*Fancy Free, The Concert, Opus Jazz, Faun;* but didn't understand what I was after in *Dybbuk* [or] *Goldberg.** One of the best gifts I gave him was *Fiddler on the Roof.* I waited to see what his reaction would be as I hadn't invited him to any rehearsals, previews, or out-of-town performances. After the opening night show, he came backstage through the theater-stage door and when he saw me in

---

* *Dybbuk* (1974, music by Leonard Bernstein) and *Goldberg Variations* (1971, music by Bach) were complex, abstract ballets.

Robbins's father, Harry. "*Fiddler* was a glory for my father," Robbins said, "a celebration of and for him."

the wings' dim lights he threw his arms around me and wept and wept and said how did I know all that.

To: Agnes de Mille[*]
November 26, 1963

Dear Agnes,

. . . Your book[†] is a beautiful volume and you write like a demon as you well know. The chapter on how choreographers work is fascinating, and the selection of photographs and illustrations are brilliant although I take exception to the

---

[*] Like Robbins, de Mille had had a successful career choreographing musicals as well as ballets, but by 1963 she had turned her focus back to ballet—or her vision of it. His response to her book reminds us—and might have reminded him—how much classical dance meant to him.

[†] *The Book of the Dance,* an encyclopedic history, which de Mille had sent to Robbins in proof. He found a number of errors in its coverage of his work, which de Mille promised to correct.

little drawings scattered on the pages which made me confused about the age level for which you were writing as did some of the captions. But it is movingly apparent throughout that your heart and dedication are behind each page.

As long as you asked me I've got to express my reservations which are naturally personal. I was upset at Doris Humphrey's book[*] and her opinions being expressed as fact, i.e. do the finale of your ballet very early in your work, dramatic material is best expressed on the diagonal etc. etc. I feel such opinion is gainful to those open to influence only when it's expressed as *possibility* rather than *dogma*. I think your book has a similar propensity. Your tremendous anti-Balanchine feeling shows through and I feel it diminishes both you and the book. I don't think there will be any doubt that the years will prove him much more than just the most prolific choreographer and your prejudice is most clearly expressed in the captions under the pictures of the two pas de deux on page 208 labeling one from a woman's point of view and the other from a man's. The captions reveal much more *your* point of view and desires than either of the choreographers and I'm unhappy that your statement will be read by vulnerable and inquisitive youngsters of our profession who are finding their way.

Your own personal dedication, gentleness, strength and understanding played a huge and inspiring part in my own growth. Your book naturally is a fascinating source of interest to those familiar with the dance, but I strongly believe that anyone who writes about the Dance has a deep weighty responsibility to the young students and potential choreographers who read and absorb the book in their quest to learn how what and why. They are the ones who are most influenced and anyone who writes a book must keep them firmly in mind and weigh one's responsibilities [for] their responses. Facts must be clearly separated from viewpoints. I admire you and respect your viewpoints and analysis but object to having any of them put down for posterity as fact.

Forgive me for this long letter. I value enormously you as a person and the contributions you have made to our art. If I didn't value and respect both I would not bother to write this and I hope you accept it in the light of my love and friendship.

Jerry

---

[*] *The Art of Making Dances,* a posthumously published book by Doris Humphrey (1895–1958), one of the pioneers of American modern dance.

To: Lincoln Kirstein
March 17, 1964

Dear Lincoln,

Wow. What a story!* If it were true, not Lucia but *I* would be very lucky if I could manage to turn out five ballets a year.

To set the record straight—I haven't promised Lucia a thing except a deep interest in the *idea* of a company whose personnel and repertory would incorporate those of Martha Graham, Ballet Theatre and my own Ballets: U.S.A. If that were ever swung, and with Dicky† as absolute artistic authority, I can foresee producing one or possibly two ballets a year. It is extremely improbable that such a plan will ever come off, but if it did the only thing it would offer me would be that chance to work with my own dancers again and some of Martha's, which is the *only* incitement it holds out to me. Outside of working in those circumstances, working with George and you is the only situation and atmosphere that interests me. You know that I think Lucia and Ballet Theatre, as it stands, is as dead an end as you can get.

I hope this letter settles once and for all my feelings and devotion to George and you and the company. I'm truly sorry that I couldn't do a new work this season for you at the Lincoln Center‡ and I wish, with all my heart, a wonderful launching of your season there. If Johnny Taras§ will let me know when rehears-

---

* Kirstein had written about a rumor that Robbins—whose ties to City Ballet had loosened drastically during his involvement with Ballets: U.S.A.—was set to rejoin American Ballet Theatre and produce five ballets for them annually. Lucia Chase had indeed recently approached him about a leadership role in the company, but after some back-and-forth he had declined for the reasons enumerated in his letter to Kirstein. Later that year (in October, after *Fiddler* opened) he wrote to Kirstein to propose doing Stravinsky's *Les Noces* for City Ballet, but Kirstein never responded.

† Richard Buckle. This scheme appears to have been more Buckle's idea than Robbins's. But already Robbins was considering what to do when *Fiddler* was behind him.

‡ New York City Ballet had announced its intention of leaving City Center for the new Lincoln Center for the Performing Arts. Robbins was currently deep in the production process of *Fiddler on the Roof,* which would open the following fall.

§ John Taras (1919–2004), a dancer and choreographer who had been Robbins's colleague at Ballet Theatre, was a ballet master at New York City Ballet.

als start I would love to oversee my ballets, and if there's any other way I can help please let me know.

All love,
Jerry

To: Richard Buckle
April 22, 1964

Dear Dicky,

. . . I went to the gala premiere of the New York State Theatre.[*] Someone described the large lobby [as] like a women's prison. It's beautiful except for the headlight chandeliers which are rather ghastly and look like cheap rhinestones. The rehearsal rooms are fluorescent lit, completely walled in and air conditioned, and leave you dry and breathless in very little time. George and Lincoln are serenading me and the company danced nervously opening night. Except for AGON which is an incredible ballet. After seeing it I don't think six million dollars[†] is enough reward for such genius. I rehearsed the company in CAGE and was shocked to find out they were dancing it a la Ballet Russe, i.e. no one knew their counts, they were all watching each other hopefully. This really shocked me as the company has always been so musical and exact, and if not great on acting theatricals etc., was superb on musicality. Doing a ballet that lasts is somewhat like creating a dish that tastes good when you first make it but then it follows you for the rest of your life and you always have to go back and cook and taste it again. These remarks are apropos of the fact that FANCY FREE is twenty years old this week and CAGE almost ten and here I am rehearsing both.

---

[*] New York City Ballet's inaugural performance in the New York State Theater (now the David H. Koch Theater), designed by Philip Johnson largely to Balanchine's specifications, at Lincoln Center.
[†] Unclear what Robbins is talking about. The State of New York gave $15 million (in 1961 dollars) to build the theater—equivalent to approximately $122 million today.

Re Shakespeare—I'm off to see Burton's HAMLET tonight and am antici-pating Scofield's LEAR.*

Otherwise nothing new except spring is popping up all over up in Snedens, and everybody at chez moi misses you and wishes you'd come over for a visit again. Write me when you can, keep well and all love.

J

Skin Log†
Sept[ember] 24, 1964

Day before yesterday Fiddler opened‡ and today resumed meetings with L, A & B§ at 2 at Lennie's at his studio.

I suggested "larger-than-life" casting: i.e. Mostel¶ & Merman for Mom & Pop; the way it had been cast in the past** only enhanced a T.V. arid antiseptic mom & pop, while warmth & humor & the comic-trying-to-get-thru-life was not only legitimately applicable, but would give us a fresh new approach & unburden us from the ghosts of Skins past. L seemed both surprised & provoked by the idea & I could see his imagination stirred by it. He warned of course about what changes in plans in writing it would make (plenty I think) but caught what I was after. B & A did so immediately & seemed "for" it.

We talked schedule—L wants to try to face a crash program of work & get it

---

* Richard Burton (1925–1984) played Hamlet on Broadway in the spring and summer of 1964; in May, the Royal Shakespeare Company's production of *King Lear,* directed by Peter Brook with Paul Scofield (1922–2008) in the title role, opened at the New York State Theater.

† Robbins's incomplete journal of work on the abortive adaptation of Thornton Wilder's *The Skin of Our Teeth,* an allegory about the history of mankind, featuring the Antrobus family of Excelsior, New Jersey, and their maid, Sabina, who becomes a beauty queen.

‡ The day after opening, there were ticket lines around the block, and *Fiddler* would go on to a then-record 3,242 performances over nearly eight years.

§ Leonard Bernstein, Adolph Green, and Betty Comden.

¶ Zero Mostel (1915–1977) had starred in *A Funny Thing Happened on the Way to the Forum* and *Fiddler on the Roof.* Mostel professed to despise Robbins for naming names to HUAC, but Robbins admired his work ardently.

** The 1942 premiere had featured Fredric March and Florence Eldridge as the Antrobuses; the 1955 revival, George Abbott and Helen Hayes; white-bread actors all.

"Hard to think of that gargantuan man not being any longer," Robbins wrote in his diary on the 1977 death of Zero Mostel, who had played Tevye in *Fiddler on the Roof* and whom he had hoped to cast in the aborted *The Skin of Our Teeth* musical.

done by Spring. I don't think it can be done but wish it could & know that only good can come from trying for it. *All* works need digesting & mulling: the more time, the better work. A crash program will force us to make decisions without the time to ravel & unravel & distract or become inspired or find the solution one is most convinced about. Plan is for us all to go away together for 10 days or so & work N & D [night and day]. Hope it's Martha's Vineyard rather than Atlantic City.

Find L. relaxed & somewhat excited. A becomes a Jewish Buddha, filling his mouth noisily with whatever was about (instead of smoking) watching me cautiously & a little afraid of criticism. B was late (mother sick), hums to herself when a rattling suggestion is made, & is the "*efficient*" one of the group: papers, notes, telephone no.s etc. Still the den mother after 20 years.

L. played some music. What a kick to hear the vitality & dynamics & even the exhibitionism of it. He *hits* the piano & an orchestra comes out. Fiddler was delicate, nostalgic, wry & tender & Jewish sad-sweet: what a change of air! He played a lovely lieder & a hilarious sequence of marches: and opening in 7/4— natch.

We meet tomorrow at noon. Today felt like early wading around—seeing if there were soft dangerous areas—or strong solid footing . . . looking about generally & scenting the size of the prey. What kind of animal would it turn out to be? large? funny? hard to land? fun to tame? a thoroughbred new species, or a hybrid mishmash—will it have no features—and different legs—& how soon will we get a glimpse of it.

Sept[ember] 25th

Met at 12 at L.B.'s Reports (re Steve & Leland*). They're excited & refreshed getting a new & clean opinion & view on all material.

Spent time discussing where & when to go. Now M. Vineyard on Thursday. L. H. will get plane.

Talked a while about casting again. Can't think of better people than Zero and Merman—but one never can at first. Spoke of Kenny Larkin & Smith for

---

* Leland Hayward was interested in producing *The Skin of Our Teeth* and would arrange for the group to go to Martha's Vineyard for a writing retreat. Not clear who "Steve" is; there is no record of Stephen Sondheim, for example, being formally attached to this project.

sets—& [?] Roberts, [Richard] Burton, [Robert] Preston, [Phil] Silvers for Pop: Nancy [Walker], Nanette F[abray] etc. for Mom; Phyllis [Newman?], Barbara H[arris], Chita R[ivera] for Sabina . . . Pat Zip[prodt] or Irene S[haraff] for costumes.

[. . .]

Found I couldn't yet sense the "style" or what I call "physical approach" to the show. With Fiddler I caught the Chagall-poetry-fantasy fairly soon. Until I know what this approach is, nothing is ordered or valid but construction & plot. But material—the "how"—isn't clear yet.

Then L.B. played Sabina's opening. Oh-oh-oh. What a hilarious opera spoof. Verdi-Puccini to the nth degree & then some. Marvelous! But what connection stylistically does it have to the Dawn-Sun number—or the lieder—or the Marches?

L pointed a finger at me & said "*I sense* you don't want Sabina to be an opera singer." I haven't said boo or peep—& actually have no idea yet because I don't know her yet thru this material. Certainly I don't want to trap ourselves as "K & I" or "Merry W" did this year, with a good-try old sport to an ex-Met diva.*   B. Harris could do it—but not till we know who Sabina is & where she's going.

Lots to talk about in Vineyard—& now I know we'll never make Feb rehearsal. But I think I'll wait till after M's V to see how far we've gotten.

During meetings, Helen Coates [Bernstein's secretary] pops in & gives the "we" bit, like a nurse. "It's time for our pictures, Lennie." "We must sign these papers now." Reminds me of Elsa Lanchester in "Dial M."† She sniffs less but smiles more. Also Lennie had his hair popped‡ while we were working. Literally!

I walked B. to the Lenox Hill hospital to see her mother & Adolph walked me home stopping at Polls§ & being absolutely indecisive about what to buy.

---

* In 1964 the short-lived Music Theater of Lincoln Center had revived both *The King and I* and *The Merry Widow* starring, respectively, Risë Stevens and Patrice Munsel—both retired Metropolitan Opera sopranos.

† Robbins apparently confused Hitchcock's *Dial M for Murder* (in which Lanchester did not appear) with *The Razor's Edge,* in which she played a secretary, Miss Keith.

‡ A folk remedy for headaches that involves grabbing handfuls of hair and pulling them until a popping sound is heard.

§ William Poll Gourmet Foods, a shop on Lexington Avenue offering high-end but un-chichi prepared foods—beef bourguignonne, tea sandwiches, country ham, chicken soup—to a clientele including Diana Vreeland, Mike Nichols, Lauren Bacall, and Joan Crawford.

Sept[ember] 28

L.B.'s at one. More talk of where to go & how—Vineyard—Thursday 1. Can foresee Adolph looking worried about whether his room's as good as ours, etc. Told all I was taking along my own private peanut butter. Will take my own tea.

Got back to "the style" of the show again & over 3 hours found L & A & B didn't know yet what it was. Pointed out 7/8 & oh-oh didn't mesh: that all various openings didn't meet. . . .

Felt lots got shifted about & moved & uprooted. Examined various theater styles—

all types make a show.[*]

Out on a Limb with Lucia[†]
March 18, 1965

On Tuesday the American Ballet Theatre will present my production of Igor Stravinsky's *Les Noces* at the New York State Theatre as part of the current season. I am deeply grateful to Miss Lucia Chase, head of the American Ballet Theatre, for the comfort of her company out on a very high limb. I've told her over and over the tree is slippery and the height tremendous, but nothing will avail. "Forward" she cries. "Danger!" yell I. "Onward" she prods me. So, here we go.

What makes this ballet so difficult to present? Well, enough musical, logistical and economic complexities to have discouraged all but two stage productions in New York, one in 1929 choreographed by Anderson-Ivantzova and the

---

[*] Despite the work retreat in Martha's Vineyard and a promised $400,000 in capitalization from CBS, *The Skin of Our Teeth* never resolved its contradictions, and the collaborators abandoned the project in December. It was "a dreadful experience," wrote Bernstein to his friend the composer David Diamond.

[†] When *The Skin of Our Teeth* flamed out and City Ballet seemed uninterested in pursuing *Les Noces*, Robbins found Lucia Chase eager to mount the ballet for a twenty-fifth anniversary gala. This essay was published in *The New York Times* under the title "Robbins on 'Les Noces'" on Sunday, March 28, 1965. A manuscript version (or versions—this is Robbins, after all) is preserved in the Robbins Papers with the title used above; in numerous cases, Robbins's original wording (including the title) and punctuation have seemed to me more vivid or accurate than those used in the published version (the *Times* made errors in transcribing tempo markings, for example), and I've chosen to silently revert to them here.

better-known one, by Bronislava Nijinska, which was presented four times in 1936.*

Consider this:

A formidably difficult score (the conductor could write a whole article on this subject alone) necessitating many extra rehearsal hours for the 50 musicians and for the choreographer and dancers;

The orchestration consisting of 4 grand pianos, a choral group of 32, 4 solo singers, and 6 percussionists;

The fact that Stravinsky asks for the orchestra to be on stage, leaving the left-over space for the dancers, making a total of approximately 75 people, 4 pianos and piles of tambourines, kettledrums, cymbals, timpani, temple bells, snares, xylophones, etc;

Also that, if this special orchestra is not placed on stage, it must be squeezed into a pit already filled with the usual orchestra needed for the 2 or 3 ballets that will be playing in repertory the same night.

If you think the above reasons seem like mere paper technicalities, let me hasten to say that I've been asked three times before to do the ballet, twice by European state theaters (the only places that ordinarily have the resources to do it) and once at a festival. In one instance, the project was dropped because the problem of placing the orchestra couldn't be solved, in another, because the singers were not available for the time needed, and in the third instance, they found even *they* couldn't afford it.

The subject? Stravinsky calls it "a dance cantata . . . a scenic ceremony on the subject of the Russian peasant wedding . . . not a dramatization or stage spectacle or reproduction of a wedding, but using ritualistic elements and presenting them through actual wedding material of popular verse: a suite of typical wedding episodes told through typical talk . . . the latter, whether [by] the brides, grooms, parents or guests is always ritualistic."

These are not necessarily happy rituals. In a Russian wedding there is as much lamentation, grieving and protestation as there is dancing and drinking. In the first half (the preparations) there is little joy: both bride and groom are constantly and emphatically reassured that it's all for the best while the parents

---

* Robbins had never seen either of these versions of the ballet.

traditionally grieve over losing their children, and the bride over leaving her home and losing her virginity. There are also passionate, almost Pagan, invocations of Saints and the Virgin to bless and help the wedding. In the second half, after the off-stage church ceremony, the rituals turn to earthy traditions. The drinking makes everyone bawdier, a married couple is selected to warm the bridal bed, and finally the marriage is allowed to be consummated while all sit outside the nuptial chamber.

The music is a masterpiece. The score is monolithic and elegant—barbaric, beautiful and frightening. This description also suits some singular mountain; trying to climb it is what it feels like when choreographing *Les Noces*. It is absolutely unyielding. It cannot be disguised or altered by the choreography. No easy parts happen along. Very few lengths of the same metered bars follow each other. Shifts from 3/4 to 5/8 to 2/4 to 3/8 are the rule and an uninterrupted length of 6/4 is the exception. The dancers must count continuously, unerringly and with unceasing concentration. Their energy in rehearsal has been exhausted as much by using their brains for computers as their muscles for dancing. For once the music starts nothing can stop it. You push a button and this terrifying machine begins to scream, launches into its lamentations and incessant chattering, shocking you with unexpected outbursts and hypnotic murmurings. Still, with its strident shrill pictures, its compulsively repetitive ruts and bumpy shifts, a strange and reverent lyricism is aroused. An overpowering tension is created by the simpleness of the material (the wedding) and by the extraordinary, bizarre, and inspiring means with which Stravinsky has expressed it.

However, the music is just one level of the work. There are also the words. Except for the final 22 bars, they are sung, spoken and shouted without cessation, a word on each note (and more often than not, overlapping words). Their sense? A montage, or rather a Joycean stream, of Russian folk songs and poems, pieces of wedding conversations, toasts, taunts, prayers, ribald folk symbols and fertility images expressed in terms of animals and all nature. Furthermore the characters have no specific choral representatives; the groom is sung by the tenor at one time, the bass another, and sometimes by the whole chorus. The text is marvelous in the original Russian. It is couched in a special ancient folk language, passionate, rugged, bawdy, all of which has proved extremely difficult to convey in the unrhymed, somewhat proper "British" English translation.

Finally, deep within the whole passionate work there rests the poignant incongruity of an intensely personal moment being subjected to the public offenses of a ritualistic social ceremony. The bride and groom have been prepared and offered up in some holy and barbaric rite which must run its course.

We are going to try putting the musicians on stage. The set is being designed by Oliver Smith, costumes by Patricia Zipprodt and, as a special blessing, Leonard Bernstein will conduct the first performance. We won't know until dress rehearsal, or maybe opening night, if our plans are practical or are acceptable.[*]

If they are not, we will try other versions (time and money permitting) in the remaining 5 performances, possibly adding a scrim between the orchestra and dancers. Maybe we will even be forced to squeeze all those pianos, singers, and piles of percussion instruments into that pit with the usual orchestra.

All the above problems have only made the work a totally fascinating and absorbing experience. I have enjoyed doing it immensely, and look forward to the next time I attempt to scale that mountain, for although I have completed the ballet, I haven't finished with it. It is too deep and complex a work not to remain challenging. There may be other routes, and I'll want to try it again if the opportunity comes.[†]

To: Leonard Bernstein[‡]
March 30, 1965

I know fellars [*sic*] are not suppose [*sic*] to send flowers to other fellars, but I'm so deeply in gratitude to you—Even without *my* efforts—it is such a moving experience when you're at the baton.

Love,

J

---

[*] Although some critics (notably *Time* magazine's) found the stage cluttered and the choreography "hectic," others agreed with *New York*'s Marcia Siegel, who declared the piece "a triumph"—and ABT's box office increased 30 percent for its performances.

[†] And he did: see pp. 337 and 385.

[‡] Bernstein had apparently got over his hurt feelings about the *Skin of Our Teeth* fiasco: he conducted the *Les Noces* premiere, and this handwritten card was enclosed with a bouquet given to him by Robbins on that occasion. The only copy is in the Bernstein Papers, Library of Congress.

Out on a Limb with Lucia: Postscript[*]
March 16, 1965

People ask me the difference between choreographing for a show and for a ballet company. In *Fiddler on the Roof,* the major dance concerned a Russian Jewish wedding while *Les Noces* concerns a Russian Christian wedding, and I put equal energy and dedication [into] both. The main difference is that in doing a ballet the atmosphere is one of such blessed purity and concentration. Nothing is more pleasurable than the singleness of the rapport of the dancers, the score and the choreographer working together toward the goal. No longer must one worry about the entire show—the book, the lyrics, costume changes, actors' problems, lyricists' reprises, composers' themes and authors' egos—not to mention producers' whims and views, orchestrations, gimmicks, etc. Just one ballet and a group of dancers dedicated to interpreting the score. This in contrast to the complexities of collaboration and of the compromises which are necessarily all part of the show. On the other hand there are no collaborators to share the problems, despair, success or failure. Neither is there that very valuable out of town try out period in which the material gets solved of its technical problems first and enough time is left for the artistic ones.

To: Richard Buckle
September 27, 1965

Dear Richard,

Thank you for your postcard, book and letter, and forgive me for not answering sooner. More than anything, I'd love to join you on your trip through Naples, Florence, etc. It sounds marvelous. But I have already completed for myself three months on the beach at the end of Long Island. It was the most wonderful holiday I've had in a long, long time and the first summer I had

---

[*] Robbins drafted this paragraph to be included in his essay on *Les Noces,* but it wasn't in the published version—possibly for space reasons, or because there was no obvious place to insert it. But it speaks to his reasons for looking away from the commercial musical theater after *Fiddler,* as well as to his positive feelings about that process.

completely for myself. The weather was superb and I swam, sailed, rode a motor-cycle, sun bathed, and carried on only moderately.

Now I'm back in the big town and am still not located.* I've been sublet-ting Fizdale and Gold's apartment which I give up next week. I almost have a house which I've been trying to buy for five months. It's a very plain simple standard but marvelously comfortable house which would take care of my needs. It's on east 81 Street and naturally it has a Richard Buckle room waiting for you. I'm not sure where I'll be this coming month—possibly with Nora and Herbie,† but if you write me in care of Palisades, New York I'll get all the correspondence.

My relationship with NYCB has broken down completely ever since LES NOCES. George, in spite of my protestations, bringing only FANFARE to London and INTERPLAY to New York. I'll have to get that straightened out.

. . . I miss you and I love you and I send you all my best wishes always,

Jerry

To: John Dexter‡
January 21, 1966

Dear John,

I suggested "The Bacchae" with some tentativeness. I love it and want to do it but have held back from pushing a production into the works because of not knowing if I am ready for it. I'm still not sure, but your enthusiastic reaction both excites and panics me. It would take me a good deal of time to arrive at all its solutions, stylistically, etc., which would be the result of a long and necessary

---

* Robbins had left his longtime rental on East Seventy-Fifth Street when the landlady took over the apartment.
† Nora Kaye had married the choreographer and director Herbert Ross (1927–2001), who created the dances for *Funny Girl,* in 1959.
‡ John Dexter (1925–1990) had been named associate director of Britain's National Theatre (now the Royal National Theatre) in 1964. He had met with Robbins while on a visit to New York and invited him—the first American to be so honored—to do a play at the National; Robbins suggested Euripides's *Bacchae.*

spading, researching, and experimenting both prior to rehearsals and deep into the production period.

Please do read *this* script and if possible the Nabokov novel on which it's based.* Most of the play is brilliantly adapted. The few flaws are not deep.. some trouble in attempting to convert descriptive passages into dialog: also the very end—Cincinnatus's last speech and the final page—is sentimentalized but need not necessarily appear so on the stage. I would appreciate your reading and returning the script to me after its consideration by the proper people. It's the only copy I have.

"The Servant of Two Masters" I couldn't do as the impression of the Italian company is too strong in my mind.† I'll get "The Hostess" and the Sartre play‡ next week.

It was very good to see you and I am deeply appreciative of the invitation and hope that something can be worked out. Please do give my best to Ken and Sir Laurence.§

Yours,
Jerry

To: Kenneth Tynan
March 7, 1966

Dear Ken,

I know the Arrowsmith¶ translation [of *The Bacchae*] and it's about the best of those existing. But there are many words, expressions, and turns of phrase

---

* *Invitation to a Beheading*. It's not clear whose adaptation Robbins was enclosing.
† Carlo Goldoni's *Servant of Two Masters,* a knockabout mistaken-identity farce, had been presented by the Piccolo Teatro di Milano at New York City Center in February 1960.
‡ Seemingly Dexter had proposed some alternatives to Robbins, but it's unclear what is referred to here; the Sartre might have been the writer's Greek-inspired *The Flies,* or *The Condemned of Altona.*
§ Kenneth Tynan (1927–1980) and Sir Laurence Olivier (1907–1989) were the literary manager and artistic director, respectively, of the National Theatre.
¶ William Arrowsmith (1924–1992) was an American classicist and award-winning translator of Petronius, Aristophanes, and especially Euripides, as well as of the modern Italian writers Eugenio Montale and Cesare Pavese.

that bother me, this in spite of the fact that I now have six different less good translations. Are you averse to exploring the possibility of a better version?

Since my last letter to you I have been haunted by the image of Peggy Ashcroft* as Agave.† Can she move at all? It's not that I want to choreograph something impossibly wild for Agave, but that she is in the throes of Bacchic ecstasy and insanity. How are our mutual schedules working out? Can I get some idea soon as I am avoiding making commitments until I hear from you.

The grapevine being what it is, my excitement about the possibility of this project has crept into some of the columns, and if anything appears forgive me, as I know it would only be proper for the National Theatre to make any announcement. When theatre columnists have called me about it I have just said we are talking about a possible commitment but that nothing is definitely settled.

With all best wishes to you, John, and Larry,‡

Sincerely,
Jerry

To: Kenneth Tynan
May 5, 1966

Dear Ken,

I've just had a flop.§ The astounding thing is that it doesn't feel any different than having a success. I worked as hard and as fully and enjoyed it all and was only disappointed that it didn't work out. But onward and upward. I'll be happy to pick up THE BACCHAE again. The date of a year from December seems okay. I'll possibly be in England some time this summer and if so I'll let

---

* Dame Peggy Ashcroft (1907–1991) was one of the leading English classical actors—on stage and film—of the twentieth century.

† In Euripides's play, Agave, the mother of the straitlaced ruler Pentheus, is a devotee of the god Dionysus (in Latin, Bacchus) and kills her own son while in a Dionysian or Bacchic frenzy.

‡ Dexter and Olivier.

§ María Irene Fornés's *Office,* a surreal comedy that reads like a Marx Brothers movie written by Samuel Beckett, played its first preview at Henry Miller's Theatre on Broadway on April 21, 1966, and closed on April 30 without ever officially opening.

you know ahead of time and maybe we can meet. Meanwhile best to everyone and kindest personal regards.

Jerry

To: Laurence Olivier
March 24, 1967

Dear Larry,

I didn't notice the pause*.. the work here has been so time and energy consuming that it seems I wrote you yesterday and you answered today.

Fall '68 is okay as a flexible plan. Would Gielgud† be interested in THE BACCHAE? It might be masked—thus he (or you) could play any role or roles or even triple parts as they were originally done. My ideas are not just formalistic but go toward a raw, religious ritual filled with hallucinations, ecstasies and poetry. Images: the great African tribal masks, Noh masks, and some awesome Fate and God masks. The piece achieves its stature not through a large and heavy production but through the intense and intimate focus of three actors playing out the roles in a fierce and meaningful ritual.

All the above are just the instinctive rumbles of my searchings. The *how* I haven't yet made concrete.

What do you think?‡

All best,
Jerry

---

* Olivier had written on March 15 in answer to a letter from Robbins. Olivier said, "It's been a bad pause, hasn't it?" and might have meant not his own delay in responding but the fact that the *Bacchae* project, first discussed in 1966, had been thrown into a seeming ten-month hiatus by Robbins's involvement in the American Theatre Lab. Robbins didn't take the hint.

† Olivier had told Robbins that John Gielgud (1904–2000), an actor who with himself and Ralph Richardson dominated the British twentieth-century theater, was under contract for three plays at the National. Olivier was "not regarding THE BACCHAE as one of those, though it is perfectly possible he could be in it."

‡ Although Olivier was receptive to Robbins's ideas and the project stayed on a slow simmer until at least 1970, the renewal of the NEA grant extending ATL's life, and the intervention of other commitments, kept Robbins from following through with *The Bacchae* for the National.

To: Robert Graves
April 25, 1967

Dear Robert,

What a wonderful letter. It was immense, and I have so much to think about after reading your thoughts both about Dionysus and your Cophetua.[*]

When I talk about a work being "literary" it has really to do with the provinces of Dance which are separate from the provinces of mime, pantomime or realistic gesture. I try more and more to make ballets which do not need any of those things. Therefore I talk about your scenario being "literary" because I don't know how to convey so much of it except through pantomime. . . . What I try to find in Dance are those things that cannot be said in words. That's why rituals excite me so, because there is always such an other thing created and evoked and placed into the atmosphere. This cannot come out of specific pantomime but perhaps through symbolic movement of an act that has finally been ritualized into some gigantic gesture (gigantic in import not necessarily in size). . . . I believe strongly in the province of Dance which evokes emotions and reactions *not* describable in words. I'm sure you know what I mean: it's like the trip under the mushroom. One can come out of it and flounder, make metaphors about it, but one can't truly pin it down. So it is with ballet, dance and ritual. Although I see what you are getting at in your scenario I don't know how to handle it.

I haven't been working on Broadway at all for the past three years. Two years ago I did a straight dramatic show which failed miserably, and I have also, since then, done Stravinsky's "Les Noces" which worked out very well. It was tremendously challenging but it had been a lifelong dream to choreograph it and I finally got it out of my system. It, too, is a ritual and I would love so for you to see it. It's a little athletic, more so than I want it to be, and I think that this is so

---

[*] Graves had sent Robbins a ballet scenario based on the legend of an African king, Cophetua, who after never feeling attraction to a woman fell in love with—and married—a beggar. The legend is referred to by Shakespeare and inspired poems by Tennyson and Hugo von Hofmannsthal, a painting by the Victorian artist Edward Burne-Jones, and numerous other works in different genres. Robbins had tried politely to say the scenario wasn't something he could work with because it was too "literary."

because my overzealous attempt to communicate *everything* about what I heard and saw in the music.

Getting back to Cophetua, there *is* a ballet in your "big subject," the change from the matriarchal to the patriarchal system. It's a fascinating subject and one that I'll have to come and spend some time with you to understand. It's really existence-shattering to think of what you are suggesting and believe in as a point of view about what's happening. I am thrilled and excited at all the ramifications of these upheaving rituals and myths.

. . . All of the Dionysic rituals are like exploring a strange land, finding clues, artifacts and trails, all of which branch out and out and out and each of which is tremendously inviting and intriguing. You must know the Villa of Mysteries in Pompeii. What's the connection between that ritual, which is both apparent and hidden in the paintings, and Dionysus' mysteries? I've always wanted to do a ballet on the Villa of Mysteries but now it seems *all* the subjects are pulling together into one work.

I must tell you now of an extraordinary event that happened at my studio* during work. I asked each member to prepare an improvised scene without words, very short and to have some point to it. I had been asking the company to work with masks, not on their faces but holding them in their hands, putting the role outside of themselves and into the mask. We've done a great deal of work on this (inspired by some aspects of NOH). Finally, one boy did a scene of an old King who comes into his throne room to say goodbye to it. He had an old man's mask in his hand which he had draped a robe around. When he performed the scene I never watched the boy but only the mask. The old man came in slowly and I could tell that his eyes were bad. He looked around the room and then he saw something which later I realized was a statue of him as a young man. Then he looked at the throne, walked over to it and, with great difficulty, sat down in it. Then he looked around the room and you could see all the memories flashing through his mind; then something disturbed him and he focused on some flunkey who was cleaning the place. The old man picked himself up carefully, stepped down off the throne and left the room with just one more look back at his throne.

* At the American Theatre Lab.

The boy who performed it has quite a remarkable talent. A few days later I was working on other aspects and I asked him to go, from moment to moment, and play the same scene as a series of animals that were possibly akin to the thoughts that were going on in the King's mind. An absolutely astonishing thing happened. The boy disappeared and converted himself (just the way I imagine Dionysus did) into a series of animals, beginning with a mouse, to a young colt, to a wounded lion, to an aged eagle, and back to the mouse as he left. It made me weep because he struck some deep and primitive core within himself and with all those watching. It wasn't at all just an act of imitating animals but he totally disappeared into the animal. His mouse was frightened, timid, anxious: his young colt struggled to get on to his feet, snorted and moved and basked in the sun, tossed his mane, galloped about: when he saw the throne he went to it like a dog after a bone, sniffing and smelling away at it; when he climbed on the throne he was an old wounded lion roaring, licking itself, smelling and keeping an eye out for what was about. His exit, as the plumed eagle, was tremendous. With his back to us he plowed his way through the skies. Without his knowing it the boy had enacted so much of what I have heard you talk about and read in some of your books. It was both frightening and exhilarating to have the New York studio changed into a tribal ceremony for those few minutes. I wish you could have seen it.

To test out what was happening I asked other members of the company to do their own scenes, changing from animal to animal. Some truly had the spirit and converted themselves before our eyes into beasts, while others, not as perceptive or vulnerable or daring, still remained humans doing imitations of rabbits, snakes etc. I so wish you had been there to see what had happened.

As for the NOH plays I am deeply deeply in some spiritual relationship to them. Don't ask me where this connection comes from. I don't know myself but having gone to Japan and watched them and studied them and read as much about them as I can, I know there's some important and meaningful connection to me. It might be just that NOH plays are rituals in the way that ballets are rituals. But I guess what appeals to me mostly is the austerity and religious atmosphere, the paring away of unessentials [*sic*]. There is a relationship between that kind of theatre and things I want to attempt. It might be the intense religious fever of it and the sense of embarking on a truly holy and perhaps dangerous journey. It has an intensity and a dedication and a solemnization which is enrapturing.

. . . This has turned out to be a whale of a letter also. If you find the time please write me again, but be sure to let me know anyway when are the good times I can come see you. I have enjoyed very much our long distance conversations on paper, but it would be more pleasurable to see you yourself. Take care and I send you my love.

Zeami [a scenario]
May 30 [1967][*]

In the darkness one hears the shrill wail of a Japanese flute broken by the metallic clunk of the drum—& the lights come up slowly on the stage of a Noh play, isolated in darkness.

On the 18 x 18 playing area a chorus of 8 men is kneeling in 2 rows on the left. Across the back of the stage 3 musicians (2 drummers & the flutist) face the audience. Gravely, ritualistically, the play progresses; slowly one begins to sense that the Noh stage is placed within a much larger setting: behind the Noh musicians there is a full orchestra, behind the 8 kneeling men is a full chorus, and seated around them on a raised low platform are other players, also masked. . . .

By the time full light is up, the contemporary orchestra has taken over the music, the modern chorus the singing, and the original Noh players disappear, leaving the full stage to Zeami and the people in his life . . . [who] will also appear in the Noh play that he writes, sections of which appear in the course of the evening. . . . There is no scenery, only exquisitely symbolic props. The time,

---

[*] This treatment for a play about the Noh actor/playwright Zeami Motokiyo is handwritten in pencil on a yellow legal pad and dated May 30 with no year mentioned. However, it can be tentatively dated because on June 16, 1967, Robbins wrote to Yukio Mishima (1925–1970), the Japanese novelist, hoping to enlist his collaboration in writing a script; Mishima was intrigued, but nothing came of it. In 1970, Mishima committed ritual suicide. Robbins saved the news clippings about the novelist's death; perhaps it's a coincidence that only a year after that he drew on some of the ideas in this scenario for his ballet *Watermill.*

place, etc. can be set by the chorus—"1390. Summer. A forest path." The aim is to portray the life as subtly and beautifully as possible—a compilation of events told thru a variety of techniques all rooted organically in the works and art of Zeami.

Zeami lived in an enormously colorful transitory period. His life is the story of change—of how the arc and span of his 80 years encompassed the arc of nature, thru youth, passion, love, marriage, thru actor—writer—director—teacher—priest—thru lover to loser, thru fame to banishment.

"The purpose of all art is to bring sweetness to the hearts of all people and to harmonize high and low."—Z[eami]

To: Robert Wilson[*]
[August 1968]

Dear Bob,

Your letter meant a lot to me. It must have had some real magic in it. I read it when it arrived, in the midst of upsets, changes, terrible decisions to make, & all that drek. A week later I picked it up to really read it—this morning—& as I read it & re-read it, and stared at the paper & studied your words, all my problems became clear to me in a sudden insight & flash—& the heavy clouds of hot anxiety lifted—all this while reading your letter. And I truly believe you sent, thru the discussion of your own search & problems, your own wish to solve them—& those wishes hit me—entered me somehow—& were transformed into a kind of thought & will that helped me.

. . . Take pictures of your structure[†]—I'd love to see it. Where is Loveland

---

[*] Robert Wilson (b. 1941), now a prominent artist and theater director, was at this time an architecture student and movement therapist who had received a BFA from the Pratt Institute and worked with Robbins at ATL designing theatrical environments and leading exercises. The two formed a close bond and Robbins was often to be found at events staged at and by Wilson's Spring Street performance space/atelier, the Byrd Hoffman School of Byrds.

[†] In the summer of 1968, Wilson built an amphitheater out of disused telephone poles, titled *Poles,* at a feminist intentional community called Grailville in Loveland, Ohio, near Cincinnati.

Christine Conrad, who lived with Robbins for two years in the 1960s, in one of a series of portraits he shot soon after they met.

and what is Grailville? What is the nearest town, city, airport? For whom do you dance, exhibit, build?

Changes are scary aren't they. Maybe not, for you—because of your age—more so for me because of habits & age. . . . And the moments of *seeing* or recognizing change, can be dismaying—because it comes from a sudden clear look at the terrain of life we've been habituating [*sic*]; *but* we can see it clearly & only because in some interior area, we are already a little distant from it whether we know that yet or ever feel it.

Well, anyway—I embrace you.

I've seen the film "Hunger"* 2 times in 2 days—& am in love with it—& think you'd get it too. I've been in Europe twice, once for 6 wks—once for 3 days—& will probably go over again next week for a week. I'm not doing "Cannibals" (1 source of the bad time passed) but am working on a musical with Bernstein, Sondheim, Guare. . . . Source—Brecht!†

Come home soon—

All love—

J.

---

* *Hunger* was a 1966 Scandinavian film directed by a Dane, Henning Carlsen, starring a Swedish actor, Per Oscarsson, and based on a novel by the Nobel Prize–winning Norwegian writer Knut Hamsun. It was released in the United States in August 1968.
† Robbins had abandoned plans to direct George Tabori's macabre concentration-camp tragicomedy *The Cannibals* and instead enlisted the up-and-coming playwright John Guare, and his own erstwhile colleagues Bernstein and Sondheim, for an adaptation of Brecht's antibourgeois one-act play *The Exception and the Rule;* it never came together.

Doctor/Chris (Notes)*
[1965]

By the way he was lifting his chin, gasping for breath, averting his eyes—the gesture of a person hesitating before jumping into a pool, [or] a man attempting to dodge into a regularly revolving door, the patient knew the doctor was trying anxiously to interrupt the narrative of the weekend's adventures of a pickup & crush on a girl at the beach. Finally the doctor managed to slip in between the sentences of reportage:

Dr.: I think I better tell you that I know that girl.

Pause. What do you mean?

Dr. (continued): You may know I'm divorced, and I've met that girl—have had a relationship with her.

Pause. The door came to a stop & doctor & patient watched each other thru 2 partitions of glass. The way out or in was on either side—but each was still unable to push on in any direction.

Patient: Well—

How long did you know her

How deeply were you involved

Why didn't you say so the first time

Why did you say maybe its her problem

Why did you say there are other girls—

What was your reaction

What do you think can be done

Who knows you are treating me

Do the Hazens†

How free are your own reactions

What do you feel about the girl now

How do you think we can cope with the problem

---

* This undated fragment was filed among Robbins's 1960s papers; testimony from Christine Conrad dates it as 1965. Robbins had returned to therapy at some point in the mid-1960s, and these notes concern a conversation he had about Conrad with his current psychiatrist, whose real name appears in the title and has been redacted here.

† The friends at whose house Robbins had met Christine Conrad.

Why did it take you so long to come to telling me

Do you always feel it better to tell the patient "the truth" immediately rather than wait till one*

Notes

October 23, 1968

This will be an attempt to put down the thoughts about existence that have concerned and occupied me over the last weeks.

Where did they start—from whence arise? I think with an article re DNA in the NY Times which stated the theory that *all* the information of physical properties concerning an individual are contained in any *one* cell of DNA in the chromosomes. This stopped me. And there undoubtedly popped into my brain the idea that this earth is just like one man . . . [and] all mankind is related, like cells within each man. Carrying this idea further out . . . [JR's ellipses] then we *each* are clearly not only related, but an intensely organic part of each other—all matter is related. . . . [W]e are each a deep related part of *everything* else . . . [JR's ellipses] and *everyone* else.

With the last belief, behavior to & towards others, & from others, becomes different for me. With it, if I can keep it, all changes & defenses drop—& I am able to become the other person if I think of them as just being another part of myself. Things, people, incidents that would usually blow me sky high are all more acceptable or understandable and I can deal with it all. It seems to allow me to drop off my ego & my super defenses to some degree—& open to me whole new sets of relationships with everything. I can begin to handle *in contact,* not *in combat,* people & places. It takes work & effort, but in truth my entire vision of the world around me has changed. [. . .] It is a deeply moving conception, & I hope one that will stay with me. My programmed instincts are otherwise. To rear up, strike back, rattle my tail; it is hard not to have that happen immediately & automatically. . . .

* The fragment breaks off here.

To: Lincoln Kirstein
March 27, 1969

Dear Lincoln,

What a lovely note!* And how generous and welcoming you are. The admiration in all dept's is mutual and I will work with you.

I ran *all* the work I made, today. It went on for some 25 minutes—and there had been so many substitute dancers that it took 11 dancers to get through it all.† Some of it is worthy. Some isn't. . . . I've enjoyed the work [and] I just hope I can straighten it all out. Maybe it will be just an 18-minute thing. *Please* look at it when you get back.

It's been good being around dancers again . . . [JR's ellipses] and it's been wonderful being able to choreograph. I'm anxious to have you & George see the opus & tell me what you think. Please give George my bests [*sic*]. *Don't* build up the work to him . . . [JR's ellipses] even you have heard exaggerations. Come home soon.

All love—
Jerry

---

* Although he'd dropped in to oversee the maintenance of old ballets of his, Robbins's association with New York City Ballet had slackened, and he had not made a new work for the company since 1956. After he agreed to do a ballet for their upcoming gala, Kirstein had written him a note of thanks and welcome.

† Originally Robbins had been going to make a simple pas de deux for the principal dancers Edward Villella and Patricia McBride but "got turned on by the music" (he told a *Newsweek* journalist) and added more pieces, and more dancers, mixing and matching participants when some of them were unavailable for rehearsals. "More, more," said Balanchine when he saw a rehearsal. "Make it like popcorn! Keep eating; keep eating."

Dances at a Gathering Notes[*]

June 24, 1969

. . . I can't tell anyone *how* to make a ballet. I can tell you how I did it, but . . . I don't believe in the written word about the creative process. No matter what I say about any moment, I'll still only be skimming the surface. Gesture is constructive. Watch anyone talking or anyone listening. To the music of the voice, a dance is happening . . . and this dance goes on all the time, without our control or knowledge.

Choreography is ordering the gestures of the unconscious (Bullshit!). It is reaching down & in & pulling out & forming the gestural relationships between people. . . . Movement must have its logic—like the sequential logic of sound in music & words. . . . Chopped up, unfulfilled, underlined gesture, constipated, unreleased, over-difficult, show-offy—not in context—reveals the gap between man & his soul.

Of course, the most difficult part is getting to trust that soul, or self. Once one trusts, one must lead it forth into the daylight. . . .

I'm going to try to write about DAAG because it's the work that came out of me with the least amount of control, certainly the least amount of pain & anxiety—& it is of all my works the most mysterious of experiences.

The physicality of accepting the music . . . not ROMANTICALLY. Because Chopin is fierce. He knew a lot. . . . He's rough & painful & loving. He is full of stabbing notes & kissing notes. He repeats & repeats endlessly—& you've got to be ready to be dragged over the corrosive landscape again & again. . . . Put your mind in his. Relax and let his world take you over. Don't do it hard or methodically. Don't do it as a lesson and a task. Don't force it—but don't fear it.

So what I do really is play [the music] ALL the time. The hi-fi goes on & on—while I'm around the house, in the kitchen—on the john—when I go to sleep & immediately on waking up. Incessantly—like not getting enough—So that it literally grooves into my senses—brainwashed. . . . I let images form . . . some-

---

[*] These notes were written after *Dances at a Gathering*'s premiere. In the wake of its success Robbins might have been asked to write about its genesis for some periodical, but given the rough, confessional flavor of these notes, it's more likely he simply wanted to try anatomizing, for himself, the steps that led to its creation.

Figure studies from Robbins's life class sketchbook, early 1970s.

times they stay—most times not—but I don't worry about it. Violette's dance[*]
I caught in one total swoop. Ride the rhythm of it and let it carry you. Imply it
all—play with it—but never give any of it away. It's all—If I wanted to I could
let loose a torrent of experience, but I'm so rich with it that my smallest gesture
will let you know how much there *may* be underneath.

I'm trying not to edit my thoughts on this paper. Because it is what happens
at a rehearsal. All the finagling, flirting, coming on, all the energy, thrusts, par-
ries, all the relationships I have with the dancers, the music, the work . . . The
first state of the paper is like the first states I'm in when I begin. The initial dive
and energetic splash into the material. Soon I'll stop thrashing in the water and
start to see which shore I want to get to, & *how* to get there, where to swim, the
nature of the water—& most of all who else is going with me, & how to take
them with me. . . .

* Violette Verdy's enigmatic solo variation to Chopin's Étude, opus 25, no. 4 was one of the most
remarked-upon parts of *Dances at a Gathering*.

EASIER WITH DANCERS

They trust themselves more than actors do. DANCERS *know* they will make it their own. ACTORS have the complication of wanting to make it their own, & their horror of exposing what *their own* is. Dancers always reveal themselves.

To: Lincoln Kirstein
May 24, 1969

Dear Lincoln,

Again thank you for your letter. It's exciting isn't it?[*] I'm somewhat bewildered by the affect [*sic*] the ballet seems to have on everybody. I have never worked so easily and fluently and I have never received such a press. I guess all I have to do is forget it and go on and not worry about why or how.

You must know that I am deeply interested and concerned with the City Ballet, primarily because the Master Choreographer is working there and what more honor and pleasure and education could one have outside of being in that surround. I just want you to know that my deep interest is there. And that whatever I can do to help you I will. It's a little early to do anything officially and it's not that I'm interested in either films or musicals at this point, but that I do feel that my working with the company closely, but in an unofficial capacity, is the best way to proceed right now.[†] I would like to see all my ballets in repertory somewhere. OPUS JAZZ has been tried by Ballet Theatre, and now by Harkness,[‡] but I don't think the latter will make it. It was choreographed for 8 marvelously swinging and understanding men and women, and as soon as any

---

[*] Although *Dances at a Gathering* received an unofficial unveiling at City Ballet's gala on May 8, its official press premiere wasn't until May 22, when it was greeted by ecstatic reviews. Robbins was ambivalent: "I am forced to . . . go ahead & do another . . . & not notice that they said the last was the capstone of my career. Great words . . . [JR's ellipses] 'capstone'—'career.' Ugh" (JR to unnamed correspondent, [1969]).

[†] During Robbins's absence from the company his old title of Associate Artistic Director had been abolished, as had that of Artistic Director: Balanchine was now simply "Ballet Master."

[‡] The Harkness Ballet was a small company founded by the Standard Oil heiress Rebekah Harkness in 1964; it was dissolved in 1975.

company has 6 of each I'll go with it, and I think that NYCB should also be explored.* But as I said to Betty† and George over a year ago, all of my ballets are available to NYCB whatever they want.

I'll come back‡ end of June and would like a few weeks' rest, then I'd like to come up to Saratoga.§ There will be two of us while you are looking for a place for me to stay (you met Christine backstage with me many times). I don't know exactly what I'll do in Saratoga as I'm still in a whirl about "Dances."

Thank you so much, dear Lincoln, for your Russian advice. I'll try to visit *all*. Most of all I do thank you so very deeply for your support and interest and belief. I'm very happy and comfortable over at the State Theatre and you have played quite a major part in making me feel so.

All best always,
Jerry

Notes (Summer 1969)¶

July 21

So "It" gets worse & better. And the tug of war, pulling on nerves, goes on. "Pain" is the name of the lovely game—get it & give it. Torture is the main action—self & other. There something is happening. . . . Frustration is the desired catalytic agent. And one could see that all is enjoyable.

But the outer & inner actions do not match. Outer: a couple: got it made: fame, success, money, popularity, attention, travels, glamor: "A Pair," goes thru public life, making it easier for each publicly to make it publicly. Success for each.

---

* Neither Balanchine nor Kirstein took Robbins up on his offer of *N.Y. Export: Opus Jazz;* it wasn't until 2005 that the ballet entered NYCB's repertory.
† Betty Cage (1917–1999) joined City Ballet in 1947 and became its "labor negotiator, certified public accountant, legal expert, mother superior, confessor, psychiatrist," in the words of Lincoln Kirstein, City Ballet's general director. Her formal title was general manager.
‡ Robbins was about to leave for a trip to Stockholm (to oversee a production of *Les Noces* for the Royal Swedish Ballet) and to Russia, accompanied by Christine Conrad.
§ New York City Ballet customarily performed for the month of July at the Performing Arts Center in the upstate New York spa town of Saratoga Springs.
¶ These notes chronicle the fraying of Robbins's relationship with Christine Conrad.

Inner: a gulf. a silence. a disaster. Faking it. The moon—barren. unable to receive or give messages. Sterile . . .

Now I must move into that no man's land between us. I will try. Now I understand there is no such thing as surrender. Because now I know I can't be "*caught*." I am. I am a separate person. . . .

August 4

Now the geography is clearer. Is *all* discovered? No more explorations? No more testings? is this all there is to it?

August 5

If I *know* I can't be caught . . . if I know I am doing what I do for & from my own desires & wishes—then I am free to really be where I am, do what I want & not refuse people because I feel I am "giving in" to them.

With Chris, I go thru that struggle all the time. I won't GIVE IN. No, not all the time . . . but the water-rises of resentments . . . mostly resenting my own feelings & desires. Keep your fucking hands off! I cry & act.

But sometimes I can recognize that she CANNOT have me . . . there is no way for her to possess me . . . she does not own me, even in the most intimate of embraces. And that's where it all is, isn't it—in bed—in possession.

Why do we stay with each other? Well something is dishonest in the relationship and until we find out what the honest thing is, we're caught.

August 8–9th [19]69

The pattern of my life is altered already.* Whether we live together or not, the form I've built must be changed from here on. The music you add to the sounds of my life changes its harmonies.

To show you my love, I break the house I live in and shatter the pattern of my life. What would you have me wear, which foods prepare? What music soothes you, which colors please your eyes. What kinds of storms are necessary: how much rope how much submissiveness; what angers, and how much kind-

---

* This loose journal entry was written as Robbins's relationship with Christine Conrad was coming asunder; the unnamed "you" seems to be Edward Davis.

ness. I will bring with me all my experience, passion, artistry, and craziness. I will leave behind what doesn't fit. I offer you all of me. . . .

You push me away, then complain of loneliness. You manufacture a scene around me & then accuse me of acting in it. But if we stop holding our breaths, stop withholding our already captured hearts, and look at all of it, admit *all* of it, we can be together.

Notes (1969)
October 30

I never mind being queer when I am in love . . . it is when I am alone that I feel the loneliness & shame. I don't feel upset because of Chris—or as if I suffered a public loss—yet I do when I feel [Edward] dumped me—as if that's more to be ashamed of.

To: Allen Midgette[*]
November 10

Dearest Allen,

There is no way of my trying to catch you up with what's happened since we last saw each other. But I do want you to know I have been thinking so very often of you. And you are not far away ever. I was sorry to miss seeing you in Rome (did you ever get my wires etc.) but here is a capsule of what's happened.

May—Open new ballet.[†] Can't wait for you to see it. New for me—and acclaimed by all—but mostly because of its loving or poetic qualities. I can't "see" it yet—too close.

---

[*] Allen Midgette (b. 1939), an artist, actor, and habitué of Andy Warhol's Factory, starred in several Warhol films and had been a friend of Robbins's since the early 1960s.
[†] *Dances at a Gathering.*

June—travel to Stockholm, to open "Les Noces." Then to Helsinki & Leningrad with Chris. Hate Russia—leave (supposed to go on to Moscow)—& come home exhausted & with some stupid Russian virus.

July–August—Spent out at Water Mill. Rent an old farm house. Summer with Chris—Very Bumpy—& tough & good at same time. But bumpy.

End of August—Split with Chris. Travel to Israel to stage Moves. Do so with [Edward Davis], friend of about a year. We have *great* time in Israel (Old Jerusalem will flip you out) & Mykonos on way back & then have to get back to N.Y.

Early Sept.—Very rough time back in N.Y. Hate it! Hate my house . . . my career . . . my "J.R. incorporated" status . . . want to change everything. Want to work at ballet more than ever . . . don't want a corporation, staff, house, etc.

Mid Sept—Given mescaline* & sent on a terrifying & destructive trip that blows apart my whole being. Lasts hard for 48 hours—& for next 3 weeks come close to suicide, murder—& total anarchy. Dr. wants to hospitalize me etc. Start then on a new work hoping I'll get my head together by having to concentrate, although till that point could still not make any sense of any music.

Late Sept–Mid Oct—Begin rehearsals. 2nd day it is going well when suddenly bam, my Achilles tendon snaps in two—& I'm in a hospital. 4 days later they operate on it, sew it together, put it in a cast, & give me lots of lovely Demerol. 10 days later I'm out of the hospital with leg in cast up to knee. Completely dependent on others (HATE IT) & in terrible state. Prognosis—from 4 to 6 months before leg capable of starting careful work.

Oct.—DEEP DEPRESSION

Learn how to walk on crutches (very tiring after little while) & how to get around on wheel chair. Try going on with new work from wheel chair. Finish 3 minutes section. Both hard & exciting to do. Result, pretty good but not personal.

Nov.—Find out it *wasn't* Mescaline, but acid & speed (a huge amount) that I was given. Still feel shaky at times—& as if the whole fall had literally exploded

---

* He and a friend were in Water Mill, and at first Robbins, entranced by tall fronds of beach grass, had pulled the stalks up and begun dancing with them; suddenly, however, he began having terrifying visions that made him curl up on the sand in a fetal position.

like a bomb under my life. I'm out of the large plaster cast now. Still on crutches & 1 leg—can drive a car—but am *very* limited in activities.

When I tripped, I had on that chocolate brown boat-necked long-sleeved pullover you gave me in Italy (Positano I think)—& you were with me so much. I keep thinking of you. . . .

So that's the brief outline of my hectic fall—called BOOM!! I've learned a lot from it. But what a hell of a hard way to learn.

Do write me.

I love you—
J

PS: This isn't really a letter . . . just a series of events to get them out of the way. I'll write again.

Notes (1970)
January 20

I've always traveled with a friend but never knew he was faithfully with me wherever I journeyed.

His disguises were so ingenious that he infiltrated my most private realms & pierced thru the sentries guarding my work, my lovemaking & my fantasies.

Over the years his presence took on a subliminal concreteness; he even entered that shadowy part of my sentience which secretly took note of some foreign presence but kept the knowledge quarantined away from any disturbing alarmed consciousness.

So his power & possessiveness increased. And he even grew bold enough to make open and startling appearances. . . .

Now I see him.

We sit face to face.

He smiles.

He says—*see,* my love.. you didn't know it, wouldn't see me, but here I am— No don't be alarmed. You know I've always been with you. Smile back. . . .

I am your lover, Death.

Yucatán–New York Journal, February–March 1970
March 11 [1970]

SNEDENS

Back from Yucatan,* † I start work on Monday on the G.V.'s.†

It's rough. I get up late . . . & can't get into NY on time. Troppo grosso.‡ Headache. Pulling it together is rough. Change rehearsal from 1 to 2.

Get into NY and over to Juilliard 1/2 [hour] ahead. Change, watch class & start.

Ugh. Nyah. Phoo.

Lots of choreography. Var[iation] 5. [The dancers] not up to it yet. Neither am I. 2–4, exhausted & down. The solid Bach doesn't give.

Think about him. I hit my head against his architecture, trying to find a way in. And klunk, down I fall—& pick myself up & walk a distance away & look again (listen), go back at full steam & klunk! Pratfall.

He only offers his math & concrete construction & says—that's how I made it—don't ask for anything else—that's how it is, baby—so go—on your own.

I can't find [the] key, spine—whatever you call it—can't get to the layer in depth to "catch on." Find the gesture—medium—my source. Can't get a finger-hold.

I go home. Think—play music. This a.m. play again. Suddenly hear a version of [variation] 5 that might work. It's the repeats that do me in. Suddenly see it with two boys splitting the material & finally coming together.

Get to rehearsal. . . . Break the variation in half. A-1 1st boy; A-2 2nd boy. B-1 1st half, boy 1, 2nd half, boy 2. B-2: both boys ending in embrace of victory.

It seemed about 1/2 as long. So clear was the feeling . . . [JR's ellipses]

---

* Robbins had gone to Yucatán for a short trip with Robert Wilson and Wilson's partner Andy deGroat; while there he'd confided to Wilson his feelings of rejection and despair but on his return threw himself into the creation of *Goldberg Variations* (see p. 287).

† Bach's *Goldberg Variations* for keyboard. The particular variation he was working on, no. 5, is fiendishly fast, complex, swirling: the player's hands continually cross and recross each other until finally coming to rest.

‡ Italian for "too much."

Oh

That's what I thought about last night & this a.m. What wasn't working was that I hadn't gotten into relationships. Who are these people—how do they relate. Do I like them. Do they like each other. Suddenly realized all that was *out* of my thinking & I was concentrating only on the math.

So

The Var[iation] 5 was about the zest of gamesmanship in friendship—& that led me straight thru Var[iation] 6 . . . [JR's ellipses] a relaxed pause—beach moment—& exit.[*]

London 1970 Journal
[October 23]

She came down the stairway into the room—& she wasn't Edna Ferber at all.[†] She had a crocheted violet shawl around her shoulders—& was a beautiful combination of chic & sloppy. Her hair, deep auburn, fell back over her ears, but some over her eyes. Her body, covered neck to boots, gave 2 messages at once. With her came a gentility—a selfless & firm tenderness firmly given to you. . . .

When we were introduced I laughed—& said But you aren't Edna Ferber at all (she'd been dead a few years—but you know with Robert anything is possible). We shook hands, and sat next to each other facing the others. I listened to

---

[*] Things were by no means as simple as that. *Goldberg* wasn't finished until the spring of 1971, and Robbins took a break from working on it to stage *Dances at a Gathering* for the Royal Ballet in London in the fall of 1970.

[†] During his London visit Robbins had been invited to a dinner at Robert Graves's house; Graves (who was beginning to exhibit signs of the memory loss that would soon engulf him) told him that one of the other guests would be Edna Ferber—an American playwright and novelist who had died two years previously, in 1968, at the age of eighty-two. Instead it was the Irish writer Edna O'Brien, then thirty-nine, whose first novel, *The Country Girls* (1960), had been banned in Ireland and denounced from the pulpit for its frank treatment of women's sexuality.

her. One of Robert's witch-white-goddesses, [giving] off the radiance and secrets of Robert's love.

December 7

Am afraid to really consult a calendar to find out how long it's been.* I know I came back from London on October 24. I know I went onto Harkness the 26th. I was there 2 weeks—then home, & have been here—.

Can't tell if it's been 1–2–3 months or weeks—All is blurred together—except seeing Edna put it in some connected place. Edna the 23rd Oct in London and Edna Dec 4th [in] N.Y. pulled the pieces together.

She does frighten me. She is intimidating and . . . [h]er appetites are apparent including the one to be hurt.

To: Robert Wilson
June 2, 1971

Dear Bob,

Well, it's over!† The thing I feel is a lot of numbness . . . the work for the past month was difficult—& not enjoyable as I felt out of connection with it . . . couldn't "feel" what I was doing..& only experienced the act of manufacturing, making patterns—& hacking my way to the end. I was deeply depressed & down on the work.. fully expected "good try" sort of reactions. I guess I don't know what it is I've made, & won't till next year when perhaps I can be a little objective. But the whole thing has given me some thoughts—& scarey ones. Like I seem to be at a point where my technique & skill can now allow me *not* to think or control the material . . . which is scarey, as I have always been so in control. I don't know what the next work will be—except

---

* While in London, Robbins had come down with strep and hepatitis (misdiagnosed) and had been given cortisone, to which he had a bad reaction. He was very ill when he returned and was hospitalized at Harkness Pavilion, part of what was then Columbia-Presbyterian Hospital.
† *Goldberg Variations,* after being delayed by Robbins's injury, then his illness, and then a musicians' strike at City Ballet, had finally premiered on May 27.

I'm pulled to Nijinsky*—in order to go into my own madness—a trip I want to take again. Most of all I'm exhausted. I need some time of quiet & being alone.

... I love you,

J

To: Ingmar Bergman
June 23, 1971

Dear Mr. Ingmar Bergman:

I wonder if you have any time to see me. I am considering doing a work in films and I need some advice. Because you are the man whose films I admire most, I am presuming on our brief acquaintance and my deep admiration to ask you if I may come see you and seek your consultation. After having turned down numerous opportunities to work within the usual system here I now can make a film† on my own terms. The film is a personal one and I would like to pursue it in the same way and with the same artistic endeavors with which I approach my ballets. But I am inexperienced in techniques, budgets, etc. Because I deeply sense the uniqueness of the pure and personal vision of *your* films, I would be most fortunate and grateful if you find yourself able to confer with me.

About the film—it is only an idea in my head—no script yet—just both strong and vague feelings similar to my feelings when I am brooding upon a ballet idea. But in spite of having done two Hollywood films (or *because* of having done them) I feel inexperienced about approaching this kind of film and hope that as a fellow writer in the arts you could help me.

---

* Robbins had been contracted by the producer Harry Saltzman, who had optioned Nijinsky's recently published diaries, to direct a film about Diaghilev's troubled star, but when Robbins had been unable to find a writer-collaborator, Saltzman had dismissed him. Robbins still harbored hopes of doing something with the Nijinsky material, however—whether a ballet or a film.
† This project appears to have been an alternative Nijinsky film (Saltzman had yet to proceed with the picture he had fired Robbins from and indeed would not do so for nearly a decade).

I am leaving for Paris and then Morocco this week . . . but I will come to see you or meet you now, anywhere, or in August or September, etc.* . . .

With affection and admiration as always,
Jerome Robbins

Journal #1†

Oct[ober] 25th 1971

There are exactly 30 pages in this book including the front & the back flyleafs. Did they know, when they made it, that if an entry a page long was made each day, one could note two months, by going over to the backside and working forward–backward in time. Which is what this is about.

For instance, as you read this, the page opposite, or the whole book, might be filled up . . . but for me putting down each word as I think & write it, there has been pure blank empty unsullied undesigned whiteness to the right of each word and line. . . . [T]he area, thought, and calligraphy ahead is forever unknown to me—but to you it's already fact whether you've read it or not. . . . For you reading it now, (which is or will be *later* for me—) the whole journey has already been taken and left the design and patterns behind.

November 9, Tuesday

. . . I'm tired of complaining, of spilling my guts & using energy to be liked. One night last week, I thought how nice it would be, how freeing, not to be liked.. or not to worry about being disliked. Maybe I'm going thru that. I don't know. I'm going thru something & can't figure it out. I also feel that my staying

---

* Although Bergman was in the middle of filming *Cries and Whispers* that summer, he wired in response that he would be "honored and happy" to discuss Robbins's ideas with him (IB to JR, July 2, 1971). They failed to meet, however, and the project went nowhere that summer; if Robbins went into his madness, it was by revisiting the scene of his 1969 acid trip in his Noh ballet, *Watermill*.
† The first in a series of twenty-five Japanese notebooks of hand-milled accordion-folded paper, with block-printed front and back covers and contrasting endpapers, which Robbins purchased from Takashimaya, a luxury Japanese retailer on Fifth Avenue. He wrote in them vertically, sometimes even circularly, as well as horizontally, in different colored inks, and decorated the pages of some volumes with watercolors or collages. One journal is entirely devoted to collages and has nothing written in it.

away from "Water Mill" is one sign of my swirling feelings. To do *my* thing. To take my clothes off.. to be myself.*

. . . Trying to get to this myself. Waiting for a dream, or an insight to clear it for me.

November 14

. . . Fighting a downer—like last fall's when I was really down with hepatitis, cortisone, etc. Just against the bleakness of my relationships—not of my life—but of the loneliness of my non-connections.

November 15th

I was traveling in Europe and was in Rome with a friend-lover.† . . . I'd taken him at night to a place I knew—it was once a church & now had been made into an ordinary not-too-popular bar. We had been caught in a terrific downpour; when we got there we were drenched thru . . . [and] because I was soaked I took my clothes off. Someone scratched my behind lightly—half play, half suggestive. I turned & there was a nondescript person there. . . . I followed him into an area which I hadn't known before & it took me a few minutes to realize it was a Turkish bath, all dark brown wood & dusky steam, not many people in view but [I had] the feeling that a lot was going on just out of sight and that you could see it if your eyes adjusted to it. The atmosphere changed, & I got out of that section, tried to find my friend, did; then couldn't find my clothes to get dressed to leave. Finally found my coat (the rest had been taken) & we both left. . . . I suddenly realized it wasn't my coat at all; in fact, it went clear to the floor like a maxi & was way over-large. But by now I had lost my way, had no money, no wallet, no cards, & was stranded in Rome, . . . worried about the amounts of charges THEY (the stealers-exploiters) would run up [on my cards].

It took a long time for the dream to wear off. Much anxiety about being lost, or rather stranded, in the hands of strangers in a foreign land, with no

---

* *Watermill*—named after the Long Island village of Water Mill where Robbins's acid trip had taken place, and inspired by the Noh plays he had worked on at ATL—was more pageant than ballet; it featured a nearly motionless, nearly naked central figure who first divests himself of his long ceremonial robe and then observes the actions of figures from his past, such as kite runners and young lovers, for close to an hour, to the accompaniment of Japanese koto and flute music.
† Robbins recorded dreams as well as events in his journals; it's not always clear which is which.

money . . . and no clothes. The anxiety was real. When I woke up I brooded a lot about it—& then came the revelation—I *want* to lose my clothes—I *want* to get rid of my OVER COAT— . . . but I have great anxiety about it. Lost——the loss of who I am—what I am—my identity so tied up with my achievements that without *my* over-coat I am frightened and helpless. HELPLESS. A word to think on . . .

TO BE COAT LESS
TO BE HELP LESS
WITHOUT MEANS   & then to take care of it myself.

I haven't said much about work. . . . Requiem* is coming along & I've blocked out 3 sections. Don't like it when it isn't "discovered" by me but just covered by me . . . which is how I feel about sections of Goldberg. So uncreative and at arm's length. A real stand-off which puts *me* off if not others. Ground out rather than created or felt . . . [JR's ellipses] all the bad spots were made during the recovery after last year's hepatitis-cortisone blow-out. But it's a scarey thing to see. Haven't got back to Watermill yet.

December 1
Made it thru November . . .

I'm alone. And can't figure it to make it otherwise. I get so tense about work because it is my only relationship. . . .

When I watch Balanchine work it's so extraordinary that I want to give up. There can't be anything more personal or out front than his work. . . .

[Undated]
"I'M AFRAID I'LL BE FOUND OUT."
  "BUT WHAT WILL BE FOUND OUT . . . THAT YOU'RE QUEER?"
  "NO. I'M NOT AFRAID OF THAT."

---

* In addition to *Watermill,* Robbins was choreographing Stravinsky's *Requiem Canticles* for the Stravinsky Festival that Balanchine had planned for the coming spring season at New York City Ballet.

"WELL, THEN, WHAT? . . . THAT YOU'LL DIE?"

"NO, NOT THAT . . . I'M AFRAID *SOMETHING* WILL DIE. . . . ALL MY WORK . . . I'M AFRAID I'M REALLY NO GOOD . . . NO GOOD AT ALL TO ANYONE IN THE WORLD . . . THAT I CAN'T LOVE . . . THAT I HAVE ONLY SELFISH FEELINGS . . . AND THAT I WILL DIE BEFORE I CAN CONNECT THE WAY MY INSIDES LONG TO CONNECT . . . AND THE IRONY IS THAT MY CURRENT FERTILITY OF PRODUCTION, AND ITS CONNECTIONS TO AN AUDIENCE ONLY INCREASES MY AWARENESS OF MY OWN LONELINESS. . . . AND I'M AFRAID THAT THAT FAILURE OF MY LIFE WILL BE KNOWN AND I'LL BE PITIED."

December 20

I guess it was what is called a homosexual panic.[*] Fag. Commie, traitor—and my reputation taken away—then who am I, and will that *ever* get into my head clearly? So I dumped down & sank back & wondered about the past wrapping me now—and how fully I recapitulated back to 1952 & McCarthy days & panic. . . . I still can't get my overcoat off.

February 5

DONE—FINISHED—or at least brought up to an opening night.[†] [The audience] began to laugh and titter and applaud at the runners across the stage—& I knew that there'd be boos & little cries of dissent—but a heavy barrage of cries—& it was surging into the heavy waves of surf and playing in the danger of it. . . . Some of my friends felt it was a big undressing—[but] I feel it could have been *more* undressed.

---

[*] On December 12, *The New York Times Book Review* had featured a review by Victor Navasky of Eric Bentley's *Thirty Years of Treason: Excerpts from Hearings Before the House Committee on Un-American Activities,* which was critical of Robbins's testimony.

[†] *Watermill* opened on February 3, 1972, and received the mixed reception Robbins reports: cheers and boos.

To: Clive Barnes[*]

February 4, 1972

Dear Clive,

It's always comforting to get a favorable review, but what is much more than comforting is to get one (favorable or not) that deeply understands what one was after. I was truly amazed at the extent to which you seemed to be piped into my head about "Watermill" and I do thank you for writing about it with that understanding and perception.

I also was happy to have you acknowledge the connections with Robert Wilson's work. I must point out however that he is not a student, graduate or even a technician of the American Theater Lab. I met Bob thru the Lab (he was recommended to me as a scenic designer!) and soon realized his immense genius. "Watermill" in many ways owes much to Bob, his thinking, influences of his talents, and his generosity of spirits. He has been as inspiring to me about the possibilities & dimensions of the art I practice as Mr. Balanchine has been. They both always open my head.

Thank you again Clive. After that stormy opening night reception your notice was like a warm fire . . . no, the warmest of fires! Thanks.

Sincerely—
Jerry

---

[*] Clive Barnes (1927–2008) was both dance and theater critic for *The New York Times* from 1965 to 1977. His review of *Watermill* (February 4), in which he mentioned its connection to the work of Robert Wilson, called it "a fantastic ballet . . . that attempts to question the art of ballet and, indeed, our concept of the theater."

To: Richard Buckle
February 11, 1972

Dear Buckle boy—

. . . Just had an opening that started out to rival "Sacre's" premiere.* Violent cheers *and* catcalls. Reviews, good. But it certainly pulled a usually lethargic audience onto their feet. And all for a very slow very quiet hour-long non-dance (or non-*ballet*-dance) work. Villella is tremendous. Strange work.

Hope this finds you well . . .

J

Stravinsky Journal†
April 27 [1972]

Talked to George.‡ I said I thought all our work was so derivative because his work was such an extreme model of perfection of the Stravinsky scores. He said Look—everything we do will look alike as the company is trained in a very special style & it will all come out like *his* style. If I were choreographing for Jack Cole dancers, it would come out looking like Jack Cole. George demonstrates & acts out all he relates. I told him of seeing Goldwyn Follies§ on TV & he *enacted* his *whole* episode with Goldwyn. He's fantastic—leaving out words & supplying gestures instead.

---

* Vaslav Nijinsky's ballet to Stravinsky's *Le Sacre du Printemps,* on May 29, 1913, at the Théâtre des Champs-Elysées in Paris, famously prompted a riot that began in the theater and spread to the surrounding streets.

† A small Italian-paper-covered journal Robbins kept of his work for City Ballet's Stravinsky Festival. Most entries are merely lists of tasks to be completed: names, times, dates, ballets.

‡ Balanchine.

§ *The Goldwyn Follies* was a 1938 Hollywood variety spectacular produced by the movie mogul Samuel Goldwyn, who had hired Balanchine to create dances for it (at a salary of $1,200 weekly). It starred Balanchine's then wife, Vera Zorina. (See p. 38.)

To: Robert Fizdale and Arthur Gold
June 15, 1972

Dear B & A—

Frantic time!* It's like being on an express train whizzing thru stations at break neck speeds—& as the stations flash by you *almost* can read the names– "Pulcinella"—gone—"Violin Concerto"—GONE—"Requiem"—GONE—& those flashes were the entire experience of visiting those places after having read about them, studied the maps, selected the sites, & restaurants you wanted to see, found out about the weather, hotels, currency, visas, inoculations etc, packed & voila—passed!

It's going at a sickening speed now. George's Violin Concerto is George at his best—& it's his top "best." I haven't seen Symphony in 3 movements:—Taras's Symphony for winds looks interesting in what I've seen. I've done the Circus Polka for 48 little gals from the school, (I'm ring-master)—& I like the Requiem very much. But none of us are having time to feel in anyway fulfilled by the experience.

George is great—& his demonstration of the title role in Pulcinella† is terrific. We haven't seen the scenery & costumes but I know they're overdue. G & I have become closer—sharing the same dressing room, ballet, & identical knee injury. I've loved helping him & know him better than ever. He seems very happy—excited & at the same time calm & patient. I'm really sorry you haven't been here to see him at rehearsals of Pul[cinella]. It's fierce, mean, peasant shrewd, evil & so admirable, a son of a bitch . . . hard, wooden, indestructible.

So you'll be back end of July. Good, how could summer be summer without you here in Watermill. I'm still not sure of my plans. Maybe the knee operation, but if I am postponing it—then I may go to Spoleto beginning of July. If you

---

* City Ballet presented its full repertory of forty ballets during the spring season, then went dark for only six days to rehearse all the new and revived works for the eight-day Stravinsky Festival. Among the new ballets premiered were *Pulcinella* (co-choreographed by Balanchine and Robbins), *Stravinsky Violin Concerto* (Balanchine), *Symphony in Three Movements* (Balanchine), *Symphony for Winds* (John Taras), *Circus Polka* (Robbins), and *Requiem Canticles* (Robbins).
† The title role in this Punch-and-Judy ballet was danced by Edward Villella; Balanchine and Robbins played two beggars in the work's comic finale, to wild applause.

aren't too full & busy it'd be fun to drive up after & visit you.[*] Could you let me know? I think I'll be driving around Italy a bit. Let me know any way what your plans are. Has your house been taken for July? (Watermill?)

Haven't seen Tanny. Speak with her sometimes. Snedens is lovely when I can get there.

All for now. Off to the express again.

Love—
Jerry

Journal #2

June 29 [1972]

ON FLIGHT TO SPOLETO

The S[travinsky] Festival is over. An extraordinary experience—it flew by at sickening speed—too fast to enjoy, savor, no less see & feel. Of course a week of wild excitement & enormous delight, true delight, backstage—of making it happen—joined together on George's clear example—"well—we'll *do* it"—& we did it with such calm and untrampling of toes—. G.B. was fantastic—knowing it would work—& to everyone's amazement, it did. If he had said we could all go to the top of the State Theater & fly off & around Lincoln Center, we would have gone & we would have flown, that's how faithful we felt & how awe struck we were by being led into such areas of incredible danger,—& sailing thru them with calm faith & quiet jubilation.

I worked hard and think I proved myself valuable not just as choreographer but in the whole production end. Had a bad time with the dancers when they left a rehearsal I couldn't get to in time because I was lighting on stage—& I didn't get my anger out and it kept festering against them. I did it wrong.

Circus Polka[†] delightful to audience but "made" to me. Dancing it—or

---

[*] Gold and Fizdale were performing in Italy.

[†] A brief jeu d'esprit for forty-eight diminutive students from the School of American Ballet dancing to music Stravinsky had composed for the elephants of the Ringling Brothers circus; Robbins, in scarlet hunting coat and top hat, was the ringmaster.

being comfortable was hard. (Must think about it.) Dumbarton[*] came out pretty much as planned, to my surprise, as I was down on it. George thought I ought not to use taps—but I did—which was hard for me to do—& I felt badly afterward going against his solicited opinion—but now I'm glad I stuck to my ideas; & I'll change it next time. It was hard but good for us. Canticles[†] came out very well—& I was pleased with its result. I was very proud of it, especially as George praises it highly & thinks it my very best work. Pulcinella was freakishly successful as it really wasn't constructed or choreographed very well. We had to fight our way out of the scenery & costumes & props—but "I.S." was with us & it worked out that night.

July 6 [1972]

The most magic of days. Today way up in the mountains, [at] Pettino,[‡] a special, thrilling beauty—watching shadows pass over the contours of 3 swelling hills, etched against the sky [here Robbins has drawn a tiny sketch of hills] & striated with different grasses—rocks—fences—a few dark green shrubs & green trees, poppies—below the coarse grain in vertical perspectives—the rock curves in & out of the contoured hills—the look of them sideways discloses new textures— breasts & bulging energy—but it makes the most beautiful of efforts of man to create beauty absolutely futile. . . .

Yesterday we[§] had lunch up in the monastery at Monteluco[¶]—& then slept in a field behind it—high up above. Then we went into town to hear some Bach Chorales on the church portico. . . .

Aidan is good. Speech comes out of him in spurts . . . he spits out & puts down & then retracts if contested. His words are exact, his head & his energies are good & beautiful & exceedingly sensitive. . . .

Every morning—or at 12—we hear a chamber concert, & the whole thing about time is even more surely put forth—for what is any second, or 1/10 of a

---

* *Dumbarton Oaks,* a 1920s-ish tennis-party ballet for a lead couple and six tap-dancing boys.
† *Requiem Canticles,* the last ballet of the festival, was set to Stravinsky's last major composition, which uses texts from the Catholic funeral Mass.
‡ Pettino is a tiny (population approximately seventy-five) village in the Apennine Mountains northeast of Spoleto.
§ Robbins was traveling with Aidan Mooney, a *Newsweek* magazine researcher, who was to become a close friend.
¶ The thirteenth-century convent at Monteluco was briefly home to Saint Francis of Assisi.

second of music unless it is related to what has gone past—& only by holding on to our memory of the last sounds does the present make any sense.

Aidan shows me a pod, green & young, so big [here Robbins inserts another tiny sketch, about three-quarters of an inch long]—& squeezes it open—& out comes red blood—brilliant orange red—but no—it's a baby poppy—but no—he unfurls it further &—miracle—compressed into it, rolled up like a Japanese paper water flower—is a *whole* poppy—shiny & damp & crushed—but when unfurled—a whole poppy.

July 8 [1972]

Left Spoleto quickly & didn't have regrets. Knew I'd come back. Talk with Aidan.. lots of talk. The P[iero] della Francesca*—suddenly elated by knowing that part of the fascinating pull was the black hole he drove the eyes to incessantly & irresistibly next to all the action. The revelation that Christ was the smallest figure & all monochromatic. That P[ontius] P[ilate] and C[hrist] were the most passive: that the center of the canvas† was the arm holding the scourge. That each 1/2 of the composition existed totally & unexceptionally [*sic*] without the other, but placed together they blew the mind. That if P[ontius] P[ilate] stood he'd be a giant . . . [here Robbins drew a schematic sketch of the painting].

The days in traveling become like instant wipe outs from moment to moment, because to each we bring intense absorbtion [*sic*]. [It] leaves no room for the last experience to remain in consciousness. . . .

July 13 [1972]

VENICE

I keep getting glimpses of a theater piece–ballet based on the Passions—the Mysteries—the Stations—all centered in my head around Judas's kiss. He comes on in a long billowing enormous cape—beige or gold—& envelops the still Christ in it—the Giotto look passes between them & hell & all breaks out. The Lord is lowered off the X, the resurrection occurs, Lazarus is raised & babes

---

* Apparently, they drove from Spoleto to Urbino, where Piero's *Flagellation of Christ*—which the scholar John Pope-Hennessy called "the world's greatest small painting"—is part of the collection at the Galleria Nazionale delle Marche.
† Actually, the *Flagellation* is painted on board, not canvas.

slaughtered. Gold, candelabras, mosaics, votive candles & those brass trichained incense light pots descend. Color is deep & splashed & light theatrical & by the end the heavens open, angels swirl, God blesses, Christ ascends, angels sing joy, Mary's robes voluminously float, clouds redden, graves open, monks pray & the dead rise. Ecce homo of Tintoretto.

Journal #3
July 18 [1972]
SARATOGA[*]

AMERICA—I can see it so much better after being in Europe & the very next day traveling in the U.S. . . .

Last night I ate at the Holiday Inn—& it was a fantastic look at the aspirations of U.S. life. The room was OK—large, light—pale yellow green patterned walls & chandeliers—box-like—& filled with American families of real middle class squares on vacation—tired & a feeling of unhappiness & no speaking between them. At no table was there joy or happiness in being together. The menu was pseudo-fancy—like the 12 Caesars† in N.Y., parchment & wood & large & promising prime steaks & spaghetti with real Italian red sauce (meat)— etc. The high for everyone was to go to the center of the room where there was a salad table (consisting of shredded lettuce & 4 bowls of dressings) & help yourself. The meal was a disaster. Steak uneatable, vegetables frozen, etc. etc. except waitress was young & direct & happy & honest. . . . [T]he piped-in Muzak had gotten stuck & was playing over & over one phrase softly—on & on & on quietly wearing away one's sanity instead of smoothing it soothingly. And finally one chandelier of the three (fake Venetian Versailles doodles) kept flickering & dimming & flashing on—when it went out the room would become absolutely

---

* Robbins had returned from Italy in time to take part in NYCB's summer residency in Saratoga.
† The Forum of the Twelve Caesars was a luxury restaurant in Rockefeller Center with an imperial Roman theme and Continental/Roman menu. Founded by Joseph Baum of Restaurant Associates, in 1957, it closed in 1975. The opening-night party for *A Funny Thing Happened on the Way to the Forum* was, aptly, held there.

quiet for only a moment as all eyes turned to it . . . then after a good long pause of consideration everyone went back eating. . . .

July 19th
Danced Pulcinella tonight—& George picked up a bouquet & knelt & handed it toward me!! They have me for another 8 years!!

Conversations & Hospital & Illness
December 1972

Florida and my father.* At night we talk. We kiss and embrace. He asks in Yiddish for God to give him five more years. . . . I tell him what wonderful things he has accomplished—from arriving here in America & working in a delicatessen for 5 dollars a month, & living in the store sleeping under the counter on a shelf—to now—living in Miami, a daughter with homes in N.Y., Vermont, and Switzerland—and 2 children and 2 grand-children—and a son who has succeeded internationally—and I tell him that it was *he* who made all this.

Journal #4
January 18 [1973]

I can't deal with my feelings. . . . Depressions are from angers—and I have lots of them. Most of all it's from unexpressed rage . . . perhaps impossible rages . . . the biggest & frightening because of Arthur Bell's account in "Playbill."† . . .

[H]ere I am trying to get my overcoat off and this happens. He's a shit & it certainly misread [*sic*] etc—but sure shits on me from all sides. I continue to go to ballet—go into lobby—etc. but paranoia of everyone knows hits me—which

---

* Harry Rabinowitz had moved to Florida with his second wife, Frieda; as he suffered increasingly from the effects of progressive heart disease, Robbins would come to visit him.
† Arthur Bell (1939–1984), a journalist and gay-rights activist, had published an article on homosexuality in the theater in the January 10 issue of *Playbill* that Robbins felt insinuated too much about his sexual orientation.

surprises me because I've always felt & behaved as if everybody knows. But I've tried to do it with some respect for myself & others & with dignity—& this man just shits on the whole thing. . . . At any rate the anger turns into depression. . . .

Journal #3*
February 24 [1973]

Another dream, the last night Sunday.†

George (who figures in most of the dreams) was starting a new, or another school or company—a new place—new everything—& I being a part of it and wanting to get into it and be in condition decided to take class, etc. So I got into light tights & shirt—almost white—cream-colored—and soft white not-new slippers & got to the bar and warmed up—& started the barre with the company & all—My toes pointed well & my legs felt good & all were surprised at my condition & I worked hard & concentrated & lots of it was difficult & uneasy-making & the sense of ill-ease & anxiety increased as I found that the company had left the class as had G.B.—& I was left at the bar with students. No one had told me that the co[mpany] and big shots had moved [on].

Journal #6
May 28 [1973]

Last night's dreams:

They wanted information. I was not going to give it. I'm not sure I had it, but my state was one of solid refusal. They were nice but numerous. Lots of white-coated doctors were about. Lights were shone in my face & conferences

---

* Robbins left off writing in Journal #3 in late autumn of 1972 and went on to Journal #4; then returned to Journal #3 to make some entries in January and February 1973.
† Robbins had just completed an unpleasant contract negotiation with City Ballet (he'd asked for a salary in return for giving them first call on his services), during which Lincoln Kirstein had suggested that the company "restudy" its arrangements with him. "I do not consider you have any particular commitment or special relationship to us," he'd said. In the end Robbins had accepted a yearly payment of $20,000 plus royalties.

were held about how to treat me. No great deference or special care. Take him to X room. There a doctor took me into a room & produced a gun-silencer-injector—he explained as how he was going to shoot-inject me at base of throat above collar-bone—it would sting for a moment—then the numbness would climb up my throat & I'd feel it hit my tongue which would twist & flip over & then as it hit my head, I'd pass out & never remember anything & in *that* period—during my blackout—I would tell all. There was no way out & as he placed the muzzle of the gun on my throat & pulled the silencer trigger & I felt the barb go in—I woke up.

Journal #7
June 27 [1973]
[SPOLETO]

Aidan, Tanny, and Randy* [are here]. The countryside is nourishment to me.

July 1
Tanny falls. Bad day.

July 2
I'm sitting in the Piazza [del] Duomo—which is like being inside your favorite painting. It's been a down day—with Tanny's leg all swollen and she wanting to stay still in her hotel room. We had a picnic there at lunch, Aidan, Randy & me.

Last night took Patty, J. Pierre & family, Helgi, Marlene, Jerry Z., Aidan, Randy to Todi†—fun, good, affectionate dinner—with Tanny on mind the whole time. . . .

---

* Aidan Mooney (see p. 298) and Randall Bourscheidt, who would later become New York's deputy commissioner of cultural affairs, had accompanied Tanaquil Le Clercq to Spoleto, in part to celebrate a program of pas de deux Robbins was presenting at the Festival dei Due Mondi.
† Todi is a picturesque town twenty-seven miles from Spoleto. Robbins's dinner guests included Patricia McBride and her husband, Jean-Pierre Bonnefoux, Helgi Tomasson and his wife, Marlene, the City Ballet pianist Jerry Zimmerman, Mooney, and Bourscheidt. McBride, Bonnefoux, and Tomasson were all dancing in the pas de deux program.

July 3

We take Tanny to the hospital & find out thru X-ray she has a hairline break in her leg below the knee. I take a look at the X-ray & almost pass out with ..with what was it—more than dismay or alarm—but maybe thru the pain of my love for her. They put her in a cast & we return to hotel. I get her to accept someone staying with her tonight in case the cast is too much. I'm for getting her back to New York—[but] her whole trip blown, when she was having such a ball! Fuck the world.

July 10

. . . Sat. night the 6th we all ate together—& had a nice time. The following morn up & get Tanny into a minibus & drive to Rome. Randy, Tanny & I play Geography all the way in & Tanny loves the way we're going. At airport all goes well—with help of a sweet Italian porter who helps carry Tanny up into plane—till we meet our Americans, a steward & stewardess & captain. UGLY. Ugly scene—hated them & their insensitivity. Pulled a big scene—& left frustrated.

    [. . . .]

    The glory of Umbria is its touching and grandiose landscape. The off-beat off-center off the square details of all one sees—be it fields, crops, trees, walls, cobblestones, towers, flowers, laundry—hit deeply & almost painfully within me.

    In Spoleto—the daily respect for me as an artist moves me—& I feel that what I have contributed to society adds to my life & becomes a part of my living. While in America the publicity of my fame seems totally apart from me—& adds nothing. One contains respect, the other, in US, contains exploitation & rat-race.

Journal #8

August 25 [1973]

Today I studied a little Italian, played a little Mozart, read 2 Hawthorne stories, read a little Tchekov [*sic*] in Italian, sketched some more in Duomo, bought paper, Digest Seltzer, washed clothes, and tried to get my head out of leaving.

At the municipal pool, Spoleto. With just a few quick strokes of a pen, Robbins could capture gesture and character.

August 26 [1973]

Another Sunday—the last—Up in the hills atop Pettino—the sun slipped off the top of the magic 5 hills while opposite mist clouds flew & cut the tops of the mountains and the sun glowed pink & gold & orange from behind & under the clouds. I cried. I realized my madness—& how I loved life and wished for death—how I roil around in my head—& in my life—& how the lack of discipline unhinges me—& *I* lack the discipline.

This book takes the place of work. (And if you *had* to do it?)

The commune wants to give me "for life" the tower on the Ponte delle Torre [*sic*].* All I must do is restore it. They say it will cost 40–50 thousand!†

Today, up in the hills, Fall came. The air changed, the trees were varied-colored, and the smell of the earth itself all told the tilt of the world. It's over. It has been important. I will miss it.

---

* The commune is the municipal government; the Ponte delle Torri is a medieval stone bridge across the Tiber. The tower, a small stone house at the foot of a steep wooded incline, is on the end of the bridge opposite the walls of Spoleto's Castello. Robbins sketched it often.

† In the end the idea of the commitment proved too much for him, and he turned the offer down.

Conversations & Hospital & Illness
December 18, 1973

FLORIDA

Dad's in a hospital. Heart. I go down to see him. 4 in a room. Next to each bed an electronic blip moves across a screen with each heartbeat, leaving an erratic blurred graph line like a series of mesas in the desert.

. . . I sit next to his bed. Night. Outside the streetlamps diminish in straight lines into the flat background. Rain. Southern-soft. Dad opens his eyes and sees me. "Gai schluffen."* I kiss him & go.

Yesterday I shaved him—& wondered when we'd have such intimacy again—& how seldom we'd had it before. He'd bother me if I was one of the 3 other men in the room with him: he coughs, spits, wipes his mouth on his nightshirt—tries, with all wires attached, to get up at night, and keeps them all awake. But oh, how his eyes light up when a nurse approaches—how he flips on the charm, humor—the energy comes smack up & he gets off a joke, a tease, & a feel—& then snaps it all off as the nurse steps away. It is hard to contact him. Today I ended writing on my pad in big letters, "COME TO MY OPENING ON JAN 31†—GET WELL." He stares at it—& then at me.

Journal #9

January 21 [1974]

I'm angry at all my life—it's a fake—& all I do is fake, false—because it isn't about what I want to be about . . . it isn't about my work, or my house or my fucking. . . . I fake it by making it seem to be about these things.

. . . I want to stop everything. I want to call a halt & change it. . . . For the first time in years my ears pound at night. But I'm not afraid. The above is a discovery not a downer.

---

* Yiddish for "Go to sleep."
† Robbins and Leonard Bernstein's ballet based on S. Anski's *Dybbuk* was—with some difficulty—finally coming to fruition. The premiere had been set for January 31 but was postponed because of Bernstein's continuing difficulties with the score; it finally opened on May 16.

Last Friday I saw "Goldberg V." with NYCB—& then went down to A.B.T. to see Fancy Free. . . . I hadn't seen FF in about 15 years. It's 30 years old. What a trip—to see the naiveness of FF after the cool clear elegance & craft & inventions of G.V. I liked what I'd made of my talent, & what I had become & what I'd made of my life. . . . FF was *full* of terrific energy, affection, some flashes of great invention, some struggles with the pas de deux—sweet—full of the '40's & influenced by movies & pop culture of the times. I had a good deal of affection for it, & the audience did, too—& I felt they had it for me. . . .

And that was my feeling on Fri.—& on Monday I *felt* what's written on the other page [above]. Both are valid—how do I put them together.

February 28 [1974]
Lennie & I—well it's a howl. Probably funny if we could see it from outside. Not much fun in it—terrible for each of us—even the see-saw of good & harmful feelings.

RULE: *ONLY* IF IT'S LENNIE'S IDEA—& HE HAS WRITTEN THE SCORE ALREADY—AND YOU LIKE IT, DO IT.

I'm sure we each think the other is impossible.[*]

Journal #11
October 23 [1974]

Balanchine teaches—& *how* he teaches—he doesn't "give" a class—it's not just a warm-up & a work out for the dancers—It is a Master Class in *how to do* & he invests each particular moment of classic & basic ballet vocabulary with a how & why & a detail of such elevated elegance & perfection. If I am known as a perfectionist, one should attend his classes. Unfortunately, one can see the attitude of the dancers still remains aloof & apart—"the old crazy man"—they *don't* hear & don't see & if he insists on a detail (each of which is basic & never

---

[*] The *Dybbuk* project was compromised by the disjunction between Bernstein's complex, more-is-more vision for the score, laden with Hasidic motifs and numerological twelve-tone passages, and Robbins's desire for a piece of abstract dance theater. When it opened on May 2, critics were underwhelmed: "a dramatic ballet without drama," said Nancy Goldner in *The Christian Science Monitor* (May 24).

ornamental) they hold it for a few poses & then drop it. What a revelation the classes are. "Each step, each movement *must* be a miracle"—a propos of port de bras—"*Breathe* your steps"—"There is no sex (no difference of the sexes) in ballet." I'm going to film it all as soon as possible.*

Journal #12

January 29–30 [1975]
Been doing a lot of thinking on *The Ordeal of Civility*.† Oh yes—yesterday watching ballet class, GB., teaching, turns to me & says, "Anglo-Saxons—English—American Anglo Saxons—careful, *nice,* polite—*dull*—*afraid* to be vulgar!!!"

. . . Full of anxiety about "G Major."‡ Started yesterday—did a few minutes but don't have it yet . . . [JR's ellipses] another dance pure ballet—not my cup of tea. O. of C. dreams last night about it . . . Anxiety about Ravel—this a.m. think about it: perfection, fear of failure, fear of being found out—found out that I'm not passing—that I am a Jew—the Yid—& now wonder if the discontent and perfectionist drive are also a part of that.

May 14 [1975]
Opening night-day. Hate it. I go over all my fantasies—Bravos—takes the Festival—then flashing & dismissed victories that get stuffed into back drawers of the head only to trip one up when the reality of bad costumes & sugary set seem to diminish the Concerto to a goody-goody. . . . I enjoy terrifically rehearsals—& hate or don't hardly enjoy performances. . . .

[O]ne is up for the knife on opening nights & I wish I were Rabinowitz instead of Robbins.

---

* Robbins did in fact film Balanchine's company class—the only visual record of his teaching work.
† John Murray Cuddihy's *Ordeal of Civility: Freud, Marx, Lévi-Strauss, and the Jewish Struggle with Modernity,* had been published in late 1974; Robbins became aware of it soon after.
‡ Robbins had begun working on a ballet to Ravel's Piano Concerto in G Major for City Ballet's upcoming Ravel Festival.

To: Lincoln Kirstein (Excerpt)
June 25, 1975

. . . The Ravel [Festival] has left me in a state of confusion. The disappointment of so many of the works which I thought were good,* and the enthusiasms of others for what I thought sometimes were the wrong reasons, plus the exhaustion (first nights are *not* for me) all have combined to put me in a black retreat. I've had poor reviews before, but there seems to be some concerted effort of the lady critic Bacchants to do in not only these recent works but things in the past they have liked! Arlene, Marcia & Nancy†—I'd like some choreographer's lib! . . .

Journal #12

June 20th [1975]
This book starts & ends with big downers. . . .
Trying to hold it all together—

June 25 [1975]
Saw Frazier‡—OUT OF SNEDENS . . .

June 26 [1975]
More thinking—
A series of rejections . . . [by] all I love & count on—
Dilemma of what do I believe in—whose instincts—etc.—
Take pills?—No—try to get out alone—& not alone—but what drugs—.
V. Redgrave.§

---

* In addition to *In G Major*, Robbins had made ballets to (and titled after) the composer's *Introduction and Allegro for Harp, Chansons Madécasses, Une Barque sur l'Océan,* and *Ma Mère l'Oye.*
† Arlene Croce of *The New Yorker*, Marcia Siegel of *New York* magazine, and Nancy Goldner of *The Christian Science Monitor.*
‡ For the past year or so Robbins had been seeing a new therapist at Columbia-Presbyterian in New York, Dr. Shervert Frazier.
§ Unclear what this reference to Vanessa Redgrave meant.

Journal #13

July 9 [1975]
Dear Diary—

Guess where I'm writing from? Oh, you'll *never* guess! I'll give you three little hints. Its near Boston—it has lots of trees & grounds & facilities (except a pool)—& the service is so good that you're almost never out of sight of one of the staff!!!

Well? . . .

No—Not Nantucket or the Cape. No—not the Ritz Carlton in Boston.

I'm a[t] McLeans*—Wheeeeeeeeeeeeeeee

I've been here a week—came on my own—was first horrified by where I was & what it meant—now I'm seduced into its tranquility & the peace of helplessness. I also know I'm not like the others—something that really bothered me when I first came in & saw the poor people on my floor.

I didn't know it was a mental hospital—& thought I'd be staying here for a rest—"find out which drugs will suit you best."

Zowie: locks—passes—crazies in the hall . . . All the edifices (edifaces) that I've erected to protect little Jerome Rabinowitz are collapsing—seem to have been wiped away in a few weeks. . . . It's so very hard to accept without falling apart that I'm in a crazy house.

I wonder about their fear of my suiciding. It's like making me think about it instead of making me think it's silly.

July 10 [1975]
Zonked out again. Last night I had 100 mg Elavil & it's now noon & I'm still sleeping. The floor is 8 ft. below my eyes & my voice has dropped all the way down. . . . It's hard to move, physically or mentally, with all this in me. In my head, now that I've separated myself from the others in this ward, I feel better about being here. . . .

---

* Shervert Frazier had recently been named psychiatrist in chief of McLean Hospital, the psychiatric affiliate of Harvard Medical School, in Belmont, Massachusetts, and had suggested that Robbins come to McLean. Robbins voluntarily committed himself on July 2, 1975.

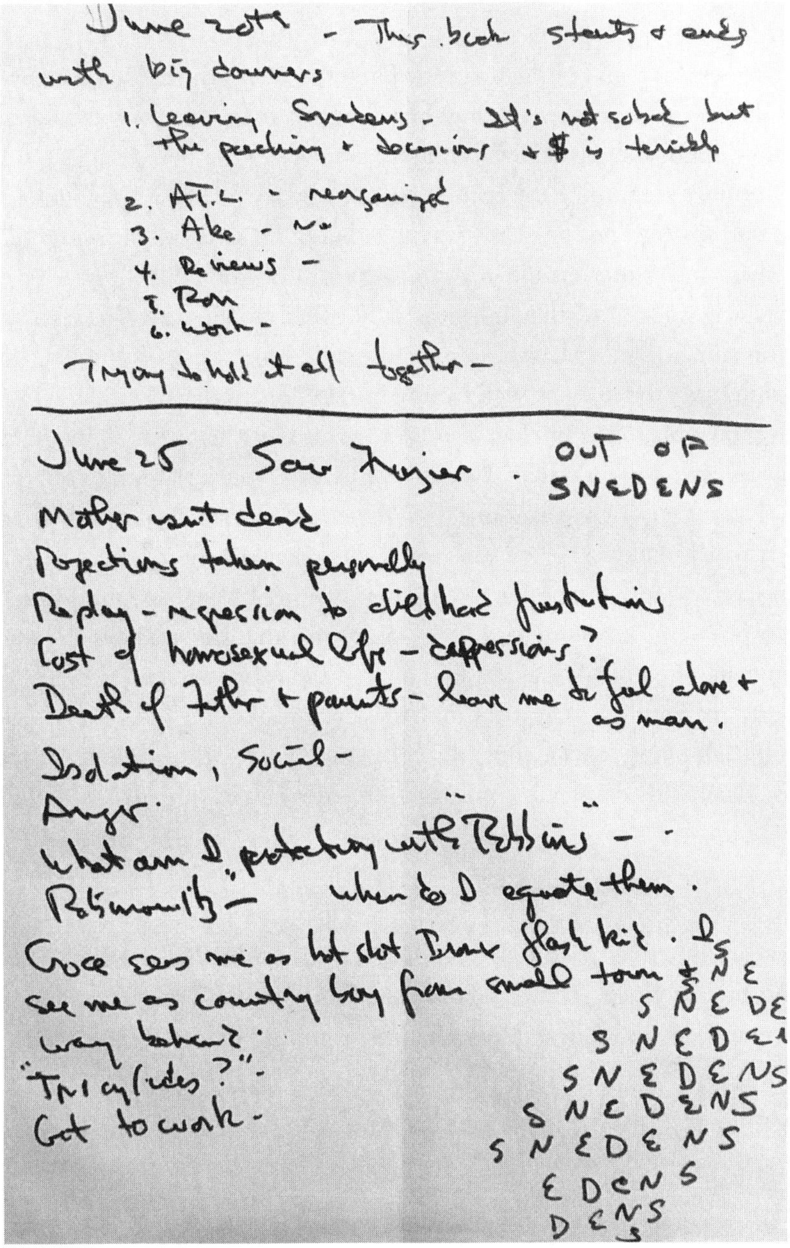

[handwritten journal page]

June 20th – This book starts & ends
with big corners
  1. Leaving Snedens – It's not sobal but
    the packing + decisions + $ is terrible
  2. ATL – reorganized
  3. Ake – No
  4. Reviews –
  5. Ron
  6. work –

I may to hold it all together –

June 25   Saw Krejer .   OUT OF
                         SNEDENS

Mother isn't dead
Rejections taken personally
Replay – regression to childhood frustrations
Cost of homosexual life – depressions?
Death of Father + parents – leave me to feel alone +
                               as man.
Isolation, Social –
Anger.
What am I protecting with "Bettina" – .
Rossmouth? –   when do I equate them.
Grace sees me as hot shot Brow flash kit . I
see me as country boy from small town #   S N E
way behind.   S N E D E
"Tricycles?"   S N E D E N
Got to work –   S N E D E N S
                             S N E D E N S
                         S N E D E N S
                           E D E N S
                           D E N S

The crack-up.

July 11 [1975]

Much better this a.m. For the first time I'm up & out of the Hall in the a.m. Last night they gave me another 100 mg. Elavil—but I guess my system could take it. And they'll probably give me 125 tonight.

Mornings seem to be the hardest part of the day for the whole floor. Trying to get started & yet not be in any way together or ready to communicate. David Story [*sic*] and Pinter* could really do the dining room up brown. (Expression?) Each walks into that room as if he were crossing a stage with an arc light on him to be scrutinized, an exposure no one wants. Rumpled, doped, unwishing [*sic*] to see or be seen by anyone else, one walks or rather gets across however possible to the kitchen door. A nurse is there helping, talking loud and clearly to each patient—like "No, Mrs. Elstrom, you just drank your orange juice, I just gave it to you, don't you remember?" Patients stand in front of the toaster, bewildered. "How to" and "where is" take the place of [the] Why that nobody wants to face. Each tries to erect invisible walls around him; each tries to pick a table no one else is at—or a table that doesn't have the remains of someone else's breakfast messily about. Few words are used. Even "Good Morning" to another patient is somehow an uncalled for invasion of privacy. Crumbs half-empty coffee cups, dirty knives, dishes with egg shells attack the senses. One, with desperate concentration, tries to get thru the meal without cracking up.†

July 23

Ron went home today with Nick.‡ He's been here—well, a long time—I can't get the days or weeks right. . . . He was fantastic in concern, care, rolling with my ups and downs, and with my changes of mind, forgetfulness, drugged-out

---

* David Storey (1933–2017) was a prizewinning British novelist and playwright whose works included *The Changing Room* and *Home;* Sir Harold Pinter (1930–2008) was the Nobel Prize–winning director, screenwriter, and playwright of *The Caretaker, The Homecoming,* and *Betrayal.* Both writers specialized in terse, gnomic dialogue conducted in an atmosphere of unease.

† At the bottom of this page Robbins drew sharply observed and funny sketches of the other inmates—a man in a broad-brimmed hat, a broad-beamed woman, seen from the rear, in bell-bottoms—labeled with their names.

‡ For some months Robbins had been in a somewhat volatile relationship with a younger man named Ron Ifft; Ifft had been staying in Robbins's house in New York and had brought Robbins's rough-coated terrier, Nick, to visit.

states, or highly-charged [ones]. . . . The only thing is as I got better he began getting sulky and baiting. . . .

July 27 [1975]

Last day at McLean . . . On rising saw Frazier at 8:30 . . . a lot zonked out—but head cleared—had packed night before & read [on] trip home. House didn't phase me! By mid-afternoon I'd done my letters, the scrapbook, & had even given the whole house downstairs a once over. Ron won't.

Undated [October 1975]

Johnny Kriza drowned.

From scenario for Fancy Free:

> His dance is much different in quality. The music is lighter, gayer, more happy go lucky, come what may, lovable. There is more warmth, humor, and almost a wistfulness about him.

October 21 [1975]

The hospital led to the drive—the drive to the park—the park to the cathedral—& the cathedral to the tower.* Each step simply opened directly, smoothly to the next. There was one thing and then there was another—& then the next, like minutes flowing into each other till some time had passed (& a crucial moment [was] unnoticeably arrived at).

But more seductively.

He didn't realize it till much later. First he looked in the church. . . . A stand announced visits to the tower—& a sign said 10:30 till 4:30. It was 4:30. He smiled ruefully at the attendant. "Too late, I guess." "No," she said, "you can still go up," as she pointed the way to the elevators. . . .

He was taken up to the 23rd floor & let out as the doors shut behind. . . . He saw a door with a sign—To the Tower.† As he stepped thru the doorway his

---

* Robbins is describing the bell tower at Riverside Church, a Gothic building overlooking the Hudson River at 122nd Street. The tower, twenty stories and 390 feet tall, houses a set of carillon bells.
† Here Robbins wrote, in brackets, "There he tried to throw himself off."

foot kicked aside a door wedge he hadn't seen and the door shut clang behind him. . . . The stairs mounted a flight, then turned sharply right—then again—then again. . . . He could hear a rushing noise getting louder. And a wind. The stairs wove in and around carillon bells. Finally he saw before him a narrow door that led out onto a small stone parapet that went around the 4 sides of the tower outside. . . . He stepped out on the parapet. It was enclosed in stone trellis lace thru which the light & wind came in. Afternoon sun. A glittering Hudson—a necklace bridge—the snaking highway, the campus, the cement quadrangle, Grant's Tomb—& there were the 2 boys still playing football he had walked past 10 minutes ago. Then for the first time he noticed that there were 2 openings, each side, to get thru, & that they were barred. He fantasized squeezing thru to get on the outer ledge—& also he saw himself wrenching himself thru the tight bars & in doing so, losing his balance & falling off the outside.

He looked at the building opposite & below him. An office building. They'd see the body. He imagined how long a fall it would be & how it would feel.

He moved on. Yes, there's Columbia below, there's the Triborough. . . . There's St. John the Divine. There's all of Manhattan—Central Park—the Guggenheim—& next, my window, only I can't get thru the bars. . . . He went around again fast and then started down. . . .

That night I had dinner, walked the dog, went to a concert, met friends. . . . I don't know if I would have jumped. Only when I got home & thought about it did I realize there'd been a search to find a way to do it. . . .

It was a dream. So much so that the next morning I had a hard time on awakening trying to remember what the event was that hung so hugely over me yesterday.

And while I am writing this, an editor, Bob Gottlieb,[*] calls and asks if we have a book in mind.

. . . If it'd been open would I have jumped?

---

[*] Robert Gottlieb (b. 1931), a writer and editor, was then president and editor in chief of Alfred A. Knopf, where he had published Lincoln Kirstein's *Nijinsky Dancing*. A passionate ballet goer, he would shortly become a member of New York City Ballet's board of trustees. It's not clear what book Gottlieb thought Robbins might have in mind.

Journal #14

January 28 [1976]

I like theater—the theater of my life—I like my life to be full of events & action & ups & downs—dramatic & fun & entertaining. [But] I haven't planned my life carefully. . . . I feel like I dipped into all of it & didn't really take charge except as it pleased me. . . . *I* made me a dancer & I made me a choreographer—& director, [but] the *personal* part of my life has been an unplanned journey.

Journal #15

March 3 [1976]

Ash Wednesday. I travel down to Philly to see *1600 Pen[nsylvania] Ave[nue]*.* It's pretty messed up. It's amazing to think of how much poor poor thinking and sloppiness have gone on in the heads of Lenny and Allen [*sic*]. Incredible that their sentiments seem un-thought thru & that finally a lousy phony "love of country" comes thru with all the intelligence they are capable of. And oh the lovely time of being out of town on a show again. The recriminations go on & back—the drinking—the lack of control, discipline, plans, clean-up, progress. The talk despair. Barclay Hotel, Rittenhouse Square, walking to the theater and seeing the Warwick, Bellevue Stratford, St James . . . , the lounge where I was in love with? [*sic*], the theater (Forrest) where the first show I was in played . . .

March 4 [1976]

More thoughts: They're in deep trouble, trying to trash their way out. Lennie never learns: he fucks around with Christ, God, and his country, forgetting his best work came out of looking warmly at life around him—On the Town,

---

* Alan Jay Lerner (1918–1986), who had written the book and lyrics for *Brigadoon, My Fair Lady, Gigi, Camelot,* and other musicals, had been without a regular writing partner since the retirement of the composer Frederick Loewe (1901–1988) and had teamed with Bernstein for this show about the men and women (above and below stairs) who had lived in the White House from 1800 to 1900. Frank Corsaro, the original director, left during the out-of-town tryouts, and Bernstein and Lerner wanted Robbins to consider stepping in.

Wonderful Town—He sees himself a Sage, Prophet, Einstein—& all gets stuffed into . . . LARGE & IMPORTANT pieces. They come out hollow, sentimental.

March 6 [1976]
Told them no. It feels good.*

March 8 [1976]
. . . The Philly experience was fruitful because I discovered how very good I am at theater, how easily my ideas & clarity flow again—that doing a show, as far as my muscles are concerned, would not be difficult, that I'm not out of practice, &—most of all—how happy I am *not* to be doing them when I see the shoddiness of 1600. . . . But I'm still undecided what to do next. . . .

March 28 [1976]
I've been to see [Twyla] Tharp twice.† She has a statement to make, "It doesn't have to be *that* way." That way being the conventions, politeness, use of music space gesture etc. of the dance & particularly the ballet dance (which she is drawn to). . . . [S]he is not a destroyer, or defiant or vulgar and offensive. She is elegant & crafted & there is a continuous delight & even dizziness in the light floating drunken heady improvisational quality of her work; eccentric & perversely independent, she noodles her way with her own idiosyncratic vocabulary thru the evenings. [But] after the first experiences of delight & exhilaration & love manifested by first viewing, . . . one gets a nagging sense of "O.K., now what? Having made your point, to what else are you addressing yourself?" One longs for variety, weight, form, & above all . . . more seriousness in her application of what she has found to the next step. All her works are divertissements, saucy, sexy, impudent. It's like a constant . . . rush or high—giddy & exhilarating—but after seeing her ballet twice, her TV, & 2 evenings I don't care

---

* With Gilbert Moses and George Faison credited as directors, *1600 Pennsylvania Avenue* opened in New York in May and played only seven performances before the producers closed it.
† Twyla Tharp had founded her own company, Twyla Tharp Dance, in 1965. In January 1976 she made the "crossover" ballet/modern-dance mash-up *Push Comes to Shove,* for American Ballet Theatre, starring Mikhail Baryshnikov. In March her own company appeared at the Brooklyn Academy of Music, and her work was the subject of one of the first "Dance in America" presentations on PBS (the broadcast aired on March 24). Robbins had been paying attention.

to see it again until she moves somewhere else. . . . [S]he does wonderful things for women. Her Jelly Roll Morton pieces* give the women a reality I never see or feel in any other's work. Martha [Graham]'s women are pious dedicated religious noble seers & monuments. George's are elegant glamorous "stars" . . . elevated, provocative, mysterious, extremely refined—a product of richness of taste & elegance. But Twyla gives you the body of women, their strength, ability, *sex,* work, co-partners to men, and adds to the body of dance & presents a full-bodied, down-to-earth woman, capable of *sharing* and abetting the man's world as an equal, uncompetitive, feminine, equally capable.†

To: Sonia Robbins Cullinen
June 21, 1976

Dear Sonia,

Well, it seems we have a lot to say to each other.‡ It isn't the pleasantest of scenes to contemplate, but maybe we should get together and get it off our chests. I don't think either of us is talking about the money really & although it may be rough, it would be worthwhile to try, both of us, to get it in the open. I'm sure each of us feels righteous & put-upon—resentful, etc. It's not to prove that one is right or wrong—but to see if we can dissolve some of the knots & tensions that have *always* been between us. Well I know you know what I'm talking about—it's not just the situation with Pop. If you want to try this, drop a note. . . .

Jerry

---

* *Eight Jelly Rolls,* a dance for two men and five women, to the music of the ragtime pianist and composer Ferdinand Joseph LaMothe, a.k.a. Jelly Roll Morton.
† Eight years later Robbins would collaborate with Tharp on *Brahms/Handel* for New York City Ballet.
‡ Robbins had written to his sister, Sonia Cullinen, in May to ask that she contribute something to the care of their father and stepmother, since the money he had given them for support had been exhausted by medical expenses. This letter is his response to her response (possibly a telephone call since there is no letter from her on the subject). As he says, it's about more than money: it's an attempt to address his family angst.

The Times of the 1930s and 1940s—Being a Jew
September 6, 1976

I didn't want to be a Jew. I didn't want to be like my father, the Jew, or any of his friends, those Jews. I twisted on the two prongs of my own anti-Semitism and the terror of others. I wanted to be safe, assimilated, protected, hidden among the Goys, the majority. . . .

My parents taught me, not directly, not openly, that it was our fate to be persecuted, separated, ridiculed, rejected. . . . They (unknowingly) also gave me the glory of being a Jew—the warmth, color, mysticism; they gave me the magic Sabbath candles, the Friday night service, the Ark, the torah. The fervent adorations of the pious, the tenacity of the faithful; only recently [have] I begun to admit my true and deep love of, and my heart's anguish at my rejection of, all that is encompassed in the Jewish soul. I am not religious. It is not a question of how or where or if I pray. My being a Jew is within the deepest part of me. . . . [But] from all of that I close[d] myself off—dismissed it, rejected it, and tore it out of me. . . . I became Jerry Robbins. . . . [And] my parents wanted me to be an American, to assimilate. I sought a career to reject all my family-culture background and to erect a protective edifice to save me from the persecution and demeaning feelings of being Jewish. . . .

[I]t was for this reason that my enormous anxieties arose in my work. This time they'll find out [that] I'm not as talented as they thought, that I'm a little Jewish kike. I covered those feelings with other reasons: it was my homosexuality that I was afraid would be exposed, I thought. It was my having been a Communist. None of these. I[t] was the terror that my career, work, veneer of accomplishments would be taken away, by HUAC, or by the critics. I panicked and crumbled: the façade of Jerry Robbins would be cracked open and behind everyone would finally see Jerome Wilson Rabinowitz.

Maybe only now can I start accepting my parents—funny they should come in second, after my accepting being a Jew.

What blew the lid off all this was reading a *review* of "The Ordeal of Civility."*

---

* John Murray Cuddihy's *Ordeal of Civility* was an anatomy and critique of Jewish assimilation in Europe in the nineteenth and twentieth centuries.

Journal #16

August 21 [1976]

Had a vivid dream about Tanny walking—isn't it terrific, she said—I cried so—& then she wanted to know the limits of her recovery, and piqueted* forward to peek into a hospital room—& in that gesture I saw all the immense talent she had for dancing.

Notes

August 2, 1977

I spoke to G.B. today about Baryshnikov.† G. is worried about the impact of such a star on the company's morale. "It will destroy dancers. OK, he says, some of them are mediocre but it holds together in our way. He'll have all the crazy people screaming for him & then writing letters because he isn't dancing every ballet or every night." G.B. seems afraid of such a star quality. I assured him M.B. was not a difficult man—could have a place in any company, any time—but is very modestly wanting to join us, stay & grow with the company.

I tried to hold my ground. Told G.B. that we have a near-capacity audience that was devoted to our repertory & artistic values. That M.B. would only enhance‡ the technical ambitions & give an uplift to the morale—not a downer. That M.B. is unassuming, easy to work with and sans temperament.

G.B. listened & said then he'd think about it. "Is like picking Vice President—very important move."

---

* A ballet term referring to a step taken onto full pointe.
† Mikhail Baryshnikov, who had defected from the Kirov (later Mariinsky) Ballet to become a principal dancer with American Ballet Theatre, had just appeared, with Natalia Makarova, in Robbins's *Other Dances,* a duet to Chopin commissioned for ABT's anniversary gala. He'd also just wrapped *The Turning Point,* a film with a screenplay by Arthur Laurents, directed by Herbert Ross and produced by Ross and Nora Kaye, in which he played a defecting ballet star. He had approached Robbins—or possibly Robbins had spoken to him—about making a move to City Ballet. Despite Balanchine's initial hesitancy, an offer was made and Baryshnikov joined the company in April 1978.
‡ This word is illegible as written; "enhance" is a guess.

To: Peter Martins
November 2, 1977

Dear Peter,

I was glad to get your letter and to receive some explanation for the use of "In G Major."* When I was told you had performed it I was very angry indeed and shot off a lot of statements . . . which had nothing to do with the ravishing way you and Suzanne perform it. In principal, I'm against the policy of excerpting ballets. . . .

It is good that you take the best of dance to the U.S. in your programs. . . . But we need each other—good dancers and good choreographers. I am against the exploitation of a public by a star when the real goods of dance are not delivered. I am also against the exploitation by managers, orchestras, impresarios, agents and sometimes dancers, of choreographers. When a symphony orchestra can afford to exist, pay its royalties, stage hands, musicians, guest stars, conductors, when impresarios can collect fees, percentage etc. from star artists, I see no reason why the creators of the works performed should not also be compensated. . . . If there ever was an economic crunch, as you suggest in your letter, the problem would fall on sympathetic ears, you know that. But to put the choreographer in the position of not being compensated for the use of his work is as unconscionable as asking the dancer to appear for free for the Art of it.

I am really very sorry, Peter, that we have had any contretemps. I do want to go on working with you, and I do want you to want to go on working with me. . . .

Sincerely,
Jerry

PS: Thanks for asking about my health.† Right now all is quiet but the doctors have a big number they're planning for December. All should go well and I'll be around and scowling again in the spring.

---

* Peter Martins, then a notable principal at City Ballet, had included the pas de deux from *In G Major*, originally choreographed for himself and Suzanne Farrell, in a touring program, without receiving explicit permission from Robbins to excerpt it from the ballet or perform it. The text of this letter is a draft retained in Robbins's archives, which contain no copy of the final version.
† Robbins had been suffering from diverticulitis, for which he had surgery later that year.

Journal #18

December 16 [1977]

Pop died today. As I was looking at a Russian gold rouble he gave me, Sonia called from Florida—he'd just passed away.* A few hours of frantic arrangements. . . . I haven't had it hit me yet. Don't know how it will go—I guess give it some time. At last, an orphan—what a sick joke. Funeral Sunday, right at graveside.

December 17 [1977]†

Done. It was very cold & snow-hailing. About 30–40 people came to the cemetery. The ceremony was brief and deep enough to solace all. Under the umbrellas, the hail bumped down, the ground became white-covered, a green grass blanket covered all but a corner of the wooden casket. I was afraid to look at anyone for fear of crying & I was trying to support Frieda.‡ When I saw Viola,§ though, I cracked up. . . . [At] home¶ drinks, coffee, lots of food & cake, talk & a slight "party" atmosphere cleared the air a bit, & things settled down. It was done & until done, I didn't realize how heavy it was. . . .

Journal #20

October 12, 1978

I turned 60. Depressing. I'm no longer a young man, or a grown man, or a middle aged man: I am an *old* man. 60! How *did* I get here. I watched everyone else at dinner last night (there were 12)** go on without concern, so realized there

---

* Robbins had just been released from the hospital after his surgery and had been unable to travel to Florida when his father's health worsened.

† The date for this and/or the previous entry is probably incorrect. In 1977, the Sunday was December 18, and it would have been difficult to make funeral arrangements in less than two days.

‡ His stepmother.

§ His favorite cousin, Viola Zousmer, with whom, as a child, he'd danced made-up ballets and reenacted scenes from silent movies.

¶ At Robbins's house on East Eighty-First Street.

** In his journal Robbins drew a seating chart of the round table in his dining room at Eighty-First Street: among the attendees were Aidan Mooney, Mooney's partner, William Earle, Nancy Hayward Keith, Daniel Stern (his friend and former neighbor in Snedens Landing), the designer Mica Ertegun, Christine Conrad, Tanaquil Le Clercq, and Jesse Gerstein, who had been living with Robbins since December 1977.

was no difference in anyone's head about me—but what a difference there was inside me. DOWN. Perhaps if the work were going better I'd be O.K.—but I'm working outside of myself.

November 9 [1978]
George B watches my Verdi*—& then says—what you're doing is very hard to do—it looks easy but only few can do it—Petipa, Noverre†—me—you!!

November 11 [1978]
Run thru of Harlequinade.‡ Gorgeous! So much life & fun, delight, invention, sentiment sans sentimentality. Misha has so much energy and devotion to his work that infuses [*sic*] everyone to dance better. . . . After the last pas de deux which closes with a kiss George said—"Maybe don't kiss; anyway, you already married." We laughed. He followed this with—"Marriage is the Death of Love"—& as he sat down beside me,—"I never go to weddings or funerals—they're the same thing."!!!!! It came off hilariously—Wilde or Coward could have gotten it off—but later when I thought of it!!

To: Leonard Bernstein
November 12, 1980

Dear Lenny,

Thank you so much for sending me the tapes and score of your latest work.§ I really like it very, very much, and I'm in love with so many of the middle movements. I'd love to do it, but I worry about it because, as you know, music tends

---

* *The Four Seasons,* set to ballet music from Verdi's *I Vespri Siciliani,* which would premiere in January 1979.
† Marius Petipa (1818–1910) was the foundational choreographer of the Russian imperial ballet tradition; Jean-Georges Noverre (1727–1810), a French dancer and ballet master, pioneered the *ballet d'action,* which evolved into the story ballets of the nineteenth century.
‡ A two-act commedia dell'arte ballet by Balanchine to *Les Millions d'Arlequin* by Riccardo Drigo, which featured Mikhail Baryshnikov (Misha) in the lead role.
§ *Divertimento for Orchestra* was composed for the centenary of the Boston Symphony and premiered in Boston on September 25, 1980.

to shrink when you add dancing to it, and the pieces themselves are so short to start with that I don't know how it would avoid resulting in broken, tiny pieces. At least, that's my reaction now. Let me know if you have any suggestions, and we'll get together. But I do love the work.

Sorry that I've only gotten to this now. I just finished the Mozart Rondo in A minor, and I like it, although like the music, it is a fairly quiet work. If you want to see it, let me know.

All my love,
Jerry

Journal #22

January 20 [1981]
[Meryl] Streep* is gorgeous, super talented, versatile, surprising, and is the only performer who can do more fill-ins and schtick than [Zero] Mostel!

January 28–29 [1981]
Peter's ballet† is good. . . . He moves too fast from pattern to pattern. If I were deep in my own work & security I'd welcome it more.‡ Because I'm in a low point it seems somewhat threatening. He's shifted the future on a bit—a real development, rather offshoot—*not* progressing it—from George. I more or less kept my own route, established prior to joining G.B. It occurs to me I am now the age George was—not quite—when he went into his 7 year slump—& he came out of it with Stravinsky Festival. I don't, haven't ever, found the Tchai-

---

* This comment is written next to a pasted-in ticket stub, dated January 20, 1981, from the Public Theater production of *Alice in Concert,* a musical version of *Alice in Wonderland* by Elizabeth Swados. Streep played Alice.

† Peter Martins, who had begun making ballets while still a principal dancer, had just choreographed a ballet to a suite from Stravinsky's theater piece *L'Histoire du Soldat.* It premiered on January 29, 1981.

‡ Robbins's last two major works (*The Four Seasons* and *Opus 19/The Dreamer*) had been warmly if not ecstatically received, but he had been spending time pinch-hitting for a sidelined Balanchine and not making his own dances, and predictably critics whined about not getting new *Balanchine* ballets and made invidious comparisons between the two choreographers.

kovsky music sparking me.* I'd like to do "the Astaire Variations." Based on the dance he did with Rita Hayworth in "I'm Old Fashioned."

March 2 [1981]

Have just "seen" Esna, Edfu, Dendera, Abydos†—& have been pushed thru all the tombs, temples & museums on this tour by the most god awful terrible little nasty man, unknowledgable, arrogant, selfish, [whose] English [is] barely comprehensible . . . a loud drone that drives us wild. [T]he best times have been away from him. . . . The cast on the tour is *upper* middle class, over middle age, & very middlebrow. . . .

Impressions: the dogs: quiet, hanging around, not begging, needing care, food, attention. All strays, they take the food, if they dare, with grave gentleness. . . . We all feed them. Adults do not beg, children do. *The ruins are awesome.* . . . Pylons rising 50–60 feet in the air. Bas reliefs 4 stories high . . . One's imagination hesitates before the awesome conjectures: What did it look like originally; how did they build it; what were the ceremonies; and above all, the terrifying proposals of what life was like then.

March 6 [1981]

. . . In the afternoon we went on a long walk thru the rotten dirty smelly & fascinating streets of an old part of Cairo. It was colorful as well as odorous & I loved it: . . . thru back alleys & past hash sellers, copper workers, weavers, bakers, butchers; old wooden latticed windows extend over the street—beeping mopeds, tired carts drawn by tired donkeys that bray out their woes & frustration; orange rinds filth & garbage strewn around; oil leaks, mud puddles, the smell of kebabs cooking, spices, urine, horse-shit, gasoline fumes, charcoal, vegetables, lemons, onions . . .

In the Cairo museum, Roman period, among the paintings done on mummies I stare through the dust-covered glass at my portrait: beard, mouth, eyes, brows, shape of face and head . . . Look, it's me. . . .

All in all it's been a strange trip. Finally it is a touching country. The past grandeur is . . . all past, crumbled, collected, respected. . . .

---

* Balanchine had decreed yet another festival, this time to celebrate Tchaikovsky, for June 1981.
† In the spring of 1981, Robbins and Jesse Gerstein went on a trip to Egypt with friends.

And personally? Content to return. Better with Jesse . . . I've been fighting to relax and accept *my* life—*my* circumstances. That's hard for me. . . .

April 1 [1981]
Breakthru. I work on Piano Pieces* & really go. Thank heaven for one good day!

April 5 [1981]
It turned out to be 4 good days. All floodgates open & off I go. It winds me up so high that I practically blow out. . . . Consider an idea for all the piano pieces as a . . . fictitious Tchai[kovsky] ballet, court scene, with grand entrée—& a series of dances, pas de deux, waltzes, character dances etc. How far to go? . . .

Yes, *up*—& confident. Why? Maybe because I finally thought . . . I'm doing well & feel confident I know what I'm doing, & if George doesn't like it, tough, or take it elsewhere. I'm speeding, & all seems possible as it seems impossible when I'm down. Fighting Poppas!

April 12 [1981]
The work streak continues. A high like I can't recall since Dances & Goldberg. Not sure yet what I'm making except the piano pieces have turned me on & I'm in tune & unafraid.[†]

So work is a high & home is not. It's terrible with Jesse.[‡] Try to talk it out. It gets only to I'm poppa & he's a son. At work George is still missing.[§]

June 13 [1981]
The Piano Pieces opened. I received a terrific reception on opening night—I got a standing ovation!! Solo. A dream come true—a wish satisfied—to prove I still was able to cut it. And along with it enough gevalt at Jesse's away—I'm horny—& as upset as if I'd had a failure! . . . I am *very* pleased when the dancers

---

* For the Tchaikovsky Festival, Robbins (who felt he had little affinity for the composer) had begun a ballet to a collection of Tchaikovsky's works for unaccompanied piano.

† In the end Robbins decided not to create a complicated structure for the piano pieces, but arranged them as he had the sections in *Dances at a Gathering* in a kind of abstract dramatic arc.

‡ Gerstein had gone from working in Richard Avedon's studio to setting up on his own and had begun occasionally seeing other men. There were predictable struggles over this situation.

§ Balanchine's worsening health caused him to be missing in action for portions of the festival rehearsal period.

compliment me & am upset at getting my wants. If I can have it, it isn't good enough. If I can do it, it isn't worthwhile. If someone loves me, they are not with good taste or else lacking in strength of character. Which means—how could they like me if they really knew me. . . . All this ain't good!

To: Oliver Smith
November 7, 1981

Well—what a wonderful letter to get, my dear, dear friend.[*] How touching, how loving, and how very flattering!

It means so much to me—your friendship & your regard of me. Strange you write now, while I, because of reading Jane B's biography,[†] have been thinking about the life we had on West 10th Street—& how lucky we all were to have had it & shared it.

Well kid—now we are Senior Citizens, Elder Statesmen, & oh-my-god The Establishment!

Oi veh—or, as Paul [Bowles] would have said—Oidel Doidel!

Oliver—a big warm hug—& all my love. I'll call soon. I think I'm starting a new work.[‡] It's come over me & I began fooling with movement & I think I'm hooked, or bit, or in it again. Feels good.

Love, dear Oliver—
Jerry

[*] Smith had written to Robbins to congratulate him on the announcement that he would be awarded the Kennedy Center Honors.
[†] Millicent Dillon's *Little Original Sin: The Life and Work of Jane Bowles* had been published the previous January.
[‡] Probably he is referring to *Gershwin Concerto,* which would premiere on February 4, 1982; see his journal entry for November 8.

Journal #22A

November 8 [1981]

I'm at the beach.* It's a wonderfully warm clear sunny day, especially for the date
& in spite of it having been icy cold & windy all week end, the house in a state
of siege by the cold & drafts & sound of wind.

This morning, I who usually rise with the sun, slept till 10, warm, lazy, safe
& cozy in the big bed, the dogs warming themselves in the sunlight doubly
reflecting off the sea. I arose, dressed, and took them for a walk. At the ocean's
edge the sand stretched out flat & packed. A cluster of wet stones, a few seagulls,
some feathers, and here and there a plastic container dotted the beach. Annie
chased a balled-up cluster of feathers as if it were a live animal, but they were
quiet dogs, not barking at each other, nipping, teasing & chasing.

Home I made breakfast, good tea, croissant & honey & I read Jane's biography.

Then I think:

Tomorrow you are to start the group work of Concerto in F.† Then *why*,
all weekend, have you refused to get the score out, the tapes, & go to work, to
study, to plan? Because when I think about the work my stomach rises my pulse
gets faster I get extremely upset & excitement isn't a good word for the exhilaration and terror that goes on within me. I know that once I pick up that music &
tape I won't be able to free myself—that it will take over; I know it has already,
but I'm not ready to admit it. . . . And also I'm scared: frightened that it won't
come out. . . . Well, I wanted to be in love or in work—to get *hooked* & now I
am—& I don't want to be disappointed by or in the work.

I have vertigo—like inner ear infection—& wonder why it came now. The
work? Or the struggles with the relationship with Jesse.

Sunday morning I was up early & lying on the couch downstairs reading
when [at] almost 10 Jesse came down. The sun was coming thru the windows

---

* In the fall of 1979, Robbins had bought a small 1930s shingled cottage on the beach in Bridgehampton, where he spent time in the summer and most weekends until it grew too cold (the house
was not winterized) with Jesse Gerstein and his two dogs, Nick and Annie, a terrier mix he had
found wandering in the subway.

† George Gershwin's Concerto in F for piano and orchestra.

toward the staircase. He came down in his light purple cotton pullover which came to his thighs, & nothing else. His black hair was tousled, his long legs stuck out below. He looked lovely in his silence.

January 15 [1982]
The Gershwin piece seems to be coming together & the company have worked *very* hard on it. . . . I started on the parts that bothered me the most & laboriously altered & redid & redid with the patience of the company. At this point it's focusing—no—*I* have focused. . . . Lesson to be learned: either know it will work out, or know you go [through] this pain . . . & accept the suffering knowing it will pass. This is a shorthand for more than I am saying.

February 5 [1982]
Gershwin opened last night. . . . Trying to pin down my feelings about it. Ok, I no longer have as heavy a feeling about the "success" or "failure." In fairness I haven't been happy with it—but there is a natural (?) piece of me that really wants it to be a smash. It *was* with the audience—but it wasn't that good.

February 25 [1982]
Jesse has been sick & after a week of my urging him to go to the doctors he fouls up all app[ointmen]t to listen to his friend Jim, the intern & heeds his advice to find out he probably has the amoebic dysentery which has been going around the gay world. . . . It's highly contagious. So far Jesse has brought home crabs, the clap, and now this!! He becomes contrite. Can he do this or that for me? I can't look at him.

Journal #24
August 28 [1982]

I dropped by to say hello George this A.M.* As I rang the bell I could see him at the piano playing at that upright. His head turned at the sound of the doorbell

---

* Balanchine had a small condominium in Southampton near the summer home of the ballerina Karin von Aroldingen and her husband, who had become trusted friends; it was only a short drive from Robbins's Bridgehampton house.

The photographer Jesse Gerstein, Robbins's lover from 1977 to 1983, photographed on a terrace in Spoleto.

& he couldn't quite see who it was. He got up—& was dressed only in an unbuttoned summer shirt & his jockey shorts. In confusion he half tried to cover himself, run for cover, see who I was, [then] the phone rang. He took care of me first: Hello—oh *Jerry!*—& then went for the phone. I put the flowers I had brought in a vase [and] made as if to go—I just stopped by to say hello—but he beckoned me in to sit & talk. His hair was astray—one eye was black—& [he was] very old & fragile looking—his Don Q come off the stage to visit him.[*] The essence?: "They want something *modernist* today—do *you* know if anyone cared who is a good *modernist*? They tell me to be patient with my eye—I said all right—I have lots of patience now—I don't want to do anything more—I did enough—now, eat, travel—& I will go to Europe—I'd like to go to Monaco—I want to be buried there—there is where I started—there I want to end—It's so nice there. [And] how are you—your health—you are doing *2* new ballets—no?

---

[*] The bruise around Balanchine's eye was the result of recent cataract surgery. In 1965 he had choreographed, and danced in, a ballet to music by Nicholas Nabokov, based on Miguel Cervantes's novel *Don Quixote,* with his muse Suzanne Farrell in the role of the Don's beloved, Dulcinea.

only one—doesn't matter. They always want something new—they don't want the old & beautiful ballets—. It doesn't matter—do something new—small. I can't do any more—my legs won't hold me up—no muscle—some people can work from a chair—not me—I must *show* them."

To: Robert Fizdale[*]
Undated [late September–early October 1982]

Dear Bobby,

. . . The news of George is not so good. . . . It has to be faced that unless there is some miraculous turnabout, the deterioration sudden[ly] and swiftly moves on. . . . [T]here is no tumor in the brain—news that is good & awful at the same time as it means pretty surely hardening of arteries in the head & lack of oxygen to it, etc. He won't have anyone stay with him, except wants Barbara[†] or Karin to be there; he has peeks [*sic*] of clarity. I saw him twice at the hospital and each time he rallied, was explicit about his illness, future; talked about ABT's strike[‡] (which now seems completely irreparable), watched TV, & seemed clear & struggling valiantly to accept & deal with what was happening. But it's unfair that Nature, having no regard for the soul, genius & contributions of that man, wreaks a swift & rather specially horrible natural destruction on his body, unconscious of the who which is contained within it. Unjust . . . [JR's ellipses] like Tanny's illness, unjust.

Meanwhile . . . as far as the Co[mpany] is concerned . . . there seems [to be] no "takeover" by Peter,[§] & some sort of communal running of it all. Of course

---

[*] Gold and Fizdale, who were friends of Balanchine's as well as admirers, had been on a concert tour in Europe; they had just attended Vera Stravinsky's funeral in Venice.

[†] Barbara Horgan was Balanchine's longtime personal assistant.

[‡] In early September, ABT's management—including its artistic director, Mikhail Baryshnikov, who had left NYCB in 1980 because of knee problems—had locked its dancers out after deadlocked contract negotiations.

[§] Although Robbins was unaware of these developments, Balanchine had expressed the belief that Peter Martins should succeed him because, as he told the City Ballet board member Robert Gottlieb, "he knows what a ballerina needs." That fall, with Balanchine hospitalized and only erratically com-it's clear to me that sooner or later someone will have to take on the burden of making decisions—Lincoln or a committee won't—& whoever does will get it in the neck. What a curious time—shifts—all shifts.

How's the *work* going—& how was your cruise—& Venice, Paris, etc.? Please write & let me know. The Hamptons were glorious this fall. I went up to Tanny's* on her birthday & we had an outdoor picnic. Fun & beautiful . . . I've been working hard on the Astaire Variations,[†] done about 8 of them—& haven't yet found the piece. The co[mpany] danced wonderfully in D.C. & that's about the news.

So dear Bobby—& Arthur—be well, enjoy yourselves—& write when you can.

All love—
Your S.P.[‡]

Journal #24

December 2 [1982]

Edith[§] died. She'd fallen about a month ago & then things went wrong. I sat with her last hours in the hospital & watched with her. It's left a hole in the galaxies. I'll get over it I know but it's a rough one. . . . (I was holding her hand when she died.)

---

petent, City Ballet's board quietly appointed Martins ballet master—the title that had most recently been Balanchine's. It was later claimed that Robbins had been asked if *he* were interested in the job but had declined it—which was not the case.

* Tanaquil Le Clercq had a cottage in Weston, Connecticut, where she spent weekends.

† Robbins had made good on his intention to create a ballet inspired by Fred Astaire and Rita Hayworth's duet in the 1942 film *You Were Never Lovelier;* the commissioned score, by Morton Gould, was a suite of variations on the song the couple dance to in the film "I'm Old Fashioned," composed by Jerome Kern with lyrics by Johnny Mercer.

‡ In the early years of their friendship Robbins, Gold, and Fizdale had occasionally referred to one another as "Secret Pals."

§ Edith Weissman had been Robbins's personal assistant for forty years—his entire career. Arguably, she knew more about him than anyone, and her death was a significant loss.

March 27 [1983]

G.B. worse in hospital—a slow elevator down. Orville Schell puts us all into a frenzy of title naming & we all get blitzed by it.* I'm not sure if my reactions were the best but I am content with the result—fair: Peter is calling it in association with me. . . .

I've been to see George about every 2 weeks. Buried angers come out toward him. Long swallowed resentments & public & private injuries surfaced in the Schell affair. I guess I was not going to remain in the company as a side-kick supplier of "other" works, no matter how it was fore-ordained by G.B. If they wanted to follow his plan they could, but *I* found it unacceptable to continue that way. The company, to keep me, would have to want my oar in its running. All expressed the same words: NYCB would be a disaster without me. OK I said: Peter is in the driver's seat. I'm next to him as associate. No one could be named Ballet-Master over me, as that referred to *making* ballets, & my record was established as senior & major over all others. . . .

April 4 [1983]

Yesterday Jesse & I finished being together for 6 years. . . . My insides go into a double or triple shock. 1st, shock of recognition that this must happen; 2nd, shock at the news itself & the feeling of deceit by him; 3rd, my feelings of rejection & the awful pain of separation & what the future can mean. . . . I can't see how to hold it together & come to the edge of deepest depression & crackup as I can get. . . . At this same time Martins is emerging with an almost brutal aggression & manipulation—at the same time I don't like Glass & can't make Astaire† work out.

---

* Surprised by Robbins's discomfiture at being left out of the decision to make Peter Martins ballet master, Orville Schell (1908–1987), chairman of City Ballet's board, was now trying to find nomenclature that would be palatable to all while naming Lincoln Kirstein general director. In the end it would be decided to name *both* Robbins and Martins ballet master in chief. Balanchine was still alive but flickering in and out of responsiveness while all these negotiations were going on.

† Robbins had been scheduled to direct the world premiere of Philip Glass's *Akhnaten* for Houston Grand Opera, but City Ballet's demands on him during the uncertain period of Balanchine's illness had forced him to withdraw. He had, however, been so inspired by Glass's score that he asked to use some of it, along with music from the composer's *Glassworks,* for a new ballet titled *Glass Pieces.* It would debut on May 12, 1983, and as happened more and more often, Robbins was dissatisfied with the ballet in the weeks before its premiere. This was also the case with the Astaire Variations, which by the time of its opening, on June 16, was titled *I'm Old Fashioned.*

What a good time!

Jesse is getting frayed at the edges. . . . I would like to send him on his way with well-wishes—I try to let him know that, but oh how it hurts, how deep a knife cuts into me. . . .

About the co[mpany]—I feel I should take a leave of absence for a while. I have no energy to want to work harder & what I do do is sterile. I go in circles. The usual complaints about work—you know them.

April 30 [1983]

George died at 4 a.m. today. I'd driven out to the beach late last night . . . determined to tell [Jesse] to pack & leave in the a.m. No sleep, but the phone at 7 a.m. lets me know (Barbara H.) that G.B. died & I tell her I'll come in right away. We dress, eat, and drive home & Jesse says nothing. . . . [B]y the time we get to the theater I just said to him, well you better start packing. . . . And at the theater all were in tears. It's terrible alternating [between] supporting & grieving.

6

Reconciliation: 1983–1998

n 1985, after Robbins unveiled a new ballet, *In Memory Of . . .*, to Alban Berg's 1935 Violin Concerto, he told a journalist, "I myself didn't consciously have Mr. Balanchine in mind in making the ballet. . . . I did think of people close to me—my secretary of 40 years, Edith Weissman, whose hand I held at the end, and Tanny, Tanaquil Le Clercq, . . . whose career was tragically cut short by polio . . . and [I] was struck by what a series of losses Berg himself had sustained in his last year—the young girl he was so deeply fond of, his citizenship, and as it turned out, his own life."*

Robbins himself was going through a complicated ritual of mourning and reconciliation, dealing with loss, age, his past, and his legacy. After the streamlined, pulsating postmodernism of 1983's *Glass Pieces,* he looked back across the decades to the music and dance styles of the 1940s with the evocatively titled *I'm Old Fashioned* (also 1983), whose choreography contains references to *Fancy Free,* and the next year, for *Antique Epigraphs,* he plundered an old score, Debussy's *Six Epigraphes Antiques,* which he'd used for his dreamy *Ballade* in 1950. He also revisited, in the same ballet, an image that had haunted him since he first saw it with his former love Buzz Miller: the implacable enamel-eyed bronze statues in the Archaeological Museum in Naples.

---

* Robbins in Alan M. Kriegsman, "Confessions of a Ballet Master," *Washington Post,* September 22, 1985. The "young girl" he refers to was Manon Gropius, Alma Mahler's daughter, dead of polio at eighteen. Although Berg, a non-Jew, did not lose his Austrian citizenship before his death, his music was proscribed by the Nazis as "degenerate" owing to his connection with his Jewish teacher, Arnold Schoenberg.

Not that he abandoned innovation—he seemed to throw out much of the ballet rule book with his kinetic collaboration with Twyla Tharp, *Brahms/Handel* (1984), and then created a spare but complex ballet to a contemporary score, Steve Reich's 1979 minimalist octet, *Eight Lines* (1985). And he made another attempt to collaborate with John Guare and Leonard Bernstein on an adaptation of Brecht's *The Exception and the Rule,* which Lincoln Center Theater produced as a workshop and which came close to delivering on the novel ideas Robbins had envisioned for the play.

Increasingly, though, there was an elegiac cast to his work and to his personal and inner lives. He and Jesse Gerstein made an attempt at reconciliation, then split again, although they remained on friendly terms. Robbins began a new relationship with a graduate student, Brian Meehan, who shared his passion for cooking and backgammon and walks on the beach. The calm of their companionship was offset, however, by Robbins's discomfiture at his increasing age ("it's pushing me up into the A.K. [*alte kocker*] territory," he complained of his sixty-fifth birthday); by strains or ruptures in some old friendships—with Arthur Laurents, Stephen Sondheim, Robert Wilson, even Leonard Bernstein; and more ominously by the terrifying plague that was sweeping through the gay world. Although four years previously no one had even heard of acquired immunodeficiency syndrome, by April 1985 the number of AIDS cases in the United States had passed ten thousand, and it was posing a literally existential threat.

In Memory Of . . . was a response to all of these things; so, in different ways, were his next two ballets, *Quiet City* (1986) and *Ives, Songs* (1988), as well as the anthology benefit program *Dancing for Life* that he organized and directed at the New York State Theater on October 5, 1987, in which thirteen dance companies participated, raising $1.4 million for AIDS research and relief. *Quiet City,* in fact, was a very specific elegy, for the young dancer Joseph Duell, who had most recently portrayed the dying young girl's sweetheart in *In Memory Of . . .* and whose tragic suicide in the winter of 1986 touched a surprisingly paternal nerve in Robbins. And *Ives, Songs*—inspired originally by the work of the late nineteenth-century American artist Maurice Prendergast and set to

Charles Ives's spiky transmutations of Victorian parlor songs and hymn tunes—revisited not just a life but a community through a series of nostalgic vignettes that Robbins described as "about me & my dancers."

Robbins had always been dismayed by the idea that his art, unlike a writer's or a painter's or a composer's, was impermanent and eradicable. And he confronted this issue in his own writing—in an unpublished essay, and in a review of a biography of the choreographer Jack Cole—in the writings and records of others, and in action. In 1987 his gifts to the New York Public Library enabled it to establish the Jerome Robbins Archive of the Recorded Moving Image, a trove of thousands of dance films and videotapes that were, he felt, the only sure way to record the truth of dance performance. In addition, in 1989, after many months of research, reconstruction, and rehearsal, he resurrected and preserved, at least for another generation, the "hit dances" from his Broadway shows in an anthology musical, *Jerome Robbins' Broadway,* that won him yet another pair of Tony Awards, one for his direction and one for the show itself.

Against his acts of preservation, however, the losses continued to mount up: the deaths of Nora Kaye, Irving Berlin, Leonard Bernstein, Nancy Hayward Keith, Robert Fizdale, and even Robbins's cherished terrier Nick; the flickering and then the fading of his relationship with Brian Meehan, with whom he broke and reconciled several times; Lincoln Kirstein's retirement from New York City Ballet; and—most painfully—the news that Jesse Gerstein was terminally ill with AIDS. Reuniting with Gerstein, Robbins took a leave from New York City Ballet to spend time with him and, ultimately, nurse him through the disease's grim final stages. He himself suffered a traumatic brain injury in a bicycle accident during this period, which left him with persistent vertigo and Parkinsonism.

As so often, work gave him a way out. A trip to Russia to oversee the Kirov Ballet's production of *In the Night* enabled him to reconnect with a wellspring of his art. In workshops he began experimenting with scenarists, actors, and directorial assistants to find a dramatic form for *The Poppa Piece,* the autobiographical theater narrative he'd been thinking about for two decades; while he was unable to arrive at a satisfactory conclusion for it, the act of staging it—even if only in a studio setting—provided some kind of catharsis. A more fulfilling experience was the transfer to City Ballet of the *West Side Story* dances that had appeared in *Jerome Robbins' Broadway,* arranged as a choreographic as well as orchestral suite—something Robbins and Lincoln Kirstein had always wanted but that Balanchine had resisted. And, possibly inspired by the Bach chorale "Es Ist Genug" (It Is Enough) quoted by Berg in the second movement of the *In Memory Of . . .* violin concerto, Robbins made three new works to Bach: a solo piece for Mikhail Baryshnikov and the White Oak Dance Project to the unaccompanied cello suites; a circular jeu d'esprit, *2 & 3 Part Inventions,* for students at the School of American Ballet; and the rollicking *Brandenburg* for New York City Ballet.

By the time of *Brandenburg*'s premiere Robbins was suffering from the aftereffects of heart-valve-replacement surgery and was becoming increasingly frail, but he kept working and kept in touch, in person and by letter, with old friends, as well as a circle of younger artists with whom he often took a fatherly tone. In the spring of 1998 he told one former dancer to bring her baby girl to the theater to see "the man with the beard" during a rehearsal break, for he was supervising the staging of his 1965 *Les Noces* for City Ballet. He'd wanted to leave this "barbaric, beautiful, and frightening" ballet, which he had once compared to "a singular mountain," in the repertory of a company that would care for it, and he did. But the effort cost him: climbing that mountain again with his reduced faculties was more than he was capable of. *Les Noces* premiered on May 20, 1998—fifty years after he had first offered himself to City Ballet—and the following day he briefly checked himself into the hospital with exhaustion. On July 25 he suffered a massive stroke; four days later he was dead.

In his will—along with bequests to lovers, friends, and family, provisions for a foundation to continue his philanthropic activities, and a trust to administer and preserve his choreographic work—he left his archives (along with an additional bequest of $5 million) to the New York Public Library, whose already rich dance collection was greatly enhanced by this gift, so much so that it was renamed the Jerome Robbins Dance Division. The entire collection is a valuable resource to dance scholars, and Robbins's own archives have been essential to his biographers and to others who have written about his contributions to dance and the theater. But there was one item missing from those archives, which Robbins himself had secreted away, seemingly daring fate to produce it at the opportune time.

This was a letter he wrote *to himself*, on his "Jerome Robbins" stationery, after coming home from a preview performance of *Jerome Robbins' Broadway*. When he finished writing it, he sealed it in an envelope, addressed it to himself, and put the envelope into the pages of a souvenir program from the show. This program, in turn, found its way into a valise, and the valise found its way into the basement of his house on Eighty-First Street; then, after Robbins's death, a member of his household preserved the valise without looking at its contents—until just months before research for this book began, when the valise was opened, the contents examined, and the letter found. Somehow he had known exactly how he wanted his story to end.

Journal #24
May 25 [1983]

3 A.M.

On again, off again—the seesaw swings up & down & even around. I ask Jesse to leave until he knows where his head is. He does. At the co[mpany] we go thru George's memorial & funeral. The room I shared with him[*] is impossible to go into. Sense of loss of a friend—& loved one. By the end of the week Jesse & I miss each other & want back & agree that to each the other comes first—that's the contract. . . . The week goes well. Glass opens[†] & to my surprise is a biggie.

---

[*] Their shared office, which Robbins had captured on videotape, panning over furniture with a reverential murmured commentary: "That's George's desk . . . that's his chair."
[†] *Glass Pieces* premiered on May 12, 1983.

So what do I know. That's Thursday . . . by Sunday Jesse's bitching at everything & resenting me so much for finding himself back with me. . . . Then *go* I say: how can you say go, he asks, cause I'm way ahead of you. . . .

What a strange period. So full of losses & upsets, & then triumph with Glass. . . .

Bodrum Journal, 1984[*]
July 3, 1984

I'm listening to Handel, Concerti Grossi, op. 6, a piece I've wanted to do for a couple of years, and have even started 5 or 6 variations.

But as I listen & imagine—images of G.B.'s ballets arise—& I think:

We all try to speak "Balanchine"—We, Peter—Helgi—Taras—even Jacques[†]— have a working understanding of his language & even how he constructs. Peter has the best grasp of the technical aspects of the language—but no matter. We all speak with the heavy accents of our own natures—& only George can spin out the seamless flow of a natural native tongue. Even when we get fluid, it still doesn't have the deep ease, knowledge, poetry & certainty of what it means to say, or the profoundly absorbed understanding of the music. We'll never pass in his language. Interesting. Peter's best work, his first, is the one that is most Peter's—the rest are artifices. Mine I can't judge—but I know that trying to "do" a Balanchine-like work is a futile effort, like trying to paint a Leonardo-like painting. I've learned a lot from Twyla.[‡] Her daring, her outrageousness, her *insistence,* her invention, the belief that all is possible, is a deep & inspiring lesson—& awakes in me again earlier & younger dares—when every second was to be invented & filled. At NYCB I've fallen backward & put [myself] asleep by trying to trust more the GB vocabulary—it's lazy—. She made me feel that

---

[*] Robbins had been invited to join the record producer Ahmet Ertegun and his interior designer wife, Mica, to cruise the southern coast of Turkey.

[†] Like Peter Martins, Helgi Tomasson, now artistic director of the San Francisco Ballet but then still a principal dancer at NYCB, had begun making dances for the company, as did the ballet master John Taras and the recently retired principal dancer Jacques d'Amboise (founder of the National Dance Institute).

[‡] Robbins and Tharp's collaboration, *Brahms/Handel* (set to Brahms's Variations and Fugue on a Theme by Handel, op. 24, orchestrated by Edmund Rubbra), had premiered on June 7.

way. Go ahead, try, *anything* is possible—turn it upside down, inside out, on its head. . . .

All this is being written on a Turkish boat, Miss Layla, in a bay as twilight descends . . . [JR's ellipses] a quarter moon, other sail boats, water sounds, sea now green & dark instead of blue & clear.

To: Robert Graves
May 9, 1985

Dear Robert,

I believe in messages—especially when they come insistently one upon the other signaling for attention.

Thus they arrived from you. First Edna O'Brien (our friendship began upon our first encounter in your home in London), arrived here in New York and at dinner, as always, we talked about you. The very next morning I received a letter from Julia Simonne[*] also talking about you. Then came a meeting with Julia and Ramon.[†] And finally, and best of all, Julia gave me your Collected Letters Vol. II, which was like being with you again.

So, dear man—I reach out to embrace you by mail. I do think of you often—how much you have given me, how many signals, messages and directions I received from being with you and how helpful, important and profound they all were.

You were particularly present with me last year when I did a ballet called "Antique Epigraphs" to music of Debussy. When I was nearly finished I realized that I'd been haunted by those bronze life size statues of dancing women—those with the enamel eyes that fix you and that see the future—the ones in Naples at the National Museum. I almost called the ballet The Dancers of Herculaneum.

---

[*] Julia Simonne, the self-described "Robert Graves' last Muse," was a principal dancer with Theatre Ballet of London and a choreographer; in the spring of 1985 she presented a series of thirteen dances at the Harkness Dance Center in New York.
[†] Ramón Farrán Sánchez (b. 1939), a Catalan jazz drummer and composer, lived on Mallorca and had become a friend of Graves's.

Since then I've done a ballet to minimalist music (enough) and have just finished another to Alban Berg's violin concerto for which I have high hopes.

As for my life, it is pleasant, quiet and I seem to ride the ups and downs of it a good deal better than before. I have a small bungalow on Long Island that looks out over the Atlantic on one side and on an enormous bay full of swans on the other. Watching sunrises, sunsets, the sky changing, and the horizon is what I do there. And walk, and let my head drift.

So dear friend, I'll say goodbye for now. My love goes with this to you. I embrace and salute you.*

With deep affection,
Jerry

P.S. I'm working on a theater piece about my father & being Jewish. It's called "The Poppa Piece" or "Robbins by Rabinowitz."

Egypt–Turkey Journal (Excerpt)†
June 28, 1985

. . . I feel I'm failing—falling toward aging—toward death. I know part of it is the giving away & giving up of money in a way I have never done before—the preparation of a will: & my last ballet.. In Memory Of.. which something tells me *is* my last ballet, there or ever—. And that, in spite of work, rework, etc., it came out of me rather like automatic writing; not easy—but outside of me, so that the completed work stood outside my own experience of it!

But more is the fatigue & decline from activity, from action, decision, from enjoyment, from participation.

Is this just a downer? Is it the unconscious break with Brian—a phase—a passing time. Even the fact that I'm writing this is something I haven't done in years.

---

* Graves had stopped writing in 1975 and became increasingly incapacitated; he would die of heart failure on December 7, 1985. This letter seems to have been Robbins's conscious farewell to him.
† To chronicle this 1985 cruise along the Turkish coast with the Erteguns, Robbins used empty pages in the notebook from his 1981 Egyptian trip.

"In 1988 it will be your big year," said Peter. What is he talking about? "You'll be 70! And we want to celebrate it!" CRASH & SHOCK. Don't push me! I've got 3 1/2 years yet. And maybe by then I'll get used to it. 70.

"You are old Father William and your hair has turned to white.
Yet you still chase after boys.
Do you think that's really right?"
Lewis Carroll?[*]

To: Penelope Dudleston[†]
August 13, 1985

Dearest Penny,

I, too, was so happy to speak to and hear you. Isn't it funny, our relationship—so odd that we have these feelings for each other. It is very comforting to me and I hope also to you.

It sounds like you're working hard with all your feelings. I guess that's what it's all about. When things are good, they are very good, and when they're not, we have to realize it's just a swing of the cycle and that we will come up on the other side.

What a wonderful letter your "Annie" recommendation is! You should be very proud of that. I particularly liked the description of your work with the company and how sensitively you handled everybody. If only we could do as well by ourselves is what often occurs to me. Whenever I get in real trouble, I try to think of what I would advise if I were my own best friend. It helps.

---

[*] What Lewis Carroll actually wrote was "You are old, Father William, the young man said, / And your hair has become very white. / And yet you incessantly stand on your head. / Do you think, at your age, it is right?" Robbins penciled in "stand on your head" over "chase after boys."
[†] Penelope Dudleston had performed the role of the young girl on the beach in *Watermill* and formed a bond with Robbins that continued after she left New York City Ballet. She had had some personal struggles but had recently supervised dances for a production of *Annie* and wrote to Robbins to share with him her recommendation from the show's director.

Life at the beach (Long Island) is very calm, quiet and frighteningly inactive in every way. Creatively I become a slug, and although I brought out lots of scores, records, videos, scripts and books, I get very little done as the days slip by very quickly. Enclosed is a little snapshot of what I look out on (the Atlantic) on a grey day. It is a continuation of the Watermill beach.

Please write again, and if you ever want to call me, please do, collect. Where I'll be for a while yet: 516/537-0418. In New York it's 212/249-4757.

I send you my love as always.

Jerry

To: Stephen Sondheim
October 30, 1985

Dear Steve,

Just got back from my trip to London and Paris and found your letter which was upsetting to me.

The D.C. interview* contained two unfortunate misquotes. One was a remark of George Perle's about Berg which was then wrongly attributed to me. In it I seemed to patronize Berg. The other was a misunderstanding of my words about you. As you can tell, Kriegsman was clearly in sympathy with my feelings about Arthur's article. He asked about your feelings, and I said in a general way you never seemed very happy about WEST SIDE STORY and that at the Dramatists Guild symposium,† there were some edges of bitching about it between you and Lenny. Thus it was given, if not correctly quoted.

---

* In an interview with Alan M. Kriegsman of *The Washington Post* published in connection with the Washington premiere of *In Memory Of. . .* , Robbins had mentioned comments Arthur Laurents had recently made about a revival of *West Side Story;* Laurents had disparaged the show, especially the film version, and suggested that new choreography might improve it. "I'm proud of it," Robbins told Kriegsman, "even if Steve Sondheim and Arthur Laurents go around bitching about it." In his letter, Sondheim complained, "You are confusing me with Arthur, which is unpleasant and unwelcome."
† A public panel discussion about *West Side Story* involving Robbins, Bernstein, Laurents, and Sondheim, reproduced in *The Dramatists Guild Quarterly* (Fall 1985).

Now to start with, I never confuse you with Arthur. Next, I don't know why you say you think I'm angry with you, no less "still" angry. If I search around for a reason to be angry, I guess I do feel the GYPSY symposium,[*] led clearly by Arthur, was a stinker of an attack, and I was glad to read that you, after some not such nice recalls, said something to the effect that I did make some valuable contributions to that show. But finally, if that quote made for any confusion in anyone's mind that you and Arthur are of the same cloth, character and talents, then I do apologize. There's no confusion in my mind, you know that. I am truly sorry that happened.

Now let's not have any Arthur Laurents further letter exchanges. If my "slamming" you (which I didn't) is an Arthur tactic, so is your response to me. Shall we both forget both and go on? I hope so. P.S. Arthur wrote me an apology!!! Well—an *Arthur* apology.

I have lots to tell you about everything I saw in London and Paris. Let's have dinner soon. I would like that.

All my love,

J

St. Bart's Journal[†]
March 2, 1986

I have been in this state before. I recognize it. . . . Inertia takes over. Sleep, & a heavy sense of isolation weigh on you like a heavy rug of nostalgia. . . .

I work a bit. The "Joe" piece I question.[‡] Can I sustain it, can the music

---

[*] At this event, another Dramatists Guild symposium attended by Laurents, Sondheim, and Jule Styne (Robbins was absent), Laurents had pointedly referred to his co-panelists as "the three people who *write*"—as opposed to Robbins (*Dramatists Guild Quarterly* 18, no. 3 [Autumn 1981]).

[†] In mid-February, Robbins had gone to St. Bart's for his customary holiday once his duties for the winter City Ballet season were accomplished.

[‡] On February 16, the NYCB principal dancer Joseph Duell had killed himself by jumping from the window of his fifth-floor apartment. His death had shattered the City Ballet company; Robbins himself began considering a ballet in Duell's memory, set to Aaron Copland's score for the film *Quiet City*.

move me, is it a good thing to do. 2 weeks ago to the day I arrived here & 2 weeks ago Joe jumped to his death. (Tolstoy, about age 10, threw himself from a 3rd floor window & nothing happened. Joe 5th—& death.) I heard of it Monday & returned Wednesday. I returned here on Thursday the following week & am waiting for my mood to change before returning to N.Y. . . . Yesterday did some work on Q[uiet] C[ity] & it helped. But my clear overpowering feelings to do the work—"The Visitation"—Joe coming back to be with us, console us, is now not as felt.

I perceive, not willingly, that the pattern is one of disinvolvement. Somewhere I feel & fear that I may not do any more ballets. Too hard for me. Too hard to invent, don't have the drive, need, search, joy & anger of creation. . . . Oi vey. Stop. This. You're just down. Joe's death hit me harder than I would think it might. I still don't want to deal with the moment of death—the need to plunge out.. to fall—to crash & destroy oneself.[*]

To: Paul Taylor
March 10, 1986

Dear Paul,

I deeply appreciate your sending me the pages from your book[†] for verification. That was very considerate of you. If you are asking everyone else in your book if you've remembered correctly, you must be getting some mail! Aren't you glad you've written it?

Well, here goes. You must know how much I admire and respect you. But I *am* surprised to find myself playing the role of Mr. Bad Boss to your wide-eyed self.

---

[*] *Quiet City* premiered on May 8, 1986; of it, *The New York Times*'s Anna Kisselgoff said that "while it is only too easy to see [its protagonist] as a surrogate for Mr. Duell, it does no service to Mr. Duell's memory, to the choreographer or to the public to do so."

[†] Paul Taylor (1930–2018), one of America's foremost modern choreographers, had written an autobiography, *Private Domain,* and wanted to check details of his account of dancing—which included breaking his nose onstage—in the ensemble of *Peter Pan.*

Here's your version. You bull yourself into a job you're not technically trained for, hurt yourself doing a back flip—not only your nose, but also your back, ankles, wrists, etc.—and you're fired because you're unable to do the necessary and required flip.

Here's my version. I'd seen you dance and thought you were terrific. I knew you were bluffing your way into the show, but out of your apparent need for a job and your insistence that you could do the back flip, gave you the job of doing it. To my horror, through your inexperience, you hurt yourself. The company carried you for a while, but the vital part had to be filled. I don't at all remember my firing you. But I've heard it before: "Is it true you fired Paul Taylor from a show?" That's the legend that's come down through the years. You could explain it now correctly.

O.K. enough. I love you. And I deeply admire your work. As I've said before to you, I hope someday you'll feel relaxed enough to come over and do something for us. Come watch rehearsals, or class—or just hang around and watch. You'll like it.

Yours,—
Jerry

P.S. *None* of my dialogue sounds like me, but the whole incident does read very funny. I made some notes on the text if you're interested.

To: Paul Taylor
March 24, 1986

Dear Paul,

Thank you for your letter and also for the changes you made in the story, which I appreciate. However, I'd like to tell you a couple of things.

Because memory does play tricks on us, I called Bobby Tucker.* Without

---

* Robert Tucker (d. 2016) played one of the pirates in *Peter Pan* and was Robbins's choreographic assistant on the show, a role he filled in several other Robbins productions including *Bells Are Ringing* and *Gypsy*. As a choreographer he was nominated for a Tony Award for *Shenandoah*.

telling him what it was about, I asked his recall of the incident. He says 1) you stupidly did more flip-flops than were called for and therefore you crashed into the wall; 2) he would never have changed my choreography because he had done that on another show and I'd laid him out for it; and 3) he has no memory of your being fired by me or anyone else. So there we are.

Paul, I don't remember firing you. It is possible that if I saw the show without the flip-flops I might have said to someone we need them and to please get them back in. What happened from there I was not responsible for.

I suppose it's Rashomon time. There's your story, there's my story, and there's Bobby Tucker's whose story was given without his knowing you were writing a book until after I had gotten his version. So love, and good luck!

Yours—
Jerry

P.S. Ballet dancers are like all dancers. Just get to know them.

Jury Duty
June 25, 1986

Saying "Here" is difficult. . . . To be present. To be affirmative. To be secure. To declare yourself. To accept & celebrate the simpleness of your duty, manhood, guiltlessness.

And that is underlying this whole experience. Just to be. Not to feel the guilt, anxiety, terror that all this holds under the wrappings.

I am called. A panel is to be picked. We go to another room. Each is questioned in private. I get thru the first day OK. The judge helped. At the second I could feel my terror rise. State your name please. The court stenographer waits. I summon up my concentration, & give my name. Speak up, the Judge says. I do. On the other side, a lawyer says, What was that please? I give my name for the 3rd time, the syllables crumbling [in] my mouth.

Oh terrors. The HUAC returns, & I can't escape the terrors of that catastrophe—the guilt, betrayal, cowardice, but most of all—the about-to-be-discovered-Jew by the Aryans. . . .

To: Penelope Dudleston
August 15, 1986

Dear Penny,

How good to hear from you. And thank you for sharing your thoughts with me.

My summer has also been bumpy. Too many illnesses with aging friends and family. My stepmother, at 89, is besieged with all sorts of illnesses and yet keeps her head up and a valiant streak of toughness and good humor about her even though she faces the ending of her mortal life and the breaking up of the home she's lived in these past 25 years. What an example for all of us. And other older aging friends show us that what's ahead is not the best by any means as we move on. Which is what I'm starting to feel myself. Having been active and so in touch with my body as a dancer, the early signs of diminishing capacities fall like blows as energies, sight, hearing, and physical strength all begin to ebb away. I try to look at it like its part of beauty and the cycle of life itself—that everything goes through this experience—but it has seemed to come upon me more suddenly than I was prepared for. Well, like they say, that's life. And I only hope I go through it as well as others I'm seeing. . . .

Sorry your summer's been a poor one. As you say, some discomfort shows something happening—baddies coming to the surface and out. And any growth is usually accompanied by some growing pains.

Stop worrying about "happiness." Just remember each day, hour and minute of your life is a passing one—and is gone forever—so enjoy *all* of it—the goodies and the baddies, and stop trying to *solve* it. It doesn't solve. At least I haven't seen it do that.

Hey good for Sly* and you. Train him *firmly* now. Whatever he learns now, he keeps as his pattern. But aren't they great pals?

I miss you and think of you. I'll be going to Europe in mid-September til mid-October. Write if you can.

---

* Dudleston had adopted a dog and was doing obedience training with him.

PS: This is more of a down letter than I feel. Sorry about it. I just came back from Florida visiting my stepmother. Forgive me.

Here comes the sun.[*]

Xo

J

To: Lincoln Kirstein
November 17, 1986

Dear Lincoln,

Thank you for your letter. . . . Yes, I wish I could do two ballets if not three, but I seem to have been in some sort of catching-my-breath respite. It's starting to lift, and I'm beginning to have ideas again. . . .

Everybody has wanted for me to do the dances from "West Side Story."[†] Many years ago, I told George I might do them for ABT and without a moment's pause, he said, "Oh, that's okay, *our* boys can't fight." This year ABT has asked for it again as have you and Peter. But I have plans for 1988 to do a Broadway show which consists of a collection of all of my commercial choreographic works. It will mark my 70th birthday, so you can see why I'm saving that material.

"Dybbuk" I question, but I'll look at it again. It was very unsatisfactory as initially it was going to be a small chamber music work about the essences of the spiritual life of the play. Instead, Lenny wrote a symphonic work (with two voices yet) without discipline, spreading over the whole story. Thus it was neither an abstract nor a story piece, just an uneasy amalgamation of approaches. I did my best to make a whole out of it, but, as you know, I was never satisfied. But I'll listen to it again.

It was so good to get your letter. And thank you.

All my love,

Jerry

---

[*] This line is preceded and followed by musical notes—a reference, probably, to the Beatles song.
[†] In 1961, Leonard Bernstein had premiered a frequently performed orchestral suite, *Symphonic Dances from "West Side Story,"* and Kirstein was hoping for a dance equivalent.

To: Frances Arkin[*]
January 5, 1987

Dear Frances,

It was good to get your note at Christmas as always. I was in Florida for a day this fall and tried unsuccessfully to call you to say hello.

I'm okay. The last part of 1986 I went to both London and Paris to stage ballets. I enjoyed my stint in Paris very much. The city never looked so beautiful to my eyes, my work went well, and so did my life outside the theater. As for life here, I am preparing for my 70th birthday (!) a Broadway show which will be a collection of all my dances in all the shows I've done. Right now I'm involved with Bernstein and John Guare working on a project we started many years ago and hope to finish this spring. My personal life is more or less the same, but with, I hope, a more even-keeled basis of dealing with it. The past few years I've seen the loss of a lot of friends, and one begins to acknowledge more clearly the shortness of the journey ahead against the length one has travelled. But I am in good shape (for my age) and a good frame of mind.

I think of you quite often and hope this finds you well. It was with great pleasure that I read your note on your card. I send you my warmest feelings as always.

Sincerely,
Jerry

---

[*] Frances Arkin, Robbins's first therapist, had retired and moved to the Miami area. He and she had stayed in touch over the years, and when he visited his father and stepmother in Florida, he also stopped in to see Arkin on one or more occasions.

Ives Journal

March 13, 1987

I bought this book[*] in Venice—to keep journals of other trips. I'm on two right now. My body is on its way to St. Barts—my head is on a fierce irrational trip on Ives & Prendergast.[†]

On Wednesday, I got on to Ives—by accident, almost. I'd seen the monotype show of Prendergast at the P.M. Whitney[‡] & became again fascinated by his work & the period & auras he evoked. It connected to the earlier search (about 3 years ago[§]) after seeing the Boston sketch book in the Lehman collection—& then going up to Boston & seeing their holdings.[¶]

Trying to fathom how to *do* a ballet on those themes (where do you go after you show the costumes & the strolling etc.). Perhaps 2 groups could [alternate]—one in the dresses & manners of the paintings—& the other, free, uncluttered dancers, perhaps in long sheer full slips to dance the feelings of those pictures. Then I tried some Ives songs sung by Fischer-Dieskau^{**}—& it was as if I hadn't heard these songs ever before.

What a revelation. They seemed perfect, made for Prendergast! But then as I listened more (Sea Gulls,^{††} Sunrise, Tom Sails Away, etc.) I wanted to just dance to them—no costumes—just compose choreography to those won-

---

* Robbins had an affinity for pretty notebooks. This one was another of the small, bindery-paper-bound ones he favored.

† Charles Ives (1874–1954) was an American composer who combined source material from the American folk and hymn-tune traditions with experimental polytonality. Maurice Prendergast (1858–1924) was an American Postimpressionist painter whose primary subject was the upper middle class at leisure.

‡ *Monotypes by Maurice Prendergast,* a show of works from the collection of the Terra Museum of American Art, ran from February 26 to April 22, 1987, at the Whitney Museum of American Art's branch exhibition quarters at Philip Morris Inc.

§ Robbins later wrote "More!" over "3 years."

¶ The "Boston Sketchbook," part of the Lehman Collection at the Metropolitan Museum of Art in New York, contains Prendergast's watercolors of activities in and around the Public Garden in his native Boston. The Boston Museum of Fine Arts has a notable Prendergast collection, and seemingly Robbins pursued his passion for the artist by traveling there to see his work.

** Dietrich Fischer-Dieskau (1925–2012), a German lyric baritone, was one of the foremost art-song singers in the world.

†† The song is actually titled "The White Gulls."

drous pieces—& I began to see another kind of ballet—in Tipton's* lighting of mists—& play the contrast of early 20th Century/late 19th century music and late 20th century ballet. That day & the next I deluged myself in Ives' songs—record after recording—reading jacket notes, the piano scores, making tapes—etc. & was in such a state of agitation, like the irrationality of the first stages of love—awe, excitement, obsessions, tremendous fear, anticipation, all carousing [*sic*] thru my head & body in such an upsetting & exhilarating way. How? How? The wish is firmly there—but *how*. I record as many songs as possible. When I follow them in the score I lose their impact thru analyzation—that comes later—& helpfully, but only after 1st reactions to the ear alone.

A day later—I get a glimmer of something. My titles—"Ives & Prendergast" "Charles & Maurice" "Songs" and titles from Ives songs etc. balance on seesaws in my head. Which way to go—pure dance—pure period—(very Tudorish† period)—& then, then—why not both—why not both together, setting each other off—making the other more clear & exciting by being both there contrasting & illuminating—appearing out of the mists—. It started with sea gulls‡—that I could imagine in the lithe young bodies of our junior boys—or an earlier image of one of Pren's paintings of lit yellow store fronts which silhouette men in overcoats & hats against which a woman with umbrella advances toward you—all dark—covered—winterized—& then wondering how it would look if out of that darkness appeared suddenly, another image of P's—the naked head & shoulders or a red headed temptress—clearly sexually. Then, if contemporary, I would use men for pas de deux etc.—as both I & P hold them back, no—P does, not I: there are indeed few men in P's works. All this is just an exciting but vague idea in my head.

———— — — ————

* Jennifer Tipton (b. 1937), one of America's most inventive and poetic designers of theatrical lighting and a winner of numerous Tony Awards and a MacArthur "genius" grant, had begun lighting Robbins's ballets in 1976, with *Other Dances*.
† Robbins means Antony Tudor—many of whose ballets were set in the late nineteenth or early twentieth century—not Tudor England.
‡ Robbins is referring to "The White Gulls," a hauntingly dissonant lament that includes the lines "Souls of men that call and cry / As they know not where to fly."

Meanwhile L'Affaire Lenny goes in & out & up & down. He's up & down & as of today I said no to a 7 wk run after a workshop.* The material is not ready, nor would be unless LB was there to help solve the problems. With JG, it's been uphill but at least he'll see what does & does not work but to commit to a run with no productions (sets, lights, costumes, orchestra) & with no satisfying script is madness. If it's just workshop & a few shows then O.K.

March 15
[ST. BART'S]

Spent the AM listening & studying the songs. The words are *so* very important that I worry about the results if the words aren't understood. Made lots of notes & the songs start to group themselves. I'm coming down from the infatuation and into the construction & analyzation of them. The *work* of making them possible to choreographing.

Most important morning notes:

Must make the choreography interesting & satisfying on its own without knowing or dependent on knowing the lyrics. Difficult!

Is there a possible sequence which follows from childhood thru adolescence, young man hood, love, marriage, the war etc.—till old age?

On Lenny. When I get back I'll see him—& tell him I'll go to work if I know he'll be involved in helping with problems as they arouse [*sic*]. And then a workshop with a fixed cut off is fine with me.

March 17
[ST. BART'S]

Spent all AM listening to tapes & trying to reference them. Will need that done. Published music who sang it, which collection, texts etc. . . .

---

* While contemplating the ballet that would become *Ives, Songs,* Robbins was also working with Bernstein and John Guare on their adaptation of Brecht's *The Exception and the Rule* (titled *The Race to Urga*); it was intended only as a workshop production, but suddenly Bernstein wanted to commit to a commercial run.

March 21
[ST. BART'S]

This AM—after I fall asleep and dream:

It's a section in N.Y.—upper west side—perhaps the area that runs behind houses, tenements—perhaps a derelict section but not too out of the way. I walk into it. No trees, or green, lots of gravel, shale, stones, coal, cinders. But its day light and the light makes strange glints on this area. There is light, & no shadows too. My footsteps crunch. It is neglected, unused, unknown or unvisited—no reason for anyone to go there. But I see, as I walk, that the glinting is strange—& many colors are there if one looks carefully, & then I realize with a shock that there are mosaics there—& in places where there have been deep excavations, the sides of the walls of them are covered with beautiful patterned mosaics, by emotion in the jeweled colors—deep ruby & purples & ambers & greens & aqua blues—they are all there if one just stops & looks carefully.

And then I hear another person's crunching footsteps—& from right angles to me from the night comes a man. He carries a rifle—looks like a hunter—explorer—is bearded, rugged looks—tallish, an old worn hat or cap on his head, some aged jacket—shoes. He approaches the edge of the shaft I'm looking in, observes the mosaics for a while, then he nods—which is an agreement of what we see—what we understand—. Then he says—"Well, we can go on now."

It is the deepest of commitment between 2 people, and completely acceptable. A bonding. It has been made together, & there is no need to talk about it. . . .

March 25
Went to the Lehman collection at Met where Dr. Szabo* showed me in private & out of glass & frames the large Prendergast Boston sketch book. What a treat.

— — — —

---

* George Szabo was the first curator of the Lehman Collection after it was incorporated into the Metropolitan Museum.

April 14–15

Listening to Bach's 2 & 3 Part Inventions. The 2nd on the CD see as a trio with the counter point seen as 1 against a couple, the single person & couple always changing.

Get to work on them!*

— — — —

Deep in The Brecht Project. Starting 3rd week. No Ives. Celebrated Seder & Pesach with Dan & his family plus Slim, Irene, Jesse.†

May 5th!!

Since April 1st I've been in a workshop production of X & R.‡ Exhausted— happy & frustrated. Fun to be working in theater—Finally Guare, a dear man, wasn't right for it, Lenny was not there§—nor was anyone else except terrific staff that'd supply me with everything I needed. It's coming to an end now.

To: Irving Berlin¶
May 27, 1987

Dear Irving,

It was good to talk with you, especially to hear the exciting news of some new songs you're working on. Anytime you're ready, let me know.

Over at the New York City Ballet, we're doing an American Music Festival in the Spring of '88. I would like to do a ballet to your music. Although the repertory of the Festival includes Copland, Gould, Bernstein, Ives, Gershwin

---

* He did get to work on them—in 1994.

† Dan Stern, Slim Hayward Keith, Irene Mayer Selznick—who had become a close friend—and Jesse Gerstein, with whom Robbins remained on good terms despite their separation.

‡ *The Exception and the Rule.*

§ Exasperated by his disagreements with Robbins or (according to Guare) in fragile emotional health, or both, Bernstein had abruptly withdrawn from the Brecht project before the workshop.

¶ Although Robbins and Berlin saw each other rarely once they weren't doing shows together, they had remained on good terms and often spoke with each other on the telephone (Berlin, by now nearly a hundred, had become reclusive in his old age).

and others, I feel it would really be a grave omission if your music were omitted. Please say yes. And please specify if you are approached by any other sources that your consent for a ballet is dependent on it being choreographed exclusively by me. I ask this because we have invited a lot of other choreographers, and without being modest, I not only am the best choreographer for it, but I also love, appreciate, and grew up on your music more than anyone else.

By the way, I do have your songbook and I'm studying it arduously [*sic*]. Please let me hear from you.* And all my love to you, dear Irving, as always.

Jerry

Ives Notebook
July 5, 1987

Sitting in the little Piazza del Mercato market square in Spoleto, having breakfast. I was noticing how many & the variety of the ways streets entered the square. From down a hill, from under an arch, from thru an ancient Roman street, up a steep walk . . . all contributing to an easy constant flow of people [of] all ages, strollers, shoppers, workers, visitors; and equally, thru the single swimming uncrowded current, were meetings, conferences, dawdlings, all flowing on a gentle tide, passing thru, passing thru.

There was, out of the corner of my eye, a woman who detached herself from others, and seemed, before I turned my head toward her, to be coming toward me. At first, as I craned my head around, it flashed on me that it was Edith,† who could be there, very simply, alive again, in this town at this moment, passing thru. And that there was, on consideration, not a thing odd, wrong, or unreal about it. There, in Spoleto, I could easily be visited by all who had passed on and there wouldn't be anything extraordinary about it. As I thought that, I

---

* There's no record of what response Berlin gave to this request. In the event, owing to Robbins's difficulties with *Ives, Songs* and the complications surrounding the launch of the *Jerome Robbins' Broadway* project (originally called *Hit Dances*), Robbins was not directly involved in the American Music Festival (see p. 360).

† Edith Weissman, Robbins's secretary, had died in 1982, but obviously he still missed her.

could see Nora* coming down that hill street, all glowing with humor & delight at bumping into me; I could see Tommy† walk by & say Hi & talk a little. Nothing would be forced or pretentious. Tudor, Ronnie Bates,‡ Michael Bennett,§ Joe Duell—(that's strange—as I wrote his name it crossed my mind that as a suicide, he might not be able to come back). . . . I knew this moment would pass—but there, under a café's outdoor umbrella, sipping tea & watching the world pass by, came a special time which, like a current of different-temperature water in a moving stream, [brought] this special and real visit from those who had died. . . .

And I thought—maybe this is what Paradise is like—the place one goes to see all one's loved ones again.

Notes for Nora Kaye Memorial, January 5, 1988
[July–December 1987]

[Nora and I] had a friend who had been in show business with us—who we'd grown up with from way back. Nora was talking to me about him & said, "You know, he said he was very unhappy about his life—& he wanted to change it. And I said to him, you can't—you can't change your life." And Nora looked at me & her eyes were clear & deep, & she said, "He can't. You can't change your life. You are what you are, aren't you. You can't change it."

---

* Nora Kaye had died of a brain tumor in Los Angeles in February; Robbins had flown there to visit with her before her death.

† Tommy Abbott, who played Gee-Tar in the original production of *West Side Story*, had become one of Robbins's choreographic assistants and, for a short time, his lover. He died in April 1987.

‡ Ronald Bates, the longtime technical director for City Ballet, who had been married to Diana Adams and who worked closely with Robbins on many ballets, died in 1986.

§ Michael Bennett, a seven-time Tony winner who had choreographed *Follies* and *Company* and directed and choreographed *A Chorus Line*, died of AIDS in July 1987.

Ives Journal

January 15, 1988

Grover withdrew from [*Hit Dances*].* Too many reasons. Felt so rejected &
abandoned—took a few days to get to my real feelings of love & loss again. Too
many, too many. At Nora's memorial (Jan 5th) I spoke of the Spoleto incident
this past summer when I imagined how easy it would be for those who had died
to casually walk past. I couldn't get thru it without tears flowing down my face.
Jesse said well you've lost so many people in recent years—I guess it all came out
& for a few days I wouldn't stop having tears. Then Nick was scheduled for [an]
operation 2 days ago. He's come thru but not without warnings that he might
not from the vets. So I was preparing myself to lose him. And then Grover;—all
on top of George, Edith, Frieda,† Tommy, Ronnie, Nora, Brian's exit—et al—

So I find myself lying in bed at night or in the morning watching my days
roll away from me & down the drain—with less & less of them left for me.
There is an end in sight. I'm heavy with that feeling—I keep going, but oh my
mortality raises its invisible barriers in constant signs every day. My eyes, my
ears, my cock, my fatigues, my desires & most of all, how I am being treated.—
How others react to me. The loneliness withers my bones. I work to not recognize it.

. . . Later—as I lay on my bed, examining the disappointment & dismay
at where I am, I thought—who are you to expect so much—what about you
deserves more than what everyone gets & goes thru—you're just another one
of all of us—& you'll come in & go out like everyone else—just like everyone
else. What did you expect—& Then I realized how fortunate I was in what I
had achieved—the position & affluence & even the friendships I had—that
my despair was caused by some terrible yearning, need, belief—that I was
an *exception* to the rules—& the moment of my superseding life's schedules,
developments—*orders* was unnatural & destructive to enjoying what I had &
where I was. Oh yes—(I just looked back at that early dream in the beginning of

---

* Grover Dale, the original Snowboy from *West Side Story,* had become a close friend and a choreographer and director in his own right; he had been expected to take a directorial role in Robbins's re-
creation of his Broadway work, a project provisionally titled *Hit Dances.* He ultimately reconsidered
and rejoined the team as co-director.
† Frieda Robbins, Robbins's stepmother, had also recently died.

this book)—no one is going to save you—no magic man or woman will become your lost & never-had parent protector.

Feb. 5th

[*Ives, Songs*] opened last night. The final reaction was great, but I thought it didn't add up as it had at varying times of rehearsal. It started to pancake during the last 3 days of dress rehearsals, which didn't have right scenery, costumes or lighting till the last day. It's slow now, & somewhat sentimental—easy answers perhaps—can't tell—but I was disappointed on the opening about its totality. . . .

Feb. 10th

Reviews are good.* So is feedback, response etc. yet *I* don't feel as good about it. What went on? Did I show my own fears & loves more than I knew I did? If someone asked me what was it about—I could easily say, it's about me & my dancers. I see them & my life, as children, as enthusiasts, as worshippers or believers, as lovers, as losers—as at last collected, loved & outside me—left alone.

March 24th

We lost Nick this morning. For the whole past week he'd been slipping away—weaker, weaker—unable to hold his head up. . . . It ripped me up to leave him

every evening at the hospital—I'd go about 5 or 6 & stayed about an hour & a half with him on my lap—or lying next to me with his head on my leg. And yesterday was the worst & this A.M. they said I should let him go. So I did & he's gone—that dearest dog—my closest friend—is gone. And my life seems so terribly poorer without him. The shocking thing is the difference from that one moment—the moment when one is

From Robbins's Spoleto sketchbook.

---

* "A ballet of sentiment that is not sentimental," said *The New York Times*'s Kisselgoff, but Marcia Siegel in *New York* magazine thought it "an honorable failure."

close to death—but *alive*—there—breathing—still holding. The piercing spirit of being here, with us, with everything still going—his blood, his heart, his chest, his eyes, his noises—still alive—alive.

And the next—when it all ends—all stops—& the living tissues change, arrest, cease functioning, close up & off, go dead—all—all—dead—& that change—the going over to other side is so vast, tremendous, uneradicable [*sic*] a change. His eyes always studied me—& he knew all. In the morning he'd come up on the bed, climb next to me, drape the upper part of his body over me, look me in the face & lift his paw which had been resting on my chest & hit me with it, looking straight into my eyes, saying—So—what's up, how are you—I'm here. I'm with you. Gone—gone. Dear, sweet, giving animal. I thank you for all you gave me. I pray for your soul, though you don't need salvation—you had no sins & no faults. If there is a heavenly place, & angelic rest—you are there now, dear dear Nick.

He was as good a dog as any could be. Understanding, loving, gentlemanly, a very manly & male dog—! He gave me so very much over his lifetime—friendship, companionship, acceptance.

May 5, 1988
The A[merican] M[usic] F[estival]* is on & fucking out everything this co[mpany] has ever stood for. The taste is abysmal, the sense of theater is nil; the ballets, all overlit & over produced, are puerile mindless fantasies of child-ish poor sad nitwits; the evenings have the least amounts of enthusiasm we've ever had in the theater—& to boot it's going to swell over & capsize our spring season & wash into the Fall.

Every evening starts with a piece of usually poor music while a really bad projection of "contemporary" art is left projected on a screen throughout; once some good songs were massacred by an inept out-of-her-water [*sic*] singer—All usually leave the audience to try to come awake & be alert after being smothered by a boring cross-purposed sound & light show.

---

* The American Music Festival, which was conceived by Co-Ballet Master in Chief Peter Martins, was a three-week showing of thirty-eight ballets, twenty-one of them new, seven of those by Martins and much of the rest by choreographers new to City Ballet—some of them, some critics suggested, unsuited to the company's strengths and aesthetic.

June 6 [1988]

For more than the last month I've been struggling with depression & despair. Mostly the show I believe. It will break me; either mind or body. I don't want to do it—no fun, no joy, no help. Old stuff—mostly mediocre dancers—I've been at it* since Jan[uary], am exhausted. . . . It's lonely here & I feel on the edge of big Depression like in 73—

June 21 [1988]

Same.

June 26 [1988]

The black broke for a while—I hope for long. Past 2 days have been up & positive about the work.

August 15 [1988]

WE BEGIN! First day of rehearsals for 22 weeks! Final press opening—Feb 26th. Here comes a trip.†

To: Leonard Bernstein

[August 1988] ‡

Dearest Lenushka—

I can't think what all our lives would have been like without you and the vast and endless gifts you have given us. And I can't think what my own life would

---

* Robbins had spent six months trying to reconstruct lost or forgotten or incompletely remembered dances from old shows with the help of cast members, stage managers, and dance captains. None had been notated or filmed, and reconstruction was often an act of collective memory.

† Originally, *Hit Dances/Jerome Robbins' Broadway* had been conceived as a research workshop, for which it was funded by the Shubert Foundation, but as the scope and appeal of what Robbins intended became apparent, the Shubert organization (along with several co-producers) made a deal to take the show to Broadway for a commercial run—offering Robbins, as a necessary inducement, an unheard-of twenty-two weeks of rehearsal (most shows get six if they are lucky).

‡ This letter is a pencil draft for a videotaped message to be sent to Bernstein on the occasion of his gala seventieth birthday celebration at Tanglewood. Robbins was unable to attend because he was in rehearsal for *Jerome Robbins' Broadway*.

have been without you, dear collaborator, inspirer, musician, theater man, and most of all, dear friend. I'm so sorry I can't be there for the celebrations, but I'm working on a show, a large part of which is yours. And I can't believe we're at the 70 mark, as nothing of the energies, excitement, or arguments (we're celebrating?) seem changed.

To: Francis Mason[*]
November 29, 1988

Dear Francis,

Thank you for the proofs of B.R. with that long & rather loving birthday greeting. It brought back amazing memories: and it was very flattering. I particularly liked Kay Mazzo's.[†] She was so young when she came to B.U.S.A. & I cared for her so much. Once I got very angry at a dancer at rehearsal, & blasted him, & then remembered Kay was in the room &, worried that the scene might upset her, I shot a glance over to where she was leaning on the barre. She *was* watching me, but her expression was one of amusement! . . . like, what a funny man he is when he gets angry. So I didn't worry about our relationship from then on.

Dorothy Bird has confused two dances[‡] I did with Anita Alvarez. Her memory of how "Strange Fruit" ended is correct *except* the ladder was used in our version of "Frankie & Johnny"!

And they all see me from their points of view, which is hardly ever how I experienced it. Rashomon time!

With best wishes—
Jerry

---

[*] Francis Mason (1921–2009) was a diplomat, museum director, critic, and longtime editor of the scholarly quarterly *Ballet Review*.
[†] Kay Mazzo had been a fifteen-year-old apprentice with New York City Ballet when she auditioned for and was accepted into Robbins's Ballets: U.S.A. company in its final season in 1961. She later became a principal dancer with City Ballet.
[‡] Both these dances were first performed at Tamiment; *Strange Fruit* won Robbins and Alvarez glowing notices when it was reprised as part of a Theatre Arts Committee benefit at the 92nd Street YMHA in New York (see p. 40).

To: Arthur Laurents
December 30, 1988

Dear Arthur,

First of all, Happy Holidays and good New Year's Wishes.

Thank you for your suggestions* and I appreciate you giving it time. At the present moment all that we are dealing with is why the fucking front curtain can't move faster. It seems all theater is now automated which means all cues have to be typed into a computer [and] nothing can move fast enough to get you a good hand.

The thing I've tried to avoid in this show is to talk about myself, career, work, etc., and just let the pieces say it for me. I think you are right when you say it has dangerous pitfalls and you are also right—it is very hard to write and it is late indeed.†

Anyway, again thank you for the suggestions and I hope your work is going well.

All love,
Jerry

---

* Robbins had called on Laurents several times during the gestation of *Jerome Robbins' Broadway*, asking for his help in reconstruction, since the songs and dances were presented in loosely connected scenes, with contextual dialogue and action. The show would start audience previews on January 9, so it seems that Laurents's most recent comments were occasioned by seeing a final run-through; any suggestions he might have had (which are not preserved) were certainly given at the eleventh hour.
† *Jerome Robbins' Broadway* opened on February 26, 1989. The next day, critics confessed to "chok[ing] back tears" (Howard Kissel, *Daily News*), called the show "brilliant, poignant and proud" (Jack Kroll, *Newsweek*), and said that Robbins "pulls off the miracle of recreating that ecstatic baptism . . . of every Broadway theatregoer's youth" (Frank Rich, *The New York Times*). It went on to run for 633 performances and won six Tony Awards, including for best direction and best musical.

Notes, Etc. (1989–1991)

March 9–17, 1989
ST. BART'S

It would be nice to be good for somebody or to somebody—nice to mean something to somebody, to help them, to do something for them. That would be nice, to feel I was important to someone personally.

That the other person would find me valuable in their life & happiness . . . [JR's ellipses] that is what I mean by "good for somebody." To be able to be needed, wanted, by someone else, for whom I could be a support, aid, comfort, lover, generous, helpful.—In whose life I would be a partner—needed.

I have given a large public (international) a huge amount of entertainment, joy, beauty, passion. That level is impersonal. I haven't accomplished being accepted on any personal level.

April 12 [1989]
The dreamer goes thru the experience alone. I can't think of any experience a man or woman goes thru where he is so totally cut off from everyone he knows and every place he knows. It is a solo journey—uniquely his, distinct, separate . . . off he goes into uncharted, unplanned, unprepared, unforeseen and uncontrolled experience. What will, what might happen? . . . no one accompanies him into the dark theater where his mind creates the plot, characters, language, landscape, etc. I sometimes used to wonder, in a dream, at how the reality of the dream was so detailed . . . & *at the same time* phantom-like, transparent—a dream.

But the aloneness of it all. Even while bodily lying within the embracing protective arms of a lover, the journey is cut off—inaccessible, *even in its telling,* to anyone else.

Somewhere I want to return to the familiar area of where I was before this surge of fame to the show. (I can't even call it by its known name—"Jerome Robbins' B'way.") Unhappy in the glare of fame & success? I am fighting it all—trying to make it disappear, go away, get off my back. I fight the producers on a new production, Equity on the rehearsal tapes, casting, changes, etc.

April 13, 1989

Anyone should be able to see that "In Memory Of . . . ," "Ives," "JR Bway" are farewell pieces; personal closing-up-shop pieces. There is some internal certainty, somewhere in my feelings, that it's coming to an end & I'd better put it in order before getting out.

So Jesse's news* is a blow to me in so many places. I can't absorb it. I can't digest it. I don't deny it—but I can't deal with my reactions to it.

April 16 [1989]

RAW!

Spent the day with Jesse . . . Now he's understanding what is happening. He's handling it well—so far—but ever so often he'll say a sentence that will break my heart. He carries it better than I would—but somewhere he must be whirling around. "I feel cheated. I'm not special. There is nothing after." I understand it better each day—drop by drop.

April 30 [1989]

I'm in bad shape. Head. It's a downer—& I'm afraid. Cut out of NYCB for at least 4 months†—felt good—felt bad—feels?—Feel the pressures of all these things down on me. The show, the ballet co., the publicity, the Tonys, articles . . .

Jesse, particularly. To sit with a *possible* 2 years' more lid on everything. He's handling it well, I think—& I try to be supportive without making him feel weak & endangered, [as if he] can't act for himself.. and try not to be suddenly too nice. Feels better getting this out.

---

* After ignoring symptoms for months (if not years), Jesse Gerstein was tested for HIV and found to be not only positive but suffering from an advanced case of symptomatic AIDS. Robbins, while not relinquishing his rekindled relationship with Brian Meehan, put it largely to one side to devote himself to caring for Jesse.

† Exhausted by the effort of mounting *Jerome Robbins' Broadway,* Robbins took a leave from City Ballet, in part to spend time with Jesse Gerstein; the two of them spent part of the summer on Ahmet Ertegun's boat off the Turkish coast.

To: Lourdes Lopez[*]

June 15, 1989

Dear Lourdes—

Excuse the paper[†]—but I wanted to write you immediately. That was a *wonderful* letter you sent me—so full of good feelings, glad tidings, and after it I felt so happy about life—& could see your eyes shining, your smiling face and all your gestures! It was *almost* as good as a visit. It does seem so very long since I've seen you. I'm sorry you've had such troubles with the foot—and happy that there seems to be an end to it.

BUT—the big news of course is your baby!! Oh how great—I can't wait to see you & it (He? She?) together. J. P. Frohlich[‡] stopped by with his ten week old who already looks & acts like J.P. So—hurry up & produce!

I haven't yet caught up with myself & rest. I'm going to Europe for a while—I hope I'll get settled down & back to where I want to work again. Right now, no. But I see the company, they look good, & are dancing well—but I miss you there! So—let's both get our act together soon & meet in the Big Studio 5 & give each other a big, warm, loving hug.

All my love to you, dear Lourdes—
Jerry

P.S. I have a new dog[§]—a stray again—who picked me up outside the Met Museum. I guess she wanted someone artistic. She's big—45 lbs—one blue eye, one brown, & is a wonderful animal—bright, alert, well trained—& stuck to my side like a twin.

You'll see her.

Love—J.

---

[*] Lourdes Lopez, a principal dancer with New York City Ballet who went on to become director of the Miami City Ballet, had originated roles in Robbins's *Four Chamber Works* and *Glass Pieces* and danced in many other works by him.

[†] Robbins was writing in his customary black felt-tip pen on a sheet of ruled legal paper.

[‡] Jean-Pierre Frohlich, a former NYCB soloist, had retired and become a ballet master with responsibility for the Robbins repertory.

[§] This was Tess, a lop-eared tan shepherd-retriever mix.

To: Lincoln Kirstein (Telegram)
August 22, 1989

DEAREST LINCOLN:

PLEASE DO NOT LEAVE,* WE NEED YOU, AND IT IS IMPERATIVE
YOU STAY WITH THE COMPANY FOR THE SAKE OF ALL YOU MADE
AND BUILT AND ACHIEVED. PLEASE DON'T GO AWAY. THIS IS A
PERSONAL MESSAGE SENT WITH ALL MY LOVE,
    JERRY ROBBINS

Irving Berlin Memorial†
[January–February 1990]

While traveling in Europe in 1949, I read of a show planned for production called *Miss Liberty*. Its creative staff were Robert Sherwood, book, Moss Hart, director, and music and lyrics by Irving Berlin. Zing like an arrow I went to the phone and called my agent and said try to get me that show. I hadn't read a script, heard a song, didn't know a thing about the casting—but I wanted to be a part of that team and most of all I wanted to work with Irving Berlin and to make some dances to his new score. My agent got me the show.

When Irving and I finally met, in a theater, I believe, we gave each other a quick intense sizing up while we shook hands and looked in each other's eyes. I felt a smile inside me and [felt] that it was reciprocated, as if we recognized something in each other. And we did. . . .

I was asked to do dances for most all of the numbers. Irving would ask me, "what are you going to do with that song?" I'd tell him what my plans were, if I knew, or that I didn't know yet, if I didn't, and we'd talk about it a lot and with Moss. Oh yes—in that score Irving included a song to be sung as the entertain-

---

* Kirstein's decision to retire had taken Robbins by surprise. He followed up the telegram with phone calls, but Kirstein "seemed adamant about his position," Robbins told *The New York Times* on September 14, and he retired on November 1. "If it were up to me, I would not accept his resignation," Robbins said.

† Irving Berlin died in his sleep on September 22, 1989. He was 101.

ment at a dance hall–beer parlor. The song was called "Mr. Monotony." I did a very sexy number which proved a great success in the show, but out of town it was clear that it was very out of place, style, character and out it went.

In 1950, a year later, I was asked to do *Call Me Madam,* again [with] Irving Berlin. . . . The only trouble for me was that there were no opportunities for me to cut loose anywhere. Out of town Irving said "Jerry, we need some more dancing. We need dancing at the beginning of Act II." Very frustrated with the few opportunities I'd had, I said "Look, just give me something to dance about and I'll do it." Stop—freeze—with a look on Irving's face. Not bad, he said. Damn good title. And the next day or two, I had it, [the song] "Something to Dance About."

Then, also out of town, he came up with a new number for Act II. And he got me into the theater and sang it for me. Nobody sings a song as well or with as much understanding and feelings or as excellently as the composer and lyricist. And Irving was good at it. The song [was] "You're not sick you're just in love." He finished, his eyes shining behind those thick glasses. Well? he said. It's just great, I said. All smiles and happiness. And how'll you stage it? Irving, I said, it's simple—they just sit down and sing it. It doesn't need anything—it's too good—it says it all and anything added would hurt. He looked startled and said O.K., try it. I did and, it worked and he never got over it. And that was the cementing of our friendship.

Oh yes, Irving put "Mr. Monotony" into *Call Me Madam.* Ethel [Merman] sang, I replicated the choreography, and history repeated itself: [the dance number] stopped the show—and came out for the same reason.

I don't know how many times I actually met & saw Irving from then on. Not much. But we had one long continuous 40-year telephone friendship. I'd get a call—"Jerry, how are you. What are you working on"—or "Jerry, now listen, I've got an idea I'm working on and when I'm ready I want you to hear it." "Anytime Irving," I'd say—"just give me a call, let me know." Or sometimes he'd swing an idea past me—for a show or a revue. . . .

When I was organizing my Broadway show* I called him and told him about it and he got very excited. And I told him I wanted "Something to Dance

---

* *Jerome Robbins' Broadway.*

About" to use in the show and as the title of the show. "No, no" he said. "Jerry, we still do a lot of business with *Call Me Madam*. No, no." Then I asked him [if I could use] "Mr. Monotony" and he said, "You do 'Mr. Monotony' and I'll pay *you*!" [So] finally we got "Monotony" on. I sent him a tape of the rehearsal of it and his family let me know he saw it and approved.

When Irving passed on, I immediately wrote the family a note—and at the end I said "he was an inspiration to all of us." I know that was right but didn't think on it until I was asked to speak today. And then the full ramifications rose to the surface. For not only was he a theater and musical artist of a superb nature, not only did he keep us, with his songs, happy, confident, [and] in love . . . beneath that was the recognition of knowing where we came from and how hard was the struggle to change our paths and make our own destinies. It was the dramatic and traumatic breaking from one's background, and enduring the anguishes as well as the triumphs of making it work—the need to express it, to say it, to dance it or paint it, [or] write it; that out of being thrust into the sink-or-swim world came the ecstasy of having to find one's own place and be recognized. I recognized [that] in him and he in me, and that story, with those drives arising from those needs, and arriving at those successes, [is] inspirational to all minority peoples in our country particularly. I believe he saw that in me, even though I am a first generation, not an original, immigrant. Thus our long and touching telephone intimacy and identification.

Well, he's gone and the comfort of his presence is gone, but his powerful jaunty redoubtable spirit abounds around us. All you have to do is hum it, or hear it, and he and his great gifts to us are immediately present as they will be long after we are gone too. Thank you, dear Irving.

To: Lincoln Kirstein
June 18, 1990

Dear Lincoln,

It touched me so very deeply to see you on stage at the final performance of the Festival.*

This is to thank you for all the years of creativity you have given me, and for the wonderful company, atmosphere, and aims of the N.Y.C.B. You should be very proud of your great contribution to its deserved and superlative achievements. Without you it would have been different. With all my thanks & with deep deep affection—

Jerry

The Poppa Piece (Prologue)†
August 14, 1984

As the audience enters they discover J.R. in a chair downstage R. He is 50-ish, dressed casually but well and calmly watches the audience assemble. Diagonally upstage, on a medical table, is a body covered with a sheet. After the audience is in, the house lights dim out, leaving lights on J.R.

J.R.

Good evening. Thank you for coming. This play is called "The Poppa Piece." Or, "Robbins by Rabinowitz and Rabinowitz by Robbins." Robbins is my legal name, Rabinowitz I was born with. So.

(Pause. Then, nodding upstage)

That's the body of my father over there. Rabinowitz. Jew. This is a Jew piece. He. The Jew there. Me, the Jew here.

---

* New York City Ballet had programmed a festival of Jerome Robbins works to mark his seventieth birthday and his forty years with the company (both of which had occurred a year and a half previously). Kirstein came out of retirement to appear onstage in a tribute.

† The text is taken from a handwritten version of the script, marked "Bridgehampton revision."

(Pause.)

I don't know about you but it seems all my life I've been dragging around a dead body with me.

(Pause.)

Well, Jews, let's get at it.

A wild blaring crazy Jewish dance music blares out, a mocking raucous Freilach.* J.R. crosses over to the table and lifts the sheeted body off of it. Then lugging it and hugging it to him he begins to dance, bouncing the body about to the shrilling music. He heaves it and throws it to and fro, jounces it up and down in time to the wailing clarinet, the cymbals and drum. A nightmare dance. Then a transition slowly takes place. The body, still sheeted, gradually bounces around by itself until both [figures] are cavorting in a harsh and furious dance, insistent, demented and separate. Suddenly the sheeted figure stops. A finger pokes its way out of the folds, next a hand, which slowly lifts a flap away from the face. First one sees a gleaming eye, then a hooked nose, a scraggly beard, rouged cheeks, a dirty collar, and finally, grimacing madly, an old payesed, yarmulked† [sic], glaring, smiling caricature of a Jew.. the Clown Jew, which steps out of its shroud. The music follows him as he begins a dance of his own . . . a rag doll figure of tzitzis, tzillum,‡ talus [sic], vest, and broken shoes. . . . [T]he flapping figure takes over the lead [and] begins to puppeteer Robbins, picking him up, pushing and pulling, kicking and cuffing him, smacking him about until at last he shoves J.R. across the stage to land back in his chair. There the clown claps a dunce cap on J.R.'s head, smacks a yellow star on his arm and hangs from his neck a rough sign: "JUDE!" He makes a grand gesture of "Voilà!" to the audience.

(Blackout.)

---

* A kind of klezmer music.

† *Payes*—or *payot*, or *payos*—are the side locks worn by some Orthodox Jewish men in addition to a yarmulke (skullcap).

‡ Robbins's rendering of "tefillin" or phylacteries, small leather boxes containing parchment scrolls inscribed with verses from the Torah, which some observant Jews strap to their arms and foreheads during weekday prayers.

Summer 1990 Notes
July 31, 1990

On rereading the original material & notes [of *The Poppa Piece*] I'm startled [by] how much of the piece has, as material between the father and son, *dancing* as its metaphor. How it returns again & again to a scene where they try to dance, dance in opposition, or dance in acceptance. There is also dance as an expression of longing & nostalgia. . . . Can understand why I ended up as a choreographer.

To: Jamie, Nina, Alexander, and Burton Bernstein[*]
October 18, 1990

Dear Jamie, Nina, Alexander, & Bertie,

Both your parents (& your brother, Bertie) would have been so proud of you yesterday.[†] In fact you did *them* proud. The thoughts you all expressed were so open, deep felt, direct & loving—without a touch of cliché or sentimentality.

We are all stunned & unbelieving of the event itself. When your life's work & some of your life itself is involved with another, as mine has been with Lenny's, you always can't see the other objectively. His talents were never a hidden or surprising thing to me, nor his energies or personality & excitement. But I never quite saw the vastness & scope of his achievements till they [were] summarized in the papers. When I received the news of his death I felt as if a big piece of my life's construction had dropped away, and I also feel that America has lost its chief energizer, maker & shaker of culture of these years. Isn't it such a tribute that all over the world there was and is such a tremendous reaction. He'd have loved all of it, and the procession thru the city. . . .

---

* Jamie, Nina, and Alexander are the children of Leonard Bernstein and Felicia Montealegre Bernstein (d. 1978); Burton Bernstein (1932–2017), a writer, was Leonard's brother. This text is from a handwritten draft in Robbins's archives.
† Bernstein had died of a heart attack caused by lung failure on October 14, 1990. Before his burial at Green-Wood Cemetery in Brooklyn three days later, his coffin was driven from his home at the Dakota, on Central Park West and Seventy-Second Street, through the city past sites significant to him.

Well it's hardest for all of you, but you have risen so beautifully to the situation. My thoughts and love are with you—& him.

Jerry

To: Mike Nichols*
November 15, 1990

Mike—

Thank you so much for your note. It came at the right moment. What a series of losses. In the most terrible of ways we got our wish—Lenny won't speak at our memorials. I guess we thought that for sure he'd go on forever, or at least beyond us. I find it impossible not to think that at any moment he'll reappear and just say, "Surprise!" . . . just can't think of that super energized person as gone—out of it.

Well—didn't mean to unload on you. Just wanted to say your friendship & opinions mean a good deal to me—& your note felt like [a] nice affection[ate] pat on the back.

All my bests,
Jerry

Notes, Etc. (1989–1991)
September 1991

Jesse's very badly off. I can't begin to describe the crippling & disfiguring he's arrived at due to his illness. A year ago, at Jim Lax's† office, we saw a man marked

---

* Mike Nichols (1931–2014), the performer and film and theater director, had written to Robbins about having seen, on a recent cross-country flight, the film of *Gypsy* (which, unlike the Broadway musical, Robbins had *not* directed). "When you build something," Nichols said, "nothing can hurt it, not even [Hollywood moguls] Mervyn LeRoy or Jack Warner. In fact, you are the third Little Pig. While the rest of us build our houses of straw and wood, you build of brick. It's something to see."
† James Lax, MD, Jesse Gerstein's internist.

with [the] AIDS look walk in, wait & then go thru into Lax's inner office: thin, haunted, marked. Jesse said after he'd gone in, to see Lax probably, "I don't want to get that bad ever." Well, he's 600° beyond that & won't give up. . . .

What we've been thru is calamitous but perhaps not so different from the horrors that lie beneath the quote, "He's got AIDS." He's been thru 2 or 4 sessions where we almost lost him—pneumonia, pancreatitis, T.B., & all the results of K.S.,* chemo, & the after-effects of the drugs to prevent further infection which have equally disastrous effects. Since April it's been downward, till today; here in the hospital he's having a permanent catheter put into his stomach—so they can feed him, hydrate him, infuse him, draw blood, etc. It's round the clock nurses, in my house, plus Mama,† staff, etc. He got very sick twice in Paris, once in Japan‡—on the way down. Now his infected mouth, no hair, great frightening lesions all over his body, thinness, swollen feet, enlarged testicles, to list a *few* of Job's torments—. I can't even remember or feel the summer even though up to a month ago we went out there [to Bridgehampton], or I limo'd him there and back. It's been an exhausting time—& only these past few weeks have I had help.

Somewhere, of course, for his sake (& mine), I wish it were over as there is apparently no way at all it'll get better—only worse, & he should not, dear God, endure more. I haven't done, or been able to do, any work since March. I did 50 min[utes] of Poppa Piece in Jan–Feb. *Good,* too. Tried again with 2nd half— N.G. but Jesse's illness was increasingly depressing & horrifying. . . . Within, I consider him gone. Support myself by thinking—this too is a part of life. . . . [JR's ellipses] others go thru it all the time, losing loved ones..& I must live it thru too. I'm not the most unfortunate man in the world.. far from it— and, Seneca: "When do we live, if not now." This experience must be eaten & digested, accepted. Life is not all pleasurable.

All that is a poor, spotty summary.

---

* Kaposi's sarcoma, a usually rare cancer that causes purple skin lesions on the body and in the mouth, is a frequent manifestation of AIDS.
† Jesse Gerstein's mother, Cassandra Einstein, a painter and filmmaker.
‡ Robbins had taken Gerstein (who had always longed to visit the country) with him to Japan for the opening of *Jerome Robbins' Broadway* in the spring of 1991.

To: Cassandra Einstein[*]
Paris, October 24, 1991

Dear Cassandra,

Yes, of course, all of the 16 items you asked for are yours. I called N.Y. and ask[ed] Lisa, Rick, Pam, etc. to collect them for you and as soon as they find them, we'll send them out.

I've just heard that you will not be coming East for the gathering of his friends and close ones. I'm sorry. I do understand your desire to have some of Jesse's ashes, but I am compelled by his expressed instructions to follow his wishes, and cannot in all consciousness [*sic*] divide his remains. He asked me to spread them on the beach which, as you know, he loved so deeply. He was always, when well, on the beach, sunning, reading, napping, swimming and taking long walks. These last summer months he always bedded down on the porch lounge, lying there under a light cover & under an umbrella, where he watched the sky, water, clouds, & shadows on the beach. He will be happy being a part of it. I hope you will accept in your heart his desire to be there. I do understand your feelings as his mother, but alas I cannot separate his remains. Even though you won't be there let's try to make this weekend not one of anything but of our love for Jesse, his life and his wishes.

Sincerely,
Jerome.

St. Petersburg–Paris Notes
April 25, 1992

We live by improvisation, a St. Petersburg man told me when I visited and worked there last March. His words were indeed accurate and could cover anything from transportation to truly fast mail, produce, communications, costs, availability of anything. For instance, lemon with your tea could easily turn into a slice of grapefruit. . . .

---

[*] Jesse Gerstein's mother (see above).

Most of all, my being there, working there,[*] was a huge improvisation on the part of the ballet company whose name changed during my stay from the Kirov to the Mariinsky Ballet, as did the theater itself change from Kirov to Mariinsky.

And oh, with what religious glory do they speak of their theater and school. It is always "our *historic* theater.. the birthplace of classical ballet, the place that produced Petipa Fokine Balanchine Nijinsky Nijinska Pavlova Nureyev Makarova and Baryshnikov" . . . as if the building itself, the walls, foundations, roofs & windows, halls and stairways . . . had given birth to the great artists of the dance. . . .

The theater itself is a large rotund edifice gaily painted green with white trim. . . . There are many stage entrances & a complex schedule of which doors are open when—each guarded by stout aging women with imposing hairdos & babushkas. . . . One early gets the feeling that the historic theater has never had a fresh, cold, or clear breeze blow through since its construction. . . .

And yet—and yet, there is a terrific pull that country has on me. I bitch about things and complain & disdain, fume & fuss . . . and yet—and yet I think I love it there. I've come back [to New York] with no plans to return and yet I am studying Russian now—a very frustrating experience. And . . . all the books I am reading are about Russia—histories, or Chekhov Pushkin Tolstoy—dance books.

Yes, it's a puzzlement. The confusion of the astounding beauties of the city, palaces, vistas, museums, ideas—the clamor of its people . . . its gray mud-splattered streets, cars, people . . . its decaying . . . buildings which clash against the brilliant repainted splendor of the yellow-ochre neo classic buildings trimmed with white . . .

After I'd been there about 10 days I invited Julia, my interpreter, and Dima, V's[†] assistant, to lunch at the Europa. . . . We ordered, drank beer, ate, gossiped & laughed a bit at things—an easy, comfortable time with new friends. We'd become close enough for Julia to ask where were you born? I said, New York, and then she or Dima asked "And your parents?" That stopped me. For I knew

---

* Robbins was supervising the former Kirov—now Mariinsky—Ballet's staging of *In the Night*.
† Mariinsky director Oleg Vinogradov.

I was about to say "Here—in Russia." I said it and they asked me where, and I explained. I already felt something going on within me as I answered their questions, and a silence followed as we all digested the information. Oh, I thought, now they think of me as Russian. One of them. Of course. That's why and where I get my talent—part of the big Motherland—. But something more was going on within me. Some large switch in my makeup . . . I suddenly realized that "some where" I certainly had more of my roots in Russia . . . that generations after generations had worked and come to manhood, had flowered or failed on this land—that years and years of living learning loving had piled up inside of me, that my more [than] 70 years of living in America had shrunk [so that I was] practically a foreigner in America compared to . . . many generations of being a Russian. The switch was thrown—and I who had boasted, prided myself as the echt American choreographer—was not one. And so many factors came together . . . the increasing love of Jewish music—folk songs—of Chopin & Russian composers—. Of how, when I started to research Fiddler, and consulted anthropological studies of life in the shtetl, I knew all of it already . . . —& most important of all how the summer I'd spent in my dad's home town in (then) Poland was such a clear & loving memory of an ideal happy happy time.

To: Edna O'Brien
May 1992

Dear Edna,

Here are words to a song (6/8 rhythm—Irish of course) caused by a look at your photo on the book* you sent. I should sing it to you as I know the rhythms and the phrases—and though I know it'll never touch Sondheim—still it's an "only one" of mine.

How much champagne do you owe me?†

---

* Probably *Time and Tide*.

† An undated letter in the files from O'Brien to Robbins explains that the two had a standing wager: champagne to be sent when the sender had gone without "a swooning heart" for some time.

Eyes still not right—but we'll see, yet!
All love.

My spirits are having a recession—
Jerry

Brush your hair back, straight back, my dearest and
Rein it in tight with a string. Right.
Clean off your face and shuck off your earrings and
Rings, beads and fancies; heels, hose and panties
Take off the red from your nails and your tootsies
Your rouge and mascara and let yourself be
Yourself
there
clean
bare
in your skin and freckles
waist, bum and heckles
It's nice, so nice—the smells and the spice
taste haste and waist, and
loose all that hobbles you
paints pads and cobbles
and let yourself be
yourself
there
clean
and
bare.

To: Andy deGroat*
March 29, 1993

Dear Andy,

I have been thinking about your work a lot since I have been back in New York and I thought you might want to tune in a little bit.

The strides you have made recently have been rather astounding. Both "Bayadere" and your "Giselle" work were so moving as giant steps in the growth of your talents, discipline, imagination, sensitivity and craft. Your visions seem to have opened up at the same time your touch is more personal and intimate.

I still am haunted by the ghost story of your "Giselle." To my eyes, it tore away the 19th century over-adorned, romanticism of the piece and left the bare, impassioned events branded on our minds and souls. This is no small accomplishment but one that I am still amazed at, fascinated by, and for which I salute you.

I like the fact that you tenaciously see your work through, beyond even audience and critical praise. As a matter of fact, when I consider your career, I have nothing but tremendous awe at the consistency of your progress and the firmness of your pursuits and the glories of your achievements.

I look forward to seeing you and your work again when I come over in June and I hope that you receive the recognition you deserve along with the opportunities to grow and pursue your mission.

All love—
Jerry

---

* Andy deGroat and Robert Wilson—with whom deGroat had worked on Wilson's *Deafman Glance* and *Einstein on the Beach*—had parted in 1976, and deGroat had moved to France, where he continued to choreograph, frequently deconstructing and revising classic ballet works.

To: Sara Levi-Tanai[*]
March 24, 1994

Dearest Sara,

It is so good to hear from you! I love your letters, and of course I love you. You send me that quality of your life to me which I find so very precious. Thank you.

My work? Well, I've been coasting ever since I left New York City Ballet in 1989 with no *new* works, but was very busy with the French Company, the Alvin Ailey Company,[†] etc., etc. Then Misha Baryshnikov asked me for a new work for himself and I said very tentatively—well, I can try, but I can't guarantee you anything. I started work on one dance and it was terribly hard. I can't move around like I used to, everything hurt, I get dizzy, etc., etc. I finished the dance and he took it away and practiced it. I looked at it and, to my surprise, I rather liked it. So I tried to do another—and then another—and then another—and ended up with *A Suite of Dances* to Bach's *Unaccompanied Cello Suites.* It worked wonderfully! Encouraged by this, I plunged immediately into a new work for a small group of students for the School of American Ballet (the school Balanchine made when he got here in 1933), the major supplier of material for the U.S. and Europe ballet companies. I finished it just today to Bach's *Inventions and Symphonies* for piano, using only 10 of the 30 pieces. I think it too is good. I learned to choreograph with my limited means, but there it is. It makes me happy. It will go the beginning of June. The students are earnest and trying very hard. I have to break down all the artifices they now have and get them just to *be,* and *dance.*

So that's my news. My life is very regular, rehearsals, rest, sleep, etc.

How are you doing? Are you working, music, pieces, etc., etc.? I hope so, as you are so talented.

I don't know when I'll come over to Israel now. It seems so hectic and upset

---

[*] Sara Levi-Tanai (1910–2005), an Israeli choreographer, was the founder of Inbal Dance Theatre. Robbins had known her since his second visit to Israel in 1952.

[†] Robbins had recently set *In the Night, Dances at a Gathering, Glass Pieces, Moves,* and *The Four Seasons* on the Paris Opera Ballet, and *N.Y. Export: Opus Jazz* on the Alvin Ailey American Dance Theater.

there and it's hard for me to know what to do. But we'll keep in touch, yes? I send you all my love and devotion and hope to hear from you soon.

X.
Jerry

Dream of Tanny*
March 24, 1994

I was walking thru a Parisian flower market. It was early—a little gray. . . . I heard a single word: Jerry. Said simply & quietly. I turned back. There stood Tanny. Tall, slim, a small straw hat perched on top of her head—a quiet look on her face—framed within all the wispy trailing plants. She held a small parasol over her head, an early spring or late fall coat lightly draped over her shoulders.

I looked at her. Her regard was all acceptance—forgiveness. I said Tanny—& walked over to her, put my arm around her, & kissed her on her lips. She was young (& older), slim, sad, clear eyed, and oh so touching. I looked at her again. Became conscious of other figures standing around. . . . I kissed her fervently again[—]it was home.

To: Maria Calegari†
April 26, 1994

Dear Maria,

You should *dance!* Just get yourself together and go in there and tell them what you will and will not do. Your years of dancing are limited. While you can

---

* In 1991, Robbins and Le Clercq had had a confrontation when he'd asked that he be given credit for his choreography of the battle of the mice and tin soldiers in a Hollywood film of NYCB's *Nutcracker*. "Over my dead body," Le Clercq had said. But the resulting frost in their relationship thawed, as so often. And until the day he died he kept one of his own photographs of her on his bedside table.
† Maria Calegari, a principal dancer who had originated roles in *Gershwin Concerto, Antique Epigraphs,* and other Robbins works, had been suffering from undiagnosed Lyme disease, but both Peter Martins and ballet master Richard Tanner were apparently unconvinced that her symptoms had a clinical basis, and they wanted her to retire from the company.

dance, you should. Don't fuss or pay attention to all the rest. It does you no good whatsoever. Your appearances in front of an audience, now, is what counts, believe me. I have many grave reservations about what you complain about, & also justified, but *do your work*. You owe it to yourself—& to your public—& to let *anyone* get in your way is a mistake. They are *small* & you are larger than they are. Don't let them be the cause of your *not* dancing. Dance *now*. As an ancient Roman said, "When, if not now, do we live?" Or dance somewhere, somehow.

Please, do think about it.

Time, *your* time, is going by fast. Use it. I hate to think of your *teaching* because of R. Tanner. It is a disgrace, to you and your work. To surrender to them is abysmal. To *hell* with them. Dance. They are small. You are great!

With love and deep concern,
Jerry

To: Maria Calegari
March 6, 1995

Dearest Maria,

How happy I was to get your note. I love hearing about what's been going on and I appreciate your allowing me to see a little of the insides. Thank you for all of that. The ballet season is over (thank God). It was a terrible one and as usual, things got thrown on stage up to the point when after the first perfor-mance of *Glass,* I yanked it. It isn't that the kids cannot dance. As a matter of fact, it's a wonderful company with lots of youngsters coming up and they do try to apply themselves. But it's a bit difficult when you are given the steps the day before you have to perform them full out. Of course, I get into everything but I must say I cannot take full credit for *Dances.*[*] The dancers themselves were so good, they fell back into the original relationships.

Next week, I start rehearsals again with a suite of *West Side Story* dances. I hope it works out. The Company (both dancers and management) have gone haywire over the attempt to try it and, although the board of directors has been

---

* Calegari had seen and admired a performance of *Dances at a Gathering.*

calling panic signs because of a deficit, they are trying to put all their dough into the effort. I myself think they're going too far but we'll see. My next gig after that is splitting the weeks at the Chatelet Theatre with the Company. We'll be doing *Watermill, Goldberg, I'm Old Fashioned* and a few others of mine. I hope the theater functions well there. . . .

Forget the decisions of the past. They're over with and done with and just concentrate on the future. I'm very happy to hear that you will be dancing again.* I feel you are missed here but I'll be glad to see you anywhere. So get in there and do your barre work, dammit!

My body is starting to go now and I have a bursitis of the hip which goes to the knee which goes to the ankle which goes to the head finally. I manage to indicate enough for people to understand what I want and I just hope this all gets better instead of worse. Please give my best to Bart† and you know you have my love and thoughts always. Stay well, be happy and I'll see you soon.

Love—
Jerry

To: Andy deGroat
November 10, 1995

Hey Andy!

What a good and what a long letter! I was fascinated by all your news. You make Lyon sound like a beautiful city—built by Italians. Now I'd love to see it.

Your description of *Nutcracker* is charming. I can't wait to see everything you describe: a red bat, a witch in a broomstick, two dancing bears on rollerskates, the long green tail of the King of Rats, and all those cowboys, Indians, snowflakes, etc. . . .

---

* Suzanne Farrell, who had started a studio company in Washington, D.C., that would become the Suzanne Farrell Ballet, was about to present a season of Balanchine ballets in association with the Washington Ballet, and Calegari would be dancing lead roles in those works.
† The principal dancer Bart Cook, who had originated roles in numerous Robbins ballets and then become a ballet master, had left City Ballet; he and Calegari were now married.

I've just roughed out the third *Brandenburg Concerto*.* It's in three pieces: the first and last are for eight boys and eight girls plus soloists, and I'm *slowly* making it a lot better. I can't show them what I want them to do so they all move around with stiff-legged movements imitating me and not my intentions. The pas de deux is fine. It is Wendy Whelan and Peter Boal† and they work beautifully. I don't know how much longer I'll be going on. I've got another pas de deux already done, and I'm going to work on a dance for four couples and see if I can do that. It's such very hard work for me now. If I stay on my feet, my hips do not lock; it's when I sit down that I get stiff all over. The kids realize that I'm not my old self and are trying to be helpful. They are a lovely bunch. I don't know how they remember all the changes I make all the time.

I'm going to the beach to close up the house this weekend. My last look at the past summer. I'll write again soon and meanwhile, all my love to you and please, Andy, take care of yourself.‡ If you need anything, ANYTHING, just let me know.

All love, and a big hug,
Jerry

To: Gerald Freedman§
9 March 1998

Dear Gerry,

Thank you for your February 26th letter. It arrived amidst my so-called two week vacation (ha-ha) which is filled with all sorts of details I must make up for

---

* *Brandenburg,* a ballet for twenty dancers, including two principal couples, made up of movements from Bach's *Brandenburg Concertos* nos. 3, 2, 1, and 6, premiered on January 22, 1997.
† Wendy Whelan (b. 1967) and Peter Boal (b. 1965) became principal dancers at New York City Ballet; he is now director of Pacific Northwest Ballet. She is associate director of NYCB.
‡ DeGroat had been diagnosed with HIV but was asymptomatic.
§ Gerald Freedman (b. 1927) had been Robbins's assistant director on *Bells Are Ringing, West Side Story,* and *Gypsy;* dramaturge for *The Poppa Piece;* artistic director of the New York Shakespeare Festival; and was currently dean of the drama school at the University of North Carolina School of the Arts. The two Jerrys, who referred to each other as "the other one," had a close working relationship.

Les Noces at New York City Ballet. Now it seems that the musicians are pulling rank and wanting to play the music themselves without knowing everything that goes into it.[*] I'll have to see if I can talk to them myself and get them to come around. And if they won't, the hell with them!

My health is better. In fact, I sleep all day long and that I'll soon be done out of by rehearsals. I'll let you know how they go.

I'm sorry this is so brief. I'm trying to answer all my notes as quickly as I can.

All my love,
Jerry

To: Lourdes Lopez
27 April 1998

Dear Lourdes,

Here's a quick answer to your lovely note. It was very good to hear from you and I miss you a lot around the company—and I'm sure others do too. So I loved your letter and all your news about Adriel[†] and the picture! Yum yum!

Sag Harbor sounds like a dream. Will you visit Balanchine's grave there? It's a nice spot. Tell Adriel the man with the beard is still around—would *love* to see you both—just call up and find out when I'm rehearsing and come on in. I still manage to keep going, a little less with each month's passage, but still going.

I miss you. Stop by. Give my love to Adriel—and a lot of it to yourself.

Jerry

---

[*] Against City Ballet practice Robbins had decided to use recorded music for *Les Noces,* given the fiendish complexity of the score, his own diminished capacities, and the difficulty of accommodating all the musicians on the stage. Apparently, the orchestra members were insulted.
[†] Lopez's daughter Adriel had been born in 1989, and Lopez had retired from dancing in 1997.

To: Himself
January 12, 1989

I'm thrilled by the show.[*] It's gone beyond my expectations. The cast & staff & spirit of it is intoxicating. Best is the reaction of the public,—from friends to civilians not in the Arts—& to sit among them in the theater & watch & feel them go with the show & the numbers. Finally it's a retrospective of theater—my theater—& I am proud [of] (as well as being surprised) by how good, tasteful [it is]. I can't get over the effect it has on friends who've seen it. They have pride in knowing me, etc. etc. Tears, nostalgia, & admiration & love. So—

So how do I feel? So pleased & content that at this point, what with *it*, my 70th birthday & the return of action with B,[†] I feel ready to die happily! Isn't that strange. I could end it all at this time of recognition & achievement & having great friends, great success, & sex returned—as contented a life as I'd want. Crazy: not when I'm depressed, but when I'm most thrilled with where I am. . . . When we used to play that game of what-would-you-do-with-your-last-24-hours if you could [do] anything you wanted & be anywhere—I used to say, well, I'd like to go on working & be at the opening of a work I knew was really good. . . .

The Poppa Piece: A Different Ending
September 20, 1980

POPPA

Qvetch! Qvetch! Qvetch! . . . Is that all there is to it? So I read dirty magazines, never ever stood up to your mother, couldn't speak English, didn't play any sports, never tried to be a model for you . . .

---

[*] Robbins wrote this letter to himself—and sealed it in a self-addressed envelope and packed *that* away in a suitcase—when *Jerome Robbins' Broadway* had just begun eight weeks of previews; the show would open on February 26, 1989, and the letter would be found, and unsealed, in the autumn of 2016.

[†] Brian Meehan.

Did I have fun?

Was life good? . . . Oi you poor thing—such a woeful tale you qvetch

out—this they did, that they did, family friend & foe.

Nu? Give me a break, kid. Give *us* a break. Give yourself a break.

Drop it. It's passed. It's over.

Now leave me be—let me rest. Stop haunting me, you, the living.

One more dance. Together now?

They dance quietly, a deep, gentle, unfighting dance. They watch each other at first, then don't need to. They dance together concentrating on the dance's spiritual quality, the beauty, & their love for the dance & what it means.

Candles are lit. People hum and pray. Kaddish is said. The lights dim out.

ACKNOWLEDGMENTS

This book would not exist without the encouragement and support of the Jerome Robbins Foundation and its trustees, Allen Greenberg, Christopher Pennington, and Ellen Sorrin. My profound thanks to them; to the editor in chief of the Jerome Robbins newsletter, Gregory Victor (who may have spent even more hours in the Robbins archives than I have); and to Victoria Ianuzzi for help with document transcription.

Jerome Robbins left his archives—both his writings and his artwork, as well as films, videos, and audio recordings—to the New York Public Library, where they reside in the Dance Division named after him at the Library for the Performing Arts at Lincoln Center. There they, and the researchers who want to consult them, are superbly looked after by Barbara G. and Lawrence A. Fleischman Executive Director Jacqueline Z Davis; the Dance Division's curator, Linda Murray; the director of the Moving Image Archive, Tanisha Jones; and Special Collections manager Arlene Yu, librarians Jennifer Eberhardt and Phillip Karg, and the rest of the wonderful staff, all of whose patience I have tried over many years. I thank them and also those at institutions farther afield where Robbins treasures are buried: especially Edward Sykes Comstock at the University of Southern California's Cinematic Arts Library, home of the Robert Wise and Ernest Lehmann archives; Mark Horowitz, Senior Music Specialist at the Library of Congress, where the papers of Leonard Bernstein, Arthur Laurents, Stephen Sondheim, and the Rodgers and Hammerstein organization are located; and Erin Hestvik at the New York City Ballet archives, which hold the papers of Tanaquil Le Clercq. And for locating or giving me material from personal collections, I'm deeply grateful to William Graves, Brian Meehan, and Ned Rorem.

Archival research is lonely work, but it was made immeasurably less so by New York University's Center for Ballet and the Arts, which awarded me a fellowship for this project in 2017. My thanks to Jennifer Homans, its founder and director; Andrea Salvatore, assistant director for programs and operations; Allan Macleod, who got my elderly MacBook to play nicely with NYU's audio and slide-projection system; and especially the Center's fellows, past and present, whose creative, analytic, and collegial spirit helped me to think about my material in new ways.

At Knopf I'm indebted to Victoria Wilson, who (as she points out) was the best possible editor for this book, and to Kathy Hourigan, Bette Alexander, Roméo Enriquez, Ingrid Sterner, Soonyoung Kwon, Jenny Carrow, Kathy Zuckerman, and Marc Jaffee for their contributions. As ever, I thank my brilliant and sympathetic agent, Eric Simonoff, who rolled his eyes only a *little* when I said I wanted to go back into the ring with Robbins a third time. And I'd like to tip my hat to Judy Kinberg, director of the documentary *Jerome Robbins: Something to Dance About*, who hired me to write its screenplay—during which it became apparent that our subject had a book's worth of things to say, by himself.

Finally, I owe a huge debt of gratitude to my husband, Tom Stewart, and our children, Pamela and Patrick, for manufacturing, or pretending, interest in stories by and about someone they've never met.

But my deepest thanks are reserved for this book's dedicatees, Aidan Mooney and William Earle, who literally opened the world of Jerome Robbins for me by sharing their memories of and insights about him over the course of two decades. I think Robbins himself would join me in saluting them.

CHRONOLOGY

A SELECTIVE LIST OF EVENTS AND WORK

1918   October 11: Jerome Wilson Rabinowitz born in New York City

1922   Rabinowitz family moves to Jersey City, then to Weehawken, New Jersey

1924   July/August: Family trip to Rozhanka, Lida District, Poland (now Belarus)

1931   June: Graduates from Alexander Hamilton School
       Autumn: Has bar mitzvah

1935   June: Graduates from Woodrow Wilson High School
       September: Enters New York University

1936   June: Withdraws from NYU; begins apprenticeship at Senya Gluck Sandor's Dance Center, where he changes his name to Robbins
       November: Sandor gets him prop work backstage at the Group Theatre during the run of *Johnny Johnson*
       Winter: Takes classes on scholarship at the New Dance Group with Bessie Schönberg

1937   September: First (Labor Day weekend) appearance at Camp Tamiment; appears in Yiddish Art Theatre production of *The Brothers Ashkenazi*; begins ballet study with Ella Daganova

November 20: Partners ballet dancer Lisa Parnova at the 92nd Street YMHA

1938   Spring: Appears in Fokine's *Prince Igor* and *Scheherazade*

Summer: Joins entertainment staff at Camp Tamiment (as Jerry Robyns)

November–December 17: Dances in chorus of *Great Lady* (book by Earle Crooker and Lowell Brentano, music by Frederick Loewe, staged by Bretaigne Windust, choreography credited to William Dollar but executed by George Balanchine)

1939   February 9–May 27: In chorus of *Stars in Your Eyes* (book by J. P. McEvoy, lyrics by Dorothy Fields, music by Arthur Schwartz, staged by Joshua Logan, choreographed by Carl Randall)

Summer: Returns to Tamiment

August: Choreographs *Strange Fruit* (to the song by Abel Meeropol) for Theatre Arts Committee for Peace and Democracy concert at 92nd Street YMHA

September 29–December 2: Appears in and contributes material to *The Straw Hat Revue* (book by Max Liebman and Sam Locke, score by James Shelton and Sylvia Fine, staged by Max Liebman, choreographed by Jerome Andrews) on Broadway

1940   April–June 29: In chorus of *Keep Off the Grass* (sketches by Mort Lewis, Parke Levy, Alan Lipscott, S. Jay Kaufman, and Panama & Frank, lyrics by Al Dubin and Howard Dietz, music by James McHugh, stage directed by Fred de Cordova, book directed by Edward Duryea Dowling, choreographed by George Balanchine)

Summer: Returns briefly to Tamiment; joins Ballet Theatre with a two-month corps de ballet contract

Fall: Joins Ballet Theatre as a full member of the corps de ballet

1941   Spring: Meets Mary Hunter, Horton Foote, and members of American Actors Company; begins writing fiction and scenarios for ballets and theater

Summer: While Ballet Theatre on hiatus, spends time at Jacob's Pillow and returns to Tamiment as "Production Choreographer"

Autumn: Promoted to soloist with Ballet Theatre, goes with company to Mexico for two-month residency

1942 January: Begins national tour with Ballet Theatre

April: Pronounced "unfit for service" by draft board; goes to Mexico for summer season with Ballet Theatre

Summer: Promoted to principal dancer; cast in title role of Fokine's *Petrouchka*

Autumn: U.S. tour with Ballet Theatre

1943 Spring/summer: Ballet Theatre commissions *Shore Leave Interlude* (renamed *Fancy Free*)

Autumn: Robbins meets Leonard Bernstein, who agrees to write score for *Fancy Free;* they collaborate long distance by letter and phonograph record

Late December: Joins Communist Party

1944 April 18: Premiere of *Fancy Free* at Metropolitan Opera House

Summer: Begins psychoanalysis with Dr. Frances Arkin; adapts *Fancy Free* into *On the Town* with Betty Comden, Adolph Green, and Leonard Bernstein

December 28: *On the Town* (book and lyrics by Comden and Green, music by Bernstein, directed by George Abbott, choreographed by Robbins) opens on Broadway

1945 January: Living at 24 West Tenth Street, close to Paul and Jane Bowles, Oliver Smith, and Leonard Bernstein; meets Robert Fizdale and Arthur Gold; begins affair with Lois Wheeler

June 1: *Interplay* (music by Morton Gould) premieres with Billy Rose's Concert Varieties and subsequently enters Ballet Theatre repertory

Autumn: Meets Montgomery Clift

December 21: *Billion Dollar Baby* (book and lyrics by Comden and Green, music by Morton Gould, directed by George Abbott, choreographed by Robbins) opens on Broadway

1946　May: Moves to 421 Park Avenue

June: Dances with Ballet Theatre in London

Summer/autumn: Working on scenario/book for *Look, Ma, I'm Dancin'!*

October 24: *Facsimile* premieres with Ballet Theatre

1947　January 19: Meets (and soon begins relationship with) Rose Tobias

March 26: Premiere of *Pas de Trois* (music by Berlioz)

May 12: Premiere of *Summer Day* (music by Prokofiev)

October 9: *High Button Shoes* (book by Stephen Longstreet, music by Jule Styne, lyrics by Sammy Cahn, directed by George Abbott, choreographed by Robbins) opens on Broadway

Late October: Relationship with Rose Tobias ends

Autumn: Joins the Actors Studio as one of its first students

1948　January 29: *Look, Ma, I'm Dancin'!* (book by Jerome Lawrence and Robert E. Lee, score by Hugh Martin, co-directed by George Abbott and Robbins, choreography by Robbins) opens on Broadway

June: Montgomery Clift relocates to Hollywood, ending his and Robbins's relationship

September 24: *That's the Ticket!* (book by Julius J. and Philip G. Epstein, score by Harold Rome, directed by Robbins) opens in Philadelphia and closes ten days later

November/December: Robbins joins New York City Ballet

1949　Named associate artistic director of New York City Ballet

January 6: Proposes *Romeo and Juliet* musical adaptation, set in Lower East Side slums and involving Catholics and Jews, to Leonard Bernstein, suggests Arthur Laurents write book

January 20: Dances in premiere of his ballet *The Guests* (music by Marc Blitzstein) with NYCB

July 15: *Miss Liberty* (book by Robert E. Sherwood, score by Irving Berlin, directed by Moss Hart, choreography by Robbins) opens on Broadway

December 1: Premiere of Balanchine's *Bourrée Fantasque,* featuring Robbins and Tanaquil Le Clercq

1950 February 26: Premiere of *Age of Anxiety* (music by Leonard Bernstein)

February 23: Dances title role in Balanchine's *Prodigal Son* (music by Prokofiev)

March 9: Dances in premiere of his own *Jones Beach* (co-choreographed with George Balanchine, music by Jurriaan Andriessen)

Mid-March: Ed Sullivan initiates investigation of Robbins's Communist ties, leading to his questioning by FBI

June: Terminates therapy with Dr. Arkin

Autumn: Meets Nancy "Slim" Hayward, wife of Leland Hayward

October 12: *Call Me Madam* (book by Howard Lindsay and Russel Crouse, score by Irving Berlin, directed by George Abbott, choreography by Robbins, starring Ethel Merman) opens on Broadway

November–December: In Paris overseeing Ballet Theatre performances of his ballet; lives with and becomes engaged to Nora Kaye

1951 March 22: Ed Sullivan publishes column urging House Un-American Activities Committee to subpoena Robbins to testify on Communism in the entertainment industry

March 29: *The King and I* (book and lyrics by Oscar Hammerstein II, music by Richard Rodgers, directed by John Van Druten, choreography by Robbins) opens on Broadway

April 19: *A Tree Grows in Brooklyn* (book by Betty Smith and George Abbott, lyrics by Dorothy Fields, music by Arthur Schwartz, directed by Abbott, choreographed by Herbert Ross, uncredited staging and choreography by Robbins) opens on Broadway

June 14: Premiere of *The Cage* (music by Igor Stravinsky) at New York City Ballet

June–October: Travels in Europe and Israel; meets Buzz Miller and (in September) Ned Rorem

November 14: Premiere of Balanchine's *Tyl Ulenspiegel* (music by Richard Strauss), with Robbins in title role

December 4: Premiere of *The Pied Piper* (music by Aaron Copland) featuring performances by Robbins, Tanaquil Le Clercq, and others

1952   January: Buzz Miller moves into Robbins's apartment on Park Avenue

February 14: Premiere of *Ballade* (music by Debussy)

February 19: Premiere of Balanchine's *Caracole* (to Mozart) with Robbins in a featured role

Spring: Provides advice and additional choreography for *Wish You Were Here* (book by Arthur Kober and Joshua Logan, score by Harold Rome, directed and choreographed by Logan), which will open June 25 on Broadway

April: Travels to Israel

May–July: European tour with New York City Ballet; during tour Robbins retires from dancing

October–December: Stages musical numbers for *Two's Company* (revue with sketches by Charles Sherman and Peter De Vries, lyrics by Ogden Nash and Sheldon Harnick, music by Vernon Duke, sketches directed by Jules Dassin), which opens on Broadway on December 15

1953   February 25: *Wonderful Town* (book by Joseph Fields and Jerome Chodorov, lyrics by Betty Comden and Adolph Green, music by Leonard Bernstein, directed by George Abbott, choreography by Donald Saddler, uncredited staging and choreography by Robbins) opens on Broadway

May 5: Testifies before a public hearing of the House Un-American Activities Committee in New York

May 14: Premiere of *Afternoon of a Faun* (music by Debussy)

June 2: Premiere of *Fanfare* (music by Benjamin Britten)

June 15: *Ford 50th Anniversary Show,* a variety special starring Mary Martin and Ethel Merman (among others), with musical numbers staged by Robbins, airs on CBS and NBC television

December: Goes to Israel to work with Inbal Dance Theatre

1954 February 2: Premiere of George Balanchine's *Nutcracker* (music by Tchaikovsky); Robbins choreographed the battle of the mice and toy soldiers

February 18: Premiere of *Quartet* (music by Prokofiev)

April 1: Premiere of *The Tender Land* (opera with music by Aaron Copland, libretto by Horace Everett, directed by Robbins)

April 12: Lena Robbins dies

May 13: *The Pajama Game* (book by George Abbott and Richard Bissell, score by Richard Adler and Jerry Ross, co-directed by Abbott and Robbins) opens on Broadway

October 20: *Peter Pan* (book adapted by Robbins from James M. Barrie, lyrics by Carolyn Leigh, with Betty Comden and Adolph Green, music by Mark Charlap and Jule Styne, directed and choreographed by Robbins) opens on Broadway

1955 February 25: *Silk Stockings* (book by George S. Kaufman, Leueen MacGrath, and Abe Burrows, score by Cole Porter, directed by Cy Feuer, choreographed by Eugene Loring, uncredited staging and choreography by Robbins) opens on Broadway

March 7: *Peter Pan* (staged for television by Robbins, with Clark Jones directing filming) airs on NBC television

Spring: Hospitalized with hepatitis; relationship with Buzz Miller ends; Robbins moves to 154 East Seventy-Fourth Street

Summer: *Romeo and Juliet* musical adaptation idea is revived, now focusing on Anglo and Latino street gangs on the West Side; Robbins collaborates long-distance with Bernstein, Laurents, and Stephen Sondheim, who is brought in to write lyrics

Autumn: In Hollywood to direct dance sequences for film of *The King and I*

1956   March 6: Premiere of *The Concert* (music by Chopin)

April: In Copenhagen to stage *Fanfare* for Royal Danish Ballet

June 28: Twentieth Century Fox's film version of *The King and I* (directed by Walter Lang) released

November: On a European tour with New York City Ballet, Tanaquil Le Clercq is hospitalized with polio in Copenhagen

November 29: *Bells Are Ringing* (book and lyrics by Betty Comden and Adolph Green, music by Jule Styne, directed by Robbins and co-choreographed by him and Bob Fosse) opens on Broadway

1957   September 26: *West Side Story* (book by Arthur Laurents, lyrics by Stephen Sondheim, music by Leonard Bernstein, directed and choreographed by Robbins) opens on Broadway

Autumn: Sets up Lena Robbins Foundation (later the Jerome Robbins Foundation) to support artists in dance, theater, and associated fields

1958   June–September: In Europe with his company Ballets: U.S.A.

June 8: Premiere of *N.Y. Export: Opus Jazz* (music by Robert Prince) at Spoleto Festival

September 4: Premiere of *3 x 3* (music by Georges Auric) in New York (Alvin Theatre)

December 13: *West Side Story* opens in London, production rehearsed and supervised by Robbins

1959 May 21: *Gypsy* (book by Arthur Laurents, lyrics by Stephen Sondheim, music by Jule Styne, directed and choreographed by Robbins) opens on Broadway

June–September: In Europe with Ballets: U.S.A.

July 3: Premiere of *Moves* (no score) at Spoleto Festival

July 12: Premiere of *Events* (music by Robert Prince) at Spoleto Festival

July 19: "Passage for Two," duet from *N.Y. Export: Opus Jazz,* performed by Ballets: U.S.A., airs on *The Ed Sullivan Show* on CBS

Summer: Leland and Nancy "Slim" Hayward part, and she comes to stay with Robbins in Spoleto; Robbins meets Robert Graves in London

November 29: *N.Y. Export: Opus Jazz,* performed by Ballets: U.S.A., airs on *The Ed Sullivan Show* on CBS

1960 January 17: *N.Y. Export: Opus Jazz,* performed by Ballets: U.S.A., repeats on *The Ed Sullivan Show* on CBS

January 31: Takes hallucinogenic mushrooms with Robert Graves

April: Begins work co-directing (with Robert Wise) film version of *West Side Story*

October 21: Fired from *West Side Story* film

1961 July 12: Premiere of *Events* (music by Robert Prince) at Spoleto Festival

December 13: United Artists' film version of *West Side Story* released

1962 February 26: *Oh Dad, Poor Dad, Mamma's Hung You in the Closet and I'm Feelin' So Sad* (play by Arthur Kopit, directed by Robbins) opens Off-Broadway

April 9: At the Academy Awards in Los Angeles, Robbins wins two Oscars for *West Side Story* (which also wins Best Picture), one for direction (shared with Robert Wise) and one for choreography (one of only four ever awarded)

April 11: Ballets: U.S.A. appears at the White House as entertainment for a state dinner given by President and Mrs. John F. Kennedy, the first dance troupe ever to do so

May: Begins renting "Ding-Dong House" in Snedens Landing, New York

May 8: *A Funny Thing Happened on the Way to the Forum* (book by Burt Shevelove and Larry Gelbart, score by Stephen Sondheim, directed by George Abbott, choreographed by Jack Cole, uncredited staging, dramaturgy, and choreography by Robbins) opens on Broadway

Autumn: Backs out of untitled Fanny Brice musical (*Funny Girl*) over script difficulties; commits to directing Brecht's *Mother Courage* instead

1963   March 28: *Mother Courage and Her Children* (play by Bertolt Brecht, directed by Robbins) opens on Broadway

July: Rejoining *Funny Girl* team, Robbins casts novice actress Barbra Streisand as Fanny Brice, then quits production again over script problems

August 27: *Oh Dad, Poor Dad* transfers to Broadway

1964   March 26: *Funny Girl* (book by Isobel Lennart, lyrics by Bob Merrill, music by Jule Styne, directed by Garson Kanin, choreographed by Carol Haney, production supervised—with additional dramaturgy, staging, and choreography—by Robbins) opens on Broadway

September 22: *Fiddler on the Roof* (book by Joseph Stein, lyrics by Sheldon Harnick, music by Jerry Bock, directed and choreographed by Robbins) opens on Broadway

September 24: Begins aborted discussions with Betty Comden, Adolph Green, and Leonard Bernstein for a musical based on Thornton Wilder's *Skin of Our Teeth*

Autumn: Donates a percentage of his royalty earnings from *Fiddler on the Roof* to the New York Public Library, in perpetuity, to establish an archive of dance film

1965 March 30: Premiere of *Les Noces* (music by Stravinsky) at American Ballet Theatre

Summer: Meets Christine Conrad

1966 January: Moves to 117 East Eighty-First Street; begins discussion with Britain's National Theatre about potential production of Euripides's *Bacchae*

April 21: *The Office* (play by María Irene Fornés, directed by Robbins) has first preview on Broadway, closes after ten performances

June: Receives one of inaugural grants of National Endowment for the Arts to set up American Theatre Lab

November: ATL begins work

1967 Spring: NEA renews ATL grant for a second year; Robbins meets Robert Wilson

Summer: Christine Conrad moves in with Robbins

1968 March: Robbins shuts down ATL; meets Edward Davis (not his real name) and begins intermittent affair with him

Spring/summer: Working on abortive adaptation of *The Exception and the Rule* by Bertolt Brecht with John Guare, Stephen Sondheim, and Leonard Bernstein

October: *The Exception and the Rule* canceled

1969 May 8: Gala preview of *Dances at a Gathering* (music by Chopin) at New York City Ballet (official premiere May 22)

June: Travels to Stockholm and Leningrad with Christine Conrad

August: Goes to Israel and Greece with Edward Davis; Conrad leaves him

September: Davis breaks off relationship

October: Ruptures Achilles tendon and has surgery

1970   January 29: Premiere of *In the Night* (music by Chopin)

      February: Travels to Yucatán with Robert Wilson and Andy deGroat

      September: Goes to London to stage *Dances at a Gathering* for the Royal Ballet; meets Edna O'Brien; contracts combination of strep and hepatitis and is hospitalized on return to United States

      May 28: Premiere of revival of Balanchine's *Firebird* (music by Stravinsky); Robbins choreographed the monsters' dance

1971   May 27: Premiere of *The Goldberg Variations* (music by Bach)

1972   February 3: Premiere of *Watermill* (music by Teiji Ito)

      February: Spends two weeks in Jamaica discussing possible ballet based on S. Anski's play *The Dybbuk* with Leonard Bernstein

      June 18: Premiere of *Scherzo Fantastique* (music by Stravinsky)

      June 21: Premiere of *Circus Polka* (music by Stravinsky)

      June 23: Premieres of *Dumbarton Oaks* and—co-choreographed with George Balanchine—*Pulcinella* (music by Stravinsky)

      June 25: Premiere of *Requiem Canticles* (music by Stravinsky)

      June 30–July 16: Travels in Italy with Aidan Mooney

1973   May 24: Premiere of *An Evening's Waltzes* (music by Prokofiev)

      June 29: Directs and partially choreographs *Celebration: The Art of the Pas de Deux,* featuring duets by Frederick Ashton, George Balanchine, Erik Bruhn (after Bournonville), Alexander Gorsky, Enrique Martinez, and Galina Ulanova (after Petipa) at the Teatro Nuovo in Spoleto

      June–August: In Spoleto; Tanaquil Le Clercq visits

      December: Harry Robbins hospitalized with heart failure

1974   May 16: Premiere of *Dybbuk* (music by Bernstein)

      October 11: Is given his dog Nick by Aidan Mooney and Slim Keith

1975   January: Reads *The Ordeal of Civility: Freud, Marx, Lévi-Strauss, and the Jewish Struggle with Modernity,* by John Murray Cuddihy

       May 15: Premiere of *Concerto in G,* later titled *In G Major* (music by Ravel)

       May 22: Premieres of *Introduction and Allegro for Harp* and *Mother Goose* (music by Ravel)

       May 29: Premieres of *Chansons Madécasses* and *Une Barque sur l'Océan* (music by Ravel)

       June 25: Moves out of Ding-Dong House in Snedens Landing

       July 2: Checks into McLean Hospital in Belmont, Massachusetts

       July 24: Leaves McLean

1976   March: Invited but declines to take over as director for *1600 Pennsylvania Avenue* (book and lyrics by Alan Jay Lerner, music by Leonard Bernstein)

       May 9: Premiere of *Other Dances* (music by Chopin), featuring Mikhail Baryshnikov and Natalia Makarova, at American Ballet Theatre's "Star-Spangled Gala"

       Summer/autumn: Begins writing autobiographical notes for *The Poppa Piece*

1977   March: Hospitalized for diverticulitis

       August: Lobbies Balanchine to bring Mikhail Baryshnikov to New York City Ballet

       Autumn: Meets Jesse Gerstein

       December: Hospitalized for diverticulitis surgery; Jesse Gerstein moves in to 117 East Eighty-First Street

       December 16: Harry Robbins dies

1978   March: George Balanchine has heart attack

       April: Mikhail Baryshnikov joins New York City Ballet

       May 18: Premiere of *Tricolore* (music by Georges Auric), co-choreographed, in Balanchine's absence, with Peter Martins and Jean-Pierre Bonnefoux

June 8: Premieres of *Fencing Dances and Exercises* (music by Handel and Biber), *Solo* (music by Telemann), and *Verdi Variations* (music by Verdi), as part of compendium program—also including a ballet by Peter Martins—titled *A Sketch Book*

1979   January 18: Premiere of *The Four Seasons* (music by Verdi)

April 8: Premiere of Balanchine's *Le Bourgeois Gentilhomme,* completed by Robbins after Balanchine fell ill, for New York City Opera

June 14: Premiere of *Opus 19/The Dreamer* (music by Prokofiev)

Autumn: Robbins buys beach house in Bridgehampton

1980   February 20: *Other Dances* airs as part of *Dance in America: Two Duets* program on WNET/PBS

July 2: *The Cage, Afternoon of a Faun,* and excerpts from *Fancy Free, The Concert,* and *Dances at a Gathering* air on *Live from Studio 8H* on NBC

November 11: Premiere of *Rondo* (music by Mozart)

1981   February/March: Travels to Egypt with Jesse Gerstein

June 4: Premiere of *Andantino* [under the title *Pas de Deux*] (music by Tchaikovsky)

June 11: Premiere of *Piano Pieces* (music by Tchaikovsky)

June 14: Premiere of *Allegro con Grazia* (music by Tchaikovsky)

September: Takes group of New York City Ballet dancers to China

December 6: Receives the Kennedy Center Honors, with Mikhail Baryshnikov introducing him

1982   February 6: Premiere of *Gershwin Concerto* (music by George Gershwin)

February: Begins discussions with Philip Glass to contribute to libretto and direct premiere of Glass's opera *Akhnaten* for Houston Grand Opera

June 16: Premiere of *Four Chamber Works* (music by Stravinsky), comprising *Septet, Ragtime, Concertino, Three Pieces for Clarinet Solo,* and *Octet*—actually *five* chamber works organized into four sections

November: Balanchine enters Roosevelt Hospital with vertigo, weakness, and increasing dementia

December 1: Edith Weissman, Robbins's assistant of forty years, dies

1983   February: Withdraws from *Akhnaten* due to Balanchine's illness and responsibilities to City Ballet

March: Threatens to resign from City Ballet when its board, without consulting him, confidentially plans for Peter Martins to succeed Balanchine; eventually they will be named joint "ballet masters in chief"

April 30: Balanchine dies

May: Robbins and Jesse Gerstein end relationship; Robbins begins seeing Brian Meehan

May 12: Premiere of *Glass Pieces* (music by Philip Glass)

June 16: Premiere of *I'm Old Fashioned (The Astaire Variations)* (music by Morton Gould on a theme by Jerome Kern)

1984   February 2: Premiere of *Antique Epigraphs* (music by Debussy)

June 7: Premiere of *Brahms/Handel* (music by Brahms on a theme by Handel, orchestrated by Edmund Rubbra), co-choreographed with Twyla Tharp

Summer: Joins Ahmet and Mica Ertegun for a cruise along the Turkish coast

1985   February 14: Premiere of *Eight Lines* (music by Steve Reich)

June 13: Premiere of *In Memory Of . . .* (music by Alban Berg)

June: Makes will

Summer: Turkish cruise with Ahmet and Mica Ertegun

1986   February 16: Joseph Duell commits suicide

May 2: *Antique Epigraphs* and *Fancy Free* air on *Dance in America* on WNET/PBS

May 8: Premiere of *Quiet City* (to music by Aaron Copland), dedicated to Joseph Duell

June 5: Premiere of *Piccolo Balletto* (music by Stravinsky)

1987   January 16: *In Memory Of . . .* airs on *Dance in America* on WNET/PBS

February 28: Nora Kaye dies

April/May: Lincoln Center Theater presents workshop of *The Race to Urga,* a play with music adapted from Brecht's *The Exception and the Rule,* by John Guare with music by Leonard Bernstein, directed by Robbins

July: In Spoleto

1988   February 4: Premiere of *Ives, Songs* (music by Charles Ives)

March 24: Robbins's dog Nick dies

1989   February 26: *Jerome Robbins' Broadway,* featuring song and dance numbers from all of Robbins's Broadway musicals, reconstructed and restaged by him, co-directed by Grover Dale, opens on Broadway after an unprecedented twenty-two weeks of rehearsals and previews

April: Jesse Gerstein diagnosed with AIDS; returns to live with Robbins; Robbins goes on leave from New York City Ballet

August: Lincoln Kirstein retires from New York City Ballet

Autumn: Leases an apartment in Paris at 58 boulevard Raspail; announces retirement from full-time participation in New York City Ballet

September 22: Irving Berlin dies

1990   Spring: New York City Ballet has festival of Robbins ballets; during rehearsals Robbins suffers concussion in bicycle accident

April 6: Nancy "Slim" Keith dies

Summer: Begins working on script of *The Poppa Piece* with Gerald Freedman

October 14: Leonard Bernstein dies

1991   Spring/summer: Rehearsing *The Poppa Piece* for a workshop presentation at Lincoln Center Theater with John Weidman as dramaturge

Fall: Cancels work on *The Poppa Piece*

October 14: Jesse Gerstein dies

1992   Spring: Travels to St. Petersburg to supervise staging of *In the Night* with Mariinsky Ballet

1994   March 3: Premiere of *A Suite of Dances* (music by Bach), a solo for Mikhail Baryshnikov and the White Oak Dance Project

June 4: Premiere of *2 & 3 Part Inventions* (music by Bach) for School of American Ballet

1995   May 18: Premiere of *West Side Story Suite* (music by Leonard Bernstein), dances from *West Side Story* as reconstructed for *Jerome Robbins' Broadway,* restaged for New York City Ballet

December 6: Robert Fizdale dies

December: Has surgery to repair the mitral valve in his heart; bequeaths his papers to the New York Public Library for the Performing Arts

1996   January 5: Lincoln Kirstein dies

1997   January 22: Premiere of *Brandenburg* (music by Bach)

1998   May 20: Premiere of *Les Noces* at New York City Ballet, where it was staged without live music (a complication beyond Robbins's capacity at this point)

May 21: Hospitalized for ten days with exhaustion

July 26: Suffers massive stroke

July 29: Dies at home at 117 East Eighty-First Street

INDEX

(Page references in *italics* refer to artworks and photographs by Robbins.)

Abbott, George, 83, 84, 96n, 102, 112, 164–5, 171n, 256n, 393, 394, 395–6, 397, 400

Abbott, Tommy, 357, 358

Academy Awards, xi, 116–17, 233, 234, 399

Actors' Equity Association, 31

Actors Studio, 201n, 236n, 237, 394

Adams, Diana, 129, 204, 222

Adler, Richard, 164n, 397

Adler, Stella, 201n, 204

Afternoon of a Faun, 113, 152, 162, 184, 220, 233, 251, 397, 404

Age of Anxiety, 84, 85, 86, 103, 104–5, *127*, *198*, 395

Agon, 255

AIDS, 335
  Gerstein's diagnosis, illness, and death from, 336, 365, 373–5, 406, 407

Alvin Ailey American Dance Theater, 380

Akhnaten, 249, 332, 404, 405

Alcott, Louisa May, 143n

Aleichem, Sholem, 117, 243, 251

Alice in Concert, 323n

Allegro con Grazia, 404

Alton, Robert, 151–2

Alvarez, Anita, 22, 35, 40, 362

American Ballet Theatre, or ABT (founded as Ballet Theatre), 23–5, 50–82, 84, 91, 121n, 171, 203, 224, 244, 245, 248, 254, 316n, 319n, 349, 393, 394, 395, 403
  Fokine's ballets for, 60–1, 64, 65
  founding of, 23, 45n
  lockout at, 330
  photographs of, xiii, *49*, *62*, *66*, *73*, *77*, *79*
  Robbins hired by, 23, 48, 392
  Robbins's audition for, 44, 45, 48
  Robbins's first choreography for. *See Fancy Free*
  Robbins's first performance with, 49
  Robbins's first principal role for (Petrouchka), 60–1, 65–7, 393
  Robbins's guest artist contract with, 95n
  Robbins's *Les Noces* presented at, 260–3, 401
  Robbins's "The Ballet Puts On Dungarees" and, 90–3
  summer season in London (1946), 95, 96, 97, 394
  summer seasons in Mexico City, 23, 50–4, 60, 61–4, 393

American Fund for Israel Institutions, 144n

American Music Festival (1988), 355, 360

American Theatre Lab (ATL), 244–5, 268n, 270–1, 273n, 294, 401

Anastasia, 184n

Andantino (performed under title *Pas de Deux*), 404

Anderson-Ivantzova, Elizabeth, 260

Andrews, Jerome, 37, 38, 392

Andrews, Julie, 233

Andriessen, Jurriaan, 395

Annie, 342

Annie (Robbins's terrier mix), 327

Anski, S.: *The Dybbuk*, 114, 170–1, 247, 251, 306, 307, 402

Antique Epigraphs, 334, 340, 381n, 405

Apollo, 24, 79, 170

Archaeological Museum, Naples, 334, 340

Arkin, Frances, 86, 100, 101–2, 103–4, 350, 395

"army game," 78n

Arrowsmith, William, 266–7

Art of Making Dances, The (Humphrey), 253

Asch, Sholem, 30

Ashcroft, Dame Peggy, 267

Ashton, Frederick, 402

Astaire, Fred, in *You Were Never Lovelier*, 324, 381n

Astaire Variations, The (I'm Old Fashioned), 324, 331, 332, 334, 383, 405

Auden, W. H., 104n

Auger, Ginette (Geneviève), 166n

Auric, Georges, 220n, 398, 403

Aurora's Wedding, 73

"baby ballerinas," 56, 92

Bacall, Lauren, 181, 183n

Bacchae, 244, 265–8, 401

Bach, Johann Sebastian, 93, 298

   Brandenburg (to his *Concertos nos. 3, 2, 1, and 6*), 337, 384, 407

   Goldberg Variations, 246, 251, 286–7, 288–9, 292, 307, 383, 402

   A Suite of Dances (to his *Unaccompanied Cello Suites*), 337, 380, 407

   2 & 3 Part Inventions, 337, 355, 380, 407

Bacon, David, 73

Bacon, Glen, 40

Balanchine, George, 22, 24, 26, 38, 47, 103, 106n, 113, 129, 130n, 136, 137, 138, 142, 147–8, 208n, 211, 222, 224, 225, 227, 247, 248, 254, 255, 277, 280, 281, 292, 294, 301, 317, 322, 324n, 337, 339, 349, 380, 383n, 385, 392, 395, 397, 402

   Baryshnikov's move to City Ballet and, 319, 403

   choreographic process of, 225, 226

   declining health and death of, 248, 249, 323n, 325n, 329, 330–1, 332, 333, 334, 338, 358, 403, 404, 405

   de Mille's *The Book of Dance* and, 253

   The Dybbuk and, 114, 170–1, 247

   Farrell as muse of, 245, 246

   Le Clercq's marriage to, 112, 113, 115, 116, 133, 190, 245

   New York City Ballet formed by, 84

   photographs of, 79, 101, 133

   Robbins's correspondence with, 192

   Robbins's creative ideas rejected by, 114, 170–1

   in Robbins's dreams, 302

   Robbins's relationship with, 114, 147–8, 265, 296

   Robbins's visit to, in his Southampton home (1982), 328–30

   Stravinsky Festival and, 246, 292n, 295–8, 323

   as teacher, 307–8

   see also specific ballets

Ballade, 113, 220, 334, 396

Ballet Caravan, 39

Ballet Review, 362

Ballets: U.S.A., 116, 213n, 214n, 218, 227n, 234, 248, 254, 362, 399, 400
    photographs of, *213*, *214*, *220*, *223*
Ballet Russe, 56, 90n, 255
Ballets Russes, 60n
Ballet Theatre. *See* American Ballet Theatre
Bancroft, Anne, 234, 237, 238–9, 240
Barber, Samuel, 196
Barnes, Clive, 86n, 294
Barnett, Robert, *99*
Baronova, Irina, *56*, 57, 92
Barque sur l'Océan, Une, 309n, 403
Baryshnikov, Mikhail, 248, 316n, 319, 322, 330, 337, 376, 380, 403, 404, 407
Bates, Ronald, 357, 358
Beat generation, 212–13
Becker, Lee, 209
Bell, Arthur, 301–2
Bells Are Ringing, 114, 115, 189n, *190*, 191, *191*, 194, 346n, 384n, 398
    photographs of rehearsals and back stage, *190*, *191*, 195–6, *197*
Bennett, Michael, 357
Bentley, Eric, 238, 239–40, 293n
Bentley, Muriel, 55, 80n, 81
Berg, Alban: *In Memory Of . . .* (to his Violin Concerto), 334, 335, 337, 341, 343n, 365, 405, 406
Bergersen, Baldwin, 35
Bergman, Ingmar, 289–90
Berlin, Irving, 83, 100, 102, 106n, 107, 109n, 196, 336, 395
    death and memorial of, 336, 367–9, 406
    Robbins's correspondence with, 355–6
Berliner Ensemble, 236
Berlioz, Hector, 394
Bernstein, Jamie, Nina, Alexander, and Burton, Robbins's letter to, 372–3

Bernstein, Leonard, 81, 96, 104n, 109, 113–14, 127, 133, 172, 173, 224, 274, 355, 393, 395, 396
    Beat generation ballet and, 212–13
    Candide and, 172–3, 184n, 193
    A Clearing in the Woods and, 172–5
    death of, 336, 372–3, 406
    The Dybbuk and, 170n, 171, 247, 251n, 306n, 307, 349, 402
    The Exception and the Rule, 245, 274, 335, 350, 353, 355, 401, 406
    Fancy Free and, 24–5, 70n, 78, 82, 83, 93–4, 393
    Gould's performance with, 198
    Les Noces premiere conducted by, 263
    Robbins's correspondence with, 89–90, 93–4, 178–9, 212–13, 231, 263, 322–3, 361–2
    Robbins's friendship with, 86, 87, 88, 182n, 335
    Robbins's tribute written for sixtieth birthday celebration of, 182–3
    seventieth-birthday celebration of, 361–2
    1600 Pennsylvania Avenue and, 248, 315–16, 403
    The Skin of Our Teeth and, 244, 256–60, 263n, 400
    trilogy idea based on *Fancy Free* and, 89–90
    West Side Story and, 114, 172–5, 178–81, 231, 343n, 349n, 394, 398, 407
Biber, Heinrich Ignaz Franz, 404
Big Knife, The, 182
Billion Dollar Baby, 83, 94n, 125n, 175n, 394
Billy the Kid, 91
Bird, Dorothy, 22, 35, 362
Bissell, Richard, 164n, 397

Blitzstein, Marc, 70n, 109, 148n, 395

Bluebeard, 60–1, 78

Blum, René, 91

Boal, Peter, 384

Bock, Jerry, 117, 243, 250–1, 400

Bogart, Humphrey, 188

Bolender, Todd, *99*

Bolm, Adolph, 55n

Bonnefoux, Jean-Pierre, 303, 403

Book of the Dance, The (de Mille), 252–3

Boris, Ruthanna, 22, 35

Bostock, Kenneth, 35

Boulanger, Nadia, 148

Bourgeois Gentilhomme, Le, 248, 404

Bourrée Fantasque, 84, 103, 136, 147, 225, 395

Bourscheidt, Randall, 303, 304

Bowles, Jane, 82n, 86, 87–8, 326, 327, 393

   In the Summer House, 109, 175n, 176

Bowles, Paul, 82n, 86, 87, 88, 101n, 140, 142, 326, 393

Brahms/Handel, 317n, 335, 339–40, 405

Brandenburg, 93n, 337, 384, 407

Brecht, Bertolt:

   The Exception and the Rule, 245, 274, 335, 353, 355, 401, 406

   Mother Courage and Her Children, xvi, 117, 234, 236–41, 243n, 400

Brentano, Lowell, 392

Brice, Fanny. *See Funny Girl*

Bridgehampton, N.Y., Robbins's beach house in, 327n, 341, 343, 374, 375, 384, 404

Britten, Benjamin, 103n, 109, 151

   Fanfare, 113, 151, 152, 184n, 187, 195, 198, 199, 265, 397, 398

Brook, Peter, 256n

Brothers Ashkenazi, The, 21, 30, 391

Bruhn, Erik, 402

Buckle, Richard, 245, 254

   Robbins's correspondence with, 233–5, 255–6, 264–5, 295

Burns, Robert Elliott, 16

Burrows, Abe, 397

Burton, Richard, 256, 259

Burton, Robert, 35

Burton, Scott, 229

Bye Bye Jackie, 89–90

Byrd Hoffman School of Byrds, New York, 273n

Cage, Betty, 281

Cage, The, 112, 125, 126, 133, 147, 148, 198, 255, 396, 404

Cahill, Gordon, Zachry, and Reindel, 120–1

Cahn, Sammy, 150n, 394

Cain, James M., 174n

Calegari, Maria, 381–3

Call Me Madam, 83–4, 86, 102, 106n, 107, 109, 111, 112, 115, 183n, 187, 368–9, 395

Camp Tamiment, 22, 23, 35–6, 37n, 39n, 40n, 45n, 55n, 362, 391, 392, 393

Candide, 172–3, 184n, 193

Cannibals, The, 245, 274

Cantinflas, 52

Capote, Truman, 194, 195

Capriccio Espagnol, 80

Caracole, 396

Carmen Jones, 77

Carnaval, 49

Carroll, Lewis, 342

CBS, 118n, 204n, 260n, 397

Celebration: The Art of the Pas de Deux, 303n, 402

Changelings, The (Sinclair), 177

Channing, Carol, 22, 35

Chanson Madécasses, 309n, 403

Chaplin, Sydney, *197*

Charisso, Nico, 35

Charlap, Mark "Moose," 163, 397

Chase, Lucia, 23, 57, 60, 72, 82n, 122n,
    254, 260

Châtelet Theatre, Paris, 383

Chekhov, Anton, 376
    "Reading Chekhov's Autobiography,"
    8–9

Chicago Lyric Opera, 23

China, Robbins's 1981 trip to, 248, 404

Chodorov, Jerome, 396

Chopin, Frédéric, 230, 246, 248, 278, 319n,
    377, 398, 401, 402, 403
    In the Night (to Chopin nocturnes),
    246, 336, 376, 380n, 402, 407
    Other Dances, 248, 319n, 403
    see also Dances at a Gathering

Christian Science Monitor, 307n

Chujoy, Anatole, 31, 33

Church, Sandra, *215*

Circus Polka, 296, 297–8, 402

City Ballet. *See* New York City Ballet

City Symphony Orchestra, 93n

Clarke, Harriet, 47

Clearing in the Woods, A, 172–7, 202

Clift, Montgomery, 85, 97n, 393, 394

Coca, Imogene, 22, 35, 38n

Coe, Fred, 250n

Cohen, Selma Jeanne, 161n

Cole, Jack, 91, 295, 336, 400

Coleman, Francis A., 89n

Comden, Betty, 82n, 83, 86, 114, 168, 173,
    191, *197*, 215n, 244, 393, 394, 396, 397,
    398
    The Skin of Our Teeth and, 256–60, 400

Comfort Corset Company, 3, 4, 12–13, 17,
    21, 25

Communist Party, 106n, 145n, 153n, 393
    nature of Robbins's affiliation with,
    84–5, 87

Robbins questioned by FBI about,
    111–12, 113, 114, 118–21, 395

Sullivan's allegations about Robbins's
    ties to, 111, 112n, 113, 118–21, 125n, 130,
    395
    see also House Un-American Activities
    Committee

Concert, The, 114, 218, 251, 398, 404

Concertino, 210

Concerto in G (later titled *In G Major*),
    308, 309, 320, 403

Conrad, Christine, 246, 247, *274*, *284*,
    321n, 401
    fraying of Robbins's relationship with,
    281–3, 284
    Robbins's therapist and, 275–6

Conrad, Karen, 44

Cook, Bart, 383

Cooper, Rex, 72, 75n

Copenhagen, Robbins's 1956 sojourn in,
    183–9, 398

Cophetua, 269, 270

Copland, Aaron, 148n, 234n, 355
    Pied Piper (to his Clarinet Concerto),
    113, 140–1, 147, 396
    Quiet City, 335, 344–5, 406
    The Tender Land, 114, 163, 165, 167, 397

Coppélia, 66–7

Corsaro, Frank, 315n

Counterattack, 118n, 119, 120

Cradle Will Rock, The, 109n

Crawford, Cheryl, 236, 237, 238, 240

Croce, Arlene, 309

Crooker, Earle, 392

Crosby, Bing, 143n

Crosse, Jenny Nicholson, 227n

Crouse, Russel, 102, 395

Cuddihy, John Murray: *The Ordeal of
    Civility*, 247, 248, 308, 318, 403

Cullinen, George (brother-in-law), 112n

Cullinen, Sonia Robbins (née Rabinowitz, sister), 3, 4, 9, 13–14, 16–17, 18, 26, 38, 80, 167n, 301, 317, 321
cummings, e. e., 4

Daganova, Ella, 391
Dale, Grover, 245, 358, 406
d'Amboise, Jacques, 339
Dance in America, 316n, 404, 405, 406
Dance Magazine, 31n, 89–90, 161n
Dance Magazine awards, 86, 204
Dances at a Gathering, 246, 278–80, 281, 283, 325n, 380n, 382, 401, 404
    staged for Royal Ballet, 287n, 402
Dancing for Life benefit (1987), 335
Danilova, Alexandra, 92
Dantine, Helmut, 74
Dark Pastorale, 196
Dassin, Jules, 150n, 396
Davis, Bette, 113, 150
Davis, Edward, 246, 247, 282–3, 284, 401
Debussy, Claude, 32, 133n
    Afternoon of a Faun, 113, 152, 162, 184, 220, 233, 251, 397, 404
    Antique Epigraphs, 334, 340, 381n, 405
    Ballade, 113, 220, 334, 396
de Cordova, Fred, 392
deGroat, Andy, 286n, 379, 383–4, 402
Dello Joio, Norman, 70n
de Mille, Agnes, 23, 54n, 71, 74, 82n, 204, 225
    The Book of Dance and, 252–3
Denby, Edwin, 86, 103, 105, 106
Depression, Great, 4, 21
Deren, Maya, 200
De Vries, Peter, 150n, 396
Dexter, John, 265–6, 267
Diaghilev, Sergei, 45n, 60n, 91, 246, 289n
Dial M for Murder, 259
Dietz, Howard, 392

Dinesen, Isak, 188n, 211
Dionysus, 269, 270, 271
Divertimento for Orchestra, 322–3
Dolin, Anton, 45, 47, 48
Dollar, William, 392
Donaldson Awards, xi, 112, 150n
Donehue, Vincent J., 166n
Don Quixote, 329
Dorati, Antal, 56
Dorso, Richard, 98
Double Exposure (McDowall), 242n
Dowling, Edward Duryea, 392
Doyle, Jerry, 120–1
Dramatists Guild, 343n, 344n
Dubin, Al, 392
Dudleston, Penelope, 342–3, 348–9
Dudley, Alice, 35
Duell, Joseph, 335, 344–5, 357, 405, 406
Duke, Vernon, 396
Dumbarton Oaks, 298, 402
Duncan, Irma, 4
Dunphy, Jack, 195n
Dybbuk, The, 114, 170–1, 247, 251, 306, 307, 349, 402

Earle, William, 321n
Egypt, Robbins's trips to, 248, 324, 341–2, 341n, 404
Eight Cousins (Alcott), 143n
Eight Jelly Rolls, 317
Eight Lines, 335, 405
Einstein, Cassandra, 374, 375
Ellis, Anita, 178
Epstein, Julius J. and Philip G., 99, 394
Ertegun, Ahmet, 339n, 341n, 365n, 405
Ertegun, Mica, 321n, 339n, 341n, 365n, 405
Euripides: *The Bacchae*, 244, 265–8, 401
Evening's Waltzes, An, 402
Events, 399

Everett, Horace, 397
Exception and the Rule, The, 245, 274, 335, 350, 353, 355, 401, 406

Facsimile, 84, 85, 96, 394
Fair at Sorochinsk, 76
Faison, George, 316n
Fancy Free, 24–5, 68–72, 74–5, 90, 91, 96, 118, 119, 226, 251, 255, 307, 313, 334, 404, 405
    adapted into *On the Town*, 83, 84, 86, 89n, 251, 393
    Balanchine's *Apollo* as inspiration for, 24, 79
    Bernstein's *Three Variations from*, 93–4
    dancers chosen for, 71–2, 79n
    danzon for, 24–5, 52n
    premiere of, 25, 71, 82, 393
    scenario for, 68–9
    score for, 24–5, 70, 78, 82, 93n, 109n, 393
    setting dance steps on principals for, 80, 81
    success of, 25, 82, 83
    title of, 71n
    trilogy idea based on (*Bye Bye Jackie*), 89–90
Fanfare, 113, 151, 152, 184n, 187, 195, 198, 199, 265, 397, 398
Fanny Brice. See Funny Girl
Farrán Sánchez, Ramón, 340
Farrell, Suzanne, 245, 246, 320, 329n, 383n
Faun, 251
FBI, 111–12, 113, 114, 118–21, 395
Feigay, Paul, 83
Fencing Dances and Exercises, 404
Ferber, Edna, 194n, 287
Fiddler on the Roof, 62, 117, 243, 244, 249–52, 254n, 256, 259, 264, 377, 400
    characters and community in, 249–50

as gift for Robbins's father, 244, 251–2
    score for, 250–1, 258
Fields, Dorothy, 392, 395
Fields, Joseph, 396
Fine, Sylvia, 38, 392
Firebird, 103, 402
Fischer-Dieskau, Dietrich, 351
Fitelson, William, 237
Fizdale, Robert, 86, 140, 141, 147n, 150, 196, 234n, 245, 265, 393
    death of, 336, 407
    photographs of, *102, 105, 169*
    Robbins's correspondence with, 101–3, 104–9, 115, 147–9, 209–12, 219–24, 228–30, 296–7, 330–1
    Weinstein's breakup with, 219n, 222–3
Fokine, Michel, 22, 49, 60–1, 64, 65, 225, 249, 376, 392, 393
Foote, Horton, 24, 54, 55, 57, 64, 150n, 392
Ford 50th Anniversary Show, 113, 397
Fornés, María Irene: *The Office*, 244, 267, 401
Foss, Lukas, 70n
Fosse, Bob, 164n, 243n, 398
Four Chamber Works, 366n, 404
Four Seasons, The, 248, 322, 323n, 380n, 404
Frankie & Johnny, 362
Franklin, Hugh, 81
Frazier, Shervert, 309, 310n, 313
Freedman, Gerald, 153n, 384–5, 406
Frohlich, Jean-Pierre, 366
Funny Girl (initially titled *Fanny Brice*), 117, 234, 235, 236, 241n, 242–3, 265n, 400
Funny Thing Happened on the Way to the Forum, A, 117, 214–15, 216, 233, 243n, 256n, 300n, 400

Gay, Madame (fortune teller), 79–80

Gelbart, Larry, 400

Gershwin, George, 196, 355

Gershwin Concerto, 326n, 327, 328, 381n, 404

Gerstein, Jesse, 248, 249, 321n, 324n, 325, 327–8, *329*, 332–3, 355, 358, 403, 404
  AIDS diagnosis, illness, and death of, 336, 365, 373–5, 406, 407
  Robbins's breakup and subsequent attempts at reconciliation with, 335, 336, 338–9, 405

Giant, 194

Gielgud, John, 268

Glass, Philip, 148n
  Akhnaten, 249, 332, 404, 405
  Glass Pieces, 332, 334, 338, 339, 366n, 380n, 382, 405

Godwin, Dwight S., 39

Gold, Arthur, 86, 102, *105*, 140, 147n, 196, 210, 211, 221, 229, 234n, 245, 265, 330n, 331, 393
  Robbins's correspondence with, 296–7

Goldberg Variations, 246, 251, 286–7, 288–9, 292, 307, 383, 402

Goldner, Nancy, 307n, 309

Goldoni, Carlo, 266n

Goldwyn Follies, The, 225, 295

Gomber, Mimi, 55

Goodman, Benny, 140–1

Gorey, Edward, 202

Gorsky, Alexander, 402

Gottlieb, Robert, 314, 330n

Gould, Glenn, 197–8

Gould, Morton, 70n, 83, 331n, 355, 393, 394, 405

Graham, Martha, 204, 225, 254, 317

Graves, Robert, 227n, 230, 287–8, 399
  hallucinogenic mushrooms taken by Robbins and, 117, 227–8, 399
  Robbins's correspondence with, 227–8, 269–72, 340–1
  The White Goddess, 230, 288

Great Lady, 22, 392

Great Migration, The, 194

Greece, Robbins's trips to, 132, 401

Green, Adolph, 82n, 83, 86, 114, 168, 173, *190*, *191*, 215n, 244, 393, 394, 396, 397, 398
  The Skin of Our Teeth and, 256–60, 400

Group Theatre, 21, 145n, 236n, 391

Guare, John, 245, 274, 335, 350, 353, 355, 406

Guests, The, 84, 85, 129n, 134, 395

Guillem, Sylvie, 247

Guthrie, Tyrone, 193

Gypsy, 62, 116, 180, 215, *215*, 216, 226, 243n, 344, 346n, 373n, 384n, 399

Halliday, Heller, 171–2

Halliday, Richard, 100–1, 163n, 168, 171n

Alexander Hamilton School, Weehawken, N.J., 391

Hamlet, 256

Hammerstein, Oscar, II, 112, 123–5, 151n, 395

Handel, George Frideric, 339, 404
  Brahms/Handel, 317n, 335, 339–40, 405

Haney, Carol, 166, 400

Harkness Ballet, 280, 288

Harlequinade, 322

Harnick, Sheldon, 117, 150n, 243, 250–1, 396, 400

Hart, Moss, 100–1, 367, 395

Hatcher, Tom, 172

Hawks, Howard, 183n

Hayden, Melissa, 104–5

Hayward, Leland, 115, 123n, 124, 163, 183, 188, 215n, 258, 399
  Robbins's correspondence with, 214–19

Hayward, Nancy "Slim." *See* Keith, Nancy "Slim" Hayward

Hayworth, Rita, 149n, 324, 331n

Helen of Troy, 23, 66

Hellman, Lillian, 193

High Button Shoes, 83, 98, 116, 394

Hit Dances. See Jerome Robbins's Broadway

Holliday, Judy, 196, *197*

Hollywood parties, 74, 229

Hoover, J. Edgar, 112, 121

Horgan, Barbara, 330, 333

House Un-American Activities Committee (HUAC), 84n, 113, 114, 318, 347, 395
  Kazan's statement to, 145
  Paramount offer and, 114, 142–3
  Robbins's decision to remain in Europe and, 113, 136–9
  Robbins's testimony to, 153n, 256n, 293, 397
  "Trial Scene" (from *The Poppa Piece*) and, 118n, 153–61

Houston Grand Opera, 332, 404

Hoyt, Harold, 118, 119, 120

Humphrey, Doris, 253

Hunger, 274

Hunter, Mary, 24, 163, 392

Hurok, Sol, 23, 50n, 57, 82n, 90, 92, 94, 217

Ifft, Ron, 312–13

I'm Old Fashioned (The Astaire Variations), 324, 331, 332, 334, 383, 405

Inbal Dance Theatre, 170, 397

In G Major, 308, 309, 320, 403

In Memory Of . . ., 334, 335, 337, 341, 343n, 365, 405, 406

Interplay, 84, 96, 195, 265, 303

In the Night, 246, 336, 376, 380n, 402, 407

In the Summer House, 109, 175n, 176

Introduction and Allegro for Harp, 309n, 403

Invitation to a Beheading (Nabokov), 266n

Island in the Sun (Waugh), 188

Israel, Robbins's trips to, 125n, 126, *131*, 131–2, 144–5, 284, 396, 397, 401

Italy, Robbins's travels in, 132, 134–6, 146–7, 297–300, 303–5, 402
  see also Spoleto, Italy

Ito, Teiji, 200n, 402

Ives, Charles, 351–2, 355

Ives, Songs, 335–6, 351–2, 353, 354, 356n, 359, 365, 406

"Ives Journal," 351–5, 358–61

"Ives Notebook," 356–7

Jacob's Pillow, 393

Japan, Robbins's 1991 trip to, 374

Jerome Robbins' Broadway (originally called *Hit Dances*), 336, 337, 338, 349, 350, 356n, 358, 361, 363, 364, 365, 365n, 368–9, 374n, 386, 406, 407

Jersey City, N.J., Robbins's early years in, 3, 7, 391

Jeux, 133

Jinx, 103

Johnny Johnson, 21, 391

Johnson, Albert, 92

Johnson, Philip, 255n

Jones, Clark, 397

Jones Beach, 395

Kahn, Otto H., 91, 92

Kanin, Garson, 243, 400

Karnilova, Maria, *62*

Karson, Nat, 46

Kaufman, George S., 397

Kaufman, S. Jay, 392

Kavan, Albia, 39, 40, *41*, 66, 75

Kaye, Danny, 22, 35

Kaye, Nora, 24, 55, 66, 72, 75n, *77*, 79, 82,
      126, 129, 148, 150n, 166, 171, 181, 203,
      221, 265, 319n, 357
   death and memorial of, 122, 150, 336,
      357, 358, 406
   Robbins's romantic relationship with,
      112, 113, 121–2, 125n, 395

Kazan, Elia, 145, 237n

Keep Off the Grass, 22, 23, 44–7, 48n, 81n,
      392

Keith, Nancy "Slim" Hayward, 115, *217*,
      321n, 336, 355, 395, 399, 402, 406
   Robbins's correspondence with,
      183–9

Kelly, Gene, 91

Kennedy, Jacqueline, 233, 400

Kennedy, John F., 116, 233–4, 400

Kennedy Center Honors, 248, 326,
      404

Kern, Jerome, 331n, 405

Kerouac, Jack, 212n

Kerr, Deborah, 177

Kerr, Walter, 150n

Khan, Aly, 149

Kiesler, Frederick, 198n

King and I, The, 112–13, 123–5, 172n, 177,
      243n, 259n, 395, 398
   photographs of filming, *174*, *176*

King Lear, 109, 256

Kipness, Joe, 98–9

Kirkpatrick, Theodore C., 119–20, 121

Kirov Ballet (later Mariinsky Ballet), 319n,
      336, 376, 407

Kirstein, Lincoln, 114, 132, 133, 136, 140,
      196n, 213, 224, 247, 255, 302n, 314,
      331, 332n, 336, 337
   death of, 407

   retirement from New York City Ballet,
      336, 367, 406
   Robbins's correspondence with, 130,
      170–1, 254–5, 277, 280–1, 349, 367,
      370

Kissel, Howard, 363n

Kisselgoff, Anna, 345n, 359n

Kiss Me, Kate, 75

Klugman, Jack, *215*

Kober, Arthur, 396

Koon, Alpheus, 80

Kopit, Arthur: *Oh Dad, Poor Dad,
      Mamma's Hung You in the Closet and
      I'm Feelin' So Sad*, 117, 235n, 249n,
      399, 400

Korean War, 106n, 111

Kraft, Victor, 87

Krahn, Meta, 55

Kriegsman, Alan M., 343n

Kriza, John, 24, 57, 72, 74, 76, 79, 81, *95*,
      95, *99*, 313

Kroll, Jack, 363n

Laing, Hugh, 74, *77*, 129, 222n

Lanchester, Elsa, 259

Lang, Harold, 24, 71–2, 76, 81, 94

Lang, Walter, 177, 398

Larkin, Kenny, 258–9

Laurents, Arthur, 75, 84, 86, 114, 116, *180*,
      184n, 216, 319n, 335, 399
   article for *New York Times* written by,
      211–12
   A Clearing in the Woods and, 172–7
   Robbins's correspondence with, 165–7,
      172–82, 363
   West Side Story and, 114, 172–5, 178–81,
      212n, 231, 343–4, 394, 398

Lawrence, Jerome, 84, 97–8, 394

Lax, James, 373–4

Le Clercq, Tanaquil, 84, 105, 147, 148,
    152n, 222, 297, 319, 321n, 330, 331, 395,
    396
    Balanchine's marriage to, 112, 113, 115,
        116, 133, 190, 245
    photographs of, *127, 133, 152, 199, 205,
        210, 211,* 381n
    polio contracted by, 116, 139n, 192, 193,
        195, 334, 398
    return to New York, 205–8, 211
    Robbins's relationship with, 85–6, 112,
        113, 115–16, 138–9, 200–8, 381n
    Robbins's correspondence with, xv, 113,
        115, 116, 125–6, 128–9, 131–9, 189–92,
        193–208, 230
    in Robbins's dream, 381
    Robbins's "moonsprite" ballet and,
        138–9, 140
    in Spoleto, 303, 304, 402
    at Warm Springs, 209n, *210, 211*
Le Clercq, Edith, 116, 195n, 208n, 222
Lee, Gypsy Rose, 116, 215n, 237n
    see also Gypsy
Lee, Ming Cho, 240
Lee, Robert E., 84, 97–8, 394
Leigh, Carolyn, 163, 397
Leisen, Mitchell, 74
Lennart, Isobel, 235, 241, 400
Leonidoff, Leon, 148
Lerman, Leo, 203
Lerner, Alan Jay, 236n, 248, 315, 403
LeRoy, Mervyn, 373n
Lester, Edwin, 163–4
Let's Make an Opera, 109
Levi-Tanai, Sara, 380–1
Levy, Parke, 392
Lewis, Mort, 392
Lichine, David, 76
Liebman, Max, 22, 392

Life, 195–6
Limón, José, 21, 81
Lincoln Center for the Performing Arts,
    254, 255
Lincoln Center Theater, 153n, 335, 406,
    407
Lindsay, Howard, 102, 395
Lipscott, Alan, 392
Live from Studio 8H, 404
Locke, Sam, 392
Loewe, Frederick, 236n, 315n, 392
Logan, Joshua, 392, 396
Long Day's Journey into Night, 193–4
Longstreet, Stephen, 394
Look, Ma, I'm Dancin'!, 84, 86, 96, 97–8,
    125n, 142n, 394
Lopez, Lourdes, 366, 385
Loring, Eugene, 23, 44, 48, 166n, 397
Los Angeles Civic Light Opera, 163n,
    166n, 168n
Lubitsch, Ernst, 166n
Lumet, Sidney, 243n
Lynes, George Platt, 106, 224
Lyon, Annabelle, 44, 55

MacGrath, Leueen, 397
MacLeish, Archibald, 92
Magallanes, Nicholas, 129, 133, 222
Makarova, Natalia, 247, 376, 403
Ma Mère l'Oye (Mother Goose), 309n,
    403
Mariinsky Ballet (former Kirov Ballet),
    319n, 336, 376, 407
Markova, Alicia, 57, 74
Martin, Hugh, 98, 394
Martin, John, 21, 25, 26, 40, 82, 162n,
    234
Martin, Mary, 100–1, 163n, 168, 171n, 397
Martinez, Enrique, 402

Martins, Peter, 323, 339n, 349, 360n, 381n, 403, 404
  as Balanchine's successor, 330–1, 332, 405
  performance of *In G Major* excerpt and, 320
Mason, Francis, 362
Massine, Léonide, 65, 80n
Maule, Michael, 71
Mazzo, Kay, 362
McBride, Patricia, 277n, 303
McCarran Act, 106n, 111
McDonald, Jeannette, 109
McDowall, Roddy, 242n
McEvoy, J. P., 392
McHugh, James, 392
McLean Hospital, Belmont, Mass., 248, 310–14, 403
Me and Juliet, 151n, 166
Meehan, Brian, 335, 336, 341, 358, 365, 386, 405
Meeropol, Abel, 40n, 392
Menotti, Gian Carlo, 148, 196n, 214n
Mercer, Johnny, 331
Merman, Ethel, 84, 102, 106n, 107, 187, *215*, 216n, 258, 368, 395, 397
Merrick, David, 215n, 216
Merrill, Bob, 400
Merry Widow, The, 259
Metropolitan Opera House, 92
  Fancy Free premiere at, 25, 82, 393
Mexico City, Ballet Theatre's summer seasons in, 23, 50–4, 60, 61–4, 393
MGM, 115
Midgette, Allen, 245, 283–5
Miller, Buzz, 113, 115, 126, 132, 148, 150n, 166, 177, 182, 189n, 209–10, 222, 223, 334, 396, 397
  photographs of, *129*, *144*, *169*
  Robbins's correspondence with, 143–7, 150–3, 167–70

Mishima, Yukio, 272n
Miss Liberty, 83, 100–1, 125n, 367–9, 395
"Mr. Monotony," 368, 369
Mitchell, Ruth, *197*, 243
Molostwoff, Natasha, 222
Moncion, Francisco, 136n, 152n, *184*, 196n
Mooney, Aidan, 298–9, 303, 304, 321n, 402
Moore, Marjorie, 47
Morris, June, 79
Moses, Gilbert, 316n
Mostel, Zero, 250n, 256, 258, 323
  Robbins's diary entry on death of, *257*
Mother Courage and Her Children, xvi, 117, 234, 236–41, 243n, 400
Mother Goose (Ma Mère l'Oye), 309n, 403
Motokiyo, Zeami, 245, 246, 272–3
Moves: A Ballet in Silence, 225–6, 284, 380n, 399
Moylan, Mary Ellen, 204
Mozart, Wolfgang Amadeus, 304, 396
  Rondo, 230, 323, 404
Munshin, Jules, 35
Muses Are Heard, The (Capote), 194
Music Theater of Lincoln Center, 259n

Nabokov, Vladimir, 229, 266
Nash, Ogden, 150n, 396
National Council of Arts, Sciences, and Professions, 118n
National Endowment for the Arts (NEA), 244, 268n, 401
National Theatre, Britain's (now Royal National Theatre), 244, 265–8, 401
Navasky, Victor, 293n
NBC, 397, 404
New Dance Group, 391
Newsweek, 277n, 363n
New York City Ballet (NYCB), 103, 126n, 129n, 130n, 254–5, 260n, 280–1, 288n, 314n, 394–5

American Music Festival (1988), 355, 360
Baryshnikov's move to, 319, 403
cancellation of 1953 fall season, 152
China trip of dancers from (1981), 404
difficulties in Robbins's relationship
    with, 265, 277n
European tours of, 103, 104–6, 112,
    115–16, 136, 144n, 147–8, 189n, 191
formed by Balanchine, 84
joined by Robbins, 84, 394
Kirstein's retirement from, 336, 367, 406
Ravel Festival (1975), 247–8, 308, 309
Robbins Festival (1990), 370
Robbins named associate artistic
    director of, 84, 100n, 280n, 394
Robbins's choreography for, 84, 85–6,
    114, 226, 246–9, 277, 395, 396, 401,
    407. *See also specific ballets*
Robbins's contract negotiations with,
    302n
Robbins's extended sojourn in Europe
    and (1951), 113, 136–9
Robbins's retirement from full-time
    participation in, 365, 380, 406
Saratoga Springs summer residencies,
    281, 300–1
Stravinsky Festival (1972), 246, 292n,
    295–8, 323, 402
succession scuffle at, 249, 330–1, 332,
    405
Tchaikovsky Festival (1981), 248, 323–4,
    404
*see also specific ballets, choreographers,
    and dancers*
New York City Center, 163n, 254n, 266n
New York City Opera, 404
New York *Daily News*, 363n
New York Herald Tribune, 126n, 150n, 162n
New York magazine, 359n
New York Philharmonic, 24

New York Post, 212n
New York Public Library, xii, xv, xvi, 336,
    337–8, 400, 407
New York State Theater (now David H.
    Koch Theater), 255, 256, 260, 335
New York Times, 21, 25, 83, 85, 162n, 211–12,
    234n, 276, 294, 345n, 359n, 363, 367n
    Robbins's essay on *Les Noces*, 260–3, 264
    Robbins's "The Ballet Puts On
        Dungarees," 90–3
New York Times Book Review, 293n
New York University, Robbins as student
    at, 21, 25, 391
Nichols, Mike, 373
Nick (Robbins's terrier), 312, 314, 327, 336,
    358, 359–60, 402–3, 406
Nijinska, Bronislava, 23, 261, 376
Nijinsky, Vaslav, 60n, 61, 90, 91, 133n, 246,
    289, 295n, 314n, 376
Nillo, David, 45, 47, 48
92nd Street YMHA, 31–3, 40n, 362n, 392
Ninotchka, 166
Noailles, Marie-Laure de, 140, 141
Noces, Les, 244, 254n, 260–3, 264, 265,
    269–70, 281n, 284, 337, 385, 400,
    407
Noh plays, 246, 270, 271–3
    Watermill and, 246, 272n, 290n, 291
    Zeami and, 245, 246, 272–3
Nordoff, Paul, 70
Noverre, Jean-Georges, 322
Nutcracker, 381, 383, 397
N.Y. Export: Opus Jazz, 213n, 218n, 220,
    224–5, 233, 251, 280–1, 380n, 398, 399
    photographs of, *213, 214*

O'Brien, Edna, 247, 287–8, 340, 402
    Robbins's correspondence with, 377–8
Odets, Clifford, 182n
Office, The, 244, 267, 401

Oh Dad, Poor Dad, Mamma's Hung You in the Closet and I'm Feelin' So Sad, 117, 235n, 249n, 399, 400
Olivier, Sir Laurence, 266, 267, 268
Omnibus, 204
O'Neill, Eugene, 193–4
On the Town, 83, 84, 86, 89n, 175n, 251, 393
Opus 19/The Dreamer, 248, 323n, 404
Ordeal of Civility, The (Cuddihy), 247, 248, 308, 318, 403
Original Story (Laurents), 178n, 179n
Oscars. *See* Academy Awards
Osgood, Larry, 202
Other Dances, 248, 319n, 352, 403, 404
Otis (Robbins's affenpinscher), *144*, 151, 152, 170
Out of Africa (Dinesen), 188

Page, Geraldine, 236–7, 238
Paige, Janis, 166
Pajama Game, The, 114, 115, 164–5, 166, 167, 173, 397
Pal Joey, 144n, 151n
Panama & Frank, 392
Paramount, 75, 114, 142–3
Paris, *123*, *139*
    apartment leased by Robbins in, 406
    Robbins's 1950–52 sojourns in, 103, 112, 121–9, 136–9, 140, 142, 143, 147–9, 395
Paris Opera Ballet, 380
Parnova, Lisa, 22, 31–3, 392
Pas de Deux (*Andantino*), 404
Pas de Trois, 394
Pavlova, Anna, 90, 91, 376
Payne, Charles, 24, 53, 54, 57, 64, 67, 76
    Robbins's correspondence with, 71–5
Pennington, Ann, 51
Perkins, Tony, 245
Perlin, Bernard, 224–7

Persichetti, Vincent, 70n
Peter and the Wolf, 55
Peter Pan, 114, 115, 163–4, 166, 168, 170, 171n, 173, 181, 397
    Taylor's account of breaking his nose in, 345–7
Petipa, Marius, 322, 376, 402
Petrouchka (or *Petrushka*), 23, 24, 60, 61, 65–7, 112, 121, 246, 393
Philadelphia Inquirer, 113
Piano Pieces, 325, 404
Piccolo Balletto, 406
Piccolo Teatro di Milano, 266n
Pied Piper, 113, 140–1, 147, 198, 396
Piero della Francesca, 299
Pinska, Klarna, 29
Pinter, Sir Harold, 312
Plautus, Titus Maccius, 211, 214n
Playbill, 301–2
Pleasant, Richard, 48
Poppa Piece, The, 86, 109–10, 114, 115, 118n, 336–7, 341, 374, 384n, 403, 406–7
    "Collecting," 109–10
    "A Different Ending," 386–7
    "A Last Conversation," 167
    "Prologue," 370–1
    "Trial Scene," 118n, 153–61
Porter, Cole, 75n, 114, 166n, 196
Prendergast, Maurice, 335–6, 351–2, 354
Preston, Robert, 259
Prince, Harold, 233n, 250n
Prince, Robert, 213n, 398, 399
Prince Igor, 92, 392
Private Domain (Taylor), 345–7
Prodigal Son, 84, 86, 106, 136, 225, 395
Prokofiev, Sergei, 106, 394, 395, 397, 402
    Opus 19/The Dreamer, 248, 323n, 404
Public Theater, 323n
Pulcinella, 296, 298, 301, 402

Quartet, 167, 220, 397

Quiet City, 335, 344–5, 406

Quintero, José, 109n

Rabinowitz (grandfather), 3, 4, 8

Rabinowitz, Harry (father). *See* Robbins, Harry

Rabinowitz, Jerry. *See* Robbins, Jerome

Rabinowitz, Lena Rips (mother). *See* Robbins, Lena Rips

Rabinowitz, Sonia (sister). *See* Cullinen, Sonia Robbins

Race to Urga, The, 353n, 406

    see also *The Exception and the Rule*

Raitt, John, 166

Randall, Carl, 392

Ravel, Maurice:

    In G Major, 308, 309, 320, 403

    New York City Ballet's 1975 Ravel Festival, 247–8, 308, 309

Razor's Edge, The, 259n

Redgrave, Vanessa, 309

Reed, Janet, 79, 81

Reed, Richard, 38, *66*, 71, 79

Reich, Steve: *Eight Lines*, 335, 405

Reid, Alastair, 230

Requiem Canticles, 292, 296, 298, 402

Resnik, Muriel, 198

Reuben, Reuben, 109

Rich, Frank, 363

Richardson, Ralph, 268n

Rimsky-Korsakov, Nikolai, 80n

Rips, Ida (grandmother), 17

Rips, Isaac (grandfather), 17n

Rips, Lena (mother). *See* Robbins, Lena Rips

Ritchard, Cyril, 168

Rittman, Trude, 125n

Rivera, Chita, *208*, 235, 259

Robbins, Frieda (stepmother), 301, 317n, 321, 348, 349, 350, 358n

Robbins, Harry (né Rabinowitz, father), 3, 4, 7, 13, 17, 21, 23, 25, 29, 30, 82n, 167, 376–7

    declining health and death of, 247, 248, 301, 306, 317, 321, 402, 403

    Fiddler on the Roof and, 244, 251–2

    Jewishness of, 14–15

    journey to America, 5–6

    photograph of, *252*

    The Poppa Piece and, 341, 370

    son's correspondence with, 50–4, 61–4

    son's personal notes about, 251–2

    son's relationship with, 7, 14–15, 223, 247, 306, 318

    son's visit to factory of, 12–13

Robbins, Jerome:

    acid trip of (1969), 284–5, 290n, 291n

    acting classes taken by, 201, 204, 394

    artwork, xiii, 4; collages, 290n; dance figure studies, *32, 33, 279*; Mexico sketchbook, *52*; Spoleto sketchbook, *305, 359*; Weehawken drawings, *6*

    ballet classes and training of, 21–2, 30, 31–2, 37, 391

    bar mitzvah of, 3, 15, 391

    born Jerome (or Gershon) Wilson Rabinowitz, 3, 391

    childhood and teenage years of, 3–4, 7–20, 391

    choreographic career launched by, 22. *See also Fancy Free*

    on choreographic process, 101, 161–2, 224–7, 269, 278–80, 286–7

    in college, 21, 25, 391

    commercial musical theater disillusionment with, 244, 264, 269

Robbins, Jerome *(continued)*:
  Communist affiliations of, 106n, 318,
    393; FBI interview and, 111–12, 113,
    114, 118–21, 395; peripheral nature
    of, 84–5, 87; Sullivan's allegations
    and, 111, 112n, 113, 118–21, 125n, 130,
    395. *See also* House Un-American
    Activities Committee
  correspondence of, xv–xvi; to Abbott,
    164–5; to Arkin, 100, 103–4, 350; to
    Balanchine, 192; to Barnes, 294; to
    Bentley, 239–40; to Bergman, 289–
    90; to Berlin, 355–6; to Bernstein,
    89–90, 93–4, 178–9, 212–13, 231, 263,
    322–3, 361–2; to Bernstein's children
    and brother, 372–3; to Bock, 250–1;
    to Buckle, 233–5, 255–6, 264–5,
    295; to Calegari, 381–3; to deGroat,
    379, 383–4; to de Mille, 252–3; to
    Dexter, 265–6; to Dudleston, 342–3,
    348–9; to Einstein, 375; to Fizdale,
    101–3, 104–9, 115, 147–9, 209–12,
    219–24, 228–30, 296–7, 330–1; to
    Freedman, 384–5; to Gold, 296–7;
    to Graves, 227–8, 269–72, 340–1; to
    H. Halliday, 171–2; to R. Halliday,
    100–1; to Hammerstein, 123–5; to
    Harnick, 250–1; to L. Hayward,
    214–19; to "Slim" Hayward (later
    Keith), 183–9; to *himself* on his
    "Jerome Robbins" stationery and
    found sealed in an envelope, 338,
    386; to Kanin, 243; to Kirstein, 130,
    170–1, 254–5, 277, 280–1, 349, 367,
    370; to Laurents, 165–7, 172–82, 363;
    to Lawrence, 97–8; to Le Clercq,
    xv, 113, 115, 116, 125–6, 128–9, 131–9,
    189–92, 193–208, 230; to Lee, 97–8;
    to Lennart, 241; to Levi-Tanai, 380–1;
    to Lopez, 366, 385; to M. Martin,
    100–1; to P. Martins, 320; to Mason,
    362; to Midgette, 283–5; to Miller,
    143–7, 150–3, 167–70; to Mitchell,
    243; to Nichols, 373; to O'Brien,
    377–8; to Olivier, 268; to parents,
    50–4, 61–4; to Payne, 71–5; to
    Rorem, 140–3; to Saddler, 45, 46–7,
    76–80, 94–7; to O. Smith, 326; to
    Sondheim, 343–4; to Talbot, 70;
    to Taylor, 345–7; to Tynan, 266–8;
    to Wilson, 273–4, 288–9; to Wise,
    232–3; to Zipprodt, 249–50
  on costumes' impact on ballet, 220
  dancing career launched by, 4, 21–4,
    26–8, 30–3, 35–49
  death of, 337, 407
  depressions suffered by, 248, 284, 291,
    301, 361
  diaries of, 247; "Diary, 1934–35," 17–19;
    "Diary, 1942," 54–7, 64–7; Mostel's
    death and, *257*
  disenchanted with his life as dancer, 114,
    142, 147, 396
  dreams of, 9–10, 151–2, 291–2, 302–3,
    319, 354, 381
  first directorial job of, 84, 98–9
  first opera directed by, 114
  hallucinogenic mushrooms taken by,
    117, 227–8, 399
  health problems and injuries of, 185,
    247, 284–5, 288, 291, 320, 321n,
    336, 337, 383, 401, 402, 403, 406,
    407
  homosexuality of, 23, 28–9, 55n, 80–1,
    85, 86, 111, 247, 292, 293, 301–2
  Jewish heritage of, 3, 4, 14–15, 16, 17, 113,
    114, 117, 131, 244, 247, 318, 341, 370–1,
    377

journals, 25, 111, 247; "Bodrum Journal, 1984," 339–40; "Conversations & Hospital & Illness," 301, 306; "Dream of Tanny," 381; "Egypt-Turkey Journal (Excerpt)," 341–2; "Ives Journal," 351–5, 358–61; Journal #2 (1972), 297–300; Journal #3 (1972), 300–1, 302; Journal #4 (1973), 301–2; Journal #6 (1973), 302–3; Journal #7 (1973), 303–4; Journal #8 (1973), 304–5; Journal #9 (1974), 306–7; Journal #11 (1974), 307–8; Journal #12 (1975), 308, 309; Journal #13 (1975), 310–14; Journal #14 (1976), 315; Journal #15 (1976), 315; Journal #16 (1976), 319; Journal #18 (1977), 321; Journal #20 (1978), 321–2; Journal #22A (1981–82), 327–8; Journal #24 (1982–83), 328–30, 331–3, 338–9; "Journal, 1939," 37–41; "Journal, 1950," 121–2; "London 1970 Journal," 287–8; "London Journal, 1971," 11–12; "St. Bart's Journal," 344–5; "*Skin* Log" (1964), 256–60; "Spring 1944 Journal," 80–2; "Stravinsky Journal" (1972), 295; typed on loose sheets of foolscap, 37n; written in Japanese notebooks of hand-milled accordion-folded paper, 290; "Yucatán–New York Journal, February–March 1970," 286–7

limericks by, 200–1, 203

marionettes and puppetry as interest of, 25–6

memorial tributes by: for Berlin, 367–9; for Kaye, 122, 150, 357

in mental hospital, 248, 310–14, 403

name changed by, 21, 391

New York residences of, 87, 198n, 321n, 338, 393, 394, 397, 401, 407

notes and notebooks: on Balanchine's response to Baryshnikov, 319; "Barbra: Some Notes," 242; "*Dances at a Gathering* Notes," 278–80; "Day-to-Day Notes Telling Story of *Mother Courage*," 236–9; "Doctor/Chris (Notes)," 275–6; "Ives Notebook," 356–7; "Nora Kaye Memorial, Notes," 122, 150; "Notes (1969)," 283; "Notes (1970)," 285; "Notes (Summer 1969)," 281–3; "Notes, Etc. (1989–1991)," 364–5, 373–4; "Notes for Nora Kaye Memorial, January 5, 1988," 357; "Poppa Piece (Personal Notes)," 251–2; "St. Petersburg–Paris Notes," 375–7; "Summer 1990 Notes," 372; on thoughts about existence, 276

photographs, xiii, 108, 136, 206, *387*; of Balanchine, *79*, *101*, *133*; of Ballets: U.S.A., *213*, *214*, *220*, *223*; of Ballet Theatre, xiii, *49*, *62*, *66*, *73*, *77*, *79*; of Baronova, *56*; of *Bells Are Ringing*, *190*, *191*, *195–6*, *197*; of Comden, *191*; of Conrad, *274*; of Fizdale, *102*, *105*, *169*; of Gerstein, *329*; of Gold, *105*; of Green, *190*, *191*; of *Gypsy* orchestra rehearsal, *215*; of "Slim" Hayward (later Keith), *217*; of himself, *108*, *210*; of his father, *252*; of Kavan, *41*; of *The King and I* filming, *174*, *175*; of Kriza, *95*, *99*; of Laurents and Sondheim, *180*; of Le Clercq, *127*, *133*, *152*, *199*, *205*, *210*, *211*, 381n; of Miller, *129*, *144*, *169*; of Moncion, *184*; of Paris, *123*, *139*; in photo booths, *99*; of Royal Danish Ballet School, *187*; of Saddler, *46*, *62*; of Steinberg, *218*; of *West Side Story*, *207*, *208*; of Yemenite folk dancers, *131*

Robbins, Jerome *(continued)*:
    poetry, 4; "Jerry Rabinowitz Poetry &
      Music Compositions," 9–11
    pronounced "unfit for service" by draft
      board, 55n, 71, 393
    psychoanalysis of, 82, 86, 87, 100, 101–2,
      275–6, 350, 393
    published articles: "The Ballet Puts On
      Dungarees," 90–3; "Out on a Limb
      with Lucia" (published under title
      "Robbins on 'Les Noces'"), 260–3,
      264
    romantic life of, 23, 24, 39, 40, *41*, 85,
      87–8, 101n, 111, 112, 113, 115, 121–2,
      125n, 245–6, 247, 248, 249, 281–3,
      325n, 327–8, 332–3, 335, 336, 401, 405
    schooling of, 3–4, 15–17, 18, 19–20, 21,
      391
    sixtieth birthday of, 321–2
    sixty-fifth birthday of, 335
    seventieth birthday of, 370
    will and bequests of, 337–8, 341
    writings: "Auditions," 42–4; "The
      Ballet Puts On Dungarees," 90–3;
      "Ed Sullivan, 1950," 118–21; "The
      Factory," 12–13; "Family Life," 7,
      15–17; "Flopping," 31–3; "Furnished
      Room," 33–5; "Grandpa," 8; "How I
      Almost Did Not Become a Dancer,"
      25–8; "Interim Years," 82, 87–8; "The
      Jew Piece," 14–15; "Jury Duty," 347;
      "My City," 88–9; "My Selves: An
      Attempt to Express My Character as
      I *See* It, by Jerry Rabinowitz, English
      12," 19–20; "Poppa: Getting to the
      U.S.A.," 5–6; "Reading Chekhov's
      Autobiography," 8–9; "Sister—
      Family Continued," 13–14; "The
      Story of Hands," 28–9; "Tamiment,"
      35–6; "The Times of the 1930s and

1940s—Being a Jew," 318; "Thoughts
    on Choreography," 161–2; "Training,"
    60–1; "Training: Yiddish Art Theatre
    and Classes," 30–1; "Untitled Stories,"
    58–60; "Working with Lenny," 182–3
    see also Poppa Piece, The; *specific ballets,*
    films, and shows
Robbins, Lena Rips (formerly Rabinowitz,
    mother), 3, 4, 9, 11–12, 13, 14, 17, 25,
    30, 38, 40, 82n, 318, 376–7, 398
    death of, 115, 167, 222–3, 397
    son's correspondence with, 50–4, 61–4
    son's poetry for and about, 9, 10–11
Robbins, Sonia (sister). *See* Cullinen,
    Sonia Robbins
Jerome Robbins Archive of the Recorded
    Moving Image, 336
Jerome Robbins Dance Division at the
    New York Public Library for the
    Performing Arts, xii, 337–8
Jerome Robbins Festival (1990), 370
Jerome Robbins Foundation, 337, 398
Rodeo, 91
Rodgers, Richard, 92, 112, 123n, 151n, 395
Rome, Harold, 99, 394, 396
Romeo and Juliet, 81
    updated to modern urban setting,
    114–15, 172–5, 394, 398. *See also West*
    Side Story
Rondo, 230, 323, 404
Rooney, Mickey, 74
Rorem, Ned, 113, 140–3, 396
Rose, Billy, 393
Rosenberg, Julius and Ethel, 106n, 111
Rosenstock, Milton, *215*
Ross, Herbert, 265, 319n, 396
Ross, Jerry, 164n, 397
Royal Ballet, 402
Royal Danish Ballet, 184n, 185–7, 190, 398
Royal Danish Ballet School, 185–6, *187*

Royal Shakespeare Company, 256
Royal Swedish Ballet, 271n, 284
Rozhanka, Poland, Robbins's 1924 trip to, 3, 7–8, 391
Rubbra, Edmund, 339n, 405
Russia, Robbins's trips to, 281, 284, 336, 375–7, 401, 407

Sacre du Printemps, Le, 295
Saddler, Donald, 24, *46*, 48, *62*, 66, 396
    photographs of, *46*, *62*
    Robbins's correspondence with, 45, 46–7, 76–80, 94–7
St. Bart's, Robbins's holidays in, 344–5, 353–4, 364
Saint-Subber, Arnold, 75n
Saltzman, Harry, 289n
Sandor, Senya Gluck, 21, 26–8, 30, 31, 81n, 391
San Francisco Civic Light Opera, 163n, 166n
Saratoga Springs, N.Y., New York City Ballet's summer season in, 281, 300–1
Sarg, Anthony Frederick, 21, 26
Sartre, Jean-Paul, 266
Scheherazade, 92, 392
Scheidt, Edward, 112n
Schell, Orville, 332
Scherzo Fantastique, 402
Schneider, Alan, 171n
Schönberg, Bessie, 391
School of American Ballet, 130n, 297n, 337, 380, 407
Schwartz, Arthur, 392, 395
Schwartz, Maurice, 30–1, 52
Scofield, Paul, 256
Seibert, Wallace, 55
Selznick, Irene Mayer, 355

Sennett, Matt, 143n
Serenade (adaptation of Cain novel), 174
Serenade (ballet), 103
Servant of Two Masters, 266
Sevastianoff, German, 57
Shah of Iran, 234
Shakespeare, William, 179n, 180–1, 187, 192, 256, 269n
Sharaff, Irene, *176*, 193, 259
She Loves Me, 243, 250n
Shelton, James, 392
Sherman, Charles, 396
Sherwood, Robert E., 367, 395
Shevelove, Burt, 400
Shubert Foundation, 361n
Siegel, Marcia, 263n, 309, 359n
Siegel, R. Lawrence, 154n
Siegmeister, Elie, 70n
Silk Stockings, 114, 166n, 397
Silvers, Phil, 259
Simonne, Julia, 340
Sinclair, Jo, 177
Singer, I. J., 21
1600 Pennsylvania Avenue, 248, 315–16, 403
Sketch Book, A, 404
Skin of Our Teeth, The, 166, 167n, 244, 256–60, 263, 400
Sleeping Beauty, *73*
Smith, Betty, 395
Smith, Oliver, 25, 82n, 83, 86, 87, 88, 96n, 98, 109, 175–7, 193, 195, 221, 258–9, 263, 326, 393
Snedens Landing, N.Y., *102*, 245, 256, 286–7, 297
    house rented by Robbins in, 234, 248, 309, 400, 403
Snow, Edgar, 85
Snuff (Robbins's dog), 134, 151n
Solo, 404

Sondheim, Stephen, 116, *180*, 214–15, 245,
    258n, 274, 335
    *A Funny Thing Happened on the Way to
        the Forum* and, 214–15, 216, 400
    Gypsy and, 215, 216, 399
    West Side Story and, 114, 180–1, 231,
        343–4, 398
Spoleto, Italy, 214–19, *217*, 296–7, 299, *329*,
    406
    Festival dei Due Mondi in, 116, 213, 214,
        227n, 303n, 398, 399, 402
    journal entries written at (1973), 303–5
    journal entry written on flight to (1972),
        297–8
    Robbins's vision of deceased loved ones
        in, 356–7, 358
    sketches at municipal pool in, *305*
    Spoleto sketchbook, *359*
Stack-O-Lee, 64n
Stark, Ray, 234n, 235n, 242n, 243
Stars in Your Eyes, 22, 45n, 392
State Department, U.S., 116, 234
Stein, Joseph, 117, 250n, 400
Steinberg, Saul, 218, *218*, 221
Stern, Daniel, 245, 321n, 355
Stevens, Onslow, 202
Stonewall riots (1969), 247
Storey, David, 312
Strange Fruit, 40n, 362, 392
Strange Interlude, 237
Strauss, Richard, 33, 93, 130, 396
Stravinsky, Igor, 93, 148–9, 227, 229,
    396
    Circus Polka, 296, 297–8, 402
    Concertino, 210
    Firebird, 103, 402
    Les Noces, 244, 254n, 260–3, 264, 265,
        269–70, 337, 385, 400, 407
    New York City Ballet's 1972 Stravinsky
        Festival, 246, 292n, 295–8, 323, 402

Petrouchka (or *Petrushka*), 23, 24, 60, 61,
    65–7, 112, 121, 246, 393
Piccolo Balletto, 406
Pulcinella, 296, 298, 301, 402
Requiem Canticles, 292, 296, 298, 402
Scherzo Fantastique, 402
Stravinsky Violin Concerto, 296
Straw Hat Revue, 22, 37–9, 392
Streep, Meryl, 323
Streisand, Barbra, 242, 243n, 400
Styne, Jule, 116, 168n, 215n, 216n, 344n,
    394, 397, 398, 399, 400
Suite of Dances, A, 337, 380, 407
Sullivan, Ed, 111, 112n, 113, 118–21, 125n,
    130, 218n, 395, 399
Summer Day, 394
Swados, Elizabeth, 323n
Swan Lake, 225
Sweden, Robbins's 1969 trip to, 281n, 284,
    401
Sweet Bird of Youth, 236
Symphony in C, 103
Symphony in Three Movements, 296
Symphony in Winds, 296
Szabo, George, 354

Tabori, George, 245, 274n
Talbot, Alden, 70
Tallchief, Maria, 112, 133–4, 225
Tamiment. *See* Camp Tamiment
Taming of the Shrew, The, 75
Tanner, Richard, 381n
Taras, John, 254–5, 296, 339
Taylor, Paul, 345–7
Tchaikovsky, Pyotr Ilyich:
    New York City Ballet Tchaikovsky
        Festival (1981), 248, 323–4, 404
    Theme and Variations, 224
Telemann, Georg Philipp, 404
Tender Land, The, 114, 163, 165, 167, 397

Terry, Walter, 126n, 162n

Tess (Robbins's shepherd-retriever mix), 366

Tharp, Twyla, 247, 316–17, 335, 339–40, 405

That's the Ticket!, 84, 98–9, 100n, 244, 394

Theatre Arts Committee (TAC), 40, 362n, 392

Theme and Variations, 224

There's No Business Like Show Business, 151n

Thirty Years of Treason (Bentley), 293n

3 x 3, 220, 398

Three Virgins and a Devil, 54

Time and Tide, 377

Tipton, Jennifer, 352

Toast of the Town, 118

Tobias, Rose, 85, 394

Todd, Arthur, 211

Tomasson, Helgi, 303, 339

Tomasson, Marlene, 303

Tony Awards, xi, 241n, 336, 363n, 365

Torn, Rip, 236

Toumanova, Tamara, 92

Tree Grows in Brooklyn, A, 112, 125, 395–6

Tricolore, 248, 403

Truman, Margaret, 109

Tucker, Robert, 346–7

Tudor, Antony, 23, 48, 65, 74–5, 225, 352, 357

Turkey, Robbins's cruises along coast of (1984 and 1985), 339–40, 341–2, 365n, 405

Turner, Chuck, 196

Turning Point, The, 319n

2 & 3 Part Inventions, 337, 355, 407

Two's Company, 113, 150, 396

Tyl Ulenspiegel, 113, 130, 136, 137, 140, 141, 142, 147, 225, 396

Tynan, Kenneth, 266–8

Ulanova, Galina, 402

Ulbricht, Otto, 55

Undertow, 91

Van Druten, John, 395

Verdi, Giuseppe:
    The Four Seasons, 248, 322, 323n, 380n, 404
    Requiem, 204–5
    Verdi Variations, 404

Verdy, Violette, 279

Villa dei Misteri, Pompeii, 134–5, 228, 270

Villella, Edward, 277n, 295, 296n

von Aroldingen, Karin, 328n, 330

Walker, Nancy, 259

Wallace, Mike, 212n

Walton, Tony, 233

Warm Springs Institute for Rehabilitation, Le Clercq's stay at, 209n, *210*, 211

Warner, Jack, 373n

Washington Post, 343n

Wasson, Robert Gordon, 227n, 228

Watermill, 82, 200n, 246, 272n, 290n, 291, 293, 294, 295, 342n, 383, 402

Water Mill, N.Y., 245–6, 291, 296, 297
    farm house rented by Robbins in, 284
    Robbins's acid trip at (1969), 284–5, 290n, 291n

Waugh, Alex, 188n

Weehawken, N.J., Robbins's childhood years in, 3–4, *6*, 11–20, 391

Weidman, John, 407

Weinstein, Arthur, 141, 150, 196, 219n

Weissman, Edith, 249, 321n, 331, 334, 356, 358, 405

West Side Story, 114–15, 116, 180, 195, 209n, 212n, 215n, 231, 234, 235n, 236n, 245, 343–4, 349, 358n, 382–3, 384n, 394, 398
field research for, 206
film version of, 115, 116–17, 179n, 228–9, 230, 232–3, 343n, 399
photographs of, *207, 208*
scheduling issues and, 172–5
writing of, 178–81
West Side Story Suite, 337, 382–3, 407
Wheeler, Lois, 85, 393
Whelan, Wendy, 384
White Goddess, The (Graves), 230, 288
White House, Robbins's appearance at (1962), 116, 117, 400
White Oak Dance Project, 337, 407
Wilder, Thornton: *The Skin of Our Teeth*, 166, 167n, 244, 256–60, 263, 400
Williams, Paul, 120–1
Williams, Tennessee, 229, 236n
Wilson, Robert, 245, 286n, 294, 335, 379, 401, 402
Robbins's correspondence with, 273–4, 288–9

Woodrow Wilson High School, Weehawken, N.J., 16, 21, 391
Windsor, Duchess of (former Wallis Simpson), 149
Windust, Bretaigne, 392
Winged Victory, 77
Wise, Robert, 117, 228n, 230, 232–3, 399
Wish You Were Here, 396
WNET/PBS, 316n, 404, 405, 406
Wolfe, Thomas, 57, 192
Wonderful Town, 114, 396
World House, 198–200
World War II, 55, 71n

Yiddish Art Theatre, 30–1, 52, 391
Yucatán, Robbins's 1970 trip to, 286, 402

Zeami, 245, 246, 272–3
Zimmerman, Jerry, 303
Zipprodt, Patricia, 249–50, 259, 263
Zorina, Vera, 38, 47, 295n
Zousmer, Viola (cousin), 321